INFORMATION, EXPECTATIONS, AND INVENTORY FLUCTUATION

FLUCTUATION

A Study of Materials Stock on Hand and on Order

NATIONAL BUREAU OF ECONOMIC RESEARCH
Studies in Business Cycles

RUTH P. MACK

INFORMATION, EXPECTATIONS, AND INVENTORY FLUCTUATION

A Study of Materials Stock on Hand and on Order

Published by the NATIONAL BUREAU OF ECONOMIC RESEARCH

Distributed by COLUMBIA UNIVERSITY PRESS, *New York and London*

1967

HD 55
.M3 c. 1

Relation of the Directors to the Work and Publications of the National Bureau of Economic Research

1. The object of the National Bureau of Economic Research is to ascertain and to present to the public important economic facts and their interpretation in a scientific and impartial manner. The Board of Directors is charged with the responsibility of ensuring that the work of the National Bureau is carried on in strict conformity with this object.

2. To this end the Board of Directors shall appoint one or more Directors of Research.

3. The Director or Directors of Research shall submit to the members of the Board, or to its Executive Committee, for their formal adoption, all specific proposals concerning researches to be instituted.

4. No report shall be published until the Director or Directors of Research shall have submitted to the Board a summary drawing attention to the character of the data and their utilization in the report, the nature and treatment of the problems involved, the main conclusions, and such other information as in their opinion would serve to determine the suitability of the report for publication in accordance with the principles of the National Bureau.

5. A copy of any manuscript proposed for publication shall also be submitted to each member of the Board. For each manuscript to be so submitted a special committee shall be appointed by the President, or at his designation by the Executive Director, consisting of three Directors selected as nearly as may be one from each general division of the Board. The names of the special manuscript committee shall be stated to each Director when the summary and report described in paragraph (4) are sent to him. It shall be the duty of each member of the committee to read the manuscript. If each member of the special committee signifies his approval within thirty days, the manuscript may be published. If each member of the special committee has not signified his approval within thirty days of the transmittal of the report and manuscript, the Director of Research shall then notify each member of the Board, requesting approval or disapproval of publication, and thirty additional days shall be granted for this purpose. The manuscript shall then not be published unless at least a majority of the entire Board and a two-thirds majority of those members of the Board who shall have voted on the proposal within the time fixed for the receipt of votes on the publication proposed shall have approved.

6. No manuscript may be published, though approved by each member of the special committee, until forty-five days have elapsed from the transmittal of the summary and report. The interval is allowed for the receipt of any memorandum of dissent or reservation, together with a brief statement of his reasons, that any member may wish to express; and such memorandum of dissent or reservation shall be published with the manuscript if he so desires. Publication does not, however, imply that each member of the Board has read the manuscript, or that either members of the Board in general, or of the special committee, have passed upon its validity in every detail.

7. A copy of this resolution shall, unless otherwise determined by the Board, be printed in each copy of every National Bureau book.

(Resolution adopted October 25, 1926, as revised February 6, 1933, and February 24, 1941)

Contents

page

CONTENTS

Tables

Charts

Acknowledgments

This book has lived with me for so long that it has become acquainted with most of my friends—a condition as trying for the friends as it has been beneficial to the book and to me. The help has worked in two ways: it has provided counsel and astute comment; it has encouraged me to trudge on.

On both scores Geoffrey H. Moore has been entirely indispensable. Thomas M. Stanback, Jr., likewise has advised me in connection with pieces of the work in earlier writings and with the draft of the present book. F. Thomas Juster has reviewed the manuscript to its advantage. Others to whom I am grateful for help along the way include Arthur F. Burns, Moses Abramovitz, Ilse Mintz, George Garvy, James W. Angell, Neil Chamberlain, Alfred Eisenpreis, and Michael Lovell. The book has benefited from review by National Bureau directors R. A. Gordon, Marion B. Folsom, and J. Wilson Newman.

The painstaking work of processing information was started by Ester Moskowitz and finished by Marilyn McGirr. H. Irving Forman tackled the job of converting too many, too wiggly lines into a clear visual statement. James F. McRee, Jr., polished prose. For all of this skilled assistance I am thankful.

Lyle C. Fitch contributed to this book, which features how businessmen react to information, formulate expectations, and learn, by exposing me to the infinite complexities of how governments do the same thing. My husband, Edward C. Mack, is the friend who has been most intimately acquainted with the work and therefore most tried by it. His stubborn encouragement has made it possible.

INFORMATION, EXPECTATIONS, AND INVENTORY FLUCTUATION

A Study of Materials Stock on Hand and on Order

Overview and Summary

The stubborn curiosity that motivates the hard labor of empirical investigation is likely to be based on a hunch about what, in a complex process, is important and what less so. This study is no exception. The thought that gave rise to it is that the size of inventory holdings and how they change is more significantly influenced by considerations other than the expected volume of sales than is generally supposed. Because of the character and extent of these influences, new concepts are required to encompass them.

Of course, such ideas are not visions flashed on a pink cloud. My study of the shoe, leather, hide sequence [1] left a legacy of preoccupation with the impact on purchasing in general, and on inventories in particular, of expectations about market conditions and about changes in other costs and the assurance with which these expectations are held. Indeed, the efforts to explain how fluctuation moves from shoes, to leather, to hides, and back again were partly flouted by the inability to picture the flows of information and of the resultant expectations which were counterpoint to, and largely cause of, the flows of output and employment.

The study attempts to come to grips with these elusive problems by viewing materials stocks on order (outstanding purchase orders) along with those on hand. When possible it examines these stocks in the light of the orders that companies receive for their own products and the shipments they make, as well as in the light of the orders they place with their suppliers which are eventually shipped to their plants.

The book is complicated as well as long. The reader therefore requires a map of the terrain to be traveled before setting out on the trip. This chapter attempts the cartographic product and it will of necessity leave much to be desired. I have worked with concepts that are unfamiliar and data that are clumsy. The argument is difficult and a summary of it is likely to float uncomfortably on the reader's mind until the pieces out of which it is built have had a chance to soak in. Nevertheless, it will be useful to know at least the subjects to be dealt with and why. I shall mainly, though not necessarily, follow the chapter sequences.

Part I of the book consists of three chapters which set the stage for the subsequent examination of time series.

A brief review in Chapter 1 of empirical work with inventory models yields no cause for complacency. Quite the contrary. The statistical representations fail to show a relationship of stocks to sales which is forceful and prompt enough to accord with the notion that businessmen are chiefly concerned with keeping stocks aligned with sales. When new orders or changes in unfilled orders are introduced, they tend to steal the show, though just why is not adequately explained.

BUSINESS FUNCTION THAT STOCKS SERVE

The unsatisfactory character of these explanations sends me back to the business firm

[1] *Consumption and Business Fluctuations: A Case Study of the Shoe, Leather, Hide Sequence,* New York, National Bureau of Economic Research, 1956.

in Chapter 2. What does managerial economics and a desultory group of discussions with businessmen indicate about the function that stocks serve? They indicate, first, that many of the functions are performed by materials or merchandise stocks on order as well as by those on hand. Besides, the chief action that controls the size of stock on hand is that of placing an order, and this necessarily likewise controls the size of stock on order. Indeed, it is the act of ordering to which managerial rules for stock management direct their attention. In consequence, the sum of materials both on hand and on order, an aggregate which I call "materials ownership," better reflects the intentions of firms than does stock on hand alone. Accordingly, for many purposes it is essential to think in terms of ownership; for other purposes each part needs separate consideration.

Understanding of how materials stocks are likely to vary during business fluctuations must be built up by detailing the several functions that stocks serve and determining for each the influences that prescribe their appropriate size.

SIX MAJOR FUNCTIONS OF STOCKS ARE IDENTIFIED

1. The first is the obvious and unique function of stocks, that of sustaining time-consuming economic processes. Assume that any process, when performed with usual efficiency, requires a stipulated time to complete, and that process-time stocks maintain the flow of goods over this period. Then, if the flow increases because of larger sales, stocks must increase proportionately (except when overtime or multishift operation permits a more intensive use of the twenty-four hours of the day, and, therefore also, of stocks).

The other five functions involve the use of stocks as one of the many ways of serving some business objective. Each of the alternative ways of serving the same purpose has a cost; the output of a dollar of such costs constitutes the opportunity cost of a dollar spent on stocks. Exhibit 1 displays a wide variety of the alternatives. How stocks vary during fluctuations in general business depends, then, not only on how stocks need to vary with changing sales (and how sales change during business cycles) but also on how the opportunity costs of stocks behave during business fluctuations.

Three of these further functions that stocks serve are:

2. Providing efficient production and purchasing lot-sizes.

3. Insurance against losing sales because of unpredictable variation in demand or other flows.

4. Smoothing operations by provision for more or less foreseeable fluctuations, such as seasonal change. Assuming that the costs of stocks and of alternatives, such as providing flexibility in processing or selling, are unchanged, stocks serving these functions need to vary substantially less than proportionately to sales. Indeed, for functions 2 and 3, stocks should change more nearly in relation to the square root of sales than to sales proper.

Neither the cost of carrying stocks nor other business costs are likely to be constant during fluctuations in sales or in general business. As the functions are examined, it seems highly probable that many stock-carrying costs per unit will undergo relative declines during prosperity. But several alternative ways of meeting variable sales, notably by flexible production schedules and overtime work, are likely to be subject to rising costs during prosperity. If so, the opportunity costs of stock fall in prosperous times both because the cost of stocks declines and because the costs of alternative ways of meeting the same management need rise.

Two further functions that stock serves are:

5. Making it possible to grasp the potential advantage (or avoid the disadvantage) of actual or expected changes in conditions in markets in which manufacturers buy materials or retailers buy merchandise. In prosperity these changes can take the form of longer lead time, poorer selections, more uncertainty about delivery dates, and rising materials

prices. This set of factors has a strong positive relationship to business conditions. Changes in stocks on order, rather than in stocks on hand, are the first line of defense against them.

6. Providing elective freedom from the tyranny of planning for uncertain events. Some uncertain events are best handled by simply providing a stock reservoir large enough to take care of them, whatever they may turn out to be. Stocks serving this function tend to rise when sales fall and vice versa. Other uncertain events cause unintended change in stock which needs to be reversed as soon as discovered. How stock of this sort relates to sales depends on forecasting and purchasing procedures such as those discussed later on.

When these observations concerning the functions of stock and the association of stocks with sales are consolidated, it becomes clear that stocks as a whole need to vary less than proportionately to sales, other things the same: of all the functions, only that of covering process time (and that not always) implies that a constant average ratio is required.

However, other things that appear to be relevant are not at all likely to remain the same during changes in business activities. Clearly, then, investigation must be sensitive to searching out how these other things do in fact change—other things such as the cost of carrying stock, the cost of accommodating unforeseen fluctuation in sales by flexible production, the opportunities for obtaining materials swiftly, surely, and at an advantageous price, and so on.

The analysis also suggests the variety of impacts that orders have on the purchasing and stock-carrying functions. Viewed from the vantage point of a particular firm, new orders for the product the company sells (here termed sales orders) can help to forecast shipment schedules and thus minimize unintended stock; outstanding sales orders reduce risk in purchasing and therefore the cost of carrying stocks. Outstanding purchase orders for materials are a type of secondary stock of materi-

als; new purchase orders convey information about total demand—demand for a company's sales plus change in stocks and materials outstanding—to the next earlier stage of production. Certainly empirical study of stocks and procurement problems must be structured so as not to confuse these diverse meanings.

A further group of implications lies dormant until the last chapter, where it is pressed into heavy service: the variety of functions that stocks serve and the variety of factors that influence their relative cost imply that sensitivity to any one factor will vary widely among different inventory goods, firms in an industry, or different industries. The resulting frequency distribution of firms with respect to sensitivity to any one factor that influences stock can have important implications concerning the process of economic change.

ANALYSIS OF AGGREGATES

These insights, based on analysis of the functions of stock viewed from within the firm, must be put to work at the level of aggregate analysis—the only level of investigation attempted in this book. Chapter 3 develops standards for statistics on ownership capable of throwing light on the vertical transmission of fluctuation in aggregate data. An illustrative table, Exhibit 2, diagrams the relation between sales orders, purchase orders, and outstanding orders of both varieties for the economy as a whole. It shows how the meaning of a given change in stock in the economy is altered by whether changes in outstanding purchase orders for several vertical steps are positive or negative.

As for the empirical materials available for study, only two areas of the economy can be represented. The first covers large department stores. For these, information on sales, stocks, outstanding purchase orders for merchandise, and receipts of and new orders for merchandise are all available. They conform to the conceptual requirements and are used for 1946 through 1963, at which time the data were discontinued.

The second set of statistics pertains to durable goods manufacturers. They are the book-value data for shipments, orders, and stocks formerly assembled by the Office of Business Economics and presently by the Bureau of the Census. Since all information for manufacturers' new orders refers to sales orders, the matching information for purchase orders (and consequently for materials outstanding), which ought to be for the same firms that submit the other information, must in fact be pieced together on the basis of sales orders for industries which presumably make the materials that other durable goods manufacturers buy. The unfilled sales orders of these materials manufacturers are, then, roughly, the outstanding purchase orders for materials of all durable goods manufacturers. By these devices, we tack together information for materials stocks on hand and on order for durable goods manufacturers and associate them with imperfectly matching information on sales orders, unfilled sales orders, and purchase orders. These figures, though very shaky with respect to absolute magnitudes, seem adequate for showing the basic patterns of changes in stocks. In any event, they are all that we have and I believe a useful tool at least for exposing a process. What, then, do the figures show?

The question is pursued in the context of two broad subjects: first, the dynamics of the inventory cycle itself; second, the participation of stocks and materials purchasing in economic fluctuation, particularly in its vertical transmission.

As always, when tools are poor, work is arduous and roundabout, and the description of it difficult to write and to read. All these miseries are unavoidable, and it is unhealthy to dwell upon them having once chosen to proceed. Part II of the book reports on how stocks and purchasing behave. Part III seeks to explain behavior, examine interrelationships with the economy at large, and consider some implications. Part of this search ventures at the periphery of what the actual data warrant. However, I make no apologies for my inability to resist the seduction of the dimly seen; if the hard-won glimpses prove of interest, further study can contrive to sharpen outlines.

EMPIRICAL DESCRIPTION OF MATERIALS STOCKS ON HAND AND ON ORDER [2]

The investigation of statistical data follows a standard form. All data were corrected for seasonal variation. Rates of change were calculated as five-month centered moving averages of month-to-month change. Specific cycles were marked on all series according to the usual National Bureau methods. Occasionally additional lesser movements seemed worth including in timing measures, and these specific subcycles were separately identified.

Amplitude measures follow, with slight variation, the standard National Bureau procedures. Timing measures compare specific cycles with matching business cycle reference dates, and, in addition, with these dates plus two additional minor movements in 1947 and 1951–52. Timing measures also compare specific cycles plus minor cycles in one series with those in another. Average timing characteristics are developed. Judgments about concurrence are based on the number of matching turns, average deviation, and the percentage of all months (1946 to 1961), during which the series compared were in like specific subcycle or cycle phase. For further details, examine Table 1 in Chapter 4.

Magnitude of Outstandings. Outstanding orders for materials are of substantial magnitude. For department stores, they are about half the size of stocks on hand; for durable goods manufacturers, they are also about half the size of all stocks and about twice that of materials stocks alone.

Judged in terms of instability, the relative importance of outstandings is far greater still.

[2] I use "materials" to refer to either purchased materials (sometimes called raw materials) of manufacturers or to all merchandise of department stores.

Comparison of the average rise or fall during specific cycles shows outstanding orders for department stores accounting for twice as much fluctuation as did stocks; for durable goods manufacturers they accounted for four times as much as did materials stocks. The contribution of inventories to instability in the flows of goods tends to be a function of the *rate* at which stocks build up or draw down. In these terms too, specific fluctuation in outstanding orders is substantially larger than in stocks of department stores and far larger than in materials stocks of durable goods manufacturers.

Leading Cyclical Pattern. For both department stores and durable goods manufacturers, materials ownership, as well as each of its two parts (materials on hand and on order) conforms to all postwar business cycles. Stocks proper tended, as frequently observed, either to synchronize or lag. But outstanding orders showed a lead of half a year or a year, particularly at peaks (and for department stores, substantial leads at troughs too).

Investment in these stocks (their rate of change) also conforms to all postwar cycles and even for stocks proper leads business cycle turns. Rates of change in total ownership reach their maxima about a year (on the average) before business in general; troughs lead by a half a year. About the same statement applies to change in outstandings alone.

Extra Cycles. Outstanding orders for both sorts of enterprises underwent contraction at the time of general fear of a postwar recession toward the end of 1946, and after the Korean boom had climbed to a peak in early 1951. They revived prior to the major cyclical peaks in 1948 and 1953, but the second peaks were lower than the first. Rates of change in all of the data for ownership and its two parts, for department stores and for durables, showed these same characteristics.

Though discontinuity in the data makes conclusions highly tentative, there are suggestions of a similar interruption of the post-1961 expansion, very early in 1962, though in this case the first peak in the ownership data was certainly far lower than the second.

Relation of Stocks on Hand to Those on Order. The evidence of the time series concerning parallelism and timing relationships between stocks on hand and on order is relevant to the dynamics of inventory fluctuation. We find first, as might be expected, that outstandings always reach peaks or troughs before stocks do. But the lead at peaks is puzzlingly long. For both department stores and durable goods manufacturers, it averages seven months; the three-months' lead at trough seems more nearly what might be expected. Rates of change for durables repeat the basic finding of long leads at peaks, though for department stores the picture was somewhat moderated.

Second, we find that stocks on hand and on order, two forms in which materials can move toward production or sales, seem to show not-insubstantial parallelism. For durable goods manufacturers, the relative height of each specific cycle rise in stocks tends to parallel that of matching cycles in outstandings. For department stores, perhaps because of distorting influences of the upward trend, it is the falls which seem related. For rates of change, particularly for department stores, similar parallelism is evident. The parallelism suggests that an understanding of the forces that cause shifts in outstanding orders can contribute to an understanding of shifts in stock.

However, the fact that outstandings turn down so early needs to be explained. At least two elements doubtless contribute. The first is a technical one: the lag of stock relative to that of outstandings may be a function of changes in the length and volume of orders carrying longest delivery periods, rather than of the average period for which all orders remain outstanding. The second concerns the group of influences associated with market expectations which have a strong influence on outstandings and seem, on the basis of independent information discussed later, to reach a peak well before prosperity starts to fade. The two parts of the explanation are, of course, related.

Early Thrust of Expansion. Characteristically, outstanding orders, and presently stocks, move strongly upward in the neighborhood of cyclical troughs in business activity. For department stores, the upward thrust in outstandings and total ownership started in the last month of recession. The period of rapid rise can be dated in various ways. But whatever method is used—whether on the basis of a wide collection of series or the ownership data themselves—the rise tails off after about a year to a year and a half. The median figure is fourteen months after the business cycle trough. The average rate at which outstandings rose during these periods of upward thrust was at least as strong as was the fall during business contraction. The termination of the thrust was followed either by decline or by slower rates of expansion.

These periods when the rise in ownership, and particularly in outstandings, seems out of proportion to other things going on in the economy are of considerable theoretical interest. The interest is heightened by the fact that the rises are early enough to give the economy a booster shot out of depression, that they cease while output and income are moving upward. Moreover, they do not always occur at the outset of a business expansion. (In 1961, for example, though outstanding materials orders for durables increased just before the trough, they did not increase relative to shipments, whereas a strong and much publicized thrust began in 1964.) The phenomenon of the thrust calls for explanation not only of how it gets under way, but also of how it stops. My effort to provide an explanation of this, as well as of some other facts we encounter, culminates in the "ecological model" of the final chapter.

Other Findings. Examination of the time series in Chapters 4–8 uncovers relationships between stocks and adjacent flows, and these are of course of critical interest to studying the dynamics of fluctuation. However, for purposes of this summary, the behavior can be reported at the point where its significance is discussed.

Part III strives to explain the observed behavior of the time series in the light of the insights afforded by the analysis of the functions that stocks serve in individual enterprises. The first of the five chapters, Chapter 9, studies the link between stocks and sales. The second examines other influences that may help to explain stock fluctuation. The next chapter brings the various pieces together in two related inventory models from which, however, multiplier effects have been excluded. Chapter 12 examines the impact of inventory fluctuation on the economy and focuses the conclusion on multiplier mechanisms. The final chapter adds to the model a description of an aspect of the process of change—the ecological interplay between business enterprises and the environment in which they operate—which appears necessary to the understanding of the time course of inventory fluctuation.

THE SALES LINK

The analysis of the functions that stocks serve in Chapter 2 suggests that stocks must change in the same direction as do sales, but not, at least in the short run, by as much as a constant stock-sales ratio implies. The analysis further indicates that many events other than a change in sales might well affect the desirable size of stocks on hand and on order. What, then, do the time series show about the actual relationship of stocks to sales?

For both durable goods manufacturers and department stores, ownership and sales underwent generally synchronous and matched fluctuations. But for department stores the relation is substantially tighter and more pervasive than for materials stocks of durable goods manufacturers. Especially impressive is the fact that the twelve specific cycle phases that were marked both for rates of change in ownership and in sales of department stores are in like phase on a synchronous basis for 84 per cent of the months covered. For durable goods manufacturers the comparable figure was 76 per cent. Change in stocks, of course, moved more tardily; it lagged change in sales by about four months for both sorts of enterprises and showed poorer correspondence.

The logic of the efficient stock-sales link calls for less than proportional change in stocks. However, the figures show more than proportional change over substantial periods when there is no reason to attribute behavior to the inability to enforce objectives. For all expansion months in sales, stocks rose at a faster rate than sales, that is, the stock-sales ratio was in rising phase 59 per cent of the months for department stores and 44 per cent for durables; the corresponding figures for the ownership ratio were 68 per cent and 37 per cent. For business cycle expansion phases, three of the four figures were substantially higher (Tables 7 and 16).

The higher than proportional rise in stocks was not, as often thought, a phenomenon of late expansion. The rise in the stock ratio started on the average within ten months of the trough in sales, for both department stores and durables. For the ownership ratio the median lag was five and six months for the two sorts of enterprises. For outstandings, as implied by the discussion of early thrusts, the ratio rose on the average within one and two months of the trough in sales for durables and department stores respectively.

The figures indicate, then, that stocks and ownership are changing in a more lively fashion than the efficient servicing of sales requires, other things the same. It would be useful to form a judgment as to the order of magnitude of this hypothetically nonsales-linked fluctuation.

To do so requires an assumption about what the efficient sales link would actually imply, and calculations were made on the basis of three such assumptions. The first sup-

poses that ownership maintains a constant ratio to sales, but one that is at trough (and therefore presumably "hand-to-mouth") levels. The other two assume a constant incremental rather than average ratio, plus a further allowance for change in buffer stocks; the incremental levels chosen were presumably generous—a two months' and a one and a half months' supply. Fluctuation in hypothetically sales-linked ownership was calculated by applying these relationships to actual fluctuations in sales. The calculations were confined to ownership because of uneasiness about applying the identical logic to stocks on hand.

Summing change for all cycle phases, the hypothetically sales-linked change in ownership was then compared with actual specific cycle change in ownership for matched phases. Sales-linked change, presuming the constant average ratio, was 69 per cent of total change in ownership for department stores and 67 per cent for durable goods manufacturers. Assuming the constant incremental ratio plus buffer, the figures were 38 per cent and 45 per cent for two months supply, 29 per cent and 34 per cent for one and a half months' supply. I conclude that a very substantial amount of the fluctuation in materials stocks on hand and on order for the two very different sorts of enterprises appears to be influenced by variables other than changes in sales.

THE IMPACT OF OTHER INFLUENCES

The examination of functions that stocks serve in Chapter 2 indicated what some of these factors may be. We noticed that changes in stock can be prompted by shifts in the costs of carrying stocks vis-a-vis those of covering in other ways the management functions that stocks serve. They can be prompted by changing expectations concerning, or actual conditions in, the markets in which materials are purchased. Moreover, whatever the specific objective with respect to sales, there are bound to be disparities between actual and desired stocks on hand and on order; some of these disparities are passive in the sense that they are tolerated; others are unintended in the sense that they are rapidly reversed.

Chapter 10 endeavors to devise empirical representation of some of these influences and to compare them with the unexplained portion of total fluctuation in ownership. Unfortunately, the means at our command are limited and afford observations chiefly for the durable goods industries, and I shall confine my summary entirely to that field. Also, I single out for discussion here only those factors for which the data seem to show impressive association.

Representation in time series can be contrived for two factors that may represent shifts in cost. Backlogs of sales orders provide a period of option during which materials can be bought further ahead with less risk of buying unneeded goods than there would otherwise be. Apparently *rates of change* in backlogs anticipate levels of advance materials buying. Back orders start to decline or rise less vigorously with interesting regularity about a half-year before the *level* of outstandings (measured in months of shipments for which they provide) start to rise or fall, respectively (Table 38, line 11). If either levels or rates of change for both sorts of unfilled orders are compared, the levels for materials lead and the associations are irregular. The time series show a very impressive association between profits of durable goods manufacturers and materials outstanding about a half a year later (Table 35, line 15). Could this suggest that unusually high profits provide a source of funds for which the relatively liquid asset, stocks, is considered a particularly appropriate investment?

Market conditions are represented by an interesting body of data collected by the Purchasing Agents Association of Chicago, most of the members of which are in durable goods industries. There are time series representing the average term of purchase orders for major materials and the speed with which vendors

undertake to deliver major materials. These two series have a very systematic and slightly leading association with the census data for outstanding orders of materials of durable goods manufacturers; 87 and 88 per cent of the months are in like phase.

Expectations that materials prices will rise could be another reason for extending materials ownership. The *level* of extension would theoretically be a function of the *rate* at which prices are expected to rise. On the assumption that expectations are based on spot prices actually experienced, one might expect parallel movements of the level of outstandings and the rate of change in the spot prices of metals. If so, of course, the *level* of prices would lag; but instead it actually leads the level of outstandings. A possible reason for this is developed in the final chapter.

These several factors which seem associated with changes in outstandings share three characteristics worth noting. The first has to do with the patterns of change: they undergo strong fluctuations which reach their peak well before those of general business; they participate very strongly in the phenomenon that I have called the first thrust of expansion; a number of series have an unusual triangular pattern—they rise at a steady rate and reverse without the customary period of retardation.

Other characteristics concern the dynamics of change. Two of the factors that have been examined seem to be primarily demand-linked —back orders for the product the company sells and profits (conceived as low-cost funds for financing stocks). One factor reflects primarily supply-linked factors—the delivery period that vendors are willing to promise. Several are obviously linked jointly to supply and demand, such as changes in prices and the varying weights in total outstandings of goods having different delivery terms.

But on further thought, *all* of the elements are potentially jointly influenced by both demand and supply. For example, delivery periods might never lengthen if buyers were not trying to build up stock; backlogs of sales orders might not accumulate if producers were able to get materials as fast as they could use them. Only if physical-capacity ceilings are clearly responsible for some of the supply limitations could one of the blades of the scissors be singled out. But the examination of the data available on plant capacity and its utilization fails to provide the basis for attributing the buildup of buying waves to physical-capacity limitations. However, at least the intensity of some movements may not be unrelated to the frequency with which plants and products bump capacity ceilings.

It is not surprising, then, to find that the dominant characteristic of all of these cost- and market-oriented influences on ownership is that they move up and down together, either as data proper or as rates of change (Table 39). There appears no way of avoiding the messy job of viewing the process in all of its complex interrelatedness.

OUTLINES OF A MODEL OF INVENTORY
FLUCTUATION

A first necessity is to endeavor to view the inventory process without an artificial separation between the impact of the sales-linked influences and of all the other influences that bear on stocks on hand and on order. In Chapter 11 we re-examine time series bearing on both sorts of influences, and consider their combined impact on stocks or ownership for each of two types of enterprises. It is not feasible to describe the empirical studies in a few paragraphs. Nor is it feasible to do more than name the pieces of a model which is presented first in a form applicable to department stores and then to durable goods manufacturing. The theory is constructed primarily in terms of materials ownership, though it can be converted at some sacrifice to apply to stocks on hand.

A basic characteristic of the apparatus is its reliance on the time lags that are actually inherent in each type of situation that is covered. The formalized lags of "period analysis"

are inappropriate, partly, because of the swift information system implicit in the focus on ownership and new orders. The natural time periods—those that characterize the time required for facts to be appreciated, action to be undertaken and completed, costs to change, and the like—pace the action-reaction patterns of the model with one exception. When expectations are important, change appears at first glance to be potentially explosive; however, the last chapter develops a theory which implies that it is not.

The model as presented in Chapter 11 covers the following elements which participate in inventory fluctuation; many of the particulars are significantly different for durable goods manufacturing and for department stores, and some of the differences are indicated in the parenthetic statements.

1. *A forecasting procedure which forms the basis of initial buying.* Description must recognize the information typically available to management and the time periods for which forecasts are actually required in view of the way in which orders are placed. (Department stores, having no advance notice of what consumers will buy, must largely rely on some sort of rule of thumb for extending past sales. Forecasts must project several months into the future for "preseason" orders, but orders of progressively shorter term can, in effect, modify forecasts. For durable goods manufacturers, the orders placed by customers often provide advance knowledge of how shipments may be expected to change. And, incidentally, knowledge of this sort is not confined to a special-order type of business.)

2. *A link of desired ownership (or stock) to expected sales* which is best formulated roughly in constant incremental, rather than average, terms. If the objective is firm, it imprints buying with an element that conforms to the rate of change in sales, and therefore has the usual tendency to lead sales proper. The larger the desired ratio, the stronger the imprint. (For department stores, the relatively large stock, and the high priority that stock

control assumes, is likely to cause the influence to be relatively large and sharp.)

3. *The desired levels of stocks or of changes in stocks are affected by changes in the opportunity costs* of serving given management objectives in other ways. The analysis and evidence suggest that these changes in opportunity costs of stocks, whether or not they are formally recognized by business managers, may tend to cause more liberal stock policies in prosperity than in recession.

4. *Choices about the timing of buying*—that is, just when materials that are expected to be required should be bought—recognize changing conditions in materials markets. Relevant conditions include what manufacturers offer by way of selections and delivery periods, and expectations about these things and about prices. (In the durable goods industries, factors effecting the timing of buying can have an important influence. The empirical data show an association between materials outstanding and vendor performance, or (with reservations) metals prices, which seem subject to this interpretation. But even for department stores, market conditions apparently influence the proportion of the seasons' expected requirements that are covered by the preseason order rather than bought much closer to the time when sales are expected to take place.

5. *Methods of defining, recognizing, and correcting errors* in materials ownership. There are at least three aspects to this problem:

(a) Inventory management itself has an opportunity cost which influences the precision with which objectives are formulated and enforced; "passive stock," in other words, may be relatively large or small. (For department stores this element is at a minimum.)

(b) The pattern of error in forecasting sales is a function of the character and the informational basis of the sales forecast and the structure of ordering procedures. (For department stores, the need to order on the basis primarily of sales of some appropriate past period means that correction of error will have the pattern of rate of change in sales. The shingled structure of orders means that orders for near delivery tend serially to correct for errors in forecast. At the same time, the seasonal characteristics of demand and ordering may tend to magnify errors and corrections. I attribute to this mechanics some of the strong parallelism between rates of change in sales and in ownership, which the data showed for department stores. For durable goods manufacturers, the informational input of forecast supplied by sales orders would presumably tend to make error smaller and in any event would have a different relationship to shipments.)

(c) Insofar as factors 3 and 4 above influence buying, errors in forming expectations about relative cost and market conditions will generate corrections in stocks on hand and on order. These corrections apply both to incorrect evaluations at the time they were made, and to changes in markets which make the actions taken no longer advisable. (The importance of this type of correction is likely to correspond to the size of the impact on stocks on hand and on order of factors 3 and 4. Consequently their impact on ownership for durable goods manufacturers is doubtless stronger than for department stores.)

This outline of the elements of an inventory model is incomplete. First, a sixth element is required—a *multiplier mechanism* covering the reaction of the economy as a whole to changes in stocks and materials purchasing; it is supplied by Chapter 12. Also required is a *spacing apparatus for the expectational aspects* of all of the elements, but particularly No. 4; this the final chapter provides.

THE VERTICAL TRANSMISSION OF INSTABILITY

The several threads in the second strand of the investigation, the impact of the inventory-purchase syndrome on the economy, are pulled together in Chapter 12, in which, along with the data previously examined, we study such information as can be readily assembled on vertical sequences in broad aggregates for output and new orders. The development of this strand is also necessary to determine the feedback to inventories of the economy's response to inventory fluctuation—a missing piece in the model previously described.

The timing and amplitude of the various series as described in Part II imply that the force exerted by the inventory-purchase complex differs at various stages of business cycles: (1) Prior to business cycle peaks and during the early months of contraction its influence is depressant. (2) Midway in the brief business contractions which have characterized the postwar economy, its leavening influence sets in. This influence gains force during late contraction and still more so during the first year of expansion, after which it is sharply subdued. (3) During the rest of expansion its force varies. It tends to be depressant while the readjustments following the cessation of the buying surge take place. But if the forces of expansion are strong enough, they tend to reactivate further investment in merchandise or materials. However, the market extension which follows is generally more moderate than the first. The 1964–65 situation is a clear exception.

The force and timing of the inventory-purchase syndrome are reflected in how demand moves from the final buyer to earlier economic stages. There is no evidence in the data examined of a tendency for turns in production to be set ahead as demand moves toward the raw-materials end of the sequence. Amplitude of fluctuation, however, is stronger at the earlier stages. As a consequence of the early thrust of inventory expansion, this increased amplitude is typically most marked early in expansion as well as, of course, during contraction.

The information conveyed by orders seems to play an important role in making this pattern possible.

Due in part to sensitivity to rates of change in the orders placed by consumers (consumer buying), retailers' orders for merchandise turn early, particularly at peaks. This anticipatory capability of retailers' materials orders, well maintained at earlier manufacturing stages, makes it possible for production starts for goods sold to consumers to increase or decrease at much the same time throughout a sequence of vertical stages. There is no need for progressively earlier action and greater amplification over the several steps of the whole vertical sequence, as conventional acceleration models seem to imply. Indeed, since individual production processes for materials tend to be reasonably swift, there is no need for production, as depicted in monthly data, systematically to anticipate sales to consumers.

For capital equipment, the orders placed by final buyers tend, as is well known, to turn early in business cycles. Those placed for materials, our data show, maintain the same pattern on the average.

It is perhaps less generally appreciated that orders for merchandise placed by department stores turn, if anything, earlier than do orders for materials placed by durable goods manufacturers. This is, of course, much earlier than consumer buying turns, particularly at peaks. Orders received by retailers' suppliers reflect the instability of both retail sales and the rate of change in merchandise ownership of retail stores. The figures reveal that the cyclical instability of the orders received by the manufacturers of the things that department stores buy is two or three times as great as that of consumer buying.

What does all this mean about the multiplier mechanisms that tend to magnify the impact of inventory fluctuation on the economy? Income multipliers are of course present in the usual sense: income associated with building up stocks is gradually distributed as it is spent and respent. The process takes time. In consequence, the multiplier impact is gradual. As mentioned before, it does not require theoretical representation in terms of discrete intervals or "periods."

A second type of multiplier is implicit in the system whereby information generates and communicates. Orders affect the plans producers make, the prices and market conditions they expect, the defensive and offensive actions they undertake. Orders affect these things differently if, on the one hand, they are interpreted as serving to build up stock or outstandings or, on the other hand, as corresponding to the flow of goods to final users. Yet for reactions of these sorts, natural time periods are not readily apparent.

In short, in a world where business conduct is based on expectations and a message circles the earth in a few minutes, what paces the speed with which expectations increase or depress activity?

Similar questions have also appeared in connection with expectations about materials markets. They are based on a network of information about market conditions in general and about what suppliers, customers, and competitors are doing. The information is rapidly conveyed. The actions that these expectations set off can be quickly formulated and executed. They affect the market and therefore subsequent expectations. Why does buying not seesaw back and forth from one extreme of opinion to another? Yet the data show that it does not.

Other bits of information in search of a theory are the ten-to-fourteen-month thrust, the triangular pattern of market extension, the long lead of peaks in outstandings relative to those of stocks, the fact that outstandings lag even the level of prices rather than showing an association with their rates of change. These are mavericks that appear at odds with obvious explanations, yet seem to fit in well enough with one that I propose in the concluding chapter.

AN ECOLOGICAL MODEL OF PRICE-TIMED BUYING

The chapter focuses on one aspect of market-oriented buying (by no means the most important one), prices; it constructs a model that describes how the expectation that materials prices will rise is capable (under appropriate circumstances) of causing a wave of price-timed buying with rising and falling phases of reasonable duration and containing intrinsic reversing mechanisms.

Price-timed ownership (a positive or negative quantity) is defined as the difference between the amount of materials actually on hand and on order when materials prices are expected to change and the amount that would be held if prices were not expected to change, ceteris paribus.

The model is constructed on the basis of a group of assumptions which, however much they require testing and further specification, are believed to be basically realistic. The assumptions refer to *structural* and *behavioral* characteristics of business situations and *market reactions*. Natural time lags are recognized where they exist. Let me present the scaffold of the argument.

Business structural characteristics: (1) Extension of stock on hand and on order predicated on an expected rise in prices (positive price-timed ownership) occurs at increasing costs and this causes price-timed ownership in any firm to have ceiling levels. (2) Firms in an industry differ with respect to their "proclivity to benefit from price-timed buying." The proclivity reflects the potential advantage to be gained from shifting the number of weeks' supply on hand and on order in accordance with expected changes in materials prices. These differing sensitivities are implied by the variety of factors that influence the advantage to be derived from price-timed buying and the highly particular pattern which they must have in a given firm. (3) The distribution of firms with respect to their proclivity to benefit from price-timed buying is such that fewer firms have a very high proclivity than have a more moderate proclivity, and probably somewhat fewer have a very low than a moderate one. Thus, for the familiar notion of the "representative firm," the model substitutes a "hill-shaped distribution of firms."

Business behavioral characteristics: These concern the circumstances that dictate a change in price-timed ownership. Desired change is effected promptly by appropriate positive buying or negative buying (reducing other buying), though there can be lags of an administrative sort. The level of price-timed ownership that is desired by a given firm is predominantly a function of (1) changing cost structures within the firm, (2) the expected rate of change in materials prices, and (3) the assurance with which the expectation is held. Assurance builds gradually in response to a number of influences, including sequential validation of previous expectations.

The structural and behavioral characteristics imply that desired price-timed ownership can be described as constituting the vertical dimension of a three-dimensional surface (Figure 5). The horizontal direction records, from left to right, progressively larger expected rates of increase in prices. The backward dimension records increasing assurance. The surface lifts moderately from left to right and sharply in a backward dimension as assurance increases. But the structural characteristics prescribe that the rise slows and finally ceases before the rear right corner of the surface is reached.

Desired changes in ownership are achieved by price-timed buying (positive or negative). For an industry as a whole, price-timed buying tends to be positive when more companies flock to move from a lower spot on the ownership surface to a higher one than move in the reverse direction. When upward movements are the rule and concentrate in the steeper portions of the surface, total price-timed buying is relatively large. But as the situation matures, the movements tend to concentrate increasingly at the flatter (rear right) part of the surface. Thus total price-timed buying declines; that is, the buying wave passes its peak. I might add that other characteristics of the model also cause or contribute to the reversal. Decline is augmented as firms start actually to reduce their ownership by

negative buying (move downward on the surface).

Price-timed buying has an impact on the materials markets and thereby on future expectations and the assurance with which they are held. Consider the impact on the market of positive price-timed buying: This addition to the buying that would otherwise occur may be conceptualized as a consequence of short-term shifts in demand and perhaps supply schedules; it thus tends to increase materials prices, lengthen delivery periods, or deteriorate selections, other things the same. These responses, though reasonably swift, are not immediate. Finally, evidence of the market responses feed back via various information systems to market participants, influencing their expectations about further change in price, the assurance with which such expectations are held, and consequently subsequent actions in response thereto.

The model, then, describes a wave in price-timed buying in terms of an ecological interplay among business firms and their environment: a changing number of firms buy changing quantities of materials to effectuate shifts in desired ownership. The buying in turn changes the very conditions toward which expectations are addressed and, communicated, gives rise to further rounds of expectations, evaluations, buying, and market impact.

But the specifics of the process prescribe that response must cumulate, accelerate, and soon decline. This results partly from the structure of proclivities and of their ceilings, partly from the fact that perception and learning are involved and take time to mature and to respond to environmental change including change in opinion, partly from the character of the market reaction, and partly from the information it generates.

The theory of price-timed buying, extended as it could readily be to cover all market-oriented buying, applies particularly to paragraph 4 of the model of inventory fluctuation previously described. It prescribes the natural time lags that are necessary to leash the potentially frenetic course of expectation-based buildups. It applies also in a more general sense to aspects of the expectation multiplier mentioned at the end of the previous section.

DIRECTIONS FOR FURTHER WORK

Since the lags are not formal but factual, the time required for the fluctuation to occur is implicitly specified by the particulars of the input concerning structural, behavioral, and market reactions. The study has suggested that the expansion phase is shorter than expansion phases of postwar cycles; the ten- to fourteen-month thrust may be more nearly typical. It would be instructive to explore by means of computerized simulation how sensitively the duration and amplitude of fluctuation vary with changes in each of the critical parameters. Interview studies could give to some of these parameters more than the airy shape which the present state of ignorance prescribes. New time series could provide aggregates against which a theory based on the behavior of individual marketeers could be checked and filled in. The study closes with a brief discussion of some of these avenues of further learning. The difficulty is that they branch so widely. The difficulty and the excitement.

Excitement lies, I think, in further exploration of how the intimacies of business problems and situations reflect and shape aggregate economic activity. One of the many aspects of this interrelationship concerns the dynamics of interplay between action, information, and expectation, between the individual and the environment. Of particular interest is what the approach can contribute to the understanding of the course of business expansions and what brings them to a close. Needless to say, the process described in the model must have very different particulars in connection with cycles in inventories and with those in consumer purchase of durables or business investment in capital equipment; yet it seems barely possible for ecological interplay to be present in one situation and absent in the others.

POSTSCRIPT FOR THE TIME-RATIONED READER

The reader, who has in the past few pages heard so much of the speed with which information travels, must find the length of this book puzzling. Should he wish to be guided by what I preach rather than what I do, I suggest the following shortcuts.

Chapter 2—Introductory and summary sections and Exhibit 1.

Chapter 3—Exhibit 2 and a glance at the description of the time series.

Chapters 4 and 5—Summary in Chapter 5 and study of Table 1, including notes to get the method of analysis. Charts 1 through 5.

Chapter 6—Summary and charts.

Chapters 7 and 8—Summary in Chapter 8 and Charts 8 and 9.

Chapter 9—First and last sections.

Chapter 10—Summary and charts.

Chapter 11—The models and the rest if he can make it.

Chapter 12—Summary and charts.

Chapter 13—If he likes models; in any event, the last section.

I. QUESTIONS AND SOURCES OF EVIDENCE

1. Gaps in the Explanation of Inventory Behavior

Inventories are a form of productive capital and as such their size must depend on the work that they are expected to perform. Viewed at an omnibus level, this work depends on the size of the vast aggregates of goods that churn through the factories and stores of the country. But viewed from within those factories and stores, many things in addition to the volume of goods that are to be processed and shipped determine the appropriate size of stocks; these include expectations about prices and other conditions in the markets in which materials are bought and finished products sold, availability and cost of funds with which to finance stocks, and all sorts of other things that influence the cost of holding stock relative to the cost of coping in some other way with the managerial objectives that stocks serve.

The many considerations that govern the size that stocks ought to be are, like virtually all determinants of economic behavior, expectations rather than precisely current, precisely known circumstances. Expectations typically diverge in some respect from reality as it unfolds. These divergences, too, govern the size of stock at a given time. Actions governing stock, then, depend on a web of expectations. The behavior of stock depends also on how expectations match the reality that comes to pass.

But expectations depend heavily on information; this is self-evident if economic behavior is "intendedly rational." In consequence, a fruitful study of the behavior of inventories must make a determined effort to admit information to full view and concern.

In this sense the investigator copies the decision maker.

Just how to achieve this ambitious objective is hard indeed to say; the study struggles with it at every turn. However, one approach is clearly indicated: orders that are received and placed by business enterprises, and the portion of each that remains unfilled at any given time, constitute an important form and source of information. In addition, unfilled orders change the actual conditions under which stock-carrying decisions are made. Outstanding orders for materials afford a secondary reserve of materials flowing toward the sales end of a production chain. Unfilled orders for the product a company sells—order backlogs—influence the risk involved in buying materials farther ahead than usual, and thus the advantage in holding materials stocks on hand or on order. At very least, then, it is essential to come to grips with the question of how to deal with the relation between orders, unfilled orders, and stocks in a meaningful way in the context of business fluctuation.

These impressions point to questions that have concerned economists for some time. The inability of the sales-stock relation alone to explain inventory behavior, and the value of unfilled orders as an assistant in doing so, are ideas that are not at variance with the direction in which the empirical study of inventories has moved in recent years. Without attempting to be systematic, it will be useful to highlight some of the major developments of this line of thought and also to point to some of the unanswered questions to which it gives rise.

THE INFLUENCE OF SALES

The point of departure for empirical analysis was a theory which explained inventory investment in terms of a constant desired association between demand and inventories. J. M. Clark, in his classic formulation of "the law of demand for intermediate products," focused on this underlying association and its prolific implications.[1] The Lundberg-Metzler formulation went on to show how the way in which expectations could be formulated, and the backwash of inevitable error on subsequent events, flouted the achievement of intentions.[2] Nevertheless he formulated desired inventory in terms of a fixed average (and he added an alternative, incremental) association with expected output.

As counterpoint to this elegant theme, empirical examination of the evidence felt its way. Moses Abramovitz' pioneer work with the scant data of the interwar years revealed a lag between change in inventories and change in output. The lag itself did not controvert the theory, but the irregularity of the association was troublesome, and Abramovitz attributed it to the different behavior and different relative importance, at various stages of the cycles, of the three levels of inventories: finished, in-process, and "raw" goods.[3]

Thomas Stanback, inspecting the richer materials of the postwar years, also found wide variations in the behavior of change in sales and change in stock.[4]

The extent to which inventories fail to be explained by their association to sales can be summarized by annual ratios of change in output to change in stocks, in constant prices.[5] Sales during the year are compared with stocks at the end of the year to allow for the lag previously discussed.[6] The calculations indicate that stocks changed in the same direction as sales in all but two of the years from 1930 to 1953 (omitting 1942 to 1945). The positive ratios ranged from 0.7 to 20.7; the average was 6.4 and the average deviation

the course of the phase—annual data do not give any indication of serious intra-phase fluctuations—it normally reaches its peak near the peak of the business cycle" (p. 378).

[4] Thomas M. Stanback, Jr., *Postwar Cycles in Manufacturers' Inventories*, New York, NBER, 1962. See particularly Table 36, p. 117. The timing comparisons were quarter to quarter; the most inclusive data were changes in final purchases (less services) and nonfarm inventory investment; stocks of manufacturers, wholesalers, and retailers were also each compared with the relevant output series. The distribution of timing comparisons was as follows:

Inventory Investment Compared to Change in Sales, Quarters (Q)	Inclusive Series	Three Other Series
Unmatched	2	4
Lead 1 Q	3	1
Lead 3 Q	0	1
Synchronous	2	3
Lag 1 Q	1	8
Lag 2 or 3 Q	2	10
Lag 4 or 5 Q		3
Total series turns	10	30

[1] J. M. Clark, "Business Acceleration and the Law of Demand: A Technical Factor in Economic Cycles," *Journal of Political Economy*, March 1917, pp. 217–235.

[2] Lloyd A. Metzler, "The Nature and Stability of Inventory Cycles," *Review of Economics and Statistics*, August 1941, pp. 113–129. Metzler credits Carl Lundberg with the conception of the model that he develops.

[3] Moses Abramovitz, *Inventories and Business Cycles, with Special Reference to Manufacturers' Inventories*, New York, NBER, 1950. The extent of the difference in the behavior of the two aggregates is interesting: "The rate of growth in output reaches a high point considerably before the end of expansion, a trough considerably before the end of contraction" (p. 378). This may be followed by a period of retarded change and sometimes an additional minor movement: "The movements of inventory investment are quite different. The rate of accumulation of inventories is typically low—usually negative—at the beginning of expansion. And whatever oscillations it may experience during

[5] Cf. R. P. Mack, comment to a paper by Franco Modigliani, "Business Reasons for Holding Inventories and Their Macro-Economic Implications," in *Problems of Capital Formation: Concepts, Measurement, and Controlling Factors*, Studies in Income and Wealth 19, Princeton University Press for NBER, 1957, p. 509.

[6] The lag implicit in using stocks at the end of the year appears to give the most stable ratios. The incremental ratio reduces the substantial cyclical fluctuation that characterizes the average ratio.

was ±5.3. The implications of this wide variation in terms of the power of sales to determine inventory investment may be brought out if actual year-to-year changes in stocks are compared with what they would have been had the incremental sales-stock ratio been constant at the median value. Average actual change was $3.6 billion; the *error* of estimating change on the basis of the constant ratio was ±$2.6 billion—72 per cent of the actual change.

Obviously, then, in order to understand the behavior of stocks, influences in addition to a presumed constant association to sales must be sought. Increasingly, in the past two decades, econometric analysis has been brought to bear on this difficult task. Different investigators have made different calculations based on different theories.[7] But recurring in recent studies are two themes which bear particularly on the general problem of meaningful analysis of the role of inventory fluctuation. One is the inclusion of unfilled orders as an explanatory variable, the other the use of distributed lags.

THE INFLUENCE OF UNFILLED ORDERS

The work of several analysts has shown that unfilled orders help to explain inventory investment. Unfilled orders must have at least some bearing on the changing expectations about market conditions on which this monograph focuses. But the difficulty with the findings of a number of studies that I would like to discuss is that unfilled orders are *too* helpful.[8] Simple correlation coefficients relating change in unfilled orders to change in variously defined stock aggregates ranged, for two investigations, from .82 to .84.[9] Beta coefficients indicate that the explanatory power of unfilled orders is roughly at a par with sales. But the actual statistics used to represent unfilled orders are heavily dominated by backlogs of sales orders in the machinery and transportation equipment industries, which on the average contribute 70 per cent of the total.[10] It is difficult to see why unfilled sales orders in these two industries should so heavily influence stock for all manufacturers (plus distributors in one investigation).

As to the explanation of the role of unfilled orders, the several investigators partly agree and partly differ.[11] Darling emphasizes

[7] For a summary and analysis of a large number of studies, see a very interesting article by Michael Lovell, "Determinants of Inventory Investment," in *Models of Income Determination,* Studies in Income and Wealth 28, Princeton for NBER, 1964.

[8] The basic references in which the work here discussed appears are: (1) Paul G. Darling, "Manufacturers' Inventory Investment, 1947–1958," *American Economic Review,* December 1959, pp. 950–963, and (2) Darling, "Inventory Fluctuations and Economic Instability: An Analysis Based on the Post War Economy," Joint Economic Committee, *Inventory Fluctuations and Economic Stabilization,* Washington, 1961, Part III; (3) Michael C. Lovell, "Factors Determining Manufacturing Inventory Investment," *Inventory Fluctuations and Economic Stabilization,* Part II, (4) Lovell, "Buffer Stocks, Sales Expectations, and Stability: A Multi-Sector Analysis of the Inventory Cycle," *Econometrica,* April 1962, and (5) Lovell, "Manufacturers' Inventories, Sales Expectations, and the Acceleration Principle," *Inventory Fluctuations and Economic Stabilization,* Part II (reprinted from *Econometrica,* July 1961); (6) Nestor E. Terleckyj, *Measures of Inventory Conditions,* National Industrial Conference Board Technical Paper 8, New York, 1960 (reprinted in *Inventory Fluctuations and Economic Stabilization,* Part II); (7) Lovell, "Determinants of Inventory Invest-

ment" (see footnote 7), and (8) Ruth P. Mack, comment on the preceding paper (*ibid.,* pp. 224–231); this comment is the direct source of most of the discussion of the next several pages.

[9] See note 8, references 1 and 3, and reference 8 (pp. 225–226).

[10] The figures are given in Ruth P. Mack, "Changes in Ownership of Purchased Materials," *Inventory Fluctuations and Economic Stabilization,* Part II, p. 86, note 8.

[11] Darling: ". . . inventory investment is more closely associated in time with receipt of the order, or more accurately with changes in the 'unfilled order' backlog, than with the delivery (sale) of the goods to the buyers. Indeed, the sale is an act of *dis*investment rather than a determinant of investment in stocks"

two causal influences: firms buy when they sell (when customers place orders), not when they ship; buffer stocks need to be greater when supply conditions tighten, which tends to be when the rate of change in backlogs is greatest. Lovell attributes the positive association primarily to the fact that an increase in backlogs anticipates an increase in production, which dictates an increase in stock. He agrees with Darling's first reason insofar as he thinks firms like to buy when they sell, as a hedge against shortages or price change. Terleckyj agrees with Lovell's first reason concerning the relevance of the link between backlogs and production.

The influence of unfilled orders on stocks has also been observed in time series without benefit of econometric analysis. To mention only one example, Stanback has displayed the impressive parallelism among stocks of purchased materials, new orders, and series that reflect the speed with which materials are delivered and the delivery terms on which pur-

chasing agents buy.[12] These in turn are closely similar to unfilled orders.[13] His explanation is complex, but he seems to emphasize the changing supply conditions that these figures feature—conditions that may be based on limitations imposed by plant capacity: "The influence of supply conditions may operate in two ways during expansions: (1) deterioration in supply conditions makes it more difficult to achieve inventory objectives, and the realized inventory investment will be somewhat less than that desired; and (2) deterioration in supply conditions influences the inventory objective itself." [14]

These studies indicate, then, that inventory investment is, roughly, equally influenced by unfilled orders and sales. At the same time, the explanations proffered do not develop agreement on the reasons why this should be so, particularly in view of the lopsided industrial composition of the statistics themselves.

UNEXPLAINED CHANGE

The problem is further complicated by what the equations fail to explain. When the time series themselves are compared, stock typically lags sales or output. The lagged association

is given an interesting interpretation by Richard Goodwin's notion of the "flexible accelerator": firms typically attempt only a partial adjustment of inventory toward its

---

(note 8, reference 2, p. 30). To the selling firm, unfilled orders give rise to "pipeline" stocks. Also, because of competitive pressures in supplying markets, "the time of greatest uncertainty for purchasing firms during business expansions, and hence the period in which their need for buffer stocks will be greatest, will tend to coincide with the period during which the *rate of increase of unfilled orders is at a peak.*" Accordingly, changes in unfilled orders are introduced to take account of "buffer stock" reactions to actual and expected conditions in markets, specifically, changes in delivery period and in the reliability of quoted delivery dates (*ibid.,* p. 33).

Lovell: "If unfilled orders represent an established demand, indeed a possible committal to deliver at some future date, entrepreneurs may well consider it advisable to carry additional stocks when unfilled orders are large as a hedge against possible shortage and price commitments. In addition, a rise in the backlog of unfilled orders may be expected to lead to

an acceleration of production that is felt first in terms of an increase of goods in process rather than a rise in the output of completed commodities" (note 8, reference 3, pp. 140–141). Lovell seems to disagree with Darling's second reason: "Conversely, if unfilled orders were only a surrogate measure for the tightness of the markets on which firms purchase their inputs, a negative relationship between orders and stocks would be revealed . . ." (*ibid.,* p. 141).

Terleckyj: "One would expect that when new orders are running above sales, and the reservoir of future business is built up, an accumulation of inventories becomes desirable, as the planned production rate rises to fill these orders. The subsequent increase in the actual production rate entails a rise in inventories concentrated in the in-process stocks" (note 8, reference 6, p. 21).

[12] Stanback, *Postwar Cycles,* Chart 9, p. 55.

[13] *Ibid.,* p. 50.

[14] *Ibid.,* p. 58.

equilibrium level in each period.[15] When this construction is used, there is an equilibrium level of stock—one which firms would not want to change, once achieved—and this differs from the actual level.

Michael Lovell reviewed a number of postwar studies and calculated equilibrium levels of stock, and what they imply about the extent to which firms attempt to adjust inventories to that level in a single period.[16] If complete adjustment were achieved, the "reaction coefficient" would be 1, but for two equations [17] for which the coefficient could be calculated it was about one-half for an entire year or about one-fifth a quarter, ". . . implying that firms in manufacturing attempt to liquidate roughly one-fifth of the discrepancy between equilibrium and actual inventories each quarter." [18] For his own effort to explain nonfarm inventory investment, 1947–59, in terms of gross national product, its rate of change, and unfilled orders, Lovell calculated differences between equilibrium and estimated (or actual)

inventories quarter by quarter. These "surplus inventories" averaged substantially larger than the quarter-to-quarter change in actual inventories, $1.7 billion compared to $1.0 billion, ignoring signs in both cases.[19] They tended to move in opposite directions, being negative when investment is positive and vice versa.

What, one is moved to ask, is the meaning of a business objective which is only one-fifth achieved in the course of three months, or one which results in nonintended stocks substantially larger than the total change in stocks? At the least, "passive" inventory investment must be very large—far larger than seems to make sense. Random disturbances and mistakes also may be partly responsible.

In any event, very much a part of the picture are the assumptions, embodied in the equation, concerning the requirements which when satisfied produce equilibrium stock. If unfilled orders [20] and demand do not in fact largely determine inventory investment, then "equilibrium stock," defined in terms of the two variables, will not, except by chance, be achieved. How realistic are the assumptions? How, in fact, is inventory investment usually determined? The next chapter aims to take some tentative steps toward an answer by looking at the business firm itself.

[15] Richard M. Goodwin, "Secular and Cyclical Aspects of the Multiplier and Accelerator," in *Income, Employment and Public Policy: Essays in Honor of Alvin H. Hansen,* New York, 1948.

[16] Note 8, reference 7.

[17] The studies were by Lawrence A. Klein, who used annual data, 1921–41, for which the reaction coefficient as calculated by Lovell was .5. (Lawrence R. Klein, *Economic Fluctuations in the United States, 1921–41,* Cowles Commission Monograph 11, New York, 1950); and Darling, note 8, reference 1, pp. 5–6; cf. Lovell, note 8, reference 7, pp. 183–184, and Mack, reference 8, p. 226.

[18] Lovell, note 7, p. 184.

[19] Lovell, note 8, reference 7, p. 187. I summed the figures only through 1959, since the last two years were extrapolations.

[20] Klein's equation uses wholesale prices rather than unfilled orders.

2. Functions and Determinants of Stocks in Business Enterprises[1]

Two attributes of stocks are critical to their management: first, stocks serve a wide variety of purposes in a business enterprise; second, they are costly to carry. These two facts mean that business firms must carry stocks, that they do not wish to carry more than they need, and that what is needed depends on the many functions that stocks serve and the influences that play upon them. What are these functions and influences? How, in view of the factors that determine the size of stocks, are they likely to vary in the course of economic fluctuations? In endeavoring to answer these questions, it will be useful to include stocks on order along with those on hand.

METHOD AND DIRECTION OF THE ANALYSIS

The Vantage Point of the Firm

The chapter examines the stock-carrying problem within business firms. Ideally it would combine economic analysis, management expertise, and descriptions by businessmen of how they operate and why, but the last approach has unfortunately gone by default in this study. As compensation in small measure, one end product of the book is a list of particular questions that need to be explored with business executives. The second source of information, management expertise, may require some justification.

There is an ample literature on inventories; it constitutes one of the major fields explored in management science or operations research. The literature is normative; it says what *should be* done. Does this bear an instructive relationship to *what is* done, the matter of interest here? I think the answer is yes. For one thing, the analysis that underlies the normative prescriptions helps to specify the relevant factors at work and thus helps the student discover what business does. For another thing, many of the prescriptions seem to have their counterpart in seat-of-the-pants judgments of businessmen. Finally, in a group of businesses, what "should be" and what "is" can differ in degree but not in basic kind. Even if actual rules have only a rough resemblance to normative rules, action is likely to resemble them more closely. Firms practicing successful procedures are imitated by their rivals, whereas firms persistently practicing unsuccessful procedures tend to disappear as Darwin has prescribed.[2]

[1] Norman Agin (MATHEMATICA and Columbia University, Department of Industrial Management and Engineering) has collaborated in the preparation of this chapter both in specific ways and by general aid and counsel throughout.

[2] Armen Alchian has gone much farther and argued that trial and error and survival of the fittest can go a long ways toward duplicating classic optimizing procedure without assuming classic rationality (which, because of uncertainty, is not even roughly realistic). "Uncertainty, Evolution and Economic Theory," *Journal of Political Economy*, June 1950, pp. 211–221.

Ownership of Materials

The first insight yielded by viewing inventories from within a business firm concerns the boundaries of the stock-carrying and procurement problem. For many purposes these boundaries appear to encompass materials on order along with those on hand—what I call materials "ownership." There are several reasons for arriving at this judgment.

Management literature speaks in these terms, often implicitly. Decision rules concern when and how much to order, and are based on correcting the difference between actual and desired stock. Obviously, if stock refers only to stock on hand, the implicit assumption is that the time required for the delivery of an order is constant and short—more rigorously, zero (since lead time affects the proper size of stocks and the forecasting error). I know of no exception in the literature to the fact that decision rules governing inventories stipulate what to order; of necessity, therefore, it is inventories on hand and on order which are thereby governed.

Sometimes authors make this attention explicit. To quote at random: "I_i = minimum stock of i at time of analysis including stock ordered." [3] "If the level system stock (stock at hand plus outstanding order) is dangerously low . . ." [4] "The foregoing analysis of optimal periodic order placement has shown that the on-hand plus on-order purchased materials inventory is brought into line each period with the prevailing usage forecast." [5]

In business firms also, reference to stocks both on hand and on order is common. It is sometimes referred to as the "position." The term "ownership" is one I encountered in discussing materials buying problems with executives in shoe and leather manufacturing concerns. Department store retailers call the same thing "in sight." [6]

The reasons why stock and procurement planning must comprehend goods on order as well as on hand will become clearer as the functions of stocks are discussed. But because the concept is unfamiliar, it may be useful to analyze it for a moment.

Production operations ordinarily involve acts that must be performed in sequence. The purpose of stocks is to provide, at each station where work is to be performed, an adequate supply of materials to facilitate efficient performance of the work at that station (under the constraint that the total system also operate efficiently, as defined).

Finished stocks supply the point where goods are ready for shipment to customers and sometimes some intermediate storage spots. Stocks in process service a number of operations that convert goods from less to

[3] Richard M. Cyert and James G. March, *A Behavioral Theory of the Firm*, Englewood Cliffs, N.J., 1963, p. 136.

[4] Yoichiro Fukeda, "Optimal Policies for the Inventory Problem with Negotiable Leadtime," *Management Science*, July 1964, pp. 690–708.

[5] Charles C. Holt and Franco Modigliani, "Firm Cost Structures and the Dynamic Responses of Inventories, Production, Work Force, and Orders to Sales Fluctuations," Joint Economic Committee, *Inventory Fluctuations and Economic Stabilization*, Washington, 1961, Part II, p. 44.

As the title suggests, the authors interest themselves in how the problems that businessmen must solve influence the size of their stocks. This and other publications by the same authors are replete with analysis and information about many of the same questions that I touch on, often in a far more impressionistic fashion, in this chapter and elsewhere in this volume. See particularly Modigliani and Franz E. Hohn, "Production Planning over Time and the Nature of the Expectations Horizon," *Econometrica*, 1955, pp. 46–66; Modigliani and Kalman J. Cohen, "The Role of Anticipations and Planning in Economic Behavior and Their Use in Economic Analysis and Forecasting," Bureau of Economic and Business Research, *University of Illinois Bulletin*, January 1961.

[6] See, for example, testimony of Vincent J. Graham, General Merchandise Controller, Sears, Roebuck and Company, in Hearings Before the Subcommittee on Economic Stabilization, Automation, and Energy Resources of the Joint Economic Committee, July 9, 1962, *Inventory Fluctuation and Stabilization:* "I am talking about the overall combination, of the inventory and the on-order, which we call in sight" (p. 29). Also "Most retailers . . . operate on a turnover basis, maintaining a flow of goods in sight related to a predetermined number of weeks or months of anticipated future sales" (p. 5).

more finished states. "Raw" materials stocks service not only the first production station but also earlier preparatory stations where cleaning, sorting, and ticketing operations may have taken place. Finally, the first appearance of goods in the establishment has been made possible by outstanding orders which have achieved their delivery date. Materials currently required in stock must have been ordered earlier by whatever time is required for delivery to take place; they must be on order during this interval in the same sense in which current finishing operations imply the previous presence of stocks of materials undergoing cleaning or sorting. Thus the essence of the work that is done by stocks is that of providing for a sequence of things to occur, each of which takes time. From the point of view of the orderly sequence whereby goods become available to the operations that a particular enterprise performs, stocks on hand and on order can be very much of a piece.

Of course, the parallelism is far from complete. Work can be performed at the discretion of the owner of stocks on hand, whereas the seller as well as the buyer make determinations about stock on order. The movement of stocks through a business has physical counterparts associated with income flows and other matters that do not apply to stock on order. The transformation effected by an order is executive and informational rather than physical.

A second reason for thinking in terms of ownership has already been mentioned—the most usual action that must be taken in order to increase or decrease stocks is to order more or fewer materials, and thus change the level of stocks both on hand and on order. Of course, if lead times were invariant, the distinction would be empty. Since they are not, the purchaser decides both what to order and, within constraints, whether to hold it on hand or on order.

In making the second decision, there are advantages and disadvantages which mean that, in effect, stock on hand has a competitive relationship to stock on order and vice versa. Stock held on order has the advantage that it does not imply carrying and financing costs. Under some circumstances purchasers may not have to live up to the commitment to accept delivery. There may be further advantages in the form of better prices and selections if suppliers are given ample time to make deliveries. On the other hand, stock on order implies uncertainty about just when materials will actually arrive and the extent to which they will meet specifications. There are other ways in which stocks on hand and on order are only partial substitutes for one another and therefore have a competitive relationship expressed by a differential price that buyers choose to pay.

Stocks on hand and on order also have a complementary relationship to one another. The complementary aspect follows from the fact that orders precede receipts. An intention to increase stocks of materials, or for that matter to increase the flow of goods toward its final state, of necessity involves some temporary increase in outstanding orders unless delivery is immediate. In this sense, outstanding orders constitute a vestibule through which materials must pass before they enter the door of factory or store. If the entrance flow is to be increased, either to add to stocks or to feed the flow of production, this "vestibule effect" will precede the increase. If, on the other hand, the intention focuses on the increase in outstanding orders, there is a "reverse vestibule effect" and the orders will eventually be delivered; when this occurs, stocks will increase as a deferred reaction to changes in outstandings, other things the same. Of course, other things do not need to be the same; the flow into production, or to customers, may have increased in line with the increase in orders for material. In this event no increase in stock need occur.

I conclude that it is essential to study stocks on order and those on hand together, as well as individually.

A "System" of Alternatives

The second major insight that the firm's-eye view affords is the wide system of alternatives of which stocks constitute a part. Carrying stocks provides one way of meeting a large variety of business problems each of which may also be met in a number of other ways.[7] Thus an alternative to solving the problem, say, of meeting variable demand promptly by means of stocks is that of doing so by flexible production schedules, and each of the two methods are pursued to the point where, other things the same, their marginal costs are equal. Similarly, an alternative to using funds for financing inventories is to use them for financing new plant capacity, and their potential earnings in one use constitute their opportunity costs for employing them in the other. To pursue this point of view it is necessary to set the cost of carrying stock against the contribution of stock to efficient business operation.

Plan for the Chapter

These generalizations point the way to how fluctuations in stocks may be probed. We need to outline the major functions that stocks serve and note by what other means the same functions can be carried out. This, along with

[7] The appropriate context in which to consider particular business problems—the system—has received growing attention in recent years. The usual conclusion seems to be that the system should be broadened. Arthur D. Hall presents this general approach in *A Methodology for Systems Engineering*, Princeton, N.J., 1962. An interesting article which makes the point for inventories is by Herbert Simon and Charles Holt, "The Control of Inventories and Production Rates—A Survey," *Journal of the Operations Research Society of America*, August 1954, pp. 289 ff. The authors discuss research relating to ordering decisions, production rate decisions, and scheduling decisions. "Since ordering and production decisions both involve this weighing of costs against gains from the holding of inventories, we should expect that fundamental research directed at either one should have applicability to the other." This, the authors say, has not been so in the past, but "Currently these two separate lines of investigation are converging rapidly" (p. 298).

information on costs, indicates how the size of stocks is determined and how it is affected by changes in the level of sales and in other relevant factors. Next we consider how the cost of carrying stock, and of the alternative ways of meeting the management objectives that stocks serve, may tend to change during business cycles.

The purpose of this last phase is not to arrive at conclusions or even firm hypotheses about cyclical behavior. Information is still too fragile for that. Rather, the analysis is intended to provide the background for understanding the evidence yielded by the examination of time series in the body of the book. The time series, it should be added, deal only with materials stock on hand and on order. But to understand the functions that these stocks serve, it is necessary to use a broader perspective for the purpose of this chapter and to cover all stocks, whether finished, in process, or purchased materials on hand and on order.

It may be useful to have the main conclusions in mind at the outset. The major functions that stocks serve are:

1. Bridging the time required for processes (economic transformations) to be performed.
2. Efficient production or purchasing lots.
3. Insurance against losing sales because of individually unpredictable fluctuations in demand or other matters.
4. Smoothing operations by provision for more or less foreseeable fluctuations.
5. Grasping the potential advantage (or avoiding the disadvantage) of actual or expected changes in conditions in markets in which purchases or sales are made.
6. Providing elective freedom from the tyranny of planning for uncertain events.

The first is, as far as I can judge, a unique function of stocks. All the other functions, in effect, "buy efficiency" by substituting the lesser cost of carrying stock for a greater cost of coping with a particular management problem in some other way.

In each case, these functions may be served by stocks at all levels of processing—from finished goods to purchased materials. They are often also served by purchased materials on order (as well as those on hand), and consequently these outstanding purchase orders must be considered along with stocks physically in the possession of the enterprise.

If we think of each of the six functions as covered by stocks serving just that function and no other, patterns of appropriate variation may be ascertained. This is, of course, an abstraction since the same physical stocks serve several functions. In any event, analysis leads to the conclusion that the efficient servicing of sales does not require stocks that vary in proportion to sales but that vary substantially less, other things the same. In other words, the stock-sales ratio could well have a pattern inverse to that of sales if nothing else changed. Yet, of course, other things do change. The analysis suggests that costs may often shift in favor of the stock-carrying alternative when business is good.

THE COST OF STOCKS

To achieve the purposes that stocks serve, the cost of carrying them must be borne. What then are these costs and how are they likely to change with business conditions?

Components of Cost

Appropriate to a decision to increase or decrease stocks are the costs that actually do change as a result of the decision—the marginal or incremental costs. Whether this solid economic rule is more honored in the breach than in practice is not clear.[8]

Physical care of physical goods includes the cost of storage, handling and guardian functions, insurance against risk of fire, theft, or other hazards. An allowance for physical depreciation may also be required. Though these costs may be substantial in some businesses, it seems likely that they usually add up to materially less than that of economic depreciation and finance. They apply to stock on hand at all stages; they do not apply to those on order.

Economic depreciation or obsolescence results from the need to immobilize resources in, and make a commitment to buy, specific inventory items. As a result there may be losses due to markdowns or other costs of having the wrong goods on hand. Though the time covered by the commitment is far shorter than for most capital investment, it nevertheless can involve a serious risk. The less is known about what sales will be (either with respect to volume or kind), and the more differentiated are the materials required for particular finished articles, the higher is the risk. It increases also with the length of time over which resources must be committed.

The risk of obsolescence starts when a commitment to purchase is made. Accordingly it applies to stock on order as well as on hand. In the former case, however, the commitment may sometimes have a modicum of elasticity which is lost once delivery takes place.

Financing costs, the cost of funds invested in stocks is calculated as a percentage, per unit of time, of the value of inventory goods. The figure is determined in one of several ways. It may be defined as an actual interest expense when stocks are in fact financed by borrowed funds. This cost, though small relative to other ways of determining financing cost, may be an important burden in com-

---

[8] Practice may differ in different contexts. For example, unused storage space may typically not be considered a charge against stocks, as it should not be; whereas unused and unusable financial leeway may be considered such a charge, at least in the management rules.

panies that are short of funds and operate with high materials costs and low value added. But even when no actual borrowing takes place, a common situation, the "opportunity costs" of funds invested in inventories are ordinarily charged against them.

This rate may be the average rate of return on invested capital for the company. It may also be considerably higher; ". . . a rate of return or imputed interest rate between ten and thirty per cent is not unreasonable." [9] Concerning one large company I was specifically told that its average return was 14 per cent and the inventory financing charge 30 per cent. The higher end of the range no doubt includes an allowance for risks of the kind discussed in the previous paragraph. But high financing rates may also serve a partly strategic managerial function in a large decentralized company. A high cost of inventories keeps management on its toes to discover other ways of achieving the objectives that inventories serve—production schedules are examined to increase flexibility; suppliers are pushed to make frequent, swift, and reliable deliveries; sales pressure aims at filling in seasonal lows.

In any event, it seems clear that the bookkeeping charge for carrying inventories has a very substantial judgmental and even strategy-linked element. If so, the formal rules, and what they yield by way of cost figures, may be only part of what upper management takes into account when it reviews the inventory position of departments and of the company as a whole. Implicit if not explicit judgment may also be made concerning the current applicability of the rules themselves.

Financing costs apply in the first instance to stock on hand only. However, if on-order positions are extended, their ultimate delivery may cause stock on hand to be larger than it otherwise would. If so, this inverse vestibule effect will imply a delayed financing cost for stock on order also. Per unit of finished goods,

financing costs are of course higher as the finished state is approached.

Cyclical Changes in Inventory Costs

The previous discussion suggests that changes in inventory costs may be of two sorts: changes recognized in explicit costing rules and changes that concern extra-rule evaluations that determine changes in the conclusions drawn from the same formal cost figures. As far as I know, there are no studies of cyclical patterns in the first type of cost, much less the second. Accordingly, only the most tentative statements are possible. However, I would like to venture the thought that, contrary to the most obvious suppositions, costs are on balance more likely to fall than to rise in prosperity.

Bank interest rates, it is true, may rise, but the difference of one, two, or even three percentage points a year is so small a portion of total stock costs in most businesses as to be of most questionable general significance. This is not to minimize the importance of these costs in some business for which funds are short and stock financing an important part of value added. Moreover, availability of credit, which is likely to parallel its costs, can seriously tend to discourage inventory investment in such businesses when credit is tight. But for many businesses, cyclical variations in the cost and availability of bank credit may be a minor influence in stock-carrying decisions except under most exceptional circumstances. In any event, painstaking empirical search has failed to establish the expected association.[10]

On the other hand, lower financing costs during prosperity are suggested by several considerations. First, the average period for which goods are held in stock is likely to fall be-

---

[9] John F. Magee, *Production Planning and Inventory Control*, New York, 1958, p. 40.

[10] See Paul F. McGouldrick, "The Impact of Credit Cost and Availability on Inventory Investment," *Inventory Fluctuations and Economic Stabilization*, Part II. The author reviews the literature on the subject, and the burden of his conclusion may be summarized in his words, "On the whole, results were disappointing" (p. 105).

cause stocks resulting from overestimating future sales are lower than during at least the early months of recession. And virtually all carrying costs are a function of the time that goods are held in stock. Second, risk of economic obsolescence is reduced by the shift from a buyers' to a sellers' market, which typically accompanies periods of strong demand; the company's customers are not as choosy.

Third, actual opportunity costs of capital are probably reduced. For one thing, the risk charge that is included in the financing rate is less for the reasons just mentioned. Further, substantial profits during peak periods may provide funds which companies are willing to invest in liquid assets but presently fear to commit to permanent capital improvements. If funds were really compartmentalized in this way, firms that customarily borrow to finance

stocks might be able to substitute more internal funds when profits were high; firms that customarily finance stocks from internal funds could dip into some portion of prosperity profits for which the alternative form of investment would be that of other liquid assets, such as financial instruments. If so, the opportunity cost would be far lower than if the alternative was investment in fixed plant. The argument implies that though the explicit rules for stock-carrying costs may remain the same, actual behavior may change. The grapevine communicates a permissive attitude from the front office. As will be seen later, the time series look as if this could be the case. In any event, for present purposes it is sufficient to conjecture that stock-holding costs will typically not have clear positive cyclical conformity.

PROCESS-TIME STOCKS

Against the cost of carrying stock is set the benefit that stocks provide. The first major type of benefit to be considered is that of supporting the time required to effect economic transformations.

The transformations may be physical—cloth and findings are transformed into a suit; they may be locational—the cloth is moved from Raleigh to Rochester; they may be executive—an order for cloth is received by the mill, recorded, scheduled, and eventually shipped. For an individual company, total processing time is meaningfully defined as the sum of all three types. It applies to stocks at all stages of processing and to materials on order.

Stocks that support some properly determined minimum time required for processing to take place are *necessities* of business existence, whatever their cost. As the next section indicates, the minimum is defined under normally prevailing efficient eco-engineering conditions. What determines this minimum size?

Determinants: Link to Sales

The amount of stocks that are required for physical transformation depends on the length of the process. If output is continuous, then some goods in each condition of processing will reside in stock at any given moment. The longer the time required for the process to be completed, the larger, relative to the output per day or week, stocks must be.

The time required for a process to take place is in one sense an engineering problem. But goods seldom pass through a production process at the maximum speed that engineering techniques would allow. Economic considerations demand that assembly belts move at rates that do not cause excessive spoilage, that goods wait until enough units queue up so that the process can be performed in economical lots, that some waiting occurs between sequential processes, and so on. All of these economic considerations must be superimposed on engineering efficiency, and therefore process-time stocks are enlarged by some admixture of "efficiency" stocks serving the many other functions that stocks perform. The point is underscored by the fact that minimum production time is also subject to some control, at a price; men and machines can be required to move more or less swiftly or production lineups can be altered. But for present purposes, the conceptual annoyances that this ambiguity involves can be kept to a minimum by thinking of process-time stocks, somewhat loosely, as those required to support the time required to move goods through the process under *normally prevailing* efficient eco-engineering conditions. These conditions are, by definition, thought of as not changing during business fluctuations, though of course they can undergo marked trends.

Process-time stocks form a significant portion of stocks of goods in process in any factory. But this is by no means the only place where they exist. Sorting, marking, packaging, carting, and storing operations, all of which take time, may be performed on goods after production has been completed and they have entered "finished" stocks. Materials stocks of "purchased goods" are also often subjected to several processes that require time, as likewise are distributors' "stock in trade."

Process time is also present for materials outstanding. The purchaser, in planning for a flow of materials designed to feed production, must consider not only the time required for the transportation of goods from the maker's shipping sheds to his own receiving docks, but also for the time required for the maker to get around to shipping it to him. The whole period is the "replenishment time" or "lead time"—the interval between placement of the order by the purchaser and replenishment of his stocks of purchased materials by the receipt of the goods.

It is particularly important in connection with this aspect of process time, which is of course supported by materials stocks outstanding, to think of the "normally prevailing efficient eco-engineering conditions" as being constant during business fluctuations. Actually conditions, needless to say, are not, since delivery periods and other aspects of market conditions tend to vary during business cycles. Perhaps the best way to identify the process-time part of outstanding orders is in terms of the amount required under "hand-to-mouth" conditions. The phrase is not meant literally; it applies under a "buyers' market"— a time, that is, when markets are unexcited.

If processing time is uniform, the size of process-time stocks (I_p) is a function of the volume of goods (D) which is required to emerge from the stockpile per calendar interval, and the time, in terms of that interval, required for processing (T).[11] Thus, $I_p = DT$. This means that if there is no change in processing time, desired process-time stocks will increase or decrease in *direct proportion to demand*. This is, of course, the model of derived demand in its generic sense, if one assumes that total stocks serve the process-time function. Actually, of course, all stocks are not caught up in the march of goods through a plant at its normal pace, and the constant ratio applies only to those that are.[12]

Other Influences

Processing time, in terms of the calendar interval in which demand is recorded, can change in two ways. First, the calendar time required for the process can change as a result of changing technology—it can take two days of processing, whereas previously it took

[11] If statistics are in dollars rather than physical units, and value is added evenly and continuously, then the value of a unit of stock will be one-half of the unit value of demand D minus the value of the equivalent unit value of "raw" materials.

[12] Another way to put it is in terms of a constant incremental ratio equal to the average ratio of process-time stocks to sales. If sales are 1,000 units, total stocks are 3,000, and process-time stocks 2,000, then as sales increase to 1,100 process-time stocks rise to 2,200.

four. Second, the relation between calendar and processing time can change; the factory can operate longer, as in a change from a one-shift to a two-shift operation. Work that took one shift two days now takes two shifts one day. Accordingly, to represent a change in process time, a correction factor is required. The ratio represents the change in the proportion of the 24-hour day or 168-hour week that processing is taking place on the same line sequence. It is the ratio of processing time to calendar time at time zero, divided by the ratio of processing time to calendar time at time 1. Thus, $I_p = \alpha DT$.[13]

The ratio α can change characteristically with business conditions. For example, if additional demand is accompanied by a second shift, α is approximately halved.[14] Thus an approximate doubling of demand can be accommodated without much change in processing stocks. Overtime work has an analogous impact, though to a far less extent. If, on the other hand, additional output is accommodated by adding parallel production lines, process time is unchanged and this means that stocks will increase proportionately to output.

Cyclical Patterns

These considerations suggest that stocks identified as process-time stocks would have an underlying tendency to maintain a generally proportional relation to sales, after allowing for the appropriate lags associated with the change in the level of output.[15] But

overtime work and multiple-shift operations (when in line sequences rather than parallel sequences) will introduce a tendency for stocks to rise less than sales during prosperous times. This could, I imagine, be quite important in some industries. Some countervailing tendency may arise if overcrowding of facilities slows up operations.

Process-time stocks on order share the tendency to change in proportion to sales, and there is no reason to expect a change in the relation of process to calendar time, α. Therefore the relation is strictly proportional, other things the same.

However, replenishment periods themselves often change. As business expands and markets tighten, suppliers tend to quote delivery dates that extend replenishment periods. Purchasers very typically accept these dates and extend their materials outstanding correspondingly, rather than pay the premium prices (including poorer selections, quality, etc.) that quick deliveries would imply. Indeed they often anticipate these market stringencies for a number of reasons, thereby further extending outstandings. These resulting stocks on order are a type of "efficiency stock" covering market prospects and are discussed below. This does not, however, exempt them from their process-time characteristics of $I_p = DT$. Thus T increases; but if D does also, stocks are a product of the two.

Assuming that there is no foreknowledge of change in demand, the lag in process-time stocks relative to shipments, both measured at book value, increases with the length of process-time and the ratio of value added to the value of product. If output is increasing, the higher unit value of more nearly completed goods will cover a smaller proportion of stocks (measured in equivalent physical units of finished goods) than the lower unit values of more nearly raw goods, which reflect the increase in demand more promptly. Therefore the ratio of stocks to output measured in dollars will be lower than when the level of output has remained unchanged during the processing time. Conversely, when output is declining, the ratio of stocks to output is higher.

---

[13] α has a value of 1 under unchanged conditions. An alternative way of formulating the concept would be to assign the value of 1 to "normal" conditions.

[14] I ignore the lower productivity of second shifts. Also, insurance stocks should be increased since the cost of stockouts in terms of lost time increases with multiple shift operation. I assume as previously that the second shift takes over where the first one ended and continues to move the same inventory pools along.

[15] The lag is present in process-time stocks as defined, though other functions of stocks also contribute.

EFFICIENCY STOCKS: THE RANGE OF ALTERNATIVES

The fundamental notion in the designation "efficiency stocks" is that of *opportunity costs*. These stocks "buy" managerial efficiency at a cost that is equal to that of the next best way of achieving an analogous marginal benefit.[16]

There are a wide variety of managerial problems that are moderated by an increase in stocks, on the one hand, or by some other management device, on the other hand, and it is to these situations that efficiency stocks apply. Correct solutions inevitably involve some combination of the two sorts of devices —the point, theoretically, where incremental (marginal) costs are equal. The range of the problems and of the devices by which they may be dealt with are indicated by Exhibit 1. For manufacturing, section 1 applies primarily to finished stock, section 2 to in-process stock, and section 3 to materials on hand and on order (see column 4). For distribution, sections 1 and 3 encompass most alternatives.

Glancing down the first column, it may be seen that one recurrent type of problem involves variability in demand; it appears at the selling stage (line 1.2), at the producing stage (line 2.1), or at the purchasing stage (line 3.1). There are many ways of dealing with this variability. For example, at the selling stage, price concessions (column 2, line 1.2.1) may encourage off-season sales, but this involves some lost revenue (relative to the full price) even if the incidence of price reduction can be narrowly contained; besides, return to normal prices may encounter customer resistance (column 3, line 1.2.1). Similarly, the extra expense of additional selling effort, including directed advertising campaigns, might help to smooth sales (lines 1.2.2 and 1.2.3).

An alternative to any of these ways of reducing sales fluctuation is simply to carry an inventory of finished goods which provides a reservoir large enough to service the existent pattern of sales. Such stocks are of two sorts according to the variability against which they protect: the first are "insurance" or "buffer" stocks, which provide for random ups and downs in weekly or monthly sales; the second we call "fluctuation" stocks, which provide for variability due to more or less predictable seasonal or other patterns of demand. Insurance stocks would afford faster delivery for perhaps a wider selection of items with a lower acceptable chance of stock-outs. Fluctuation stocks might cover higher seasonal peaks as alternative to the methods in column 2 applied to smoothing the monthly pattern of demand. Both sorts of stocks may provide alternatives to price concessions or sales pressure in dealing with variability of demand at the selling stage.

Another alternative is that of doing nothing (line 1.2.7) and simply tolerating the cost of disappointing or turning away customers. Somewhat analogous situations reappear at the earlier stages of the sequence of operations that a company performs. At the purchasing stage the stock function of insuring against variable demand is served both by stocks on hand and on order. (Column 4b indicates when this is or is not the case.)

Stocks also permit production or buying to take place in efficiently sized batches. Job lots that are too small (line 2.2) involve high labor costs and machine down-time (column 3). Larger job lots imply larger "lot-size" stocks (about half the size of the lot) and resultant inventory costs (column 4). Orders too have optimal sizes. The high unit purchasing costs that result when orders are too small

[16] The notion of stocks that "buy efficiency" was used and emphasized in Magee's very useful *Production Planning and Inventory Control*. I have borrowed from his analysis in a number of other ways as well.

EXHIBIT 1

Business Problems Which Can Be Dealt With by Methods That Include an Increase in Stock

Problem (1)	Method Other Than Increasing Stock		Stock Method[a] (4)
	Method (2)	Type of Cost Involved (3)	
1. *Selling*			*Finished Goods Stocks*
1.1 Sales promotion	1.1.1 Price adjustments	Possible lost revenue	Ins., Fl.
	1.1.2 Selling pressure	Sales costs	Ins., Fl.
	1.1.3 Advertising	Advertising expense	Ins., Fl.
1.2 Variable sales (expected or random)	*Reduce variability:*		
	1.2.1 Price concessions	Lost revenue Difficulty in reversing policy	Ins., Fl.
	1.2.2 Selling pressure	Selling; costs	Ins., Fl.
	1.2.3 Advertising	Advertising expense	Ins., Fl.
	Predict variability:		
	1.2.4 Research	Research cost	Ins., Fl.
	Shift variability:		
	1.2.5 Buy vs. make	Higher cost	Ins., Fl.
	1.2.6 Counteract via requiring advance orders	Lost sales or selling expense minus the advantage of preknowledge of sales	Ins., Fl.
	1.2.7 Accept the cost of stock-outs	Lost sales	Ins., Fl.
1.3 Achieving an optimal selling price if prices are expected to rise	1.3.1 Forgo opportunity to wait	Lost revenue	MP
2. *Producing*			*In-Process Stocks*
2.1 Variable demand (expected or random) for completed product	*Reduce variability:*		
	2.1.1 Reducing sales variability as above	Costs as above	Ins., Fl.
	2.1.2 Support finished inventories	Finished inventory costs as above (col. 4)	Ins., Fl. Un.
	Meet variability:		
	2.1.3 Add facilities	Capital expense with risky payoff	Ins., Fl.
	2.1.4 Buy rather than make	High cost	Ins., Fl.
	2.1.5 Achieve more flexible production	Labor cost Idle capacity cost Too small job lots as below	Ins., Fl.
	2.1.6 Accept the cost	Lost sales	Ins., Fl.

(continued)

EXHIBIT 1 (concluded)

Problem	Method Other Than Increasing Stock		Stock Method[a]
	Method	Type of Cost Involved	
(1)	(2)	(3)	(4)
2.2 Job lots that are too small	2.2.1 Accept the cost	Labor cost Machine down-time	LS
3. *Purchasing*			*Materials Ownership*[b]
3.1 Variable demand	*Reduce variability:*		
	3.1.1 Reduce variability of production or sales as above	Costs as above	Ins., Fl., H, O
	3.1.2 Support finished and in-process inventories	Cost of inventories as above (col. 4)	Ins., Fl., H Un.
	Meet variability:		
	3.1.3 Reduce order-lot size	Costs as below	Ins., Fl., H, O
	3.1.4 Demand fast deliveries	High purchase price	Ins., Fl., H
	Accept the cost:		
	3.1.5 Accept	Production delays, etc.	Ins., Fl., H, O
3.2 Variable receipts: risk of tardy or unavailable goods of desired specification	3.2.1 Pay premium prices for desired goods	High purchase price	MP, Ins.
	3.2.2 Accept the cost of late, short, or incorrect deliveries	High-cost manufacture	MP, Ins., H, O
	3.2.3 Support inventories of "raw" materials	Cost of inventories (col. 4)	Un, H, O
3.3 Order lots that are too small	3.3.1 Accept	High-cost purchasing	MP, H, O
3.4 Achieving an optimal purchase price	3.4.1 Forgo the advantage	High-cost purchasing	MP, H, O
3.5 Supplier-announced increase in replenishment period	3.5.1 Pay premium price elsewhere	High-cost purchasing	PT, H, O

Note: Most of the entries are probabilistic; that is, they involve the *chance* of costs rather than sure costs.

[a]Type of stock involved: process time (PT), lot size (LS), insurance (Ins.), fluctuation (Fl.), market prospect (MP), unplanned (Un.), on hand (H), on order (O).

[b]The "Stock Method" can utilize material stocks either on hand or on order, except in the case of 3.1.2 and 3.1.4.

must be balanced against higher stockholding costs for larger order sizes (line 3.3).

Other management problems in connection with which stocks can "buy efficiency" include variability in receipts of goods of desired specification (line 3.2) and the need to sell at what is judged to be the highest possible price (line 1.3) and buy at the lowest (line 3.4).

In each case, the problem arises out of actual or anticipated changes in the condition of the markets in which finished goods are sold or materials are purchased. One way to cope with the problem is to carry larger stocks of goods on hand and on order. Increases in these "market-prospect" stocks involve costs which are alternative to those of other devices —paying premium prices for swift deliveries (line 3.2.1), accepting the higher manufacturing cost of, say, substandard materials (line 3.2.2), or (because of failure to anticipate a rise in prices) buying at future hypothetically higher prices rather than at present low ones (line 3.4).

Further study of Exhibit 1, which is intended to be amply illustrative rather than entirely comprehensive, may be rewarding, but its basic message has been brought out: stocks are one of a number of management devices for solving a number of management problems. Efficient solutions involve the proper combination of the stock and other alternatives. They involve, also, a proper combination of the other alternatives which are often partial substitutes for one another. How much of each to use depends on comparison of incremental costs at the margin of decision. We need to examine the character of these appropriate comparisons.

The subject is adorned by an elaborate and highly technical literature, which constitutes a large part of the work in operations research and management science. Most of it applies to stocks of finished goods and those that serve primarily what I have called the lot-size, insurance, and variability functions. It specifies the optimal size of stocks serving designated purposes. At the growing edge of

study, interrelations are taken into account, though often mathematical solutions are indeterminate.[17] *Changes* in the cost functions receive very little attention.

The basic results of these studies are learned at business schools. Restricted aspects of them are embodied in nomographs and simplified tables for the use of stock clerks.[18] How often they are actually used in their full quantitative form by business is difficult to say. However, some sort of qualitative consideration of the relevant factors can hardly be avoided.[19] But what-

---

[17] For relatively nontechnical summaries, see J. F. Magee, "Guides to Inventory Policy," *Harvard Business Review*, January–February 1956, March–April 1956, and May–June 1956; D. W. Miller, and M. K. Starr, *Executive Decisions and Operations Research*, Englewood Cliffs, N.J., 1960, Chapter 10.

For a swift idea of the range of problems dealt with, see Robert Dorfman, "Operations Research," *American Economic Review*, September 1960, pp. 589–598; J. Laderman, S. B. Littauer, and Lionel Weiss, "The Inventory Problem," *Journal of the American Statistical Association*, December 1953, pp. 717–732.

Good comprehensive treatments are available in many books, including M. K. Starr and D. W. Miller, *Inventory Control: Theory and Practice*, Englewood Cliffs, N.J., 1962; G. Hadley and T. M. Whitin, *Analysis of Inventory Systems*, Englewood Cliffs, N.J., 1963; T. M. Whitin, *The Theory of Inventory Management*, Princeton, N.J., 1963.

More advanced treatment, including work with dynamic models and efforts to explore interreactions among inventories at various stages or serving various purposes, is contained in K. J. Arrow, S. Karlin, and H. Scarf, *Studies in the Mathematical Theory of Inventory and Production*, Stanford, Calif., 1958.

[18] See, for example, Joseph Buchan and Ernest Koenigsberg, *Scientific Inventory Management*, Englewood Cliffs, N.J. The preparation and use of these devices are described on pp. 263–277 and many applications given. See, for example, pp. 72–73, 152–153.

[19] John F. Magee, research director of the Operations Research Group of Arthur D. Little, Inc., refers to the question in "Guides to Inventory Policy, Functions and Lot Size," *Harvard Business Review*, January–February 1956. He discusses the matter in connection with optimum lot-size formulas: "Even though formulas for selecting the optimum lot size are presented in many industrial engineering texts, few companies make any attempt to arrive at an explicit quantitative balance of inventory and change-over or set-up costs." He speaks of the difficulty of calculating these costs in many companies and particularly their marginal cost: "Oftentimes companies therefore attempt to strike only a quantitative balance of these costs to arrive at something like an optimum

ever the extent of their direct use, or use in a common-sense approximate way, their particular value here is primarily analytic. They help to indicate, as I mentioned at the beginning of this chapter, what factors are relevant to inventory control and approximately in what way. Thereby they should help to suggest how inventories may be expected to behave during business fluctuations.

The essential point is that the correct solution for the management problems involve almost universally some *combination* of supporting the cost of stocks and of recourse to one or more other devices. Solutions should proceed according to traditional economic principles of equimarginal advantage, whereby the combined costs are minimized. They must be analyzed separately for each of the five sorts of efficiency stocks: lot-size, insurance, fluctuation, market-prospect, and error stocks.

THREE TYPES WITH DAMPED ASSOCIATION TO SALES

Lot-Size Stocks

THE NEED SERVED AND RELATION TO LOT SIZE

These stocks permit bunching of processing or ordering in efficient lots as suggested in lines 2.2 and 3.3 of Exhibit 1. Bunching for processing applies most particularly to goods in process, but it can also apply to such preparatory processes as are performed on purchased materials; finished-goods stocks may also present a bunching problem particularly in connection with appropriate lot sizes for shipping. For example, the cost of machine processing is ordinarily increased by a change-over in the work performed by a machine. Costs include the labor of setting up the new operation, and often labor inefficiency in getting into the swing of its production (shake-down cost); the fact that equipment is idle while the change is under way gives rise to a further opportunity cost. All these costs occur less often when lots are large than when they are small; on a per-unit-of-output basis, they are, in other words, inversely associated with the size of lots. Inventory costs, on the other hand, are directly associated with lot size. Stocks that serve the lot-size function range between a maximum of the lot sizes and a minimum of zero; assuming a uniform rate of withdrawal, they average one-half the lot size.

Orders for materials also need to be assembled in economical bunches: order quantities. Otherwise costs of processing the order, receiving it, and particularly the cost of transportation mount; quantity discounts may be foregone. For stock on hand, associated stocks will again tend to equal one-half the size of the order. But for stock on order the withdrawal rate is necessarily discontinuous; the whole lot is delivered at the same time or at a stipulated discrete time. As a result, outstanding orders associated with economical order quantities are larger relative to the lot size than are stocks on hand.[20]

DETERMINANTS

The choice of the appropriate lot or order size (which, divided by about two, is also the choice of the average inventory size) selects the point at which the *sum* of the cost of carrying stock and of supporting the setup costs, as described above, is at a minimum. Where the point is located depends on the pattern of substitution of stock costs for setup costs. Figure 1 depicts such a pattern. It is

of minimum-cost re-order quantity" (p. 9). I take it that the distinction is between an accurate and a very approximate optimization. However, the article was written ten years ago and there has been a large increase in "calculating" over the period.

[20] The size of stocks, I, is a function of lead time (T weeks), lot size (L units) and utilization rate (D units). Without specifying the particulars, note that when $L = TD$, $I = L$. When $L < TD$, $I > L$; when $L > TD$, $I < L$.

FIGURE 1

Optimum Lot Size

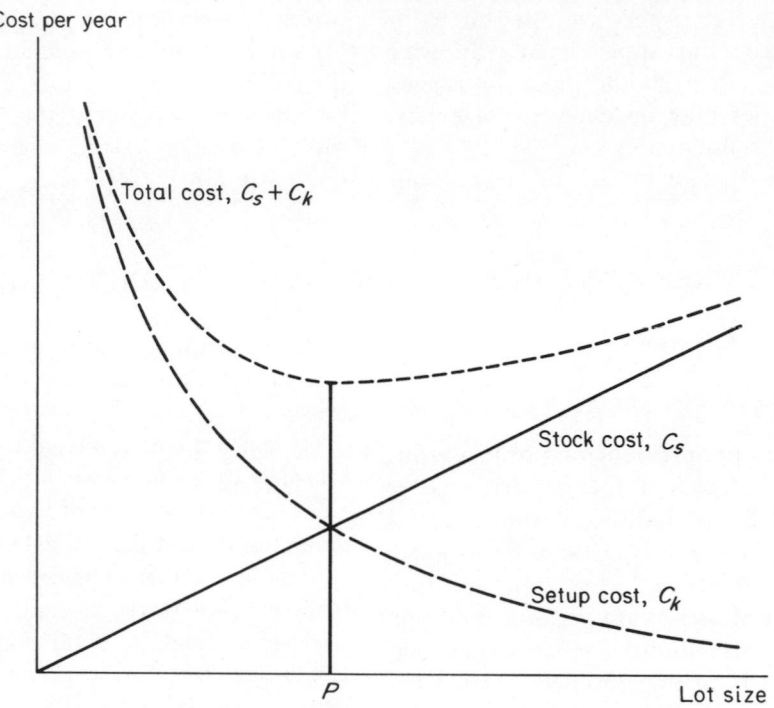

characteristic that as stocks increase, they "buy" marginally a declining reduction in setup costs. The optimum size of lots is located where the slopes of the two curves are equal and opposite, which is also the low point on the total-cost curve.

The curves compare the cost, over some period of time (say, a year) for each possible lot size, of the carrying charge for stock on the one hand and the setup costs on the other hand. Stock cost per year in dollars C_s increases more or less proportionately to the size of stocks (assuming the unit value of the stocks is constant) and the stock-cost curve, $C_s Z/2$, is a straight line. The setup cost C_k is a constant; cost per year is this constant multiplied by the number of setups that need to occur—a function of the year's demand D and lot size Z. Thus the setup cost per year varies with lot size according to the formula $C_k D/Z$. The sum of the two $C_k D/Z +$ $C_s Z/2$, represents total cost. To obtain the point of minimal total cost—the point where marginal costs of the two alternatives are equal—we find the derivative of total cost, and set it equal to zero.[21] Thus,

$$Z = \sqrt{2C_k D/C_s}$$

The formulations of the previous paragraph apply also to order-lot-size with the costs of placing, shipping, receiving, and accounting

[21] I have used (with a minor change) the notation given in David W. Miller and Martin K. Starr, *Executive Decisions and Operations Research*, Englewood Cliffs, N.J., pp. 249–250. Chapter 10 has an excellent brief discussion of certain aspects of the inventory problem; see pp. 244–280.

The assumptions as to the nature of the two types of costs in the square-root formula imply that the point p in the diagram is at the intersection of the two curves. However, the basic argument holds under a range of assumptions which do not necessarily imply that lowest total costs occur at the lot size at which two cost curves intersect.

for an order substituted for setup costs. If orders are delivered immediately, order-lot-sizes will affect only the size of stocks on hand. However if lead times are present, the size of stocks on order will also be influenced, as indicated in note 20, above, and the textual discussion.

The construction carries two important messages: First, optimal lot size or its associated stocks on hand or on order vary proportionately to the *square root of sales*. The square-root relationship derives from the character of the lot-size term. Setup or order cost, a constant which is multiplied by the number of orders per year, approaches infinity as the lot size approaches zero. Second, optimal lot size increases (or decreases) if setup or order costs increases (or decreases) in proportion to the square root of the lot costs.

PATTERNS OF CHANGE

These conclusions would presumably apply to changes in sales and relative costs associated with business cycles. Consider what they may be. Sales or shipments tend to conform to cyclical fluctuations, so the rules just mentioned would cause a damped positive reaction of stock. The relative cost structure is also likely to shift in response to changed level of sales and collateral conditions. Setup costs tend to rise when plants are busy. When a plant is operating on a tight schedule, actual cost of labor for resetting and other purposes is likely to be higher than when many workers have extra time for which they have to be paid in any event. Similarly, when factories are well utilized, down time for machines has genuine opportunity cost, which is not the case when machines are idle. In terms of Figure 1, this means that the setup cost (C_k) curve shifts upward. If so, the optimum lot size will be larger than previously, even if there is no shift in the cost of carrying stock. However, as I indicated earlier, I believe that the realities (though perhaps not the bookkeeping) of stock costs may actually decline. If this were the case, the C_s curve would

drop and the optimal point would indicate a still larger lot size.

Insurance or Buffer Stocks

The uncertain pattern of sales, or procurement, and even production schedules, calls for stocks that insure against cost of failing to meet demand. Demand in the sense relevant to stock problems occurs at each station where work is performed. It consists of the desired flow of materials into that operation. Thus the schedule for production starts is the demand relevant to stocks of purchased materials after preliminary operations have been completed. Demand at each station is subject to random variability, but the greatest variability, and an important source of variability at other stations, is at the point of final demand.

The risk of failure to meet demand is a function of the variability of the actual demand per relevant time interval—a day, or week, or month. The cost of protection against stockouts increases rapidly as 100 per cent insurance is attempted. Accordingly, policy objectives, explicitly or implicitly, designate a tolerable incidence of stockouts. Stocks, then, must be adequate to meet, at all times, a demand of a size which is exceeded no oftener than this acceptable frequency, say, 2 per cent of the time. Insurance stocks per se cover the variation from the mean level.

But in order to insure this adequacy, the frequency with which stocks are replenished must also be considered. The problem is perhaps most critical at the purchased-materials stage, where the replenishment period can be relatively long and there is no leeway supplied by anterior stocks.

DETERMINANTS

The critical determinants, then, of the size of insurance stocks of, say, "raw" materials on hand and on order are (1) variability of demand, (2) replenishment period, (3) tolerable percentage of stockouts, and, in some cases, (4) the time between orders.

Assume experience shows that demand averages 1,000 units a week and ranges between 900 and 1,100. It is larger than 1,080 units only one per cent of the time. Then if mean demand plus 80 units were always on hand, customers would be disappointed on the average only one time in one hundred and this would be the insurance stock required. If the level of sales, mean demand, increases, the range of variation is also likely to increase to something more than the 80 units, but typically the increase is less than proportional. When actual distributions are not known on the basis of the company's history, it may be approximated by a Poisson distribution for which the standard deviation is the square root of the mean. Reference to standard probability tables indicates that $D + 2.326\sqrt{D}$ approximates the stocks that would insure against the same level of stockouts as above. According to this formula, the 1 per cent level of stockouts would be covered by stocks of 1,073 units (rather than the 1,080 units that the previous example assumed that experience had shown); larger levels of demand imply an increase to cover the new mean level plus an insurance factor that increases according to the square root principal.

To effectuate this degree of insurance, it is of course necessary to consider how fast goods can be procured, that is, the replenishment period, T. It is the mean demand plus likely variation over this entire period which must be *on hand and on order* at the beginning of the period; thus required ownership is $DT + 2.326\sqrt{DT}$.[22]

A number of implications of the formula are of interest. First, insurance or buffer stocks

consist of stock on order as well as on hand; second, the impact on stock of the variability of sales tends to be muted by the square-root relationship or probably something like it; third, insurance stocks must also keep a constant incremental relationship to sales (the DT term); fourth, the size of the increment depends on the length of the replenishment period; fifth, if the replenishment period varies, the size of buffer stocks on hand or on order will vary proportionately.

PATTERNS OF CHANGE

As to the cyclical pattern of these variables, that of sales is obvious enough, but how about the variability of sales? Other things the same, it seems reasonable to assume, as has the previous discussion, that random components do not increase proportionately. But they may indeed even decrease if the unforetold fluctuation of required shipments to customers is reduced by increasing lead time (and the resulting increase in backlog of orders) for the articles the company makes (Exhibit 1, line 1.2.6). If so, the size of insurance stocks could be reduced.

There seems every reason to suppose that an increase in lead time for sales orders will be a favored choice of the several ways by which sales can be tailored to available capacity. It is more easily reversed than a rise in price. Nor will it typically alienate customers if many competitors are doing likewise. At the same time, it produces several benign results affecting stocks. It is likely to reduce the cost of carrying stock by markedly diminishing economic obsolescence, since requirements are known farther ahead. It reduces the need for buffer stocks, since the variance of the shipment schedule is reduced. The last two results have an opposing influence on the size of stocks: the first decreases it and the second tends to increase it because of lower cost. The net result is unknown.

The same logic just applied to sales orders (and unfilled order backlogs) applies to purchase orders (and outstanding-materials or-

---

[22] The formula applies to an ordering system in common use, the "two-bin system." If the "order-cycle system" is used, the time between orders, N, must be covered and the formula becomes $D(T + N) + 2.326\sqrt{D(T + N)}$. This tends to increase stock on hand somewhat, though stock on order is the same under either system. For a discussion of the two systems see, Whitin, *The Theory of Inventory Management,* pp. 44, 48.

ders) since these are the sales orders of some other company, the supplier. And the previous discussion showed that the size of total ownership of materials responds in a somewhat more than proportionate fashion to the relative change in the lead time for materials. How much of the impact will fall on stocks on hand rather than on order is a question that will be discussed later.

Fluctuation Stocks

The pattern of monthly sales often varies in ways that can be at least roughly foretold. Seasonal patterns, for example, may be reasonably well understood. The expectation of a strike may demand some advance preparation. Far more hazardous and infrequent prophecies about cyclical conditions and trends are, willy-

nilly, incorporated in decisions concerning the size of plants and other things which carry implications about accommodating change via inventories or via overtime work.

Assume, for example, that sales of a given enterprise have a strong seasonal peak toward the end of the year. The cumulative pattern of shipments is shown in Figure 2 by the dotted line. For the year, shipments are 1,200 units and the monthly amounts are indicated by the slope of the line month by month. What path should production follow? If production costs were the only consideration, they would be minimized by the smooth flow implicit in equal monthly lots of 100 units—the path shown by the diagonal solid line. But if this course were followed, inventories would pile up during the first part of the year and then gradually reduce to zero by the end of

FIGURE 2

Cumulative Forecast Shipment, and Two Production Schedules

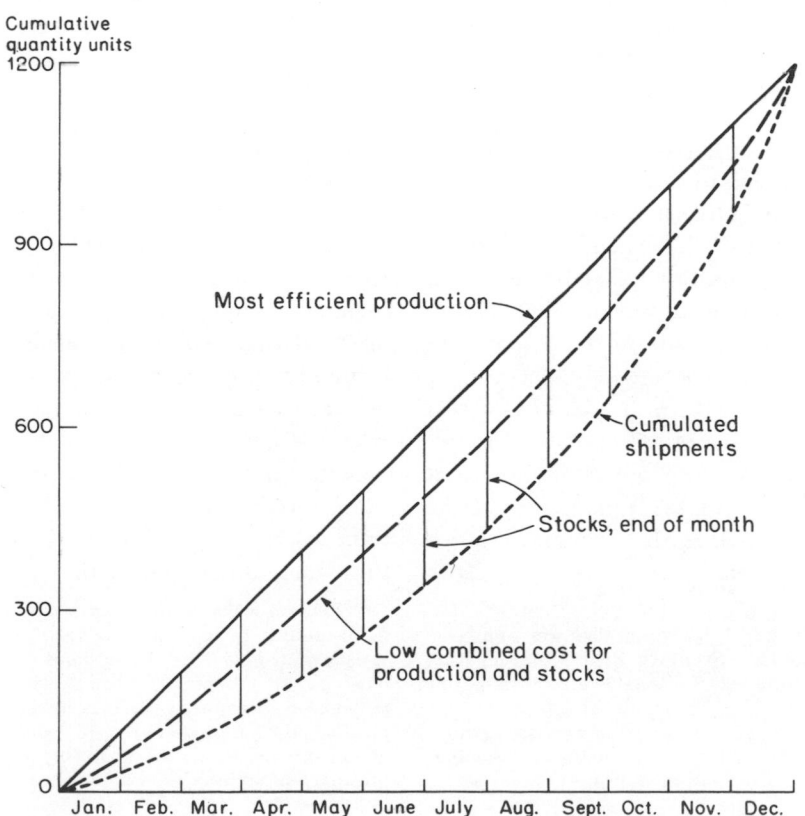

the year. The size of inventories month by month is shown by the vertical lines on the chart.[23] The carrying costs of these stocks constitutes the opportunity cost of this most efficient production schedule. However, the combined costs of inventory and production are almost inevitably lower at some path intermediate between the two shown, perhaps that of the dashed line. This is especially true in view of the uncertainty that would in practice surround the sales estimate.[24]

A similar type of construction applies to purchased-materials stocks that provide a way of coping with expected seasonal variability in production requirements, or in the sales of retail stores. Materials on order perform an identical function for less immediate requirements. They do so, moreover, without corresponding financing and storage costs.

Just how fluctuation stocks vary with the level of sales is not subject to general formulation. However, the cost of the inventory alternative would tend to increase linearly with the size of stocks as for lot-size stocks depicted in Figure 1. The alternate or opposing cost would tend to be convex to the origin, since ordinarily at least a substantial component of costs would be of the relatively fixed variety. This implies that efficiency of substitution of stocks for the alternative would increase as stocks increase, and increase also as sales increase. Thus, though the square-root relations of stocks to sales would not apply, at least stocks should increase substantially less than proportionately to sales.

Changes in the relative cost of holding stocks and of supporting uneven production schedules would presumably affect fluctuation stocks in much the same way that it affects lot-size stocks. If so, these stocks would tend to increase, other things the same, during expansion. On the other hand, the expansion phenomenon of larger backlogs of sales orders can flatten the required-shipments curve in Figure 2, thereby decreasing optimal stock.

MARKET-PROSPECT STOCKS

Market prospects concern the purchaser's estimate of conditions in markets in which materials are bought. The estimate may be based on sure knowledge; for example, the seller may simply have stipulated that he now will promise delivery in four weeks, whereas formerly the period was two weeks. It may, at the other end of the confidence spectrum, be based on highly uncertain guesses about how delivery periods or prices are likely to change. Delivery periods are a "process time" that must be bridged by stocks. If the length of the period changes, so does the amount of stock required to cover the delivery process. However, as stated earlier, it is useful for analytic purposes to distinguish between the time associated with customary efficient eco-engineering conditions, loosely called hand-to-mouth conditions, and departures from that time associated with particular conditions in the materials markets. Stocks associated with the former are process-time stocks, and those which accommodate the departures are market-prospect stocks.[25]

Note, however, that if market prospects cause replenishment periods to lengthen, then the ownership covering the longer period has the same association with expected sales as

[23] John Magee uses virtually the diagram here presented in "Guides to Inventory Policy, Anticipating Future Needs," *Harvard Business Review*, May–June 1956, p. 32.

[24] For a discussion of the impact of various patterns of sales, see Morton Klein, "On Production Smoothing," *Management Science*, April 1961.

[25] The reader may think that the distinction could more usefully be made on the basis of delivery periods as stipulated by the seller and actions primarily initiated by the buyer. But as will be seen as the evidence is examined, there is so intimate and complex an association between the supply and demand blades of the shears that a distinction along these lines is not useful.

does any process-time stock—it will fluctuate in direct proportion to sales volume. However, market-prospect ownership may reflect changes other than in lead times—in expected prices, or selections, for example; and for these the constant relation to sales does not necessarily apply.

Action based on market prospects is sometimes branded as "speculation." This is a misnomer. Most business life is necessarily speculative, and it serves no useful purpose to single out changing market prospects (including that of expected change in materials prices) as particularly so, and consequently a "bad thing." The purchasing agent should aim to insure that required materials of the desired quality are on hand at the desired place and time, and at the lowest possible price. This objective has its counterpart in the size of stocks of materials on hand and on order. Changes which have occurred, or which he anticipates, in the speed and reliability of deliveries, in their quality, in the range of selections, or in the prices he will pay must influence his behavior. Proper regard for these matters is as much a part of efficient business operation as is attention to future sales, or indeed to any unsure event which will perforce leave its impact on profits. Therefore, though there may be some difference in emphasis, it seems correct to include market-prospect stocks under the general heading of stocks that "buy efficiency."

Determinants

Two sorts of determinants of ownership linked to actual or expected conditions in the materials markets need to be covered. The first group concerns the judgment about what those conditions are, the second, how the judgments affect ownership.

Three types of conditions likely to engage attention are those bearing (1) on prices, (2) on delivery conditions, and (3) on quality, variously defined. These matters are considered more carefully in Chapter 10, but a preview is needed here.

One reason for an increase in ownership is the expectation that materials prices will rise (Exhibit 1, line 3.4). If the expectation were certain, it would be appropriate to increase ownership until the carrying cost of the last increment of stock over a specified period of time equaled the expected increase in price during the period. Thus, under certainty, the *level* of ownership is associated with the expected rate of *change* of prices. If a price expectation is unsure, the expected increase in prices required to instigate a given level of ownership must be greater than if the expectation is certain.[26]

Two other sorts of expectation that may motivate an increase in market-prospect stocks is the belief that the replenishment time for goods of desired quality will lengthen or quality, including selections, will deteriorate (Exhibit 1, line 3.2). These expectations confront management with four alternatives: materials on hand can be increased; orders for the more distant deliveries can be placed; premium prices can be paid for rapid delivery if and when the expectation proves to be correct; adverse quality and delivery schedules, should they materialize, can be compensated for at some other level of the enterprise. These matters involve costs which need to be balanced against the cost of increasing the amount of stocks on hand and on order.

But a judgment is also required (probably most typically an implicit judgment) about how the cost of extending ownership may itself have changed. Risk is a chief part of the cost of outstandings—risk of buying the wrong thing or paying the wrong price. But, as the following section explains, it is likely that risk costs will decrease at just the time when markets are expected to tighten.

Location and Size

The list of factors that motivate market-prospect stocks implies that they may be found

[26] This subject is discussed at some length in Chapter 13.

anywhere in a business. Even finished stocks may be involved under appropriate circumstances—circumstances that make it important to buy materials advantageously and preferable to hold them in finished rather than raw state. But the emphasis falls on purchased-materials ownership, and especially on materials on order. Thus, when markets are expected to tighten, materials stocks on order are likely to increase. But stocks on hand can have a competitive relation to stocks on order in that the additional buying may carry short delivery dates. In any event stocks on hand are likely to have the complementary association of the inverse vestibule effect: they will tend to increase as the larger orders are delivered. The matter is somewhat complicated and deserves a moment's thought.

Consider first a situation in which the only change in market conditions is that delivery periods are expected to lengthen; sales are expected to be unchanged and are precisely foretold. Under this admittedly highly unlikely circumstance (delivery periods for materials are probably never expected to lengthen without some expected increase in sales of finished goods), the change in ownership could be almost entirely confined to outstandings. Figure 3 describes materials ownership at a sequence of one-week periods (horizontal axis). Requirements are reviewed and orders placed every two weeks at the beginning of the week. Orders are all delivered exactly at the end of the expected term—first at the end of two weeks, and later (starting with the order of week 7) at the end of four weeks. Stocks on hand are the shaded portion of the diagram and are of two sorts. First, there is some minimum loosely defined amount which is required at all times; it covers insurance stock, error stock, and everything else; it is shown as the unsegmented band at the bottom of the columns. Second, there is a variable stock intended to cover two weeks' expected sales.

Beginning at the left, picture the purchasing agent who starts with his required two weeks' stock on hand plus the minimum, and contemplates what he will order. He should cover expected sales for weeks 3 and 4, since the orders will not be delivered until week 3. The forecast sales for those weeks are shown on the right vertical axis. He places the orders shown by the dashed line at the extreme left. Now time ticks on. In the first week sales use up one week's supply. During the second week, sales continue at the same rate and draw down variable stocks to zero at the end of week 2. At the beginning of the third week, the orders placed at the start of week 1 are delivered, as shown by the dotted vertical line. At the same moment the purchasing agent once again reviews the scene and places orders to cover forecast sales for weeks 5 and 6 (dashed line). The process repeats until the beginning of period 6. Variable stock on hand has averaged one-half of sales over the order period. Stocks on order are uniformly two weeks' supply.

But now the expected delivery period doubles; orders placed at the beginning of week 7 with the regular supplier will not be delivered for four weeks—the beginning of week 11. If the purchasing agent simply placed orders covering forecast sales for the period, by the beginning of week 11 sales would have cut into the minimum safety band for stock on hand to point P. Accordingly he places orders covering weeks 11 and 12 with his regular supplier; finds a manufacturer or jobber who will deliver one week's supply of his expected needs in one week and another in two weeks. For this he pays through the nose, but no matter. At the end of two weeks, the beginning of week 9, at his usual order period, he now contemplates expected sales for weeks 13 and 14, and orders these requirements. As a matter of fact, his orders over this period should be somewhat larger than I have described since the longer replenishment period implies larger potential sales variance and therefore larger insurance stock. I simply indicate their impact by a slightly larger (responding to a square-root principle) mini-

FIGURE 3

Materials Stocks on Hand and on Order During Sequential Weeks
as Delivery Periods Change

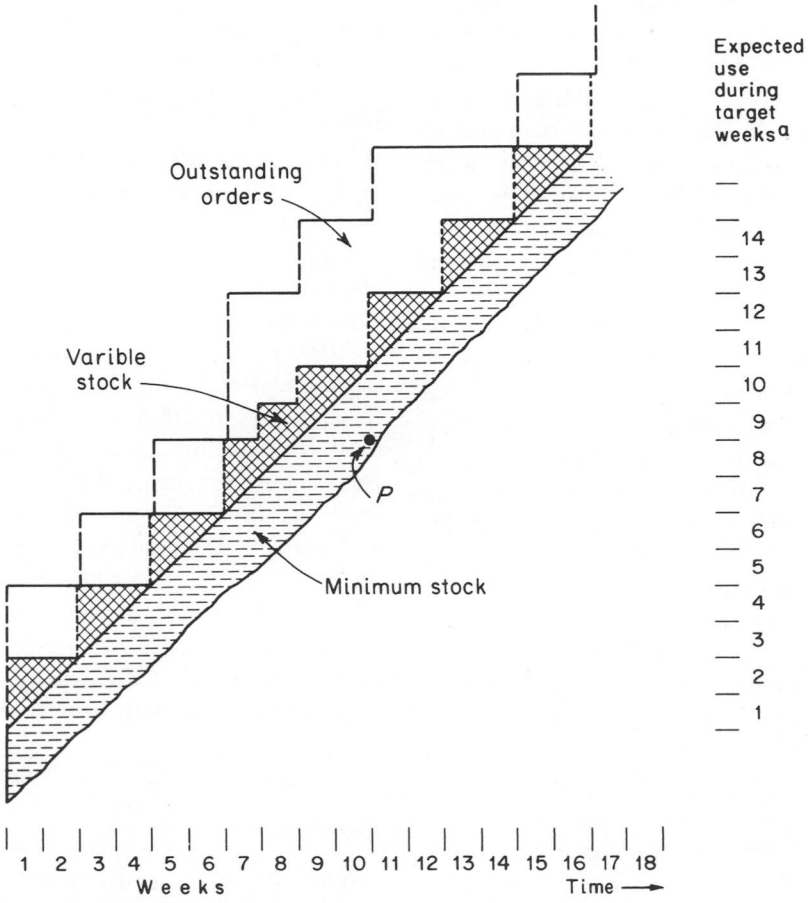

a Weeks are numbered successively from the present.

mum-stock. Over this period of the longer replenishment period, outstandings nearly double, in line with the doubled period. But stocks on hand increase only during the period of transition in weeks 7 and 8 (except for the variance buffer).

At the beginning of period 13, the scene shifts. The union contract has been signed, or whatever, and the purchasing agent expects deliveries to return to their customary two-week period. Accordingly he places no new orders but waits for the previous ones of two

weeks ago to arrive. He starts ordering in the customary fashion (adjusted to reduce the variance buffer) at the beginning of week 15.

Figure 3 is concerned with market prospects confined to sure and correct estimates of a change in the delivery period, sales unchanged and correctly forecast. If sales had also been expected to increase when delivery periods did, the vertical distance for expected sales for weeks 9 and thereafter would have lengthened, and outstandings, starting at week 7, would have been larger by four times the weekly increase plus some allowance for the increase in the buffer. Beginning in week 9, the slant of the bottom of the columns, indicating weekly use, would become steeper. But again, so long as sales are correctly forecast, stock on hand can still cover one week's sales on the average (except during the transition). Change in ownership is confined almost entirely to stock on order. Even when sales are expected to decline, an increase in stock on hand could be forestalled by appropriate changes in new orders *if the decline had been correctly forecast.*

The example has dealt with market prospects focused entirely on delivery periods. But if some of the advance buying had been intended to take advantage of selections which were expected to deteriorate, though delivery periods did not lengthen, the additional purchases would move into stocks on hand and increase their size over the longer period covered. If forestalling an expected increase in prices had been the target, the buyer would no doubt prefer to delay deliveries until the material was needed, thereby reproducing as nearly as possible the patterns described in the diagram. But the seller might be quite unwilling to cooperate. The steel industry, for example, has for some years refused to fix prices on customers' orders until their date of delivery.

Finally, uncertainty influences what happens. For one thing, sales cannot be exactly foretold, as we have been assuming. As a result, if forecasts were too optimistic, variable stock on hand will be larger than desired when orders are delivered and contrariwise if they were too pessimistic. However, in the latter case orders for "at once" delivery can often correct the discrepancy. For another thing, the fact that delivery periods, and anything else, cannot be forecast with certainty means that a planned flow of outstandings intended to meet contingencies needs to be reinforced by provisions in terms of stock on hand.

Cyclical Fluctuation

For each of the various sorts of stocks, some influences affecting their size are often external to the sales history of the particular company—changing labor cost and labor availability, financing costs, for example. But in the case of market-prospect stocks these external influences tend as we have seen, to be powerful in their impact. Therefore it is important to know the circumstances that cause them to vary significantly.

Do lengthening delivery periods ordinarily accompany rising demand? Or must plant capacity be fully utilized first? Do rising materials prices usually accompany large order backlogs? Do these things occur at quite different times in different industries or do they tend to cross industry lines and be broadly present? Unfortunately there is little empirical work on the basis of which to answer these and many other relevant questions. The time series to which we turn presently move toward some very tentative answers.

But a few guesses can be tendered on the basis of the logic of the procurement problem in business firms and a few investigations.[27]

[27] Tangential evidence on absence of parallelism between a firm's buying, production, and, sometimes, selling is scattered through the literature on individual industries. It also appears in market reviews in current periodicals, of which the *Commercial & Financial Chronicle,* starting well before the turn of the century, and, more recently, *Business Week* are notable examples. It is seen on financial pages of newspapers.

There have been a few studies of individual industries in which these problems have appeared to play an important part. Cf. Thomas M. Stanback, Jr., "Short Run Instability in the Cotton Broad Woven Goods Industry, 1946–51," unpublished Ph.D. dissertation, Duke University, 1954; Bert G. Hickman, "Cyclical Fluctuations in the Cotton Textile Industry," unpublished Ph.D. dissertation, University of California at Berkeley, 1951; Ruth P. Mack, *Consumption and Business Fluctuations: A Case Study of the Shoe, Leather, Hide Sequence,* New York, National Bureau of Economic Research, 1956. Explicit analysis of buying waves appears in *ibid.,* Chapters 9 and 16; also in Ruth P. Mack and Victor Zarnowitz, "Cause and Consequence of Changes in Retailers' Buying," *American Economic Review,* March 1958, pp. 19–22; Mack, "Business Expectations and the Buying of Materials,"

I might add that the evidence developed in this book has turned out to be entirely in line with these suppositions.

The willingness to extend the number of weeks for which materials are purchased is fostered by (1) increasing and reasonably strong demand, (2) increasing backlogs of orders for the product the company sells, (3) conditions in markets in which materials are bought that suggest rising prices and a reduction in the speed and certainty with which materials of desired quality can be bought and delivered. All three developments are interrelated.

Rising demand for the product an industry sells has a multiple relation to prospects in the markets in which the industry buys. Favorable market prospects are encouraged by rising demand, since materials markets are not likely to tighten when demand is slack and demand for materials is derived from demand for the products in which the materials will be incorporated.

If strong and rising demand for the product a company sells causes increasing backlogs of unfilled orders, a further link to materials markets is forged. With orders on the books, the purchasing agent can elect *when* to buy materials. He can buy them at the time the sales order is written or he can wait more nearly until the time when materials are needed to meet production schedules. During this entire "period of option," the deliberate timing of buying is relatively free of two important elements in the cost of advance buying—that of buying the wrong thing and of paying the wrong price. Indeed, *failure* to buy materials when sales orders are written could imply the risk of paying the wrong price, if the price at which materials were eventually purchased was higher than the materials cost embodied in the selling price of finished goods.

But though favorable demand for final products is necessary to optimistic expecta-

in Mary Jean Bowman (ed.), *Expectations, Uncertainty, and Business Behavior,* New York, 1958, pp. 106 ff.

tions about the materials markets, it is not sufficient to it. These markets themselves are a tracery of signs and footprints that the purchasing agent reads daily. Telephone wires, salesmen, competitors, trade journals, selling floors, affairs in industries buying the same materials—all contribute to the sensitive reporting that helps to form the judgment about whether this is a good time to buy short or long of requirements and to what extent.

One consideration may be that of paying the right price. Another, and usually more important, is the need to have physical goods where they are wanted when they are wanted, and in the assortments and quality wanted, in view of the prevailing or expected delivery conditions. But typically the two considerations dictate doing the same thing—buying ahead or refraining from doing so—at the same time.

These considerations on which market expectations are based in an individual firm are at any given time likely to change in similar ways for most firms in an industry. The judgments are actually addressed, for the most part, to conditions in sales and materials markets as a whole, rather than simply to the affairs of the customers or suppliers of a particular firm. Consequently, an entire industry is likely to move toward an increase in market-prospect stocks more or less at the same time.

The analysis has indicated that when materials markets are expected to tighten, stocks on order increase. If extension is dictated by actual or expected lengthening in delivery periods, stocks on order will increase proportionately. If extension is caused by expectation of rising prices, the quantitative dimensions are obscure. If optimistic market prospects occur when sales are rising, and they are not likely to occur at other times, sales and delivery periods interact in their impact on stocks on order. Stocks on hand increase because of the need to increase buffers; they may increase as an alternative response to optimistic expectations; they are likely to increase as the larger outstanding orders are delivered and move through the plant, the inverse vestibule effect. These are the direct effects; there are many indirect ones, among which are those associated with errors in guesses about market prospects and about sales over the longer period for which commitments have been made.

UNPLANNED STOCKS

Imagine a firm whose executives were thoroughly versed in management lore. They knew all about the appropriate size of stocks serving each of the five purposes that I or anyone else have described. They understood their interrelations and the cost structure of their own business. Theoretically, then, stocks could be set and kept at optimal levels.

But stocks would not in fact be at these theoretical levels. Instead "unplanned stocks" would exist. They would exist, first, because it was not worthwhile to plan for the last little contingency. They would exist, second, because most plans involve only partially foreknown future events, and cannot, therefore, except by luck, be precisely executed, a failure to which some ineptitude is also likely to contribute.

However, the theoretical levels themselves do not apply in most firms because ignorance obscures knowledge necessary to plan the proper size of stocks and to enforce such plans as are formulated. Ignorance, then, is a third reason for unplanned stock.

Passive and Unintended Stock

We can group unplanned stocks that result from ignorance and from the limits to advantageous planning, and think of them as "passive." [28]

[28] Cf. Ruth P. Mack, "Characteristics of Inventory Investment: The Aggregate and Its Parts," *Problems of Capital Formation,* Studies in Income and Wealth 19, Princeton University Press for National Bureau of Economic Research, 1957, p. 480: "Passive inventory investment or disinvestment takes place in part because plans about the proper size of stocks are hardly ever precise figures; instead, they are ranges, and variation within the range or band is a matter of indifference. Passive stock change also occurs when

Passive stocks reflect the decision not to decide. They result from the election that further control of stocks, given the degree of control that actually could be achieved, is not worth the executive time and other costs that would be involved. Thus they are always a matter of degree. Stocks are never passive in the sense that there are no limits to their size, but only in the sense that the limits are much broader than usual and only roughly determined. Passive stocks, then, constitute a residual category after process stocks and the other efficiency stocks have been provided for. They are included in Exhibit 1, primarily in lines 2.1.2, 3.1.2 and 3.2.3—coping with variability in demand at one level by carrying stocks at a later level, or with variability in supply by carrying stocks at the same level.

Note that the difference between unplanned and insurance or fluctuation stocks is somewhat subtle, and there are doubtless several ways of drawing the line between them. My own thinking focuses on the impact of uncertainty and the cost of information. If all relevant factors were known and if their impact could be evaluated at reasonable cost, then it would be worthwhile to plan the size of any stock and there would by definition be no passive stock. But for many purposes it seems clear that relevant factors cannot be assessed with sufficient accuracy to justify the *executive time* that would be involved in planning, and in enforcing the plans to the degree necessary for the planning to pay off.

business objectives that focus on other matters than the appropriate size of stocks nevertheless affect their size." Some of this last group I would now exclude because attention to opportunity costs means that this behavior may represent a close weighing of relative costs of the two means of promoting efficiency.

Of course, what is feasible differs from time to time and firm to firm. Several decades ago stocks of finished goods were more commonly passive than they are today. Both management expertise and computers have made it feasible to plan their size within far narrower limits than formerly. The cost of planning can be reduced by rules of thumb, and if they are poor rules it is a question whether they define planned or passive stock. As we shall see later, the constant average stock-sales ratio may sometimes fall in this category. My point is simply that in matching empirical evidence with the presumptions of management theory, or the firm's-eye view of the procurement problem, it is realistic, I believe, to have in mind, in addition to the various explicit functions that stocks serve, and for which explicit planning is called for, the further category of stocks which in view of the uncertainties of the real world are the tail unwittingly wagged by the dog. It does not pay to try to plan them except in most approximate terms.

The second type of unplanned change in stock, unintended stock, results from the failure to *enforce* plans. Stock change of this sort constitutes divergence from plans. The divergence is recognized by the firm as errors which need to be reversed. It is unintended in the sense that it is not tolerated for long. Unplanned stock change of this sort has long been acknowledged in economic analysis. The distributed lag mentioned in the previous chapter is one way of coping with it at an econometric level.

Positive or negative unintended stock results in part from management lags. Discipline may be inadequate to enforce instructions; information may be poor or tardy. Unintended stocks may also result from the fact that the correct size of stocks is typically a function of conditions at a later period than the time when action that partly determines their size is taken. If the relevant conditions are incorrectly anticipated, some part of the actual change in stocks will be unintended. The relevant conditions may be the level of sales. If materials are bought on the basis of an incorrect forecast of sales, stocks will not conform to plans and the divergence must be corrected. We shall see that the definition of error, and consequently the efforts to reverse it, appear to differ in connection with stocks of department stores on the one hand and materials stocks of durable-goods manufacturing on the other. The relevant conditions may also be changes in opportunity costs of the sort that we have discussed. Those concerned with market conditions are particularly subject to forecast error, and consequently unintended change in ownership based on erroneous expectations can be an important type of error stocks which subsequent action endeavors to reverse.

Location and Patterns of Change

Unplanned stocks of either the passive or unintended sort can of course occur at any point in the productive process. When they are of the unintended variety, efforts to reverse them can take the form of changes in selling prices or changes in purchasing of materials. Since the latter method is a very usual one, and since it can take effect quite swiftly, it seems reasonable to suppose that errors in materials stocks on hand will imply a compensating change in stock on order, outstandings, and vice versa, and the sum of the two, ownership, will be less subject to unintended change than either component. The time series that we shall be examining support this supposition.

Patterns of change in passive stock are hard to anticipate, but in general it seems likely that they will be unresponsive to the things that prescribe changes in stocks and thus will tend to have generally inverse cyclical patterns. But there may also be a tendency for this inverse behavior to be less than it otherwise would be because of a shift in attitudes. When business is good there is a general feeling both on the part of management and customers that service rather than economy is called for. At such times, there also is a natural tendency for stock problems to take care of themselves. This may hide for a while the fact that unplanned stocks are in effect gaining relative to the rest. The general effect would be to dampen the possible countercyclical behavior of these stocks.

For unintended changes, errors associated with incorrect forecasts of sales depend on how sales forecasts are made and how errors are adjusted; and these things we do not know. Many surveys have shown that changes in sales tend to be underestimated. If so, when sales are rising, error stocks may tend to be negative. At the onset of recession, on the other hand, the level of sales is likely to be overestimated, since not to do so would imply that prized accomplishment, prophesying the turn.

Yet here again adjustment is not likely to be overswift, and in the meantime stocks are larger than optimum; that is, error stocks are positive. The effect might well be exaggerated by the fact that replenishment periods tend to be long around business peaks and consequently the period for which sales must be forecast long.

There is no need to rehearse how failure to anticipate delivery periods, materials prices, or any other events, such as strikes or weather, can cause stocks to be larger or smaller than they would be had the event been correctly foreseen. But it is important, in view of the great emphasis in the literature on sales forecasts, to remember that these things too must be forecast if inventory holdings are to be optimal.

SUMMARY AND CONCLUSIONS

The first chapter pointed to unsolved problems in aggregative analysis of inventory investment. Efforts to solve them must be based on what businessmen actually try to do, and that is what the present chapter has attempted to discover. It will be useful to summarize this discussion, keeping the purpose of aggregative analysis in mind. What has been learned about how stocks are likely to change in the course of fluctuation in economic affairs? Particularly, what has been learned about how to study these changes and their causes?

The first set of conclusions concern how the information conveyed by orders can be integrated with the stock-carrying problem. Unfilled orders for a particular firm are of two sorts: the orders for materials which the supplier has not yet filled are a secondary materials stock; the unfilled orders for the product that the company makes affect the risk and other costs of carrying stocks or other assets. The new orders placed for materials afford a net picture of the current procurement situation as the company views it; new

orders received for the product the company makes are a major source of information on which future plans are founded. That new orders for materials are the orders for the product that another company makes is no reason to smudge the differences in the informational content and the action implications of the same piece of paper viewed from the two points of view. This point is further developed in the next chapter.

Here it is prelude to a specific conclusion: it is necessary to examine materials stocks on order along with those on hand. Like stocks anywhere in a productive process, stocks on order provide availability at the appropriate time to a particular processing station. Further, none of the functions that stocks serve are unaffected by a change in the time required for orders to be delivered. Therefore, the correct size of stocks on hand must be determined with a view to how fast new orders arrive. At the same time, the length of the replenishment period is itself one of the choices that the purchaser must make in terms of trade-offs between stocks on order and stocks on hand, or between other ways of handling procurement problems.

This line of thought explains why it may be useful to confine empirical analysis of time series to stocks of materials rather than to all stocks. The focus forgoes the advantage of a comprehensive analysis of stocks on hand. But it enjoys the advantage of studying the relation between materials on hand and those on order, without confusing the picture by the different price levels of "raw," in process, and finished goods.

The effort to understand the forces shaping the cyclical patterns of stocks has been built up in three parts: (1) by picturing the functions that stocks perform, (2) by spotting the influences within a business and external to it to which stocks need to react in order to do their job, (3) by speculating as to how these factors may vary during business fluctuations.

The functions of stocks are, on the one hand, to support the time required for an operation to be performed and, on the other hand, to buy efficiency by substituting a lesser cost of carrying stocks for a larger cost of accomplishing the same management purpose in other ways. Both of these functions and each of the subfunctions of buying efficiency are sensitive to the volume of sales, but their degree of sensitivity varies.

How stocks move relative to sales is a basic determinant of their cyclical behavior; therefore, it will be useful here to list the functions in the order of their sensitivity to sales. I start with the most sensitive. The analysis is phrased in terms of stocks serving each function. In actuality, of course, the same physical inventories can serve several functions.

1. *Process-time stocks* support the time required for economic processes to take place when they are executed with usual efficiency in an eco-engineering sense. The processes include the physical transformations involved in preparation of materials, processing, and preparing to sell; they also include the time normally required between the writing of an order for materials and their delivery to pur-

chasers. Stocks serving this function tend to maintain a constant proportional relationship to the volume of sales unless the use of overtime or multiple-shift operations changes the relation of process time to calendar time. Since increased plant utilization is likely to take these forms during prosperity, process-time stocks on hand, other things the same, are likely to change somewhat less than in proportion to sales during business expansions and contractions. Process-time stocks on order would presumably tend to maintain a strictly proportional relation, other things the same.

2. *Market-prospect stocks* reflect the opinion that market conditions may depart from the hand-to-mouth condition. Insofar as delivery periods lengthen, the additional stock on order will cover the expected volume of sales over the additional period for which provisions are made; thus the impact of changing delivery periods and sales have a multiplicative relation. Insofar as changing market conditions affect judgments about prices, selections, or the like, the association with sales of either stocks on hand or on order is indeterminate.

3. *Fluctuation stock* has a pattern not subject to general formulation; it is likely to be somewhere between that of insurance and process-time stocks.

4. *Insurance stock* per se has something like a square-root association to sales. But since mean demand over the replenishment period must also be on hand or on order at the start of the period, a constant incremental relation is also present which would need to be covered by stock of some sort.

5. *Lot-size* (including order-size) *stock* has an approximately square-root association.

6. *Unplanned stock* provides a break in the link to sales except within a broad band. This may tend to give the passive aspect of unplanned stock an inverse association with sales proper, other things the same. For the unintended portion, resulting from the inevitable failures of control instruments in the first instance, the inverse pattern could feature the

rate of change in sales if forecasts tended to be conservative.

Differences in the functional character of the sales link imply differences in the impact of changing sales on stocks at the several stages of processing. Likewise, shifts in particular opportunity costs have more influence on stocks at one place in a business than at another. The numerical functional listings just set down will serve to illustrate these varying impacts. Stocks of finished goods are likely to be weak in functional classes 1 and 2, and strong in 3, 6, and perhaps 4. In-process stocks are likely to consist of all functional classes, though perhaps usually less of 2 and 6. Materials stocks will also be of diverse sorts, with perhaps the exception of 6, but with special emphasis on 2; materials stocks on order will be particularly dominated by 1 and 2. The emphasis on the higher-numbered functional classifications for finished stocks is in accord with statistical findings that they characteristically show a damped positive or inverse association to sales. It suggests that cyclical behavior of the stocks at the several stages will respond to different influences and that separate analysis of each sort is bound to be useful.

A chief implication of the analysis is that the link to sales, other things the same, does not prescribe a constant ratio to sales of stock on hand or of both stocks on hand and on order. The stock-sales ratio should, purely on the basis of efficient servicing of sales, have a pattern inverse to that of sales.

Just how marked the inverse pattern would be depends on matters such as the size of passive stocks, the length of replenishment periods, sales variance, and the like. Of all the stock functions that have been described, the only one requiring as much as a proportional association to sales is process-time stocks, and these only if there were no increase in operations in line sequence. All the rest, unplanned stock particularly, would tend to dampen changes in the level of stock relative to that of sales, other things the same.

A second finding of the analysis is that many other objective considerations can influence the size of stocks and how they change. They include changes in the costs of carrying stocks and of all of the alternative methods of achieving the efficiencies which stocks can provide. Thus as business improves, the unit costs of carrying stock may decline because of lower financing costs and lessened risk of obsolescence when sales and perhaps backlogs of orders are rising. On the other hand, the cost of competing ways of coping with management functions that stocks serve may rise in prosperity. For example, flexible production schedules encounter higher hire-and-fire and other labor costs, small-lot buying requires premium prices when suppliers are busy, and fast replenishment periods can only be achieved at premium prices or by sacrificing selections and quality. Such changes would tend to accentuate the rise in stocks during prosperity. Thus the stock alternative becomes more desirable because of both lower costs and higher productivity.

But the changes that occur during business fluctuations are not simply the function of objective situations and how they impinge on business decisions concerning buying and carrying stocks. Situations must be observed and appreciated, and this is a subjective process that may have patterns of its own. Even objective facts must filter through this learning process before they affect decisions. But we have seen that expectations as well as facts affect ownership decisions, and these are particularly sensitive to how information is generated, collected, and appreciated. Certainly there is some sort of group process involved in how expectations are formulated and acted upon. Whatever it is, changes in ownership, especially changes associated with market prospects, must bear its stamp.

The examination, then, of the functions that stocks serve has opened up a wealth of possibilities. The picture is much in need of the verification, modification, and enrichment which empirical study of the management of stocks in business firms could supply. But instead, such empirical studies as are undertaken in this book make use of aggregative time series alone. They are confined to stocks of materials. However, they utilize information on stocks both on hand and on order, thereby making it possible to observe elements affecting stocks which otherwise would remain invisible or hopelessly obscured.

Study of the time series should help to sharpen the picture of fluctuation and its possible causes. We have seen that materials stocks on order and on hand can be influenced by a very considerable number of occurrences normally associated with rising and ebbing tides in business or industry affairs. The changes involve expectations and the information on which they are based as well as actual events of many sorts. One cannot say now how significantly these influences will impinge on the size of stocks, but the analysis has served to indicate that if stocks behave in one fashion it is likely to imply one sort of relative weighting of a number of causal factors, whereas if they behave in another fashion a different weighting system is implied.

This is not as meager a result as it may seem. We shall see that the aggregate time series for stocks and ownership do appear to change far more than the sales-service link alone implies. This over-responsiveness does seem to bear a strong resemblance to changes in market conditions and other influences to which this chapter has pointed. New and unfilled orders received and placed tell distinctive yet interrelated stories.

In addition, more subtle implications of our study of business problems fall into place in the interpretation of the behavior of aggregates. Aspects of that behavior are not entirely explicable in terms of the objective facts of the business environment and how they change. First, they seem to reflect a process that involves expectations and how they are formulated, acted upon, and how these actions generate new information and further expectations. And certainly this learning and reacting process has kept winking at us from behind every fact that has been reported. Second, there is an implication of the material here presented which it has not been possible to display without further complicating a too complicated story. It is this: where the functions that inventories serve are so numerous and so intimately involved in the *particulars* of business problems, sensitivity to any single influence will vary greatly among different inventory goods, different firms, and, of course, different industries. If so, aggregate response to change in any single influence will have to creep over a frequency distribution of firms that reflects these varying sensitivities —a time-consuming process. This notion is one of the cornerstones in my final explanation.

3. The Problem of Aggregative Analysis of Ownership

Of the several questions that require empirical study, to which the previous chapters point, this monograph deals with only one: What can be learned about "inventory cycles" by studying ownership of materials—materials on hand and on order? [1]

The investigation is undertaken at an aggregate level. Stocks of materials on hand for the economy as a whole are the sum of those in all business enterprises. But for materials on order, the relation between microcosm and macrocosm is a bit more complicated. The difficulty concerns the relation between unfilled orders received and outstanding orders placed. Within the individual firm it is simple enough to distinguish between backlogs of sales orders and materials on order but not yet received. But for the economy as a whole, outstanding sales orders of one business are the outstanding purchase orders of some other business. These somewhat confusing relationships can be examined by means of a vertical sequence of operations.

A VERTICAL SEQUENCE EXAMINED

Stocks are a reservoir of goods having an inlet and outlet stream. Stocks of materials, for example, have an inlet stream, goods received from suppliers; and an outlet stream, goods on which production is commencing. When receipts are larger than utilization rates, stocks of materials increase; when smaller, they decrease. The change in stock over an interval of time is equal to the inlet minus the outlet stream over the period (with minor adjustments for wastage).

Outstanding purchase orders are likewise a reservoir having an inlet and outlet stream; the inlet is new purchase orders placed with suppliers; the outlet, the physical receipt of goods. The difference between these two flows is the change in outstanding orders (with adjustments for cancellations).

Change in the ownership of materials during, say, a month comprehends changes in outstanding purchase orders plus changes in stocks of purchased materials. It is the difference between the volume of new orders placed during the month with a firm's suppliers and the volume of goods on which production is commenced that month; the receipts of materials cancel out since they reduce outstanding orders and increase stocks on hand by an equal amount. The relationships are shown in Exhibit 2.

The exhibit is concerned with steps prior to the movement of goods to final users. Thus, for consumer goods, orders placed by individuals (commonly called retail sales) constitute the top line of the table. For durable pro-

[1] "Ownership" has a legal implication that is not fulfilled in the case of stock on order. For this, though there often is a legally enforceable commitment to purchase, title has not yet passed to the purchaser and therefore he does not actually own the merchandise. There appears to be no word that is exactly correct for both stock on hand and on order, and accordingly I use the approximation, ownership.

EXHIBIT 2

A Vertical Sequence of Flows and Stocks
(equivalent units of finished goods)

Flows of Goods or Orders	Case I	Case II	Stocks of Goods or Orders	Changes in Stocks or Orders Case I	Case II
Consumer					
1. Orders placed	100	100			
Retailer					
2. Orders received (sales)	100	100			
3.			Unfilled sales orders	0	0
4. Shipments	100	100			
5.			Stock	0	+2
6. Receipts	100	102			
7.			Outstanding purchase orders	+4	−4
8. Orders placed	104	98			
Manufacturer					
9. Orders received	104	98			
10.			Unfilled sales orders	−(+4)	−(−4)
11. Shipments	100	102			
12.			Finished stock	0	+1
13. Production	100	103			
14.			In-process stock	+2	−1
15. Starts	102	102			
16.			Purchased materials stock	+1	−1
17. Receipts	103	101			
18.			Outstanding purchase orders	+2	−5
19. Orders placed	105	96			
Importer or Raw-Materials Dealer					
20. Orders received	105	96			
21.			Unfilled sales orders	−(+2)	−(−5)
22. Shipments	103	101			
23.			Stocks	−1	+1
24. Receipts	102	102			
25.			Outstanding purchase orders	0	0
26. Orders placed	102	102			
Miner, Rancher, or Farmer					
27. Orders received	102	102			
28.			Unfilled sales orders	0	0
29. Shipments	102	102			
30			Finished stock	0	0
31. Production	102	102			

ducers' goods, whose final use is by a business firm, the top line of the table would represent the orders placed by the purchaser expecting to install the machinery. Stopping the table at this point reflects the thought that stocks of consumer goods in the hands of individuals or families, or stocks of durable capital goods in the hands of producers, respond to very different influences from goods moving through the operations of production and marketing. Final product is excluded throughout this analysis.

The first two columns show, at some particular time, the vertical steps in the production, shipment of, or orders for goods which could apply to the economy as a whole or to steps whereby cotton is converted to bath towels, steel into screws, or cattle hide into shoes. Each step constitutes the inlet for one stock of goods or orders, and an outlet flow for another. The changes in stocks or orders that result from differences in the volume of inlet and outlet streams are shown in the second set of columns. All figures represent physical units of finished goods or of its constituent materials.

In order to keep the agents identified, steps that constitute virtually two sides of the same coin are listed separately. In the case of receipts and shipments there is similarity but not identity: receipts of purchases follow the same time pattern as shipments by the supplying manufacturer except for changes in time in transit (cf. lines 6 and 11). In the case of orders, there is actual identity: purchase orders placed, say, by a retailer are actually the same instruments as the sales orders of the supplying manufacturer (cf. lines 8 and 9). Consequently, changes in the outstanding orders of a customer placed with one supplier are, precisely, changes in the unfilled orders of the supplier. Convention records an increase of these pools of orders with a positive sign. But an increase in outstanding orders is thought of by the purchaser as precursor of an increase in ownership responsibility. An increase in unfilled orders may be thought of

by the supplier as a remission of ownership responsibility—it passes to his customer. Increases in stocks all represent an increase, other things the same, in ownership responsibility. To maintain consistency of thought and record, then, a change in unfilled sales orders is subtracted algebraically from an increase in stocks or in outstanding purchase orders.[2]

This means that, for a vertical sequence as a whole, the net change in orders that are unfilled or outstanding is close to zero. At the finished end, we exclude changes in unfilled sales orders for goods which will be shipped to the final user, whether consumer or business purchaser of durable capital; at the crude end, the miner or farmer does not typically place purchase orders for basic stock. For intermediate orders, all the rest in the vertical sequence, outstanding and unfilled orders are exactly equal and opposite to one another.

Yet it seems clear that the presence of unfilled (or outstanding) orders and how they are changing is highly material to the power of purchasing to generate or respond to instability. Consider an example.

Assume in both cases I and II that retail sales have been rising during the course of a general cyclical expansion. The retailers in case I think that sales will continue to rise. They underestimated the rise when advance orders for the current season were placed and therefore they must try to get merchandise delivered swiftly. They think competitors are in a similar situation and that stocks in the pipelines are also low, and this may cause a rush for goods and some difficulty in obtaining highly desirable merchandise surely and promptly. If this occurred, prices might also rise; indeed manufacturers have been threatening that present prices would not hold except for preseason purchases. Consequently,

---

[2] Inventory position is defined this way by Hadley and Whitin: "The inventory position is the amount of stock-on-hand plus on order minus backorders. . . ." *Inventory Systems,* p. 46.

they think it wise to increase the proportion of expected season's requirements which are ordered now for delivery in two or three months, instead of waiting for a month or so and then ordering these goods for immediate delivery. They also scout around and find some extra goods for "at once" delivery. Their total current orders (line 8), therefore, those for immediate delivery and for advance delivery, are four units larger than current sales (line 2). Outstanding orders have risen by four units (line 7). Stocks have not changed (line 5) because, though they were drawn down by unexpectedly large sales, they were built up by the additional market-prospect-linked orders for at-once delivery.

The manufacturers, whose production was adjusted to current retail sales, have felt the increase in demand. New orders and unfilled orders have risen. They have responded by increasing production starts (line 15); moreover, they are buying (line 19) more than they are selling (line 9) and more than current receipts (line 17); these in turn are larger than production starts. The fact that manufacturers are buying more than they are selling, in spite of the fact that they are receiving more advance notice (more orders carrying advance delivery dates), may express a willingness to increase stocks because the relative cost of carrying them has declined. For one thing, because of the increase in backlogs, there is less danger of buying or producing an article that will not sell. Also the pressure to raise output may put a premium on steady employment and larger production lots, both of which imply some increase in stocks. In addition, manufacturers, like retailers, are expecting either delay in deliveries or rising prices or both. Perhaps, if it is the bath towel-cotton sequence, the published estimates of the cotton crop may now look as if the crop had previously been overestimated. Supply, then, may be smaller than was formerly expected as well as demand stronger, thus further increasing the likelihood of scramble for goods. As a result, sellers all along the line be-

come tougher traders as buyers become more eager. In effect, short-term demand schedules shift upward and to the right. There is movement along supply schedules; but these schedules also shift upward and to the left as suppliers become less anxious to sell goods which may rise in value. If the example, instead of applying to the bath towel-cotton sequence, applies to the screw-steel or shoe-hide sequence, the chances of shifts in supplying schedules may perhaps be somewhat less. In any event, supply schedules for crude materials have the classic upward slope. Accordingly, larger requirements are attracted to central markets from further distances, as purchased scrap steel, country hides, and imported hides are induced by higher prices to augment the pseudo-byproduct supply of home-produced scrap and packer hides. But, in any case, the sensitive prices of crude materials rise.

The exhibit shows receipts of raw material dealers (line 24) responding only slowly to increased demand since supply is inelastic and inflexible. Their receipts are a little higher than sales of retailers and lower than the receipts of manufacturers. Stocks of dealers decline. Perhaps if the sequence involved hides or steel, at least the orders placed by dealers would be higher because of the efforts to import hides from abroad and to collect larger quantities of scrap metal.

The example has pictured typical occurrences during an upward phase of a business cycle. Efforts to fill the pipeline augment the upward surge. Though consumer buying is increasing, the buying of retailers and manufacturers increases more, since stocks buy more efficiency than formerly, requirements are found to have been underestimated and delivery periods are expected to lengthen and prices to rise. At the later stages of production, swelling demand takes the form of an increase in outstanding materials orders and of stocks of purchased material—an increase, that is, in ownership of materials. At the earlier stages, increased buying endeavor, meeting resistance of inflexible supply, presses on the price structure. The increasing orders, order backlogs, delays, and price increases support the expectation of increasing tensions and cause further buying at later stages and further price increases at earlier stages.

Contrast this picture with one which might apply in case II. Though sales have been rising, retailers had expected them to rise more and had made provisions based on these too-optimistic expectations. These errors have caused stocks to be quite high and they have increased two units more (line 5). Buying, it is thought, should now be cautious. For, if, as seems likely, other retailers have had similar experiences, markets will soften and goods become easier to obtain on short notice. With this possibility in mind, buying is cut back substantially. Retailers' orders are cut to two units less than sales and total ownership declines by two units—a four-unit decline in outstanding orders minus the increase in stock on hand of two units associated with the error in estimating sales (line 7 + line 5).

Manufacturers learn of the changed opinion of retailers from the reduction in their orders as well as from trade sources. Their production starts are now equal to their shipments, but they expect shipments to decline not only because orders have, but because retail sales are probably lower than shipments to retailers because retailers' stocks are rumored high. The decline in their backlogs of sales orders (line 10) increases the economic risk in holding stock. Furthermore, the continued rise in materials prices has started to pinch margins so that the idea is gaining currency that prices are too high. If so, many manufacturers are thinking that "you cannot make money" with prices where they are because margins are too narrow; yet they fear the effect on sales of any effort to raise selling prices in line with increased costs. Accordingly, they reduce their purchasing in the hope that materials prices will come down and goods can be picked up later at a better price. In the example, manufacturers' purchase orders (line 19) are reduced more than is their selling (line 9). Their ownership of purchased

materials (line 16 + line 18) is cut drastically—new orders are six units less than production starts. The rising finished stocks of manufacturer and dealer, and the presently undesired increase in retailers' stocks, all evidences of errors in guessing demand, cause buyers all along the line to be less patient than previously; by the same token, sellers are more willing to listen. Demand and supply schedules shift. If prices do not fall, at least they cease to rise. This reinforces expectations of further weakening. Here, as in case I, output and shipments at the earlier stages are little affected as yet by the changed buying interest. Since production and shipments all along the line are still increasing, income payments to consumers are ample to support the current level of sales. But if the situation holds its present shape, production will be curtailed; then income payments will be reduced even though stocks may still rise for a while.

The examples that we have been considering have concentrated, to their injury, on very limited aspects of even the central data under consideration. But in spite of their deficiencies, they serve, perhaps, to suggest the meaning of the several sorts of information about stocks and orders.

Notable is the fact that in the tabular example none of the difference between case I and case II is reflected in net change in stocks. Change in stocks in all hands is +2 in both cases.

The force of buying endeavor, given the level of final demand, seems to be evidenced most immediately and accurately close to the purchasing operation. It is evidenced by changes in outstanding purchase orders and in stocks of purchased materials. Most accurately, it appears in the sum of the two—changes in ownership of materials.

In the exhibit, the difference between case I and case II is well represented by the fact that changes in materials ownership for retailers and manufacturers are +4 and +3, respectively, in case I, whereas the corresponding figures for case II are −2 and −6.

THE CONCEPT

Definition

Ownership of materials combines stocks of purchased materials of manufacturers, or merchandise stock of distributors, with orders for these materials that have not yet been received by the purchaser—purchase orders outstanding. My basic notion is that stocks and outstandings should not necessarily be combined, but simply studied together.

The concept is intended to aid in the exploration of the complex of events comprehended under the rubric, inventory cycle.

It is not unusual, as we saw in Chapter 1, to study outstanding or unfilled orders in connection with inventory cycles. However, the concept that I use differs from the usual one in three ways:

1. It views unfilled orders from the point of view of the buyer rather than the seller; thus it concentrates on purchase orders outstanding rather than on unfilled sales orders.
2. It combines purchase orders outstanding with stocks of purchased materials (including merchandise stock of distributors, which henceforth will not be named separately) and thus deals with purchased materials on hand and on order. For many purposes, however, it is useful to separate the two components; there need be no rules on this score.
3. It excludes outstanding purchase orders of the final buyer of durable producers' goods.

It is customary, of course, to exclude from the concept of inventories the buyers' stock of durable producers' goods—the installed machinery of manufacturers or others. But the unfilled orders for these goods in the form of unfilled sales orders received by producers of durable goods are ordinarily included in the analysis of unfilled orders. Indeed, statistics on unfilled orders are dominated by this segment of the total. I exclude them because many of the influences to which they respond may be different from those that affect orders for goods intended to be resold or processed. Their impact on sales and stock decisions is, as we saw in Chapter 2, also different.

Aggregation

A comprehensive aggregate of materials ownership for the entire economy would aim at summing, for all enterprises, materials stocks on hand and on order. "Materials stocks" is meant to cover "stock in trade" for distributors; for manufacturers, it is often referred to as stocks of "purchased materials" or "raw" materials (with "raw" signifying a state prior to processing by the enterprise rather than truly raw). "Enterprise" could be defined in a number of ways—an establishment, a financial or management unit such as corporation or firm, a major division of a corporation in one industry field. The choice is likely to depend on available data.

A vertical sequence of types of establishment for which materials on hand and on order need to be included follows.

Manufactured Goods Destined for Consumer Use
1. Retailers
2. Wholesalers and dealers in finished products
3. Manufacturers of finished products
4. Dealers in intermediate products
5. Manufacturers of intermediate products
6. Manufacturers of raw materials
7. Dealers in raw materials

Manufactured Goods Destined for Business' Final Use
Line 1 would typically not apply. (Perhaps trucks and farm machinery are major exceptions.) Line 2 would also not apply in the common case of direct sale by manufacturer; otherwise the list is the same.

Construction

Lines 1 and 2 would apply in connection with do-it-yourself trade and work by private contractors. Line 3 is replaced by the construction company, which is the last business agent who sells to the final user, whether consumer, business, or government.

Ideally, one would like to provide statistical representation of each major vertical stage for all industry. Moreover, it would be desirable to provide information for several vertical sequences. At the very least, since the backward transmission of demand must be different for goods having different patterns of final use, it would be valuable to have separate chains for consumer nondurables, semidurables, and durables, and business capital equipment, particularly for sorts having very long production periods and consequently long intervals by which orders can precede delivery. Separate chains, appropriately designed, could provide information about the dynamics of the process, such as the impact of multiplicity of stages, of size of firms, of overcapacity.

The data should be in terms of equivalent physical units required per unit of finished product. Thus, if dollar figures had been used, they would need to be adjusted for the value added as processing and distribution are completed.

Unfortunately the statistical realities put an end to these daydreams. The basic building blocks that are required are data on sales, stocks, and outstanding purchase orders *for the same companies.* As far as I know, this information is available for a single group of companies, a sample of large department stores, but as of the end of 1963 the "is" must be changed to "was." The series was discontinued, temporarily, it is hoped. All the rest of such data as there are on orders or unfilled orders applies to sales orders, so that for a particular company stocks can be matched with backlogs of sales orders but not with outstanding purchase orders. All available data are in book value and none in the physical units in terms of which the analysis has been phrased. As beggars then, not choosers, with what statistical rags can the analytic skeleton be clad?

THE DATA

Beginning in 1939, the "Merchandising Sample" of large department stores had submitted monthly information to the Federal Reserve System concerning (among other things) sales, change in stocks, and change in outstanding orders; and from these figures the System also calculated stocks, outstanding orders, receipts, and new orders. About two hundred stores participated. It is usual for retail stores to carry inventories at retail prices rather than at purchase price, and this is the meaning of book value for the department store data. It has the advantage of coming closer to the notion of "equivalent finished units" than does the usual book value concept. These figures, then, provide one small sample for line 1 of the previous enumeration—retailers' stocks and outstanding orders. Unfortunately there is no satisfactory way of matching them in other lines of the vertical sequence.[3]

The second pool of information concerns

[3] The outstanding purchase orders of department stores are the unfilled sales orders of their suppliers. These would be chiefly manufacturers of finished goods (line 3), and very occasionally wholesalers (line 2). To carry the sequence backward another step, then, the outstanding purchase orders for line 3 are primarily required. Since all data for manufacturers are for sales orders, the outstanding purchase orders of finished goods manufacturers would have to be estimated on the basis of the unfilled sales orders of their suppliers, manufacturers of semifinished or crude products which enter into the finished goods that department stores use. However, the data for manufacturing, to be discussed presently, do not provide the appropriate industry breakdown except for the textile group.

manufacturers. It consists of monthly statistics on shipments, inventories in three stages of manufacture, and change in the unfilled orders of the product the company sells; from the latter, new sales orders are computed. The data were collected by the Office of Business Economics of the United States Department of Commerce until the work was transferred to the Bureau of the Census in 1957. Although some totals are available, industry breakdowns cannot be carried back earlier than 1947, or 1946 in some cases. The sample consisted of 3,100 companies in 1948–49, but declined to 2,400 in 1953 and to 1,650 in 1957.[4] Reporting is on a corporation, not an establishment, basis.

This body of information has recently undergone a serious overhauling, and the old series was revised back to 1953. However, the new data were not available in time for use in this study. Indeed, it is a moot point whether in any event they should have been used for a study covering the period from 1946 to 1962. I would have been inclined not to.[5] Needless to say, the new series is greatly superior to the old, when, beginning January 1962, the basic information was supplied by the new enlarged sample in which many corporations submitted reports for each of several major divisions.

Because the individual companies report sales orders and not purchase orders, the data can picture materials on hand and on order only if it is possible to match the materials stocks of one set of companies with the unfilled orders of the companies from whom the first group buy their materials. For example, the materials stocks of shoe manufacturers (chiefly leather) could be matched with the unfilled sales orders (for leather) reported by tanners, which would typically also be the outstanding purchase orders of shoe manufacturers, tanners' customers.

However, for nondurable goods, virtually no vertical sequences could be isolated, and therefore the data could not be used. For durable goods, the prospect was a little more hopeful. Nevertheless, the discussion of what can and cannot be done is exceedingly tedious.

[4] The sample is discussed in *Manufacturers' Shipments, Inventories, and Orders: 1947–1963 Revised*, U.S. Department of Commerce, Series M3-1, p. 12. The figure for 1953 is from *Statistics of Business Inventories*, Report of Consultant Committee on Inventory Statistics, Organized by the Board of Governors of the Federal Reserve System at the Request of the Subcommittee in Economic Statistics of the Joint Committee on the Economic Report, November 1955, p. 170. Not all of the 2,400 companies reporting in 1953 supplied monthly figures. For the durable goods industries, the annual sample supplying annual or quarterly data was estimated to cover 72 per cent of the estimated total manufacturers' shipments, and the monthly sample 48 per cent; the coverage of the monthly series for eleven industry groups varied from 80 per cent for motor vehicles and equipment to 7 per cent for lumber and furniture. The median was 50 per cent (*Statistics of Inventories*, p. 171). For unfilled orders it is lower, though how much is hard to say. For the new sample, for example, 65 per cent of the shipments reported by the sample in the durable goods industries was reported by firms that also gave information on unfilled orders (*Manufacturers' Shipments*, p. 11, Table E).

[5] Thanks to the courtesy of the Office of Business Economics in making unpublished material available, we had thirty-four industry breakdowns, about the same number now available in the new sample, though it is hoped eventually to expand the tabulations to fifty-five industries (*Manufacturers' Shipments*, p. 15). The new series is based on a sample of 4,000 companies, and efforts have been made to get divisional reports for the large diversified companies—about 375 of them (*ibid.*, p. 8). The divisional reports make it possible to approximate the establishment basis of reporting, and accordingly the Annual Survey of Manufacturers now provides the benchmark figures. (The old series was linked to Bureau of Internal Revenue figures, which are, of course, on a corporate basis.) The old series, for each industry group that was tabulated, was revised back to 1953 on a monthly basis (*ibid.*, p. 14). A chief aspect of the revision was the shift to the Annual Survey of Manufacturers base. However, the actual reporting sample is for entire corporations only, and this frequently does not provide an adequate means of interpolating annual benchmarks on an establishment basis. As a result, it was necessary to resort to a variety of estimating devices. (See discussion, *ibid.*, p. 14.) Whatever the limitations of these devices for the purpose of estimating stocks and shipments (for which some parallel information exists), they are greatly magnified in the case of orders. All in all, since my study focuses on the 1946–62 period, it seems preferable to stay with sow's ear rather than turn to the silk purse at best for about half of the period.

Moreover, the final outcome, which is far from a desirable one, adds a feeling of frustration to the tedium. One thing stands out in garish clarity—our statistics are not constructed on a principle which is prepared to yield exactly the information we need.

Two large industry groups chiefly make durable finished products. They are the machinery industries and the transportation equipment groups. Their unfilled sales orders are for the most part either those placed by distributors who sell autos,[6] household appliances, and the like, mostly to consumers, or farm equipment and standard machines for business use, or those placed by business firms buying capital equipment often for their own use. In either case, these unfilled orders should not be included in the aggregate materials ownership for manufacturers. (The first group would, of course, properly be included as outstanding purchase orders of distributors, but the stock data are missing for them.) Other major industry groups make parts or semifinished or crude materials that enter into the production of the two finished groups. They are primary metals (ferrous and nonferrous), fabricated metals, and some of the miscellaneous group. It would seem, then, that our basic tactic should be to use the unfilled sales orders of these intermediate groups as estimates of the outstanding purchase orders of the finished-product groups. Their materials ownership would then be this plus purchased materials stocks for the finished-product groups. Of course, this tactic bows without even a demurrer to the fact that stocks cover all materials and outstandings only those of durable goods. Since this difficulty is present in any approach using existing data, it will be ignored.

But the difficulty of matching figures to the requirements of this general scheme counsels some modification of it. The difficulties are:

1. Many companies in the intermediate group sell to one another, and therefore their sales orders are not all purchase orders of the finished-goods industries.

2. A not inconsiderable portion of the finished-product group actually make intermediate products such as parts used by other divisions of the same company or other companies, and the sales orders of these companies are really purchase orders of a finished-goods manufacturer in just the same sense as are the sales orders of firms in the intermediate-industries group.

3. Manufacturers that must be classed primarily in the intermediate group make some products that are not sold to finished-goods manufacturers in the machinery and transportation equipment industries. Examples are construction materials sold to construction companies, or products of any sort sold to industrial or institutional users, wholesalers, or even retailers.

Accordingly, one cannot isolate a substantial part of the outstanding purchase orders of the two broad finished-product groups by looking at the unfilled sales orders of the intermediate group. The latter include too much because of 1 and 3, and too little because of 2. Moreover, the misplacement of an industry subgroup (with respect to the finished product vs. materials criterion) that distorts the measurement of outstanding orders also distorts the materials stock part of ownership. The defects are large. This can be seen simply in the fact that the book value of shipments of the intermediate groups in 1956, as defined in the previous paragraph, summed to 97 per cent of that of the finished product group, thereby suggesting, absurdly, that, according to the logic of the classification scheme, value added by finished-goods manufacturers was 3 per cent. On the basis of the sample breakdowns that are available (I refer to the unpublished material), there is no way to eliminate what does not belong and add what does. The difficulty may be analyzed by using the far finer breakdowns and establishment data assembled in the course of the work on the Federal Reserve Board Index of

---

[6] No unfilled orders for automobiles are presumably recorded by auto manufacturers.

Industrial Production, and this confirms the negative conclusion.[7]

An alternative scheme seems preferable for most purposes. It abandons the effort to isolate two parts of the durable goods industries—those making finished products and those supplying these industries with materials. Instead, it estimates ownership for all durable goods manufacturing. We have data on outstanding sales orders of all corporations manufacturing durable goods—the sum of both groups previously mentioned. We also have their materials stocks. Concerning their outstanding purchase orders, we know the following:

1. They should not include the vast majority of the unfilled sales orders of machinery and transportation equipment industries; and these can actually be removed, though in so doing we also remove unfilled sales orders for machine parts or materials manufactured by this group which ought to remain.

2. They should not include the unfilled sales orders of manufacturers of construction materials or other goods sold to jobbers or construction companies which do not undergo further manufacture; about this nothing can be done.

3. They should include the unfilled sales orders of all the rest of the reporting sample of durable goods manufacturers, and these figures we have.

4. They should include the unfilled sales orders of dealers, miners, or importers who sell materials to durable goods manufacturers (this would be particularly important for the manufacturers of crude materials); these figures are unavailable.

Following this procedure, then, outstanding purchase orders of all durable goods manufacturers are somewhat too large by the inclusion of 2 and too small by the exclusion of 1, 3, and 4.[8] The materials stocks on hand are appropriately represented. Unfilled sales

---

[7] Calculations were made in terms of the production weights assigned to each category that needed to be singled out. The weights were developed in the course of the 1959 revisions of the Index of Industrial Production. They represent value added in 1957 (*Industrial Production, 1959 Revision*, Board of Governors of the Federal Reserve System, 1960, pp. 29–30). The FRB tables, "Series in Industrial Production Index," which give "market classifications" for each industry subdivision (*ibid.*, pp. S-3–S-11) were summarized to conform with the industry classifications available in the OBE unpublished data. In this way one could see, for example, that for 4.61 weight assigned to "aircraft and parts," 2.57 were for finished goods ("equipment") and 2.04 for parts. In addition to these data, use was made of the information in the 1958 Census of Manufacturers, *Distribution of Manufacturers Sales*. The calculations are at best little more than informed guesses concerning general orders of magnitudes concerning what one would like to measure on *an establishment basis*. The actual OBE data are, of course, on a company basis, and this can make very substantial differences. For example, auto parts manufactured by separate companies as reported to OBE were *far* smaller than by separate establishments as calculated by FRB. In addition, the small samples reporting to the OBE sample in some industries sometimes mean that the companies actually reporting are poor representatives of the industry group.

However, for whatever they are worth, my calculations for the adjustments required under points 1, 2, and 3 in the text involved adding 8.8 weight points

(intermediate products in final-products industries) to the groups' unadjusted weight for the intermediate-goods manufacturers of 22.5, and subtracting 18.3 points (the sum of a number of different adjustments). The net decrease of 9.5 points brought the intermediate-group weight down to 13.0. The final-products group, which started with a weight of 26.1, was decreased by 8.8 points (for intermediate products in final-products industries) and increased by 5.2 (for final products in the intermediate group), causing a net decrease of 3.6 to a final figure of 22.5.

Shifts of this order, or indeed half this order, cannot be ignored unless it were safe to assume that materials and unfilled orders for all industries behaved alike. Very little could be done to meet the difficulty. Auto parts could have been shifted to the intermediate group, but the company reports failed to isolate most of this group (as indicated by comparison of FRB and OBE weight) and none of the other intermediate products in the finished-goods group were covered by separate OBE industries. The furniture industry could not be shifted to the final-products group because it had not been tabulated separately from lumber for most of the interval covered. Instrument manufacturers were left in the intermediate group, though the industry title suggests that they produce final products. There were two reasons for the decision: first, separate tabulation for the group did not start until 1954; second, a substantial part of the output of the actual companies in the sample consisted of parts rather than finished products.

[8] Evaluation of the sins of this calculation was similar in many respects to the procedure described

orders, shipments, and new sales orders are appropriately given by the totals for the durable goods industries. The figures are, I believe, the best that can be devised for the period prior to 1962 and adequate for preliminary exploration of the fluctuation of materials on hand and on order in durable goods manufacture.

For January 1962, I shift to the revised series compiled by the Bureau of the Census. The industry groupings are roughly comparable to those previously used, but the actual company reports not only are greatly expanded but differ since divisional information makes it possible to make a better assignment of the output of large integrated companies to the major fields that their work covers. For these and other reasons, I have made no effort to reconcile the differences in the two sets of data. Instead the new series have been set at the same level as the old for January to June 1962, and used without further ado beginning January 1962. (The data are discontinuous December 1961 to January 1962.) The procedure implies that subtle judgments concern-

ing the location of turning points and the like cannot be made after 1962, and our measurements and summaries therefore end in 1961. However, the charts and discussions take the later evidence into account.

The calculation turns its back on some potentially useful information. Perhaps the most regrettable neglect is that of separate tabulation for the consumer durables industries, for which unfilled sales orders would be outstanding purchase orders of distributors. Combined with appropriate retail sales and stocks, this would be valuable evidence on how fluctuations in consumer buying are altered as they become incorporated in the buying of retailers and wholesalers. Also, by using the unfilled sales orders for the two groups of manufacturers, one could, in effect, compare the outstanding purchase orders for consumer durables bought by distributors and for capital equipment bought by dealers and final users. Both these comparisons would, of course, be greatly enriched if it were possible to contrast also the outstanding purchase orders for producers of finished consumers' and producers' goods. Needless to say, the latter calculation is impossible. But the division at the finished-goods stage is also foiled by the character of the actual reports.[9]

in the previous note. Two of the difficulties were shared by both calculations—those caused by intermediate products made by finished-goods manufacturers, and those caused by products made by the intermediate-products industries that are sold to construction companies and industrial or institutional users or distributors (since for these, unfilled sales orders are not outstanding purchase orders of any covered company). One difficulty of the previous calculation is not present here: the outstanding sales orders of the intermediate group that sell to one another are properly included. One difficulty is present here and not in the previous calculation: outstanding purchase orders for materials bought from miners, dealers, etc., should be included and cannot be. My estimates on the basis of the production data show the need for an adjustment downward by 11.3 index points and upward by 12.7. The net increase of 1.4 points, which is negligible, is, however, produced by a gross shift of 25.0 points, which is only slightly smaller than the gross shift of 27.1 points in the rejected calculation. But the redeeming features of this one is that the shifts should be measured against the base of all durables, 48.6, where in the other the appropriate base was 22.5, the unadjusted base of intermediate products alone. Further, for this concept, the defect is confined to outstanding orders. Stocks of materials or other stocks are correctly represented, as are shipments and new orders.

[9] The possibility of dividing materials producers into two groups is ruled out by the fact that even without the subdivision they cannot be adequately isolated. (See footnote 3 above.) But the difficulty goes deeper than this, and even the improved data now available may well not solve it adequately. Even the detailed level of the FRB sample and establishment data gives small representation to materials used in the durable consumer goods industries, which have a total weight of 3.67, and always as a part of contributions by the same industry subgroup to some other market classification. No subdivision for primary metals is undertaken for the FRB index; indeed, the distinction may well be meaningless at that level of production. This means that, at best, the consumer-producer break would have to be justified for what the analysis of the sales orders of the finished goods producers could show.

However, here, too, the separation could not be achieved on the basis of the company data. The new divisional reporting system should change this sad story. The obvious groups to include among the consumer group are (1) radio and communications, (2) household machinery, (3) motor vehicles, (4)

Questions, then, concerning the behavior of materials on hand and on order are to be addressed to two relatively small pools of information—those supplied by department stores, which are conceptually appropriate; those supplied by durable goods manufacturers for which appropriate concepts are only partially attained. It is clear that these are about the best data available. But this does not mean that they are good enough. However, I do indeed believe that they are good enough to support useful exploratory work.

Why? It is not easy to display the complex and dissimilar elements of which the judgment (perhaps one should say the partly intuitive judgment) is compounded.

There is, for one thing, information about the figures—information of the types discussed

furniture. However, the actual data available in no case were adequate to serve a useful purpose. The output of the reporting companies in (1) was far more heavily weighted with industrial than with consumer products. For (2), the chief producers of household machinery were classified in a different section of the machinery industries. As for (4), reports for furniture companies were not tabulated separately from those for lumber until 1954. But the worst difficulty was for (3), the group which on the surface seemed clear, the motor vehicle group. The industry had huge backlogs of orders in the early fifties, which must have been associated with defense contracts written by the auto manufacturers, whereas their outstanding orders for automobiles are presumably small or not recorded as such. Thus the outstanding orders of the largest group of consumer goods manufacturers were large, variable, and actually associated with non-consumer goods business.

in the previous footnote; there is information about the reporting samples conveyed to me by the people who have striven to evaluate and improve them (and even the very character of these strivings is not immaterial); there are observations about how the data behave—the reasonableness of the way that parts of the total relate to one another, and to parts of parts, and to outside evidence.

Into the judgment seeps, no doubt, some wishful thinking. (An investigator is constantly horrified by the crafty ways in which he contrives to find relevance and order.) The judgment also scans the relation between the tools and the work to be done. The figures are for many reasons, including their level of aggregation, suited at best to box the compass of the problem rather than to explore in depth any single direction. Perhaps most reassuring is the realization that the shortcomings of the data are capable of obscuring meaningful information, but it is hard to see how they conceivably could produce the many sorts of sensible relations which, in fact, they show. Their greatest difficulty is that they must remain at a level of aggregation which is truly inappropriate to the problem under study.

Finally, there is a time dimension to be considered. The strategy of scientific advance often means that a good question answered badly may be a necessary prelude to a good answer some years later. Without further apologies, then, we turn to the effort to observe and understand how the time series behave.

II. THE BEHAVIOR OF OWNERSHIP AND ITS PARTS

4. Materials Ownership, Durable Goods Manufacturers

The task that now confronts us is primarily descriptive. It is necessary to learn how the several sorts of materials stocks on hand and on order behave, and how that behavior relates to fluctuations in flows of goods or flows of orders for goods.

Of course, description has no place to start or stop unless it is related to a question. Two sorts of questions alternatively provide the frame of reference that makes description feasible. The first is, What does the behavior of the data suggest about possible causal interrelations? Second, How do the activities of stocks participate in economic instability? Efforts to answer these questions form the substance of Part III.

Here they provide the point of view which guides how the behavior of the various time series is explored. This and the following chapter each constitute an examination of some particular type of information, and focus on data on stocks and outstanding orders proper, expressed in dollars or as ratios to sales; durable goods manufacturers are examined here and department stores in Chapter 5. Chapter 6 looks at rates of change in stocks—

inventory investment. Chapters 7 and 8 concentrate on the relation between adjacent flows and the stock pools that they feed or drain.

The impact of stocks and, with many qualifications, of unfilled orders on the flows of income and output in the economy is measured primarily by the amount that they increase or decrease, period by period; it is measured, in other words, by rates of change. However, the level of stocks and of unfilled orders constitutes a resource (and in some senses an obligation) both for the economy at large and for the individual company, and thus influences and reflects a wide variety of judgments. It is necessary therefore to acquire a firm understanding of characteristic movements of stocks and unfilled orders proper.

Accordingly, we examine, for manufacturers of durable goods, the levels and patterns of fluctuations, during postwar years, of materials on hand and on order. In the second section we review how these patterns relate to those of shipments of manufacturers to their customers.

THE LEVEL OF OWNERSHIP

Manufacturers of durable goods carried "raw" materials on hand or on order, the book value of which averaged about $20 billion during the seventeen years 1946–62. Monthly sales (shipments) averaged about half that amount— about $10 billion; that is, the book value of stocks covered about two months' sales. How-

ever, direct comparison of the two figures is misleading. In durable goods industries, materials typically constitute about half of the value of final sales; the rest of the value accrues in the course of manufacturing.[1] Con-

[1] This estimate is based on the relation between costs of materials and value of shipments for about

sequently, materials stocks on hand and on order, carried on the books at $20 billion, might have represented on the average the material required for about four months' sales.

Of total goods on hand and on order, stocks of materials on hand constituted about a third; outstanding orders of materials represented the other two-thirds.[2]

CONFORMITY AND TIMING

Business Cycles

The level of ownership underwent strong cyclical fluctuations, as the top curve in Chart 1 shows. Comparison with the shaded areas, which mark periods designated as business recession according to the National Bureau's business cycle chronology, indicates that ownership tends to conform with general business conditions with a persistent lead at peaks. Table 1 sharpens the visual comparisons. The columns of section A show timing at each business cycle peak and trough; in the B and C sections, various summary measures are given. Typically, durable goods manufacturers ceased expanding their ownership of materials well before peaks in business activities occurred; the median lead[3] was four and a half months (line 1, column B4). During business cycle recessions, on the other hand, declining ownership continues just about up to

the trough in business with a lead or a lag of no more than two months.

Extra Movements

Line 2 of the table uses the "subcycle" reference scheme. It consists of the business cycle dates plus two additional movements found in many economic events. The first was part and parcel of the transition from a war to a peace economy. Recessions have notoriously followed wartime expansion. As some of the more drastic aspects of the adjustment subsided in late 1946, the usual postwar recession was thought by many to be due. Of the executives responding to a questionnaire distributed by *Fortune* magazine in May 1947, 74 per cent said that they expected conditions to worsen. Rendigs Fels in a study of "Recognition of Cyclical Turning Points" discusses this episode as one of the most blatant examples of "false declarations" of cyclical turns. He notes that:

> In May 1947, in separate statements, two professors from the same university used almost identical language, one saying, "The long expected and long advertised recession is here," the other saying, "Beyond question, the long advertised recession is here." A month later, a news magazine with a large circulation said, "The nation's bumper crop of economic forecasters could now relax, tuck their thumbs in their vests, and say, 'We told you so.' The recession had officially begun."

Also, there appears to have been confirmation as the year rolled on. Fels recounts that:

> The mean of the forecasts of industrial production made in September by the group of forecasters

thirty-five of the larger industries covered in the durable goods field. The basic data were those of the 1958 *Census of Manufacturers*, Vol. 1, Table 3, pp. 1–6 ff. Value added is shipments minus cost of materials, which include also supplies, fuel, purchased electricity, and construction work. The median ratio for the various industries of value added to shipments fell in the upper portion of the .45–.49 size group. In view of the padded (for our purpose) definition of materials costs in the Census, the 50 per cent figure for values added is far more likely to be too low than too high. If so stocks represent a somewhat larger number of weeks' supply than the text suggests.

[2] The analysis of the OBE data in the previous chapter makes it clear that there is a wide margin of error in these figures. Certainly any finding that is dependent on fairly close measurements ought to be rejected. Fortunately the evidence throughout is sufficiently gross to be most unlikely to be vulnerable to errors in the figures.

[3] The term median is used to apply to the average of the middle two or three observations.

CHART 1

Ownership, Stocks, and Unfilled Orders, Durable Goods Manufacturers, 1946–64

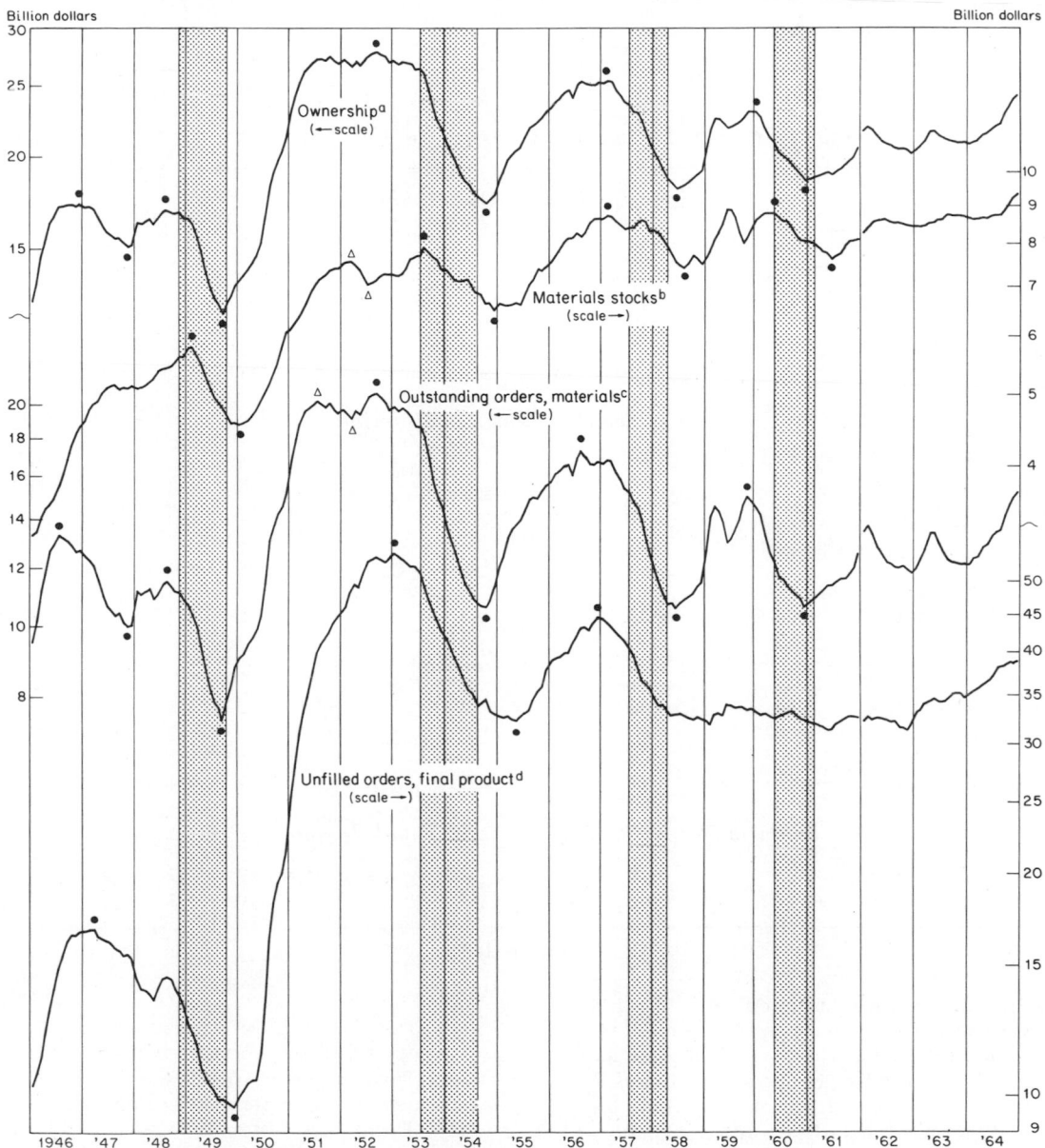

Note: Shaded areas represent business contractions. Specific cycle turns are marked by dots, additional minor turns by triangles.

a The sum of lines 2 and 3.   b Purchased materials stocks for all durable goods industries.
c Unfilled orders for fabricated metals, primary metals, and other durables.   d Unfilled orders for machinery and transportation equipment.

TABLE 1

Timing: Stocks on Hand and on Order, Durable Goods Manufacturers, 1946–62

Section A: Months Lead (−) or Lag (+) for Matched Turns[a]

Chronology[b]

Line	Reference Series[c]	P (1/47)	T (7/47)	P 11/48	T 10/49	P (2/51)	T (6/52)	P 7/53	T 8/54	P 7/57	T 4/58	P 5/60	T 2/61
	Specific Series: Ownership												
1	Business cycles			−3	−1			−10	+2	−5	+2	−4	−2
2	Subcycles	−1	+4	−3	−1	⊕	⊕	−10	+2	−5	+2	−4	−2
3	Outstanding orders	+5	0	0	0	⊕	⊕	0	0	+6	0	+2	0
4	Unfilled orders, final product	−3	⊕	⊕	−3	⊙	⊙	−4	−7	+2	Ω	Ω	−5
	Specific Series: Stocks of Materials												
5	Business cycles			+3	+3			+1	+4	−5	+4	0	+4
6	Subcycles	⊕	⊕	+3	+3	+13	+1	+1	+4	−5	+4	0	+4
7	Ownership	⊕	⊕	+6	+4	Ω	Ω	+11	+2	0	+2	+4	+6
8	Outstanding orders	⊕	⊕	+6	+4	+8	+4	+11	+2	+6	+2	+6	+6
9	Unfilled orders, final product	⊙	⊙	+23	+1	⊕	⊕	+7	−5	+2	⊕	⊕	+1
	Specific Series: Outstanding Orders												
10	Business cycles			−3	−1			−10	+2	−11	+2	−6	−2
11	Subcycles	−6	+4	−3	−1	+5	−3	−10	+2	−11	+2	−6	−2
12	Unfilled orders, final product	−8	⊕	⊕	−3	⊕	⊕	−4	−7	−4	⊕	⊕	−5
	Specific Series: Unfilled Orders, Final Product												
13	Business cycles			−20	+2			−6	+9	−7	⊕	⊕	+3
14	Subcycles	+2	⊕	⊕	+2	⊕	⊕	−6	+9	−7	⊕	⊕	+3

(continued)

[a]Specific series are matched with the indicated reference series (see note c) in accordance with the standard NBER rules. A double relaxation of rules is marked r; it applies to cases for well-conforming series in which two like turns are matched, though an unlike turn lies between them. The figure is underlined when subcycle chronology is the reference series, a minor cycle in the specific series has entered a comparison; or, when two individual series are compared, a minor cycle in either series has entered a comparison. When the business cycle chronology provides the reference, minor specific cycle turns are ignored. The meaning of other symbols is:

⊕ = Turn in the reference series does not appear in the specific series.

Ω = Turn in the specific series does not appear in the reference series.

⊙ = There is no turn in either series in the neighborhood of the chronology date.

[b]Chronology dates are business cycle reference dates. In addition, four minor subcycle dates, enclosed in parentheses, are added to form a subcycle chronology.

[c]Reference series are of three sorts: (1) the business cycle chronology as shown in column heads, excluding the dates in parentheses; (2) the

TABLE 1 (concluded)

Line	Reference Series[c]	Number Matched			Median[e]			Average Deviation[f]		All Turns		Timing Adjust-ment[g]	% Mos. 7/46–12/61
		−	+	0	P	T	All	P	T		Wt'd		
							Specific Series: Ownership						
1	Business cycles	6	2	0	−4.5	+0.5	−2.5	2.0	1.8	1.9	1.9	−2,−3	82
2	Subcycles	7	3	0	−4.0	+1.0	−1.5	2.2	1.8	3.0	2.1	−1,−2	75
3	Outstanding orders	0	3	7	+2.3	0	0	2.3	0	1.4	1.1	0	89
4	Unfilled orders, final product	5	1	0	−1.7	−5.0	−3.5	2.4	1.3	2.0	1.9	−3	78
							Specific Series: Stocks of Materials						
5	Business cycles	1	6	1	+0.5	+4.0	+3.0	2.2	0.2	2.0	1.3	+3	89
6	Subcycles	1	8	1	+1.3	+3.7	+3.0	4.3	0.9	2.8	2.6	+3	82
7	Ownership	0	7	1	+5.0	+3.0	+4.0	3.2	1.5	2.4	2.4	+4	82
8	Outstanding orders	0	10	0	+6.7	+3.3	+6.0	1.5	1.3	1.9	1.4	+6	81
9	Unfilled orders, final product	1	5	0	+10.7	−1.0	+1.5	8.2	2.7	5.8	5.4	+1,+2	70
							Specific Series: Outstanding Orders						
10	Business cycles	6	2	0	−8.0	+0.5	−2.5	3.0	1.8	3.9	2.4	−2,−3	70
11	Subcycles	8	4	0	−6.0	+0.5	−2.5	3.8	2.3	4.1	3.1	−2,−3	74
12	Unfilled orders, final product	6	0	0	−5.3	−5.0	−4.5	1.8	1.3	1.5	1.5	−4,−5	77
							Specific Series: Unfilled Orders, Final Product						
13	Business cycles	3	3	0	−11.0	+4.7	−2.0	6.0	2.9	7.8	4.4	+2,−2 to −6	61
14	Subcycles	2	4	0	−3.7	+4.7	+2.0	3.8	2.9	4.2	3.3	+2	56

subcycle chronology as shown in all column heads; (3) particular series whose specific cycles and minor cycles constitute the reference dates for comparison.

[d]The number of months during which the specific series is in like phase with the reference series is expressed as a percentage of the total number of months covered between dates as given.

[e]Median is the average timing of the center two or three turns.

[f]Average deviation from the median. The "weighted" (wt'd) average is the deviation from the median for peaks and for troughs separately, weighted by the number of turns.

[g]In determining months in like phase a timing adjustment is made which maximizes confluence. Before counting the months in phase, the specific series is in effect moved to the right to allow for a lead and to the left to allow for a lag if by so doing the percentage of months in like phase (as rounded) is increased. If the months in phase are as large or larger without an adjustment, this is indicated by a "timing adjustment" of 0.

In some cases we wish to know the percentage of months in phase on a synchronous basis, regardless of whether the percentage in phase is thereby maximized. If so, the "timing adjustment" is given as "none."

referred to as Set A in this investigation predicted a decline from a high in the first half of the year, the decline to continue for the year and a half covered by the prediction and to aggregate more than 10 per cent—clearly an amplitude of cyclical proportions. What is worse, every single forecaster in the group predicted a decline in industrial production.[4]

In view of the customary lag in forecasts relative to actual turns,[5] it is not surprising that a wide variety of time series showed a downturn which seemed to center in January. I had dated the upturn in July.[6]

The second episode was associated with the Korean War, which occasioned a burst of business activity in the second half of 1950. It culminated early in 1951; February was selected as the most representative month. Troughs in many sorts of activities occurred in June of 1952, though a number, particularly in nondurable goods industries, started to recover almost a year earlier.[7]

The large majority of the economic time series with which this monograph is concerned had specific cycle turns which appeared to be associated with the Korean episode and a number also with the postwar phantom recession.[8] Occasionally, movements in individual series at these or other times do not qualify as specific cycle turns according to National Bureau rules, yet do seem clear interruptions of the current cyclical phase. It has seemed unwise to lose sight of such movements for the purpose of describing the basic behavior of the times series during business cycles or

for comparing one series with another. Accordingly, additional "minor specific subcycle" turns have occasionally been selected; they are shown on the charts by triangles.[9]

Subcyclical Timing

Timing at subcycles, as line 2 of Table 1 indicates, includes behavior at both *business cycle and the two minor subcycle* turns. Ownership as a whole conformed to the first of the extra (minor) movements largely because of the strong drop in outstandings after the abnormalities of wartime expansion receded. But in the later phases of the Korean War, ownership leveled rather than dipped. The timing of ownership with respect to the reference subcycle chronology was virtually the same as previously described for business cycles only—a clear lead at all peaks, and mixed and therefore average synchronous behavior at troughs.

Characteristically, the two parts of ownership, stocks and outstandings, turn at different times. Stocks tend to lag the subcycle or cycle chronology, and by more at troughs than at peaks (median lags of four and one months,

---

[4] Rendigs Fels, "Recognition of Cyclical Turning Points," unpublished paper, National Bureau of Economic Research, 1963, p. 32.

[5] Fels found it typically to be between three and six months (*ibid.*, p. 32).

[6] Ruth P. Mack, "Notes on Subcycles in Theory and Practice," *American Economic Review, Proceedings*, May 1957, pp. 164–167; also, NBER, Annual Report, May 1957, pp. 53–56.

[7] *Ibid.*

[8] Turns in individual series selected by the National Bureau in accordance with standard procedures are referred to here as elsewhere as "specific cycle turns." They are marked on all charts by crosses placed above (peaks) or below (troughs) the curve.

[9] Note that selection of these minor movements, like the selection of specific cycles themselves, is constantly confronting marginal decisions. For example, the 1949-53 expansions in stocks of materials and outstanding orders, the second and third curves on Chart 1, were interrupted by a brief contraction early in 1951 or 1952 which was marked as a subcycle. For outstanding orders, the decision teetered on the margin, but the turns were marked. Ownership (top curve) had a slightly less clearly delineated hesitation at that time, and this was not marked. The marginal character of the selection of specific cycles is also evident when, for example, the extra movements in outstanding orders or ownership associated with troughs in 1947 are compared with other specific cycles in the same series or with the minor subcycles marked in material stocks in 1950-51.

The decision not to mark a movement can also be based on reasons other than that it is too mild. A strike affects stocks outstanding, orders, and sales, yet the phenomenon as a whole has a number of highly particular characteristics. For this reason I have consistently not marked the interruptions of expansion in 1959 associated with the steel strike; these occurred in many series.

respectively, line 6). Outstandings lead strongly at peaks (median lead of six months, line 11) and virtually synchronize at troughs. They share the business cycle pattern previously described for ownership. Direct comparisons between stocks and outstandings confirm the character of the difference. Line 8 of the table indicates the lead or lag of stocks at each turn in outstandings. The median lag is seven months at peak and three at troughs. And a lag of six months is the median for all turns.

Moreover, the relationship is reasonably systematic. The average deviation from the median for all turns is only 1.9 months—1.4 months if the average deviation for peaks and troughs is computed separately and then averaged (line 8, last column of section B). The chart also suggests substantial parallelism in the two series once the inflated unfilled orders of the immediate postwar years had been somewhat reduced and stocks correspondingly increased. (This counterpoised behavior appears again in 1952 and during the protracted steel strike in 1959.) Section G of the table indicates that from mid-1946 through 1961 the two series are in like specific cycle phase for 81 per cent of the months, after allowing for the average tendency for orders to lead by half a year. If comparisons are confined to 1948 and thereafter, 88 per cent of the months are in like phase. Apparently, then, outstandings exhibit substantial parallelism to materials stocks and lead them by a considerable interval, particularly at peaks.

A further indication of correlation appears in the impression that matched episodes in the two series seem to have about the same rank order with respect to their severity. The episodes to be compared can be selected by turning to Chart 1 and selecting matching expansion phases in materials stocks on the one hand and outstanding orders for materials on the other. They are the rises starting in late 1949 or early 1950, in late 1954, and in 1958; the first lap of the post 1961 expansion can also be included by selecting the top of the

first rise in 1962 (which, however, has not been considered as a candidate for a specific peak because of the discontinuity of the data discussed in Chapter 3, page 64).

For both stocks and outstandings the specific cycle amplitude of the four expansions grew successively less. Also, in each case the amplitude for stocks was small relative to outstandings—between a quarter and a third the size; the average ratio was 29.8. This relationship remained remarkably stable. If this figure is used to estimate the rise in stocks by applying it to the rise in outstandings for each episode, the estimates on the average are within ±9 per cent of the actual figure.[10]

The long lead and considerable parallelism of the two series have interesting implications. The parallelism seems to support the suggestion to which the analysis of business problems pointed—that outstandings and stocks on hand had an intimate dynamic interrelationship. However, the length of the lead of outstandings is puzzling. The average number of months' supply held as stocks on order has probably not exceeded four months since 1947, or two and a half since 1953.[11] If this average tenancy period is the critical figure, it would seem that a decline or rise in outstandings would be transmitted to materials stocks via the inverse vestibule effects in far less time than leads at peaks ranging from six to eleven months imply. It will be useful to keep this puzzle in mind in the hope that additional information bearing on it will be uncovered.

[10] The ratios of the specific rise in stocks to those of outstandings during four matched episodes were 24.9, 33.2, 31.2, and 29.0. The average of these figures is 29.8. For each episode the rise in outstandings in dollars was multiplied by 29.8 to estimate the rise in stock for the corresponding periods. The estimated rise was divided by the actual rise and subtracted from 100 to get the percentage error or estimate. The errors for the four episodes were +19.4, −10.2, −4.0, +2.6.

[11] The estimates are based on doubling the ratio of unfilled orders to sales on the assumption that materials represent about half the value of final product and value added the other half.

Unfilled Sales Orders

By way of digression, it is interesting to compare unfilled orders for final products (the unfilled sales orders of the transportation equipment and machinery industries) with the outstanding orders placed by these companies for materials (goods produced by the fabricated metals, primary metals, and "other durables" industries). Total unfilled orders for the durable goods industries is the sum of those for the two groups. As the two lower curves on the chart suggest, the book value of unfilled orders for final products since 1951 averaged about twice that of the materials.

A comparison of the two curves throws light on the relation between unfilled orders for the product a company sells (often referred to as "back orders" or backlogs of unfilled orders in management literature) and unfilled orders for the materials a company buys (called materials orders outstanding, outstandings, or stock on order). The latter are, of course, "back orders" of producers of materials.

The two groups of unfilled orders behaved very differently. The decline in backlogs that followed the buildup of World War II was interrupted in 1948 for materials, but not appreciably for final products. There is another sharp contrast after the Korean War, when the continued upward movement of orders for final products indicated that production did not catch up with shipments of machinery and transportation equipment (including automobiles) for almost two years after balance had been restored in orders and shipments of materials. The huge backlogs of orders for durable equipment must certainly have tended to cushion the jar to economic expansion created by the post-Korean declines in many other lines. The 1954–58 movement was found in both series, but this time the percentage movement of final products was weaker than that of materials. From 1958

through 1962, unfilled orders for final products remained virtually constant, while those for materials moved in conformity with the cyclical tides of the period as well as with the temporary dip of early 1962. In general, it is clear that outstanding orders for materials respond sensitively to even minor business fluctuations, whereas those for finished machinery and transportation equipment take much more to set them in motion. As a result, many of the movements in outstanding orders for materials are unmatched by similar ones for final products. Line 12 of Table 1 shows that only six turns could be matched.

These facts about behavior do not seem out of line with the firm's-eye view. The size of back orders for the product a company sells affects the risk involved in advance orders for materials. Consequently it is reasonable to find that the former never fluctuated without corresponding fluctuations in the latter. However, since the presence of sizable back orders is only one of the things influencing ordering policy for materials, there is no reason why materials buying cannot undergo fluctuations, manifested in changing outstanding orders, at times when back orders for final product are level.

Perhaps also reflecting the variety of influences that shape the course of materials outstanding, turns in outstandings always preceded those in unfilled orders whenever they occurred. The median lead was five months (Table 1, line 12). Thus backlogs of sales orders were still increasing when purchased materials outstanding had already started to decline; similarly, backlogs were still falling when outstandings had started to rise.

These facts seem to support the general notion that it is useful to separate unfilled orders for final products and for intermediate products, at least until the character and cause of their heterogeneity is more adequately understood.

TABLE 2

Reference Cycle Amplitude of Stocks and Outstanding Materials Orders,
Durable Goods Manufacturers,[a] 1946–62
(billion dollars)

	A: Rise or Fall (−) During Reference Phases						
	Contrac-tion 11/48– 10/49	Expan-sion 10/49– 7/53	Contrac-tion 7/53– 8/54	Expan-sion 8/54– 7/57	Contrac-tion 7/57– 4/58	Expan-sion 4/58– 5/60	Contrac-tion 5/60– 2/61
1. Ownership	−4.09	13.61	−8.59	5.83	−4.70	2.10	−2.04
2. Materials stocks	−.91	3.04	−.86	1.47	−.43	.81	−.78
3. Outstanding orders	−3.18	10.57	−7.73	4.36	−4.28	1.29	−1.26
4. All stocks	−1.48	11.98	−2.29	7.77	−2.20	2.65	−1.50

	B: Average Rise or Fall (−) During Reference Phases					Amplitude as % of Amplitude of Materials Stocks[b]		
	Per Phase		Per Month[a]					
	Expan-sion (1)	Contrac-tion (2)	Expan-sion (3)	Contrac-tion (4)	All Phases (5)	Expan-sion (6)	Contrac-tion (7)	All Phases (8)
1. Ownership	7.18	−4.86	.205	−.462	.219	402	651	390
2. Materials stocks	1.77	−.75	.051	−.071	.056	100	100	100
3. Outstanding orders	5.40	−4.11	.154	−.392	.222	302	552	396
4. All stocks	7.47	−1.87	.213	−.178	.204	417	250	364

Note: The measures are those of standard NBER business cycle analysis.

[a]Per month amplitude measures are the sum of the rises divided by the total number of months of cyclical expansion and analogously for contractions. For the total, falls (carrying a negative sign) are subtracted from total rises and divided by the number of months between first and last peak or trough.

[b]Per month amplitude of each series as a percentage of the corresponding figure for materials stocks.

AMPLITUDE

Ownership and each of its components underwent substantial cyclical fluctuation. Stock on order had a far wider amplitude of movement than did stocks on hand. During the three reference cycle expansions occurring between 1948 and 1962, the book value of stocks on order increased on the average by $5.4 billion (Table 2, column B1) and during the four reference cycle contractions fell on the average by $4.1 billion. The corresponding figures for materials stocks on hand were $1.8 and $.8 billion respectively. Thus the cyclical rise in outstandings was, on the average, about three times that of materials stocks and the fall

TABLE 3

Average Specific Cycle Amplitude Per Month of Materials Stocks on Hand and on Order,
Durable Goods Manufacturers, 1946-62

	Date of First and Last Peak or Trough (1)	No. of Cycles (2)	Amplitude Per Month ($ billion)[a]			Amplitude as % of Amplitude of Materials Stocks		
			Expansions (3)	Contractions (4)	All Phases (5)	Expansions (6)	Contractions (7)	All Phases (8)
1. Ownership	P 12/46 to P 2/62	5	.308	−.367	.333	417	456	436
2. Materials stocks	P 2/49 to P 5/62	4	.074	−.080	.076	100	100	100
3. Outstanding orders	P 7/46 to P 2/62	5	.280	−.304	.291			
	P 8/48 to P 2/62[b]	4	.293	−.328	.309	396	408	404
4. All stocks	T 1/46 to T 5/61	4	.233	−.225	.231	315 120[c]	279 135[c]	302 126[c]

[a]Amplitude measures are the sum of the rises minus the sum of the falls divided by the number of months between the first and last peak or trough. Thus the rise and fall during each specific cycle (carrying a negative sign) are weighted by its duration.

[b]The amplitude of outstandings beginning 8/48 is compared with that of materials stocks in order to match the time periods as nearly as possible.

[c]Amplitude for outstandings as percentage of all stocks.

about five times (columns B6 and 7).[12] The level of outstandings proper, it will be recalled, was only about twice that of materials stocks. The first part of Table 2 gives the phase-by-phase figures.

Even compared with total stocks of durable goods manufacturers, outstandings show striking fluctuations. Comparison of the last two lines in the table indicates that during contractions (column B7) the cyclical amplitude of the average book value of outstanding orders for durable materials was over twice that of total stocks of the durable goods industries (stocks of finished and in-process goods and materials) and about three quarters of it during expansions. If these book-value figures were converted to months of supply (a conversion that would raise the weight of raw and in-process materials relative to finished goods), the ratios would be substantially higher.[13]

Reference cycle amplitudes are influenced by the degree to which each series conforms to business cycles. This element can be removed by comparing amplitude during cycles specific to each series. Table 3 gives the figures. Comparison of column 5 in the two tables shows that a substantial portion—between two-

---

[12] The difference in the relationship for rises and falls was partly due to the fact that there was little trend rise in book value of outstandings and a substantial one in stocks.

[13] Also, it will be recalled that the series excludes materials bought from dealers or other nonmanufacturers.

thirds and three-quarters—of the total specific fluctuation in these several stockpiles occurred during the times of general economic fluctuation as designated by the reference subcycle chronology. The tables also show that the relative instability of outstandings compared with stocks is somewhat greater when the full specific rises and falls of each aggregate are taken into account than when the reference framework is used (compare column 8 in the two tables). Apparently, if outstandings have the capacity to influence economic events, their influence will tend to reinforce the business tides.

FIRST THRUST OF EXPANSIONS

Outstanding orders seem to share the characteristics often observed in stocks—they fall at a faster rate during business contractions than they rise during expansions, thereby suggesting that they push things down with more force than they lift them up. The average monthly rate of rise of outstanding orders during the expansion phases of business cycles (beginning with the 1949 troughs) was $160 million per month; during contractions the monthly rate of fall averaged $400 million.[14]

But further examination reveals an interesting variation on this usual theme: outstanding orders rise with far more vigor in the early months of expansion than in the later ones. This impression is also conveyed by Chart 1.

Table 4 formalizes the comparisons by using a three-part reference framework. Business cycle expansions are divided into two pieces and contractions are treated in the conventional way. The first sections of expansions are delineated by the additional minor peaks that were mentioned earlier—January 1947 and February 1951. We also select two further dates. The first, December 1955, was a candidate subcycle peak which was considered in the course of the work on subcycles, but it was rejected because the break in expansion was not sufficiently diffused among different sorts of economic activity. However, many series appeared to reach temporary peaks in their expansion at about that time. The second date, March 1959, marks the time when the anticipatory action associated with the steel strike a few months later seemed to reach its zenith. Note that these four peak dates occurred fifteen, sixteen, sixteen, and eleven months after the previous business cycle reference troughs marked in 1945, 1949, 1954, and 1958 respectively. It is interesting, incidentally, that these periods are quite uniform in length and also typically a bit longer than postwar contractions (compare columns 5 and 15). Table 4 indicates that in three of the four episodes the total cyclical rise in outstandings had been effected during these first periods—the standing at subpeaks is usually higher than at subsequent peaks (columns 7 and 8). For all of them, the average monthly rate of expansion was entirely comparable to that of contractions (bottom two lines, columns 12 and 19).

The large proportion of the rise that occurred in the first phase of expansion could be due in part to the strong tendency for outstandings to experience peaks ahead of the business cycle high points. Table 5, therefore, converts the comparisons to a specific cycle basis. The specific cycle peaks or troughs in outstandings that are matched with business cycle peaks or troughs provide the dates for columns 1, 2, 10, and 11. The first period of thrusts is selected as the months when, in the course of its first specific cycle rise in reference expansion, the rate of rise in outstandings has reached its maximum and declined to the halfway mark between its maxi-

[14] The figures are based on standings for the single month of peaks and troughs and are rounded to tens of millions of dollars. They are therefore not identical to those in Table 2, line 3, columns 3 and 4.

TABLE 4

Amplitude of Outstanding Materials Orders During Reference Cycle Phases and First Subcycle Expansion,[a] Durable Goods Manufacturers, 1946-62

Reference Dates			Interval (months) Trough to:		Standings ($ billion)[b]			Rise ($ billion)			
								Total		Per Month	
Trough (1)	Peak (2)	Sub Peak[a] (3)	Peak (4)	Sub Peak (5)	Trough (6)	Peak (7)	Sub Peak (8)	Cycle (9)	Sub C. (10)	Cycle (11)	Sub C. (12)
Expansions											
1/46[c]	11/48	1/47	34	(12)[d]	9.5	11.1	12.5	1.6	3.0	0.05	0.25
10/49	7/53	2/51	45	16	7.9	18.6	17.9	10.7	10.0	0.24	0.62
8/54	7/57	12/55	35	16	10.7	15.2	15.5	4.5	4.8	0.13	0.30
4/58	5/60	3/59	25	11	10.7	12.2	14.5	1.5	3.8	0.06	0.35
Average, 1/46 to 2/61			34.8					4.6	5.3	.13[e]	.39[e]
Average, 11/48 to 2/61			35.0	14.3				5.6	6.2	.16[e]	.43[e]

Reference Dates		Interval (months) (15)	Standings[b] ($ billion)		Fall ($ billion)	
Peak (13)	Trough (14)		Peak (16)	Trough (17)	Total (18)	Per Month (19)
Contractions						
11/48	10/49	11	11.1	7.9	-3.2	-0.29
7/53	8/54	13	8.6	10.7	-7.9	-0.61
7/57	4/58	9	15.2	10.7	-4.5	-0.50
5/60	2/61	9	12.2	10.8	-1.4	-0.16
Average, 1/46 to 2/61					-4.2	-.40[e]
Average, 11/48 to 2/61		10.5	11.8	10.2	-4.2	-.40[e]

[a]Two of the dates are part of a previously selected subcycle chronology; two are otherwise chosen.

[b]Standings are for the single month of peak or trough. Therefore figures may differ slightly from those of Table 2, where standings are three-month averages.

[c]First month for which data are available.

[d]The interval from the business cycle trough in October 1945 was fifteen months.

[e]Sum of the rises (falls) divided by the total number of months of expansion (contraction) covered.

TABLE 5

Amplitude of Outstanding Materials Orders During Selected Specific Cycles and First Period of Rapid Thrust[a], Durable Goods Manufacturers, 1946-62

					Expansions								
					Rise ($ billion)[b]								
			Interval (mos.) from Trough to:		Total		Per Month		*Contractions*				
Specific Dates							Cycle Expansion	Thrust	Specific Dates		Interval	Fall ($billions)[b]	
Trough	Peak	Top of Thrust[a]	Peak	Top of Thrust	Cycle Expansion	Thrust	(6÷4)[c]	(7÷5)	Peak	Trough	(mos.)	Total	Per Mo.
(1)	(2)	(3)	(4)	(5)	(6)	(7)	(8)	(9)	(10)	(11)	(12)	(13)	(14)
1/46[c]	8/48	6/46	31	(5)[d]	2.0	3.4	0.06	0.68					
									8/48	9/49	13	−4.1	−0.32
9/49	9/52	4/51	36	19	13.2	12.1	0.37	0.64					
									9/52	10/54	25	−10.0	−0.40
10/54	8/56	6/55	22	8	6.6	3.3	0.30	0.41					
									8/56	6/58	22	−6.6	−0.30
6/58	11/59	3/59	17	9	4.4	3.9	0.26	0.43					
									11/59	12/60	13	−4.4	−0.34
1/46 to 12/60			106	41	26.2	21.7	.25	.53					
9/49 to 12/60			75	36	24.2	19.3	.32	.54			73	25.1	.34

[a]Only those specific cycles are included whose troughs are matched with business cycle reference troughs. The first period of thrust starts at the specific trough and ends at the month when, in the course of its first specific cycle rise of reference expansion, the rate of rise (as measured by a five-month centered average of month-to-month change) has reached its maximum and declined to halfway between its maximum and zero. Failing the necessary information for the first period, the peak date of the first specific cycle was used.

[b]Based on standings for the month of peak or trough only.

[c]First month when data are available.

[d]Period from beginning of the data, not from the previous trough.

mum and zero.[15] The intervals ranged from eight to nineteen months, and the shorter figure seems more typical. Comparison of columns 9 and 14 of Table 5 shows that the monthly rates of rise during these periods of first thrust are stronger than during contraction. A large part of specific cycle expansion usually occurred during these first episodes (compare columns 6 and 7).

After the first two thrusts, outstandings declined for a while and then rose again, thus producing extra movements which, as mentioned previously, were also found in many other economic areas. In 1959, too, the thrust was followed by a temporary decline, but its

[15] The selection was made on the basis of a five-month moving average of month-to-month change as shown in Chart 6, below. Some time after outstandings proper have reached their specific cycle trough associated with the reference cycle trough, the rate of rise in outstandings reaches a peak. Some months later outstandings cease to rise. (The five-month average crosses the zero line on its way down.) The month when the five-month average has declined to a figure closest to one-half its peak level marks the termination of the first specific cycle thrust.

CHART 2

Relations Among Outstanding Orders, Stocks, and Shipments,
Durable Goods Manufacturers, 1946–64

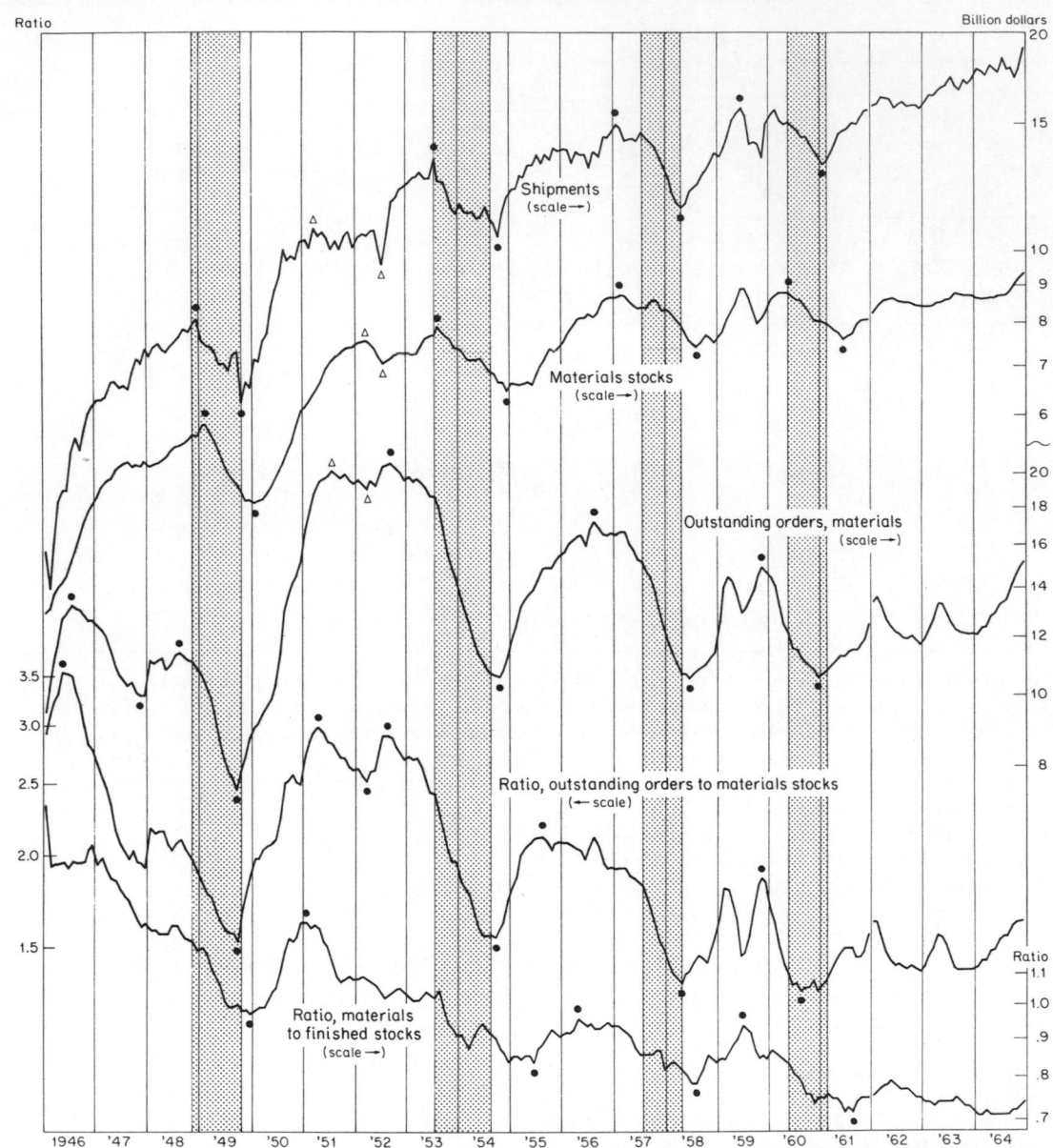

Note: Shaded areas represent business contractions. Specific cycle turns are marked by dots, additional minor turns by triangles.

short duration and close association with the extended steel strike gives it a somewhat colloquial interest. The movement that ended in 1955 resulted in a flattening rather than an actual downturn.

In general the figures suggest that insofar as an increase of materials on order tends to stimulate more ordering than would otherwise take place (and consequently more business activity), the chief impact of stimulation occurs in the first year or year and a half of expansion.

Though stocks of materials on hand also tend to flatten by the middle of expansion, the strong early upward surge of materials on its way to factory floors concentrates particu-larly in the most responsive portion of ownership—outstanding orders. The proportion of total ownership that consists of outstanding orders rises to a peak early in expansion and then flips downward. This can be seen in the next to the last curve in Chart 2, the ratio of outstanding orders to stocks of materials. The bottom line in the chart suggests that a similar pattern characterizes the relation of materials to finished stocks. Taken together, the curves seem to depict a moving bulge in the pipelines of materials; it starts in the first section, the outstanding orders for materials, and slips toward later sections as expansion continues. During contraction it moves much farther in that direction.

RELATION BETWEEN SALES AND STOCKS

The economic meaning of the size of a stock reservoir depends in part on its relation to the flow of goods or services to which it is linked.

Any business must, of course, maintain some sort of positive association between the volume of stocks and sales. But the analysis of Chapter 2 suggests that it is not at all clear what that association is likely to be. It is the joint result of the physical necessities of servicing sales (and the sales relation alone is most efficiently handled by a less than proportionate change in stock), changes in opportunity costs which may or may not parallel sales, changes in expectations about market conditions, and errors which it is not worthwhile to reverse immediately. Obviously, then, it is pertinent to ask how these ratios actually behave. Do stocks tend to maintain a systematic relation to sales or shipments and, if so, is it a constant one or one that is positively or negatively associated with shipments? How about these relations for outstanding purchase orders or ownership as a whole? What is the meaning, in terms of business problems and practices, of such relationships as the time series show? In this section some gross behavioral characteristics are exhibited. In Chapter 9 we explore the question of "why."

Parallelism in Sales and Stocks

The behavior of shipments and of stocks both on hand and on order in durable goods manufacturing are compared in the first three lines in Chart 2 and detailed timing comparisons appear in Table 6.

The chart reveals a family resemblance between shipments and stocks of materials on hand and on order. But it certainly suggests that stocks on hand follow shipments more closely than do stocks on order. The latter, as the analysis of earlier chapters suggests, are likely to reflect, among other things, conditions, or expectations about conditions, in the markets in which materials are bought and sold. The eye picks up notable differences in the contours of the waves in outstandings and shipments (curves 3 and 1), whereas stocks on hand move more similarly to shipments (curves 2 and 1). Table 6 supports these impressions. In line 4 of section C we see that during 84 per cent of the months from mid-

TABLE 6

Timing: Shipments, Durable Goods Manufacturers, 1946–62

| | | Section A: Months Lead (–) or Lag (+) for Matched Turns[a] | | | | | | | | | | |
| | | Chronology[b] | | | | | | | | | | |
Line	Reference Series[c]	P (1/47)	T (7/47)	P 11/48	T 10/49	P (2/51)	T (6/52)	P 7/53	T 8/54	P 7/57	T 4/58	P 5/60	T 2/61
		Specific Series: Shipments										
1	Business cycles			+1	0			0	+2	–6	0	–11	–1
2	Subcycles	⊕	⊕	+1	0	+1	+1	0	+2	–6	0	–11	–1
		Specific Series: Ownership										
3	Shipments	Ω	Ω	–4	–1	⊕	⊕	–10	0	+1	+2	+7	–1
		Specific Series: Stocks of Materials										
4	Shipments	⊕	⊕	+2	+3	+12	0	+1	+2	+1	+4	+11	+5
		Specific Series: Outstanding Orders										
5	Shipments	Ω	Ω	–4	–1	+4	–4	–10	0	–5	+2	+5	–1
		Specific Series: Unfilled Orders, Final Product										
6	Shipments	⊕	⊕	–21	+2	⊕	⊕	–6	+7	–1	⊕	⊕	+4

		Section B: Average Timing of Turns									Section C: Percentage of Months in Like Phase[d]	
		Number Matched			Median[e]			Average Deviation[f]				
										All Turns	Timing Adjust- ment[g]	% Mos. 7/46–
Line	Reference Series[c]	–	+	0	P	T	All	P	T	Wt'd		12/61
		Specific Series: Shipments										
1	Business cycles	3	2	3	–3.0	0	0	4.5	0.8	2.6　2.6	0	80
2	Subcycles	3	4	3	–1.7	+0.3	0	4.1	0.9	2.3　2.5	0	84
		Specific Series: Ownership										
3	Shipments	4	3	1	–1.5	–0.5	–0.5	5.5	1.0	3.2　3.2	–1,0	72
		Specific Series: Stocks of Materials										
4	Shipments	0	9	1	+4.7	+3.0	+2.5	4.7	1.4	2.9　3.1	+2,+3	84
		Specific Series: Outstanding Orders										
5	Shipments	6	3	1	–1.7	–0.7	–1.0	5.3	1.5	3.4　3.4	–1	73
		Specific Series: Unfilled Orders, Final Product										
6	Shipments	2	2	0	–9.3	+4.5	–1.7	7.8	2.5	7.3　5.6	–1	62

For notes see Table 1.

1946 to the end of 1961, shipments and materials stocks are in like phase after allowing for a lag of either two or three months. For both ownership and outstanding orders, the association with shipments is nearly synchronous on the average (or leading slightly for outstandings), and this is an interesting fact. However, the months in like phase are low (72 or 73 per cent). For all these data, troughs behave systematically; average deviations in the timing of shipments and the stock or outstandings series are very small (column B8). It will be recalled that this was also characteristic of the association of materials stocks (and, to a lesser extent, the other stock data too) with troughs in business cycles, and the statistical reason is simply that it is also true of troughs in shipments. The economic meaning, on the other hand, is equivocal since the reversal in the stock aggregates could very well be causally associated with change in sales *or* in the business climate, or both.

Stock-Sales Ratios, Trend and Fluctuations

In any event, it is certainly no surprise to see manufacturers increasing their raw materials on hand and on order when their shipments to customers rise, and decreasing them as they fall off. But how about the particular character of the association? Chart 3 addresses itself to this question by depicting the ratios of end-of-month stocks to shipments during the month. The shaded areas show the periods when business cycles were in falling phase. These curves tell, I think, a very interesting story.

First, a word concerning their level and trend. One would like to gauge the size of stocks in terms of the number of months' sales for which they provide. But this is not shown by the ratio because, as suggested earlier, stocks are measured in terms of the value of "raw materials" and shipments in terms of the value of finished goods, and consequently, to make a unit-for-unit comparison, the value

of materials must at least be doubled.[16] Thus the scale for the center three lines should be multiplied by two to indicate approximately the number of months' sales for which provisions have been made. So viewed, materials stocks on hand typically constitute about five weeks' sales (stock-sales ratio of .6 in the chart) for the period as a whole. But the trend has been downward, and this is not merely a reflection of early adjustments to peacetime conditions. Though there may have been some stabilization in the fifties, the last several years have seen a further decline to about one month's provisions (ratio of .5).

Materials on order were, for the period as a whole, substantially larger than those on hand; they averaged just short of two and a half months' sales, and, as the discussions at the end of Chapter 3 indicate, this must be regarded as a rough approximation. They shared the downward trend relative to sales, but to a more marked degree.

In view of the relative decline in both stocks of materials on hand and on order, the constant relation of total stocks to shipments may seem surprising (bottom curve). Yet actually it probably is more of an explanation than a contradiction. Stock in process kept a relatively steady relation to shipments. The increase in finished stocks relative to stocks of materials—and relative also, and particularly so, to outstanding orders for materials—can be interpreted as reflecting a long-term shift from a seller's to a buyer's market.

Turn now to the cyclical patterns of the stock-shipments ratio, which, if my interpretation is correct, may also have some bearing on their trends. A swift glance at Chart 3 answers one question of some general import. Ignoring trends, are stocks-sales ratios approximately constant? They are not. The vertical scale of the chart is proportional and has the

---

[16] The reason, to repeat, is that an examination of census data for a number of major durable goods industries suggests that, very typically in durable goods manufacture, the value added by manufacture is about equal to the cost of the materials and fuels.

same dimensions as that used for the previous charts. Accordingly, the picture suggests that the magnitude of fluctuation in the ratios is substantial. (Compare it with that of the data proper in Chart 1.) Table 7, lines 1, 4, and 7, shows the average standing of the ratios, converted to estimated weeks' supply, at their specific peaks and troughs, 1948 through 1961.[17]

On the average, materials represented one more week's supply at peaks than at troughs in the ratio (column 3), about one-fifth more than the five-week supply typical at troughs (column 4). For ownership and outstandings, an additional four weeks' supply was usual, and this constituted about one-third more for ownership and one-half more for outstandings than the average position at troughs. Clearly, then, if manufacturers were trying to achieve a constant relation between sales and any of the three stock aggregates, they were not succeeding. Moreover, there is no reason to suppose that they could not do so if the objective carried a sufficient priority. For ownership, adjustment to a desired figure could be achieved almost immediately by appropriate changes in new orders; even for stock of materials on hand, foreknowledge of demand, often supplied by advance sales and orders, would make it possible to gauge materials buying so as to validate a stock objective if it were worth the cost.

Relationship of Ratios to Shipments

But granted that the figures suggest that a constant sales-stock ratio is not a high-priority management objective, what are the characteristics of the relation that actually does obtain? Is it, for example, the inverse relation of the ratio to the level of sales which would be produced if the single factor influencing stocks

were an efficient link to sales, other things the same? Here again, the answer is no.

Study of Chart 3 makes it clear that the ratio of materials stocks to shipments is increasing during substantial periods when shipments are increasing too. These are certainly periods when stocks could be cut down if it were clearly desirable to do so. A similar remark applies to the ratios for ownership and stocks on order. Column 5 of Table 7 shows that the three ratios (for stocks, outstandings, and ownership) are in rising specific cycle phase during 44, 47, and 37 per cent respectively of the months when shipments are in rising specific cycle phase. Column 4 indicates, in lines 2, 5, and 8, that the range between the high and the lows in the ratio, which are reached when sales are rising, is, of course, less than their total specific cycle range (lines 1, 4, and 7), but nevertheless not insignificant; the high is 110 to 146 per cent of the low.

The particular times in the cycles in shipments when the ratios rise and fall are worth some attention, and Table 8 gives the figures. The specific cycle lows in the stock-shipment ratio occurred after shipments had started to rise, indeed never less than seven nor more than twelve months thereafter (Table 8, line 7). Typically, the last few months' fall in the ratio was due to the fact that though stocks were rising, shipments were rising faster. But it is noteworthy that this situation did not last for long: within the first year of the expansion in shipments, stocks started to rise faster than shipments (the ratio began to rise). An exception, however, was the phase starting in 1961, when the ratio flattened for a while and then continued to fall.

The ratio was usually still rising—that is, the number of months' supply held in stock was increasing—when shipments reached their peak and started to decline. But since stocks themselves reversed very promptly, the continued rise of the ratio was due to the fact that stocks did not fall *as fast* as shipments. Again, the last complete expansion phase, the one with a peak in 1959, was an exception.

---

[17] I use the assumptions that materials constitute half of the price of finished goods and that there are four and a third weeks to the average month. Accordingly, the monthly book-value figures are multiplied by 8.67.

TABLE 7

Average Amplitude and Conformity of Stock-Shipment Ratios During Expansion Phases Variously Defined, Durable Goods Manufacturers, 1948–61

Line	Ratio to Shipments	Reference for Expansion Phase In Ratio	Standing of Ratios, Weeks[a]				% Months When Ratio Was in Rising Specific Phase During Expansion Phases of: [b]	
			Standing at		Peaks Minus Troughs[c]	Peaks as % of Troughs[c]	Shipments	Business Cycles
			Troughs (1)	Peaks (2)	(3)	(4)	(5)	(6)
	Materials							
	Stock							
1		Ratio[d]	5.0	6.0	1.0	121		
2		Shipments[e]	5.0	5.5	.5	110	44	
3		Business cycle[f]	5.0	5.9	.9	119		52
	Outstandings							
4		Ratio[d]	8.2	12.5	4.3	152		
5		Shipments[e]	8.2	10.6	2.4	146	47	
6		Business cycle[f]	8.2	12.5	4.3	152		44
	Ownership							
7		Ratio[d]	13.5	17.9	4.4	133		
8		Shipments[e]	13.5	16.9	3.4	125	37	
9		Business cycle[f]	13.5	17.9	4.4	133		34

[a]The individual standings are two-month averages of monthly data for peak (trough) month and the higher (lower) of the two adjacent months. If the peak (trough) was erratically high (low), a three-month centered average was used. Monthly data were converted to weeks by assuming that there are 4.5 weeks per month. The figures average the individual standings for the fourteen years from the beginning of 1948 to the end of 1961.

[b]These are the same measures as those appearing in section C of the timing tables except that they are confined to the periods when the reference scheme (specific cycles in sales for column 5 and business cycle chronology in column 6) is in rising phase. Comparisons are made without a timing adjustment.

[c]Based on average standings (not on standing for each phase averaged).

[d]Standings are taken at specific cycle peaks and troughs in the ratio.

[e]The peak standing is that of the high reached in the ratio during each specific cycle in shipments. Trough standing is that of the specific cycle trough in the ratio that is matched with each specific cycle trough in shipments.

[f]The peak standing is that of the high reached in the ratio during each business cycle expansion. Trough standing is that of the specific cycle trough in the ratio that is matched with each reference trough.

TABLE 8

Timing: Stock-Shipments Ratios, Durable Goods Manufacturers, 1946–62

		Section A: Months Lead (−) or Lag (+) for Matched Turns[a] Chronology[b]											
Line	Reference Series[c]	P (1/47)	T (7/47)	P 11/48	T 10/49	P (2/51)	T (6/52)	P 7/53	T 8/54	P 7/57	T 4/58	P 5/60	T 2/61

Specific Series: Ratio of Ownership to Shipments

Line	Reference Series	P (1/47)	T (7/47)	P 11/48	T 10/49	P (2/51)	T (6/52)	P 7/53	T 8/54	P 7/57	T 4/58	P 5/60	T 2/61
1	Business cycles			⊕	+8			−24	+4	−12	+8	−6	⊕
2	Subcycles	⊕	⊕	⊕	+8	+5	⊕	⊕	+4	−12	+8	−6	⊕
3	Shipments, all durables	⊙	⊙	⊕	+8	+4	⊕	⊕	+2	−6	+8	+5	⊕
4	Ownership	⊕	⊕	⊕	+9	−14	⊙	⊙	+2	−7	+6	−2	⊕

Specific Series: Ratio of Purchased Materials Stocks to Shipments

Line	Reference Series	P (1/47)	T (7/47)	P 11/48	T 10/49	P (2/51)	T (6/52)	P 7/53	T 8/54	P 7/57	T 4/58	P 5/60	T 2/61
5	Business cycles			+3	+10			+4	+11	+8	+12	+8	⊕
6	Subcycles	+7[r]	+8[r]	+3	+10	+10	+8	+4	+11	+8	+12	+8	⊕
7	Shipments, all durables	Ω	Ω	+2	+10	+9	+7	+4	+9	+14	+12	+19[r]	⊕
8	Stocks	Ω	Ω	0	+7	−3	+7	+3	+7	+13	+8	+8	⊕
9	R:ownership to shipments	⊕	⊕	+3	+2	+5	⊕	⊕	+7	+20	+4	+4	⊙
10	R:outstanding to shipments	⊕	⊕	⊕	+11	+5	⊕	⊕	+12	+20	+4	+14	⊙

Specific Series: Ratio of Outstanding Orders to Shipments

Line	Reference Series	P (1/47)	T (7/47)	P 11/48	T 10/49	P (2/51)	T (6/52)	P 7/53	T 8/54	P 7/57	T 4/58	P 5/60	T 2/61
11	Business cycles			⊕	−1			−24	−1	−12	+8	−6	⊕
12	Subcycles	⊕	⊕	⊕	−1	+5	⊕	⊕	−1	−12	+8	−6	⊕
13	Shipments, all durables	⊙	⊙	⊕	−1	+4	⊕	⊕	−3	−6	+8	+5	⊕
14	Outstandings	⊙	⊕	⊕	0	0	⊕	⊕	−3	−1	+6	0	⊕
15	R:materials stocks to shipments	⊙	Ω	Ω	−11	−5	⊕	⊕	−12	−20	−4	−14	⊙

(continued)

TABLE 8 (concluded)

Line	Reference Series[c]	Number Matched			Median[e]			Average Deviation[f]		All Turns		Section C: Percentage of Months in Like Phase[d]	
		−	+	0	P	T	All	P	T		Wt'd	Timing Adjustment[g]	% Mos. 1/48– 12/61

Section B: Average Timing of Turns spans the Number Matched, Median, and Average Deviation columns.

Line	Reference Series[c]	−	+	0	P	T	All	P	T	Wt'd(1)	Wt'd(2)	Timing Adjustment[g]	% Mos. 1/48–12/61
	Specific Series: Ratio of Ownership to Shipments												
1	Business cycles	3	3	0	−14.0	+6.7	−1.0	6.7	1.8	10.3	4.2	None	51
2	Subcycles	2	4	0	−4.3	+6.7	+4.5	6.2	1.8	5.8	4.0	None	54
3	Shipments, all durables	1	5	0	+1.0	+6.0	+4.5	4.7	2.7	3.5	3.7	None	60[h]
4	Ownership	3	3	0	−7.7	+5.7	0	4.2	2.4	6.7	3.3	0	64
	Specific Series: Ratio of Purchased Materials Stocks to Shipments												
5	Business cycles	0	7	0	+6.0	+11.0	+8.7	2.2	0.7	2.7	1.6	None	51
6	Subcycles	0	11	0	+7.5	+9.7	+8.0	2.0	1.5	1.9	1.8	0	48
7	Shipments, all durables	0	9	0	+9.0	+9.5	+9.3	5.4	1.5	3.7	3.7	0	41[h]
8	Stocks	1	7	1	+3.7	+7.0	+7.0	4.9	0.5	3.2	3.0	+7	79
9	R:ownership to shipments	0	7	0	+9.5	+4.3	+5.3	6.4	1.8	4.6	4.4	+5	69
10	R:outstandings to shipments	0	6	0	+13.0	+9.5	+11.5	5.3	3.3	4.3	4.3	+11, +12	73
	Specific Series: Ratio of Outstanding Orders to Shipments												
11	Business cycles	5	1	0	−14.0	+2.0	−3.5	6.7	4.0	8.0	5.3	0	57
12	Subcycles	4	2	0	−4.3	+2.0	−1.0	6.2	4.0	5.2	5.1	0	60
13	Shipments, all durables	3	3	0	+1.0	+1.3	+1.5	4.7	4.4	4.5	4.6	0,−1,+1,+2	63
14	Outstandings	2	1	3	−0.3	+1.0	0	0.4	3.3	1.7	1.9	0	79
15	R:material stocks to shipments	6	0	0	−13.0	−9.5	−11.5	5.3	3.3	4.3	4.2	−11,−1	73

For notes a through g, see Table 1.

[h]Adjustments that maximize percentage in phase are, respectively, line 3: +2, 68 per cent; line 7: +9 or +10, 72 per cent.

The ratio did not rise during the expansion in shipments starting in 1958; it fell most of the time.

Materials stocks on order, measured in months of sales, declined uninterruptedly from wartime highs until the end of the 1949 recession. Thereafter they had two bold rises with subsequent bold falls and a less bold episode in 1958–60. Both troughs and peaks in these waves occurred much earlier than in the stock-on-hand ratio, and the outstandings-shipment ratio therefore tended to reach troughs much closer to the upturn in shipments than did the stock-on-hand-shipments ratio; indeed it even turned earlier than shipments at two of the three comparisons (Table 8, line 13). In other words, a rise in shipments and an increase in the number of months' supply on order tended to occur around the same time. Chart 3 shows another fact worth noting. Apparently the rise in materials outstanding that started early in 1961 was no greater than necessary to maintain a constant number of months' sales on order. The ratio slid continuously downward from late 1959 to the beginning of 1964, when it again turned up.

Behavior During Business Cycles

The tendency for stocks to rise when sales do is a well-explored aspect of business cycle dynamics. If stocks tend to rise even faster than do sales, this tendency for stocks to add to or partly generate cyclical fluctuation would thereby be emphasized. Accordingly, it is interesting to ask how the stock-sales ratio behaves during business cycles and particularly during cyclical expansions. Do stocks of materials tend to rise faster than shipments at times when business as a whole is expanding? If so, there is a tendency to add an element to the leavening influence.

Column 6 of Table 7 is addressed to this question and it shows that materials stocks are rising faster than shipments (which, of course, also tend to rise during expansion)

during 52 per cent of the months of reference expansion 1948 through 1961. The range of fluctuation comprehends very nearly all of the conforming specific fluctuation in the ratio (compare lines 1 and 3, column 4). Materials stocks on order, because of the long leads at peaks, were rising for a smaller proportion of cyclical expansion than stocks on hand; the figure was 44 per cent, which, though smaller, is still not insubstantial. However, the full impact of the specific rise in the ratio occurred during months of cyclical expansion; peaks occurring during expansion were about 50 per cent higher than troughs—an extra four weeks' supply (Table 7, line 6, columns 3 and 4). Generally similar observations apply to total ownership.

Manufacturers' purchasing of materials, then, tended to add to other forces of expansion not only by causing an absolute rise in materials on hand and on order but a rise proportionately greater than that of the rise in shipments of finished goods.

The behavior of purchasing at the very start of cyclical expansion is interesting. In 1949 and in 1954 the outstandings-shipment ratio began increasing one month before the cyclical trough dates. Accordingly, part of what I have called the first thrust of expansion consisted in this increase in the number of weeks' supply on order. For materials on hand, the number of weeks' supply went down at first, and, as we shall see in Chapter 9, this is not without significance. But a few months before the terminal dates of periods of "thrust," stocks started to rise relative to sales and continued to do so for some months after the outstandings-shipments ratio started to decline.

The expansion starting early in 1961 was different in several respects from the earlier postwar movements. Though outstanding materials orders rose as usual about the same time that business reached its low, they did not rise relative to shipments. (It will be recalled, incidentally, that unfilled orders for final product did not rise at all.) The stock-sales ratio likewise did not start to rise within

CHART 3

Relation of Stocks and Unfilled Orders to Shipments,
Durable Goods Manufacturers, 1946–64

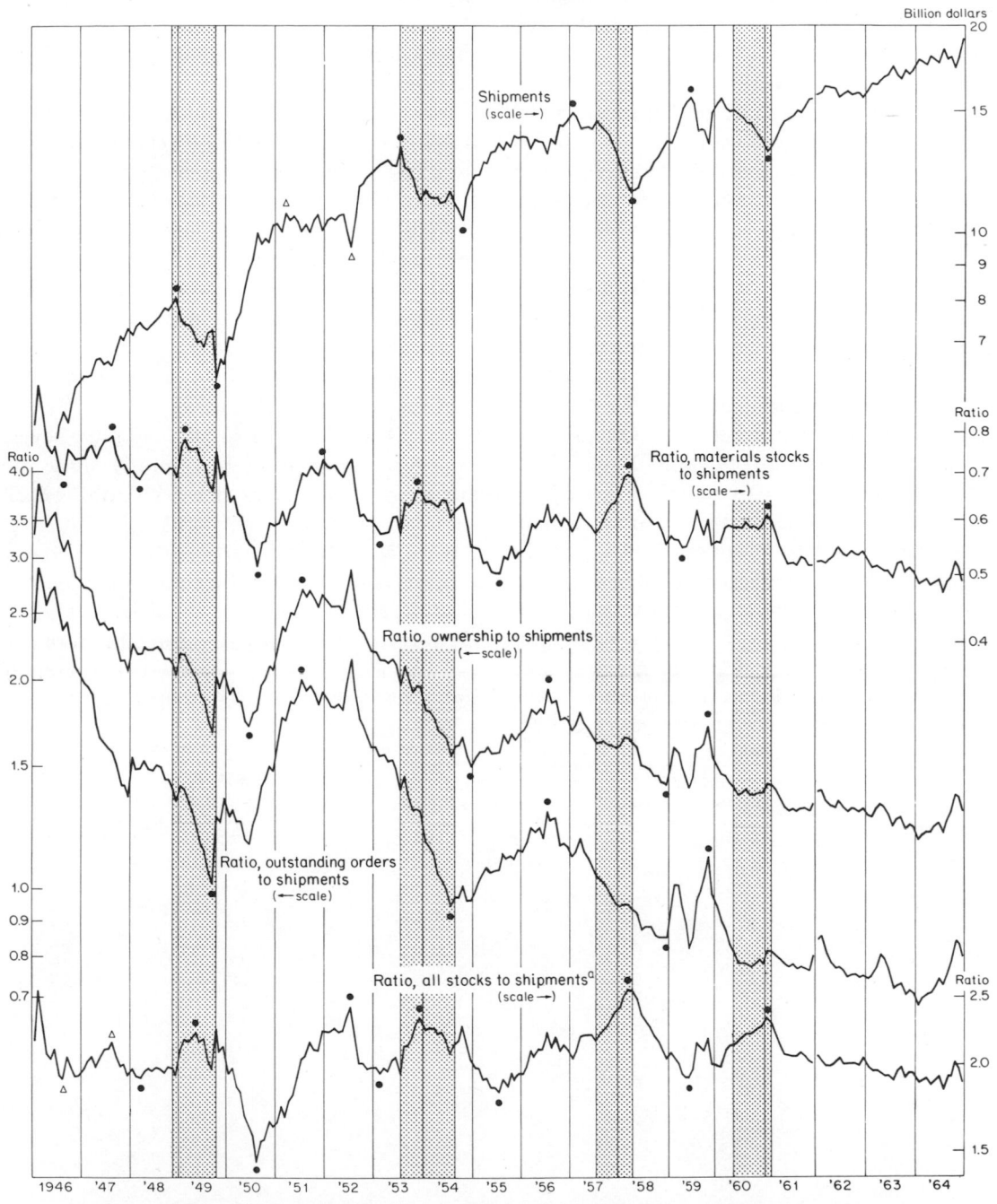

Note: Shaded areas represent business contractions. Specific cycle turns are marked by dots, additional minor turns by triangles.

a Ratio of finished, in process, and materials stocks of all durable goods manufacturers to shipments, all durable goods manufacturers.

the usual eight to twelve months after busi-ness troughs were acknowledged (Table 8, line 5 or 6). Can this taming of inventory movements be explained in terms of the firm rein on stock management afforded by electric data processing? Before this popular explana-tion is accepted, we shall need to move as far as possible toward understanding some of the factors other than sales which seem to influence materials ownership. Chapter 11 returns to the question and recommends a different answer.

The facts that have been assembled describe the character of the participation of durable goods manufacturers' stocks of materials on hand and on order in business fluctuation, one of the two questions to which the behavior of the time series are referred. Outstanding orders for materials appear to be large—about half as large as all stocks and twice as large as materials stocks. The facts point to movements that correspond to business cycles, to the presence of two minor movements in outstand-ings, to leads in the outstandings segment. We have seen also that the amplitude of fluctua-tion is strong—greater than can be accounted for by fluctuations in shipments alone, even assuming that it was actually necessary for

stocks to increase or decrease as much as ship-ments, an assumption which Chapter 2 denied. We saw also that whatever stimulating influ-ence on the economy is generated by increases in outstandings was particularly strong in the first year of expansion.

Most of these observations also have some bearing on the dynamics of change in stocks on hand and on order, the second major ques-tion concerning which information is to be assembled. Of particular interest in this con-nection is the large size of outstandings, their tendency to parallel stocks though with a lead which at peaks is longer than can be readily explained. The early thrusts likewise require explanation in terms of the business problems that they reflect.

It will be useful to summarize these several findings somewhat more carefully since they are hard to fasten in memory. However, the summary will be more useful if it also covers a parallel study of department stores. Behavior is more noteworthy if it is found in enterprises as different as the large retail store and the manufacturer of heavy equipment. Insofar as a characteristic is not repeated in these very different industries, it is useful to try to learn why.

5. Merchandise Ownership, Department Stores

A moment's thought about the function of stocks and purchasing, in the framework of Chapter 2, impresses one with the importance of this whole constellation of management problems in a retail store. The vast number of articles that are bought, their high degree of specificity and the consequent need to foresee exactly what articles customers will want, the difficulty of disposing of customers' rejects, the necessarily large stocks that must in any event be carried—these and many other characteristics of the business make it clear that good purchasing and good stock management are prerequisite to good profits for a department store. Moreover, it seems evident that the specifics of good purchasing and stock management, their costs and opportunity costs, *could* be quite different in connection with the merchandise stocks of department stores on the one hand and the materials stocks of durable goods manufacturers on the other hand. Accordingly, it is important to examine the empirical evidence with an eye cocked at both possible similarities and differences in the two types of enterprises. The differences particularly may be helpful in salting the slippery tail of causation when, in Chapter 9, we try to examine it.

"Merchandising data" reported by department stores to the Federal Reserve System include information on outstanding orders as well as on stocks. The totals, which we have called ownership, are sometimes referred to by retailers as "in-sights," [1] and it is not, incidentally, without interest that retailers have a word for it.

THE LEVEL OF OWNERSHIP

Total ownership averaged four months' supply during the thirteen years from 1949 to 1961. And it is interesting, though I can attach no specific significance to it, that this seems to be about the same figure as for the materials of durable goods manufacturers. However, the distribution between stocks on hand and on order was very different for the two types of enterprises. For department stores, stocks constituted about 70 per cent and outstanding orders 30 per cent of total pipeline goods "in-sight."

CONFORMITY AND TIMING

Waves in ownerhip, Chart 4 suggests, conform quite neatly to business cycles. Ownership and each of its two components show the two extra cycles at the time of the phantom postwar recession and of the Korean War. During the former, sales did not decline.

Table 9 shows in the last two columns, lines 2, 6, and 11, that all of these stock series dis-

[1] See Chapter 2, note 6.

CHART 4

Ownership, Stocks, and Outstanding Orders, Department Stores, 1946–63

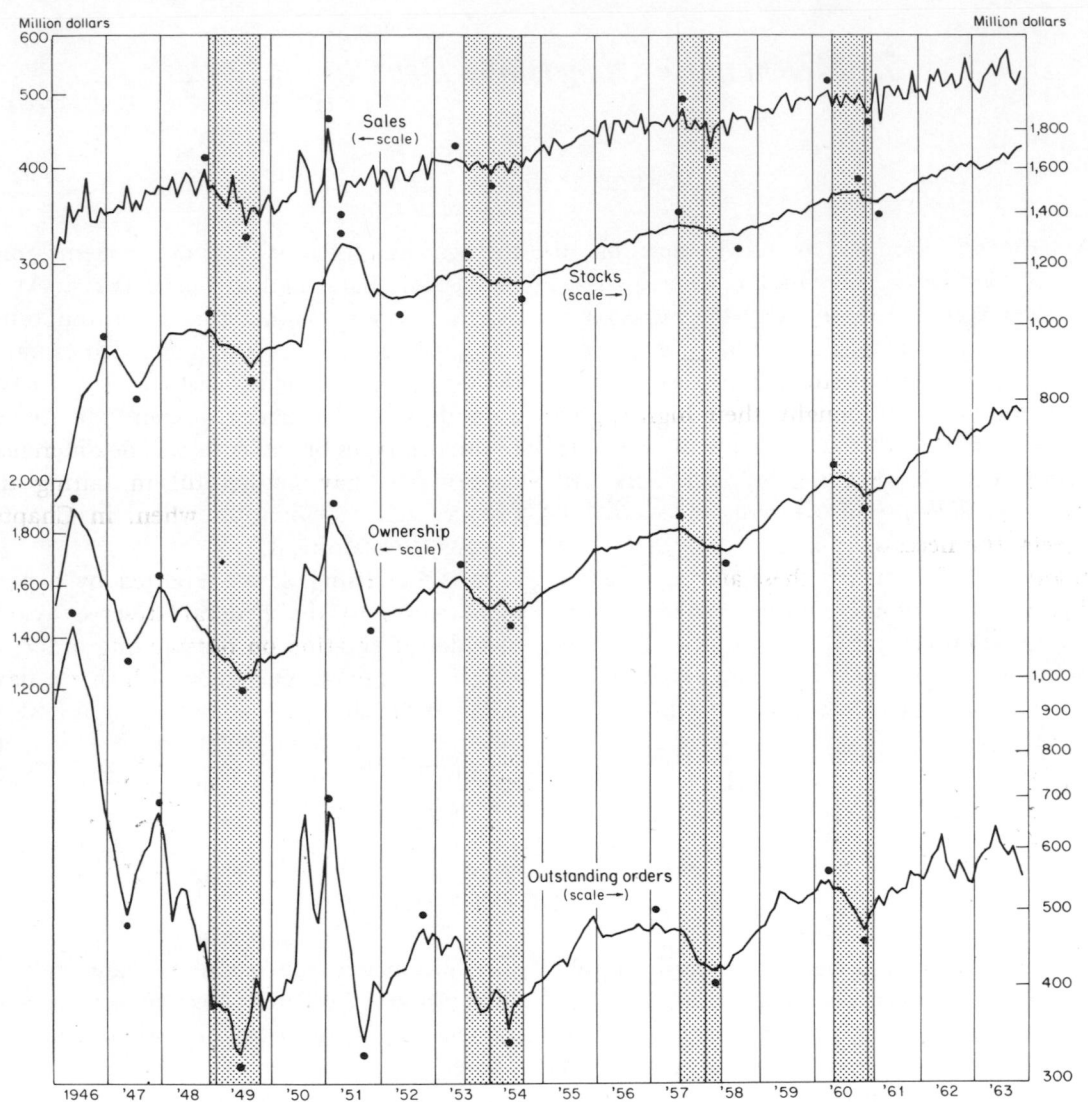

Note: Shaded areas represent business contractions. Specific cycle turns are marked by dots.

play reasonable conformity with the subcycle chronology, after adjustment for characteristic timing relationships. Stocks on hand show a strong association on a synchronous basis; 91 per cent of the months from mid-1946 through 1961 are in like phase. Outstanding orders lead by an average of four months. Ownership is, of course, intermediate, with a median lead of two months. Since 1948, peaks in ownership and in the business subcycle chronology have all been virtually synchronous. Troughs have tended to lead (line 2). Outstandings for department stores, like those for durable goods manufacturers, tend to lead substantially more at peaks in business affairs than at troughs. But unlike durables, the pre-

TABLE 9

Timing: Stocks on Hand and on Order, Department Stores, 1946–62

Section A: Months Lead (−) or Lag (+) for Matched Turns[a]

Chronology[b]

Line	Reference Series[c]	P (1/47)	T (7/47)	P 11/48	T 10/49	P (2/51)	T (6/52)	P 7/53	T 8/54	P 7/57	T 4/58	P 5/60	T 2/61
	Specific Series: Ownership												
1	Business cycles			−11	−4			−1	−3	0	+1	0	−2
2	Subcycles	−8	−2	−11	−4	0	−8	−1	−3	0	+1	0	−2
3	Outstanding orders	0	0	0	0	+1	+1	+8	0	+5	+2	+1	0
4	Ownership, durables	−7	−6	−8	−3	Ω	Ω	+9	−5	+5	−1	+4	0
	Specific Series: Stocks												
5	Business cycles			0	−2			+1	0	0	+4	+6	+1
6	Subcycles	−1	0	0	−2	+2	−1	+1	0	0	+4	+6	+1
7	Ownership	+7	+2	+11	+2	+2	+7	+2	+3	0	+3	+6	+3
8	Outstanding orders	+7	+2	+11	+2	+3	+8	+10	+3	+5	+5	+7	+3
9	Stocks, durables	Ω	Ω	−3	−5	−11	−2	0	−4	+5	0	+6	−3
	Specific Series: Outstanding Orders												
10	Business cycles			−11	−4			−9	−3	−5	−1	−1	−2
11	Subcycles	−8	−2	−11	−4	−1	−9	−9	−3	−5	−1	−1	−2
12	Outstanding orders, durables	−2	−6	−8	−3	−6	−6	+1	−5	+6	−3	+5	0

(continued)

TABLE 9 (concluded)

Section B: Average Timing of Turns

Line	Reference Series[c]	Number Matched			Median[e]			Average Deviation[f]				Section C: Percentage of Months in Like Phase[d]	
		−	+	0	P	T	All	P	T	All Turns	Wt'd	Timing Adjustment[g]	% Mos. 7/46– 12/61
	Specific Series: Ownership												
1	Business cycles	5	1	2	−0.5	−2.5	−1.5	3.0	1.5	2.5	2.2	−1, −2	79
2	Subcycles	8	1	3	−0.5	−2.5	−2.0	3.3	2.0	2.8	2.7	−2	82
3	Outstanding orders	0	6	6	+1.0	0	+0.5	2.2	0.5	1.5	1.3	0, +1	90
4	Ownership, durables	6	3	1	+0.7	−3.0	−2.0	6.5	2.0	4.6	4.2	−1, −2	71
	Specific Series: Stocks												
5	Business cycles	1	4	3	+0.5	+0.5	+0.5	1.8	1.8	1.8	1.8	0, +1	82
6	Subcycles	3	5	4	+0.5	0	0	1.7	1.3	1.5	1.5	0	91
7	Ownership	0	11	1	+4.0	+3.0	+3.0	3.3	1.0	2.2	2.2	+3	87
8	Outstanding orders	0	12	0	+7.0	+3.0	+5.0	2.2	1.5	2.5	1.8	+5	84
9	Stocks, durables	6	2	2	+0.7	−3.0	−2.5	5.1	1.4	3.5	3.3	−2	77
	Specific Series: Outstanding Orders												
10	Business cycles	8	0	0	−7.0	−2.5	−3.5	3.5	1.0	2.8	2.2	−4	79
11	Subcycles	12	0	0	−6.5	−2.5	−3.5	3.5	1.8	3.0	2.7	−4	81
12	Outstanding orders, durables	8	3	1	−0.5	−4.0	−3.0	4.7	1.8	3.4	3.2	−3	78

Notes to Table 9

^aSpecific series are matched with the indicated reference series (see note c) in accordance with the standard NBER rules. A double relaxation of rules is marked r; it applies to cases for well-conforming series in which two like turns are matched, though an unlike turn lies between them. The figure is underlined when subcycle chronology is the reference series, a minor cycle in the specific series has entered a comparison; or, when two individual series are compared, a minor cycle in either series has entered a comparison. When the business cycle chronology provides the reference, minor specific cycle turns are ignored. The meaning of other symbols is:

⊕ turn in the reference series does not appear in the specific series.

Ω turn in the specific series does not appear in the reference series.

⊙ there is no turn in either series in the neighborhood of the chronology date.

^bChronology dates are business cycle reference dates. In addition, four minor subcycle dates, enclosed in parentheses, are added to form a subcycle chronology.

^cReference series are of three sorts: (1) the business cycle chronology as shown in column heads, excluding the dates in parentheses; (2) the subcycle chronology as shown in all column heads; (3) particular series whose specific cycles and minor cycles constitute the reference dates for the comparison.

^dThe number of months during which the specific series is in like phase with the reference series is expressed as a percentage of total number of months covered between dates as given.

^eMedian is the average timing of the center two or three turns.

^fAverage deviation from the median. The "weighted" (wt'd) average is the deviation from the median for peaks and for troughs separately, weighted by the number of turns.

^gIn determining months in like phase a timing adjustment is made which maximizes confluence. Before counting the months in phase, the specific series is in effect moved to the right to allow for a lead and to the left to allow for a lag if by so doing the percentage of months in like phase (as rounded) is increased. If the months in phase are as large or larger without an adjustment, this is indicated by a "timing adjustment" of 0.

In some cases we wish to know the percentage of months in phase on a synchronous basis, regardless of whether the percentage in phase is thereby maximized. If so, the "timing adjustment" is given as "none."

dominant timing even at troughs is that of a lead, however short.[2]

[2] A corollary is that at troughs the various stock series for department stores regularly lead those of durable goods manufacturers. The figures are given in lines 4, 9, and 12 of the table. This could reflect a closer control of stocks in retail stores because of the critical importance of stock management to successful store operation. However, the conclusion would be premature since Table 15 will show that the same tendency to lead at troughs characterizes retail sales compared with shipments of durable goods manufacturers. But here again the meaning must be considered in the light of the fact that the advice about an upturn in customer buying has taken place at just about the same time for department stores (via their sales) and durable goods manufacturers (via their sales orders, that is, orders received). As will be seen later, four troughs occur synchronously or within one month in the two series, and department stores lead at one turn—in 1951. Thus the figures do not seem to throw much light on the dynamics of stock management. However, we can, I think, con-

For department stores, as for durable goods manufacturers, the two parts of ownership—stocks and outstanding orders—display the same three relationships. First, turns in outstanding orders precede those in stocks. They lead at each turn, as Table 9, line 8, shows. (The table shows the lag of stocks instead.) Second, the lead is somewhat longer at peaks than at troughs. The median for all turns is five months, with seven as a typical figure at peaks and three at troughs. The difference is quite persistent.[3] In view of the fact that orders

clude that the impact on the economy of the small segment of consumer buying represented by large department stores may, for whatever weight it had, have tended to shorten the duration of contractions.

[3] When the timing at each peak is compared with the previous and following troughs, peaks lead nine times and lag and synchronize one time each. The

average only about one month's sales, the length of this lead is puzzling and demands explanation after the rest of the evidence is in.[4]

Third, stocks and outstandings display strong correspondence in the timing of specific fluctuation. Eighty-four per cent of the months between mid-1946 and the end of 1961 were in parallel phase after allowing for a lead of five months (line 8, section C). If the allowance is based on the characteristic behavior at peaks and at troughs separately—leads of seven and three months respectively—

the percentage of months in phase rises to 89.

A glance at Chart 4 suggests that the correlation in amplitudes for matched cycles in stocks and outstandings, noted for durables, may be absent or at least harder to detect where the relative sensitivity of stocks and outstandings to trend and cyclical influences is so exceedingly different. This question is discussed in the course of the next section along with other matters bearing on amplitude.

AMPLITUDE

As Chart 4 suggests, ownership undergoes substantial cyclical fluctuation. The two components, outstandings and stocks, play about an equal part in the fall during business cycle contractions, whereas stocks play a far more important part in the rise during expansions; this is true whether concern focuses on change per phase or per month. The figures are given, phase by phase, in Table 10 and summarized in section B (see particularly columns 6 and 7, line 3).

The specific amplitude as measured in Table 11 highlights the intrinsic variability of each series. Average monthly rises or falls during *specific* cycle expansions or contractions show that outstandings fluctuate somewhat more in absolute terms (lines 2 and 3, column 5 or 8) than do stocks, which are, it will be recalled, on the average about two and a third times as large for the period as a whole. Rises in outstandings are much smaller relative to rises in

stocks than are falls (line 3, columns 9 and 10).

At first thought, it seems possible that cancellations in outstanding orders when business recedes might be largely responsible for the asymmetrical behavior. But there is an alternative explanation involving the arithmetic of combining a shared upward trend influence for two series for which cyclical volatility differs.[5]

Comparing amplitude for matched phases of outstandings and stocks (a duplication of the measure for durables described in Chapter 4, note 10), contractions in the dollar volume of stocks are found to have almost exactly half the amplitude as those of outstandings (in spite of the far larger size of total stocks).

average deviation of 2.2 at peaks and 1.5 at troughs is also small enough (in view of the length of the leads) to cause the differences to be taken seriously. When the difference in characteristic timing is taken into account, the average deviation is reduced from 2.5 to 1.8 (columns B9 and 10).

[4] For department stores, unlike durable goods manufacturers, it will be recalled, the statistics are able to give the size of outstandings and stocks relative to that of sales without equivocation.

[5] When this is the case, the cyclically sensitive series can have contractions which are relatively larger compared with those of the insensitive series than are their respective amplitudes of expansion. Assume two series have an upward trend of 2 per cent a year. Series A starts at 300, series B at 100. The pure cyclical component is 5 per cent of each cycle phase for series A and 20 per cent for series B. Expansions last two years and contractions one year.

		Expansion			Contraction		
		Trend	Cycle	Total	Trend	Cycle	Total
Series A	300	+12	+15	+35	+6	−15	−9
Series B	100	+4	+20	+24	+2	−20	−18
Ratio A/B				.69			2.0

TABLE 10

Reference Cycle Amplitude of Stocks and Outstanding Orders, Department Stores, 1946-62[a]
(million dollars)

A: Rise or Fall (−) During Reference Phases

	Contrac- tion 11/48− 10/49	Expan- sion 10/49− 7/53	Contrac- tion 7/53− 8/54	Expan- sion 8/54− 7/57	Contrac- tion 7/57− 4/58	Expan- sion 4/58− 5/60	Contrac- tion 5/60− 2/61
1. Ownership	−84.0	299.7	−89.0	292.3	−80.0	273.7	−50.0
2. Stocks	−62.7	260.7	−42.7	207.3	−30.7	159.0	−20.0
3. Outstanding orders	−21.3	39.0	−46.3	85.0	−49.3	114.7	−30.0

B: Average Rise or Fall (−) During Reference Phases

	Per Phase		Per Month[a]			Amplitude as % of Amplitude of Stocks[b]		
	Expan- sion	Contrac- tion	Expan- sion	Contrac- tion	All Phases	Expan- sion	Contrac- tion	All Phases
1. Ownership	288.6	−75.8	8.24	7.21	7.95	138	194	149
2. Stocks	209.0	−39.0	5.97	3.72	5.33	100	100	100
3. Outstanding orders	79.6	−36.8	2.27	3.50	2.62	38	94	49

Note: The measures are those of the standard NBER business cycle analysis.

[a]Per month amplitude measures are the sum of the rises divided by the total number of months of cyclical expansion and analogously for contractions. For the total, falls (carrying a negative sign) are subtracted from total rises and divided by the number of months between first and last peak or trough.

[b]Per month amplitudes of ownership and outstandings as percentage of the corresponding figure for stocks.

For expansions, however, there was little or no correlation.

Returning to the character of typical amplitudes of fluctuation, several contrasts between department stores and durable goods manufacturers have been noted. Table 12 converts specific cycle measures to relatives of the average standing of the data over each cycle. Accordingly, the figures give an approximate percentage variability which affords comparison among various sorts of enterprises and statistics.

Outstandings of both department stores and durable goods manufacturers undergo fluctu-ations that involve an average rise or fall of about 2 per cent a month relative to their average level (lines 1 and 4, last column). Stocks of durable goods manufacturers fluctu-ate about half as violently—about 1 per cent of their average level per month—and those of department stores still less so. But the general impression that the table conveys is one of rather surprising similarities in the relative degree of instability of the outstand-ing orders of manufacturers of durable goods and of department stores (see lines 7 and 8). Durable goods manufacturers, after all, them-selves have large changes in backlogs of cus-

TABLE 11

Average Specific Cycle Amplitude, Stocks and Outstanding Orders, Department Stores, 1946-62

| | Period Covered (1) | No. of Cycles (2) | Amplitude Per Phase[a] (million dollars) | | | Amplitude Per Month[a] | | | Amplitude as % of Amplitude of Stocks[b] (million dollars) | | |
			Expansion (3)	Contraction (4)	All Phases (5)	Expansion (6)	Contraction (7)	All Phases (8)	Expansion (9)	Contraction (10)	All Phases (11)
1. Ownership	T 5/47 to T 12/60	5	297.0	183.9	240.4	13.62	−17.02	14.75	159	243	183
2. Stocks	T 7/47 to T 3/61	5	193.3	71.5	132.4	8.55	−7.01	8.07	100	100	100
3. Outstanding orders	T 5/47 to T 12/60	5	152.1	158.7	155.4	7.84	−12.02	9.53	92	171	118

[a]Measures are based on the standard NBER business cycle analyses; per month amplitude is the "weighted" average: the sum of the rises minus the sum of the falls divided by the number of months of expansion or contraction between the first and last peak or trough dates included.

[b]Per month amplitude of ownership and outstandings as percentage of the corresponding figure for stocks.

tomers' orders on the books; they buy materials which are not typically style sensitive or perishable, materials whose prices may well undergo substantial fluctuations. Merchants, on the other hand, sell on demand; they often buy highly style-sensitive goods, and at prices which often remain unchanged during a season.

Perhaps these differences in business problems are reflected in the *proportion* of total provisions that are carried on hand compared with those carried on order, rather than in the way in which each type of reservoir *fluctuates* relative to its average level. But if so, implications follow. The amplitude of ownership as a whole is greater for durable goods manufacturers than for department stores because the more volatile part, outstanding orders, is relatively far larger. This means that suppliers of durable goods manufacturers are confronted with a stream of new orders that fluctuate more extremely than those received by the suppliers of department stores.

FIRST THRUST OF EXPANSIONS

For department stores, as for durables, most of the impact of rising outstandings was spent early in business expansions. Using the same dates to delineate the first segment of expansion that were applied to manufacturing, the story of Table 4 repeats itself in Table 13.

Outstanding orders show these thrusts most sharply. Indeed, they reach their major cyclical highs before the beginning of 1947 and at the peak of the Korean boom. Beginning in 1948, the average monthly rate of rise during all of these first stretches, which lasted for a year

TABLE 12

*Average Specific Cycle Amplitude Per Month in Cycle Relatives,
Materials Stocks and Outstanding Orders, Department Stores
and Durable Goods Manufacturers, 1946-62*

	First and Last Peak or Trough Date	Amplitude Per Month, Cycle Relatives[a]		
		Rise	Fall	Average Rise and Fall
Department Stores				
1. Outstandings	5/47 − 12/60	1.69	−2.56	2.04
2. Stocks	7/47 − 3/61	.75	−.65	.72
3. Amplitude of outstandings as % of stocks		225	394	283
Durable Goods Manufacturers				
4. Outstandings	7/46 − 2/62	2.01	−2.22	2.11
5. Stocks	2/49 − 5/62	1.04	−1.08	1.06
6. Amplitude of outstandings as % of stocks		193	206	199
Amplitude for Department Stores as % of Durable Goods				
7. Outstandings		84	115	97
8. Stocks		72	60	68

[a]Cycle relatives give rises or falls expressed as a percentage of the average monthly standing of the series, cycle by cycle.

to a year and a half (longer than total contraction) was much higher than the fall during contractions—$10.2 and $3.2 million per month respectively (bottom line, columns 9 and 14).[6]

Comparable figures for total ownership are shown in the upper half of the table. Though the amplitude of movement is about double that of outstandings, the first subcyclical rises again show monthly rates of decrease that are

[6] It seems preferable to exclude the period prior to the peak in 1948 from the averages because of the distortion imparted by the postwar adjustments; outstandings declined during the reference expansion.

much faster than is the rate of increase during contractions—$20.8 and $7.8 million per month respectively.

Table 14 eliminates the influence of differences in business cycle conformity by using a specific cycle framework. The terminal dates for the first thrusts are selected by the same rule used for durable goods manufacturing; they last between fifteen and nineteen months for outstandings and fourteen to twenty months for ownership. Here again, both for outstandings and for ownership, the monthly rate of rise during the periods of thrust was as fast or faster than the rate of fall during

TABLE 13

Amplitude During Reference Cycle Phases and First Subcycle Expansion,[a]
Ownership and Outstanding Orders, Department Stores, 1946-62

Expansions									Contractions				
Reference Dates			Interval (months) Trough to:		Rise ($ million)[b]				Reference Dates		Inter-val (mos.)	Fall ($ million)	
					Total		Per Month						
Trough	Peak	Sub Peak[a]	Peak	Sub Peak	Cycle	Sub C.	Cycle	Sub C.	Peak	Trough		Total	Per Mo.
(1)	(2)	(3)	(4)	(5)	(6)	(7)	(8) 6÷4	(9) 7÷5	(10)	(11)	(12)	(13)	(14)
Ownership													
1/46[c]	11/48	1/47	34	(12)[d]	−124	27	−3.6	2.2					
									11/48	10/49	11	−88	−8.0
10/49	7/53	2/51	45	16	292	556	6.5	34.8					
									7/53	8/54	13	−92	−7.1
8/54	7/57	12/55	35	16	302	222	8.6	13.9					
									7/57	4/58	9	−81	−9.0
4/58	5/60	3/59	25	11	281	118	11.2	10.7					
									5/60	2/61	9	−66	−7.3
Average	11/48 to 2/61		35	14.3	292	297	8.3[e]	20.8[e]			10.5	81.8	−7.8[e]
Outstanding Orders													
1/46[c]	11/48	1/47	34	(12)[d]	−521	−299	−15.3	−24.9					
									11/48	10/49	11	−16	−1.5
10/49	7/53	2/51	45	16	34	263	0.8	16.4					
									7/53	8/54	13	−43	−3.3
8/54	7/57	12/55	35	16	84	106	2.4	6.6					
									7/57	4/58	9	−45	−5.0
4/58	5/60	3/59	25	11	105	71	4.2	6.4					
									5/60	2/61	9	−29	−3.2
Average	11/48 to 2/61		35	14.3	74.3	146.7	2.1[e]	10.2[e]			10.5	33.2	−3.2[e]

[a]Two of the dates are part of a previously selected subcycle chronology; two are otherwise chosen (see discussion of Table 4 in text).

[b]Based on standings for the single month of peak or trough.

[c]First month for which data are available.

[d]The interval from the business cycle trough in October 1945 was 15 months.

[e]Sum of the rises (falls) divided by the total number of months of expansion (contraction) covered.

TABLE 14

Amplitude During Specific Cycle Phases Matched with Reference Cycles and First Period of Rapid Thrust,[a] Ownership, and Outstanding Orders, Department Stores, 1946-62

Expansions									Contractions				
			Interval (months) Trough to:		Rise ($ million)[b]								
					Total		Per Month					Fall ($ million)	
Specific Dates							Cycle Expansion	Thrust	Specific Dates		Interval		
Trough	Peak	Top of Thrust[a]	Peak	Top of Thrust	Cycle Expansion	Thrust	(6÷4)	(7÷5)	Peak	Trough	(mos.)	Total	Per Mo.
(1)	(2)	(3)	(4)	(5)	(6)	(7)	(8)	(9)	(10)	(11)	(12)	(13)	(14)
Ownership													
1/46[c]	12/47	5/46	23	(4)[d]	63	366	2.7	91.5					
									12/47	6/49	18	−343	−19.1
6/49	6/53	2/51	48	20	385	624	8.0	31.2					
									6/53	5/54	11	−134	−12.2
5/54	7/57	12/55	38	19	319	239	8.4	12.6					
									7/57	5/58	10	−85	−8.5
5/58	5/60	7/59	24	14	285	196	11.9	14.0					
									5/60	12/60	7	−86	−12.3
Average, 12/47 to 12/60			36.7	17.7	329.7	353.0	9.0	20.0[e]			11.5	162.0	−14.1[e]
Outstanding Orders													
1/46[c]	12/47	5/46	23	(4)[d]	−261	240	−11.3	60.0	12/47	6/49	18	−343	−19.1
6/49	10/52	1/51	40	19	147	346	3.7	18.2	10/52	5/54	19	−122	−6.4
5/54	2/57	11/55	33	18	127	130	3.8	7.2	2/57	3/58	13	−61	−4.7
3/58	4/60	6/59	25	15	126	107	5.0	7.1	4/60	12/60	8	−74	−9.2
Average, 12/47 to 12/60			32.7	17.3	133.3	194.3	4.1	11.2[e]			14.5	125.0	−10.3[e]

[a]Only those specific cycles are included whose troughs are matched with business cycle reference troughs. The first period of thrust starts at the specific trough and ends at the month when, in the course of its first specific cycle rise of reference expansion, the rate of rise (as measured by a five-month centered average of month-to-month change) has declined to a point halfway between its maximum and zero. Failing the necessary information for the first period, the peak and the first specific cycle were used.

[b]Based on standings for the month of peak or trough only.

[c]First month when data are available.

[d]Period from beginning of the data, not from the previous trough.

[e]Sum of the rises (falls) divided by the total number of months of expansion (contraction) covered.

CHART 5

Selected Operating Ratios, Department Stores, 1946–63

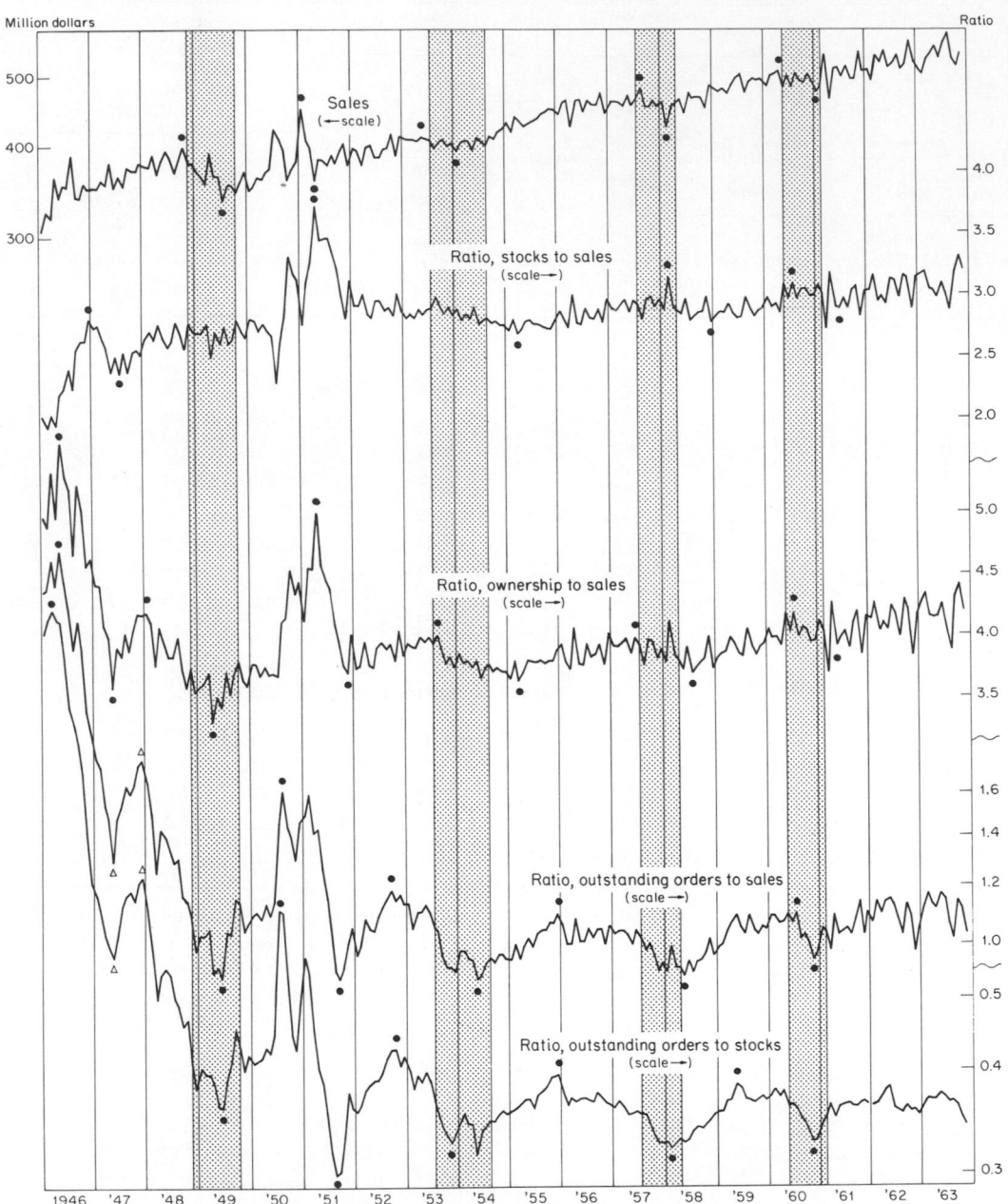

Note: Shaded areas represent business contractions. Specific cycle turns are marked by dots, additional minor turns by triangles.

contractions (compare columns 9 and 14).

Several of the ratios in Chart 5 seem to reassert an association between the volume of goods on order and these first surges of expansion. The level of outstandings, in terms of months' sales (ratio of outstanding orders to sales), curve 4 of the chart, reaches virtually its cyclical highs at or before the end of the first spurt of expansion. The same is true of the ratio of outstandings to stocks, the bottom curve.

The marked activity of outstandings in the first part of expansions, and the leveling or sometimes the fall followed by a subsequent resumption, seem to convey the special quality of behavior generated by decisions which relate to procurement rather than to sales. Sales (top curve) continued to rise throughout 1947; their fall after the Korean speculative episode was sharp and brief; they continued to rise after the end of 1955 and early 1959. Nevertheless, department store buying changed in a fashion which caused an extra wave in the first two cycles and an early flattening in the later ones. Obviously there is a great deal to learn about why this should be.

RELATION BETWEEN SALES AND STOCKS

Parallelism in Sales and Stocks

One would expect that the usual need of any business enterprise to keep stocks in line with the volume of sales in some systematic fashion would be especially acute in connection with the cumbersome stock-carrying functions of retail stores. Accordingly, the broad parallelism between sales and stocks, shown in Chart 4, is no surprise. Table 15, line 5, shows that stocks lag sales on the average by about three months; allowing for this lag, 80 per cent of the months are in like phase. Because sales do not drop in 1947 though stocks do, 82 per cent of the months are in like phase starting at the beginning of 1948. Outstanding orders have a somewhat less regular association with sales partly because of long leads at peaks and a slight tendency to lag at troughs. When stocks on hand and on order are summed, the association is not very different from that of stocks—80 per cent of months are in phase for the whole period, and 84 per cent starting in 1948. However, six of the ten turns are within one month of one another. This could reflect a deliberate effort to have "in-sights" rise when sales rise and fall when they fall. But if the possibility of a deliberately enforced systematic association is not ruled out, what is the character of the system?

Stock-Sales Ratios

The ratios of Chart 5 tell the story. Stocks, as noted earlier, represented about three months' sales, and outstandings one month's. The number of months' sales carried in stock on hand and on order has perhaps been subject to a slight upward trend since 1949.[7]

The chart also shows that retailers have not tended to carry a constant number of weeks' supply either on hand or on order. The ratios move in clearly defined cycles. Table 16, line 1, indicates that stocks on the average were 1.5 weeks' supply higher at peaks than at troughs in the ratio, about 13 per cent more than the nearly twelve weeks' supply that characterized troughs. For outstandings (line 4), peaks were 44 per cent higher than troughs. Total ownership, which would seem to be the most readily controlled aggregate, was 2.1 weeks', or 13 per cent, higher at its peaks than at troughs. Though the differences are

[7] During the war stocks fell and outstandings rose relative to sales, so that the early postwar years moved back toward more usual relationships.

TABLE 15

Timing: Sales and Stocks on Hand and on Order, Department Stores, 1946–62

		Section A: Months Lead (–) or Lag (+) for Matched Turns[a] Chronology[b]											
Line	Reference Series[c]	P (1/47)	T (7/47)	P 11/48	T 10/49	P (2/51)	T (6/52)	P 7/53	T 8/54	P 7/57	T 4/58	P 5/60	T 2/61
		Specific Series: Sales											
1	Business cycles			–1	–3			–2	–7	+1	–2	–1	–1
2	Subcycles	⊕	⊕	–1	–3	–1	–14	–2	–7	+1	–2	–1	–1
3	Shipments, durables	⊙	⊙	–2	–3	–2	–15	–2	–9	+7	–2	+10	0
		Specific Series: Ownership											
4	Sales	℞	℞	–10	–1	+1	+6	+1	+4	–1	+3	+1	–1
		Specific Series: Stocks											
5	Sales	℞	℞	+1	+1	+3	+13	+3	+7	–1	+6	+7	+2
		Specific Series: Outstandings											
6	Sales	℞	℞	–10	–1	0	+5	–7	+4	–6	+1	0	–1

Section B: Average Timing of Turns

		Number Matched			Median[e]			Average Deviation[f]				Section C: Percentage of Months in Like Phase[d]	
										All Turns		Timing Adjustment[g]	% Mos. 7/46– 12/61
Line	Reference Series[c]	–	+	0	P	T	All	P	T		Wt'd		
		Specific Series: Sales											
1	Business cycles	7	1	0	–1.0	–2.5	–1.5	0.8	1.8	1.5	1.2	–1, –2	92
2	Subcycles	9	1	0	–1.0	–4.0	–1.5	0.6	3.8	2.5	2.2	–1, –2	83
3	Shipments, durables	7	2	1	+1.0	–4.7	–2.0	4.0	4.7	4.4	4.4	–2	76
		Specific Series: Ownership											
4	Sales	4	6	0	+0.3	+2.0	+1.0	2.7	2.6	2.7	2.7	+1	80[h]
		Specific Series: Stocks											
5	Sales	1	9	0	+2.3	+5.0	+3.0	2.1	3.6	3.0	2.9	+3	80[h]
		Specific Series: Outstandings											
6	Sales	5	3	2	–4.3	+1.3	–0.5	3.7	2.3	3.5	3.0	0, –1	75[h]

For notes a through g, see Table 9.

[h] For the period January 1948 to December 1961, the percentage of months during which shipments and each stock series were in phase was: ownership 84 per cent, stocks 82 per cent, and outstandings 79 per cent.

TABLE 16

Average Amplitude and Conformity of Stock-Sales Ratios During Expansion Phases Variously Defined, Department Stores, 1948-61

Line	Ratio to Sales	Reference for Expansion Phases in Ratio	Standing of Ratios, Weeks[a]				% Months When Ratio was in Rising Specific Phase During Expansion Phases of:[c]	
			Standing at		Peaks Minus Troughs[b]	Peaks as % of Troughs[b]	Sales	Business Cycles
			Troughs (1)	Peaks (2)	(3)	(4)	(5)	(6)
	Stock							
1		Ratio[d]	11.7	13.2	1.5	113		
2		Sales[e]	11.7	12.8	1.1	109	59	
3		Business cycle[f]	11.7	13.1	1.4	112		64
	Outstandings							
4		Ratio[d]	4.0	5.7	1.7	144		
5		Sales[e]	4.0	5.7	1.7	144	59	
6		Business cycle[f]	4.0	5.9	1.9	148		57
	Ownership							
7		Ratio[d]	16.1	18.2	2.1	113		
8		Sales[e]	16.1	17.9	1.8	111	68	
9		Business cycle[f]	16.1	18.1	2.0	113		74

[a]The individual standings are two-month averages of monthly data for peak (trough) month and the higher (lower) of the two adjacent months. If the peak (trough) was erratically high (low), a three-month centered average was used. Monthly data were converted to weeks by assuming that there are 4.5 weeks per month. The Figures average the individual standings for the fourteen years from the beginning of 1948 to the end of 1961.

[b]Based on average standings (not on standing for each phase averaged).

[c]These are the same measures as those appearing in section C of the timing tables except that they are confined to the periods when the reference scheme (specific cycles in sales for column 5 and business cycle chronology in column 6) is in rising phase. Comparisons are made without a timing adjustment.

[d]Standings are taken at specific cycle peaks and troughs in the ratio.

[e]The peak standing is that of the high reached in the ratio during each specific cycle in sales. Trough standing is that of the specific cycle trough in the ratio matched with each specific cycle trough in sales.

[f]The peak standing is that of the high reached in the ratio during each business cycle expansion. Trough standing is that of the specific cycle trough in the ratio matched with each reference trough.

not dramatic, they are systematic. Apparently, then, if retailers were trying to keep a constant number of weeks' supply on hand, they did not achieve it.

Moreover, further study of the ratios suggests that the maintenance of a constant ratio could hardly have been an all-important management goal. Stocks increased more than sales at times when there is no reason to assume that the result was undesired, since the ratio rose during a substantial part of the time when sales were rising. At such times, stocks are not likely to pile up for the reason that goods did not move as rapidly as they were expected to at the time when they were purchased. As column 5 shows, the ratio for ownership was rising 68 per cent of the time that sales were rising, that is, the number of weeks' supply in sight was increasing; for stocks alone, the figure was 59 per cent. The timing measures of Section A, Table 17, line 4, show that the rising phase of the ownership ratio started no more than seven months after the trough in sales on all but one occasion and even led once; the average was a lag of five months (column B5). The fact that the ratio also stopped rising a few months before or after the peak in sales—the average timing was synchronous (column B4)—suggests that things were not seriously out of hand at peaks either. Stocks on hand also started to rise well within the first half of expansion phases in sales (line 9); Chart 5 perhaps provides a clearer view.

The rises in the ratio were not negligible during the periods of rising sales. For outstandings and total ownership, very nearly the whole specific variability in the ratio occurred when sales were rising (compare Table 16, lines 4 and 5, 7 and 8, column 4); for stocks, the highs during rising sales were 9 per cent higher than the troughs (Table 16, line 2, column 4). The meaning of these figures depends on the standard against which they are compared. As we saw in Chapter 2, a constant ratio should be read as itself implying stocks that are larger than need be for ef-

ficient servicing of rising sales, other things the same. Just how much higher is a question that needs to be asked later on.

It is clear enough without going into specifics that when, during cyclical expansion, stocks or ownership increase not only in line with sales but more so, the general impact on the economy, at least at the time, will be stimulating. And Table 16 shows that the full impact of expansion in the ratio actually did occur during business expansion (compare lines 1 and 3, 4 and 6, 7 and 8). Moreover, the stock-sales ratio was rising 64 per cent of the months designated as business expansions, and the ownership ratio rose 74 per cent of these months (column 6).

The stimulating impact of the rise in total ownership for department stores, unlike that of ownership for durable goods, continued into the neighborhood of peaks in expansions. Since 1949, the ratio turned within two months of the four business cycle and minor peaks (Table 17, line 2).[8]

Outstandings, though not stocks, also appeared to conform to periods of thrust as defined by the chronology previously described. (The terminal dates were February 1951, December 1955, and March 1949.) Study of Chart 5 indicates that retailers not only increased outstandings at these periods but increased them relative to sales. The ratio of outstanding orders to sales roughly reached its maximum height for the phase by the end of the periods of thrust. During the rest of business cycle expansion, the number of months' sales on order either declined or remained about the same.

[8] The ownership-sales ratio for department stores has a very irregular association with that for durable goods manufacturers; it lags as often as it leads (Table 17, line 5). The irregular association may be caused by the strong influence of department store ownership of stocks on hand rather than on order; for durable goods manufacturers, stocks on order dominate the pattern of ownership. For each of the two segments of ownership the ratios for department stores, with the exception of one synchronous turn, always turned earlier than for durable goods manufacturers (Table 17, lines 10 and 15).

TABLE 17

Timing: Stock-Sales Ratios, Department Stores, 1946–61

Section A: Months Lead (−) or Lag (+) for Matched Turns[a]

Chronology[b]

Line	Reference Series[c]	P (1/47)	T (7/47)	P 11/48	T 10/49	P (2/51)	T (6/52)	P 7/53	T 8/54	P 7/57	T 4/58	P 5/60	T 2/61
	Specific Series: Ratio of Ownership to Sales												
1	Business cycles			−10	−6			+1	+7	−1	+3	+2	+3
2	Subcycles	−8	−2	−10	−6	+2	−7	+1	+7	−1	+3	+2	+3
3	Ownership	0	0	+1	−2	+2	+1	+2	+10	−1	+2	+2	+5
4	Sales	℧	℧	−9	−3	+3	+7	+3	+14	−2	+5	+3	+4
5	R:ownership to shipments dur.*	℧	℧	℧	−14	−3	℧	℧	+3	+11	−5	+4	⊕
	Specific Series: Ratio of Stocks to Sales												
6	Business cycles			⊕	⊕			−27	+7	+7	+8	+2	+4
7	Subcycles	−1	0	⊕	⊕	+2	⊕	⊕	+7	+7	+8	+2	+4
8	Stocks	0	0	⊕	⊕	0	⊕	⊕	+7	+7	+4	−4	+3
9	Sales	℧	℧	⊕	⊕	+3	⊕	⊕	+14	+6	+10	+3	+5
10	R: material stks to ship., dur.*	−8	−8	⊕	⊕	−8	⊕	⊕	−4	−1	−4	−6	⊕
	Specific Series: Ratio of Outstanding Orders to Sales												
11	Business cycles			−11	−4			−10	−3	−19	+1	+2	−3
12	Subcycles	−8	−2	−11	−4	−6	−9	−10	−3	−19	+1	+2	−3
13	Outstandings	0	0	0	0	−5	0	−1	0	−14	+2	+3	−1
14	Sales	℧	℧	−10	−1	−5	+5	−8	+4	−20	+3	+3	−2
15	R: outstandings to ship., dur.*	℧	℧	℧	−3	−11	℧	℧	−2	−7	−7	−8	⊕
16	R: stocks to sales	−7	−2	℧	℧	−8	℧	℧	−10	−26	−7	0	−7
	Specific Series: Ratio of Stocks to Sales												
17	R: ownership to sales	+7	+2	⊕	⊕	0	⊕	⊕	0	+8	+5	0	+1
18	R: outstandings to sales	+7	+2	⊕	⊕	+8	⊕	⊕	+10	+26	+7	0	+7

(continued)

TABLE 17 (concluded)

| | | Section B: Average Timing of Turns | | | | | | | | Section C: Percentage of Months in Like Phase[d] | |
| | | Number Matched | Median[e] | | | Average Deviation[f] | | | All Turns | | |
Line	Reference Series[c]	- + 0	P	T	All	P	T		Wt'd	Timing Adjustment[g]	% Mos. 7/46– 12/61
		Specific Series: Ratio of Ownership to Sales									
1	Business cycles	3 5 0	0	+3.0	+1.5	3.5	3.2	3.9	3.4	+1, +2	74
2	Subcycles	6 6 0	−1.5	+0.5	−1.5	3.7	4.8	4.2	4.2	+2	73
3	Ownership	2 8 2	+0.5	+1.5	+1.0	1.3	3.2	2.0	2.2	+2	88
4	Sales	3 7 0	0	+5.3	+3.0	3.6	4.1	4.5	3.8	+3	70
5	R: ownership to shipments, dur.*	3 3 0	+4.0	−5.3	0	4.7	5.8	6.7	5.2	0	60
		Specific Series: Ratio of Stocks to Sales									
6	Business cycles	1 5 0	−5.3	+6.3	+5.5	13.8	1.5	7.2	7.7	+5, +6	67
7	Subcycles	1 6 1	+2.0	+5.5	+3.0	2.0	2.8	2.9	2.4	+3	75
8	Stocks	1 4 3	0	+3.5	+1.5	2.8	2.0	3.1	2.4	+2	74
9	Sales	0 6 0	+4.0	+9.7	+5.5	1.3	3.1	3.2	2.2	+5, +6	65
10	R: material stks to ship., dur.*	7 0 0	−7.0	−5.3	−6.0	2.2	1.8	2.1	2.0	−6	74
		Specific Series: Ratio of Outstanding Orders to Sales									
11	Business cycles	6 2 0	−10.5	−3.0	−3.5	5.5	1.2	5.1	3.4	−3, −4	62
12	Subcycles	10 2 0	−9.0	−3.0	−5.0	4.7	2.0	4.5	3.3	−5	71
13	Outstandings	4 2 6	−0.5	0	0	3.8	0.5	2.2	2.2	0	86
14	Sales	6 4 0	−7.7	+2.0	−1.5	5.7	2.6	5.9	4.1	−1, −2	63
15	R: outstandings to ship., dur.*	6 0 0	−8.7	−4.0	−7.0	1.5	2.0	2.3	1.8	−7	75
16	R: stocks to sales	7 0 1	−7.5	−7.0	−7.0	6.8	2.0	4.4	4.4	−7	65
		Specific Series: Ratio of Stocks to Sales									
17	R: ownership to sales	0 5 3	+3.5	+1.5	+1.5	3.8	1.5	2.6	2.6	+1, +2	70
18	R: outstandings to sales	0 7 1	+7.5	+7.0	+7.0	6.8	2.0	4.4	4.4	+7	65

For notes a through g, see Table 9.

*Line 5: ratio ownership to shipments, all durables; line 10: ratio of purchased materials stocks to shipments, all durables; line 15: ratio of outstanding orders for primary metals and other durables to shipments, all durables.

SUMMARY

The forces that govern the volume of materials stocks on hand and on order appear to generate fluctuations having a number of pervasive characteristics. The following observations apply to enterprises as different as durable goods manufacturers and department stores:

1. Average holdings of goods on order were, on the average, about half the size of stocks on hand for department stores or of total stocks of durable goods manufacturers. They were about twice the size of durable goods manufacturers' stocks of materials. Because the book value of stocks on hand underwent an upward trend and outstandings did not, the latter declined somewhat relative to stocks over the period as a whole.

2. Ownership, outstanding orders, and stocks for durables and department stores conform to all postwar business cycles.

3. Outstanding orders for durables and all the stock series for department stores show the two extra movements, one at the time of the postwar phantom recession (1947) and another after the early impact of the Korean War (1951).

4. Outstandings or ownership tend to synchronize or lead either the usual business cycle chronology or the combined minor and cycle dates, the subcycle reference chronology. The lead for durable goods manufacturing is stronger at peaks; for department stores, stronger at troughs. Merchandise stocks of department stores and materials stocks of durable goods manufacturers tend to synchronize or lag. Outstandings for both types of enterprises have strong leads at reference peaks. Of the eight business cycle timing comparisons at peaks for the two series combined, four were leads of eleven to nine months, two of six or five months, and two of three and one months respectively.

5. Turns in outstanding purchase orders of durable goods manufacturers regularly lead turns in their backlogs of unfilled sales orders.

6. For both durable goods manufacturers and department stores, the time series give evidence of possible causal interrelation between stocks on hand and on order of a sort that seems reasonable. For one thing, outstandings lead stocks and by more at peaks than at troughs. For another thing, there is substantial parallelism in the direction of change, particularly if the characteristic differences in peak and trough timing are allowed for. There even appears to be a quite constant relation between the amount of rise in outstandings and the subsequent rises in stocks for durable goods manufacturers. For department stores, possibly because of the distorting influence on the comparisons of the strong upward trend, it is rather the amount of fall of outstandings that gives some indication of the severity of the associated fall in stock.

But the picture takes a puzzling turn by showing a lead, particularly at peaks, which seems much too long to be explicable in terms of the direct or inverse vestibule effect. For both department stores and durable goods manufacturers, the median lead of outstandings relative to materials stocks was seven months at peaks and three at troughs. Of the eleven timing comparisons at peaks for the two sorts of enterprises, leads of eleven or ten months occurred three times, of eight to six months six times, of five and three months two times.

7. The absolute rise or fall of outstandings of durable goods manufacturers during business cycles was far greater than that of materials stocks—about four times as large; indeed it was as large as for all stocks, twice as large during contractions. For department stores, because of the much smaller size of outstandings, the absolute rise or fall of out-

standings during all business cycle phases was about half that of stocks, but the fall was equal to that of stocks during reference contractions.

8. The total instability experienced and communicated is recorded in the specific rather than the reference measures. These also show that the book value of outstandings rose or fell more than that of materials stocks. It was again about four times as great for durable goods and a little better than equal for department stores.

9. If fluctuation is expressed as a percentage of their average level, cycle by cycle, most of the difference in the specific instability of outstandings in department stores and durable goods manufacturers disappears. These measures of relative variability show that outstandings for both sorts of enterprises tend to rise or fall during their specific cycles by a little over 2 per cent per month. Stocks vary at about half that rate, more nearly a third of it for department stores.

10. Outstanding orders for both durable goods manufacturers and department stores shoot up strongly and rapidly as business prosperity gets under way. Whether reckoned on the basis of amplitude during first segments of expansion having some general currency or on the basis of the periods of thrust of expansion in outstandings itself, the monthly rate of rise tends to be at least as large as the rate of fall during reference or specific contractions.

11. The termination of the thrusts may be followed by either a temporary decline or by a slower rate of expansion.

12. These periods of rapid rise occupy, on the average, the first fourteen months of expansion. The figure is the same whether they are dated on the basis of observation of a wide variety of economic time series or on the basis of data for manufacturers or department stores alone. Incidentally, on the same double basis, business cycle contractions averaged ten months in length. Thus the period of upward thrust tended to be a bit longer than the total period of contraction. Using three sets of

dates—those based on department stores, on durable goods manufacturers, and on the wide variety of data—the nine determinations of the three post-1949 periods of thrusts were: eighteen months one time, sixteen or fifteen months five times, eleven or ten months three times.

13. The volume of ownership that is needed is of course vitally influenced by the volume of sales; its behavior therefore needs to be interpreted in terms of the number of months' sales which it services. Efficient service requirements of business might well imply that stocks change somewhat less than do sales and outstandings at least no more, other things the same. Instead, the data show that stocks rose more than proportionately during substantial parts of the intervals when sales were rising.

The more than proportional rise began quite early in expansion. For department stores and durables, the lags were about the same. Outstandings started to rise more rapidly than sales only on the average a month or so after sales themselves started to rise. For stocks, the median lag of the turn in the ratio relative to that of sales was ten months. For ownership it was five months for department stores and six months for durables. The distribution of lags for individual turns was reasonably compact. For ownership, five of the eight comparisons for the two sorts of enterprises showed lags between four and eight months, and there was only one longer lag—fourteen months. For stocks, five troughs in the ratio came within five to ten months of that of sales or shipments, and only two lags were as long as twelve and fourteen months respectively. For outstandings there were four short leads and only one lag longer than five months.

Contrary, then, to the common impression that more than proportional rise in stocks is a phenomenon of late expansion only, it is clear that, for both sorts of enterprises, it started in outstandings almost immediately and in materials stocks proper within half to one year after sales started to rise. Stocks rose about three-fifths of the entire time that department store sales rose and over two-fifths of the time that shipments rose.

14. But quantitatively the more than proportional rise in stocks is subtle. It might pass relatively unnoticed in business management channels. Confined to periods when sales were rising, peaks in the ratios, either for durables or department stores, were about 10 per cent higher than troughs. For outstandings, the difference was of an entirely different order of magnitude—about 45 per cent for both sorts of enterprises.

These observations bear on both of the major groups of questions that need to be asked. On the one hand, much of the information describes the way in which ownership and its parts participate in economic fluctuation. Indeed, it seems clear that in addition to *reflecting* prosperity and recession, owner-ship and its parts are potentially also *active participants* in economic fluctuation. Note the systematic leads (paragraphs 2, 4, 5), the extra cycles and early thrusts (paragraphs 3, 10, 11, 12), the more than proportionate increase in stocks during expansions (paragraphs 13 and 14). They are potentially able to play a role of some importance because they fluctuate with considerable vigor and are large in their absolute impact (paragraphs 1, 7, 13).

But the observations also hint at behavior that may help to understand how change takes place and why. The systematic and leading relationship of outstandings relative to stocks (paragraph 6), the greater volatility of outstandings (paragraph 8), the early thrusts (paragraphs 10 and 12). At this stage of the work these facts present, rather than unravel, puzzles. Both the facts and puzzles will be stored away for future use.

6. Rates of Change

The capital asset, stocks, is a means to the end of production and consumption of goods. Its absolute size is relevant to its capacity to perform this function, as is its relation to the flows of output that it serves. This was the point of view on which the previous two chapters focused, since they examined the levels of stocks and stock-output ratios.

But stocks are not merely an enabling factor. Their increase or decrease can itself be a target, or at least a consequence, of production. As such they are directly involved in the dynamics of business decisions. These decisions have a direct effect on employment and income; they may have many indirect effects. The magnitude of the impact often depends on the *rate of change* of stocks over a period of time.

For example, the time-rate of change in stocks, inventory investment, measures the direct impact of stocks on the flow of goods and of incomes in the economy. During a specified time interval, incomes are paid out to generate an addition to stock, other things the same; a decrease in stock absorbs income (to effectuate their purchase) without creating it by the payments associated with the production of the goods purchased. Further effects of the time-rate of change in stock (and here the level of stocks is doubtless also significant) include their influence on expectations, on tensions in markets and on prices. The various sorts of initial impacts ripple in rings of subsequent or "multiplier" effects, and this applies not only to the much discussed income multiplier but to expectational and market-impact multipliers as well.

Rates of change in outstanding orders, unlike stocks, do not constitute the measure of some aggregate direct impact on the relation between current income and product flows. They may have this effect later if their deliveries result, other things the same, in larger or smaller stocks. In any case, they have many other direct and indirect effects which may take place immediately or subsequently. For one thing, they represent a commitment on the part of the seller to undertake future production. Present implications include influences on market conditions, on prices, and on producers' judgments as to whether to increase or decrease production, buying or selling. But consideration of these complicated effects of change in materials on hand and on order had best be put off until their behavior has been visualized.

For the purpose of describing the time-rates of change, we select one month as the basic period. Because month-to-month change is characterized by a heavy erratic component, all data are smoothed by a five-month moving average.[1] I use the term "investment" interchangeably with that of "change" or "rate of change" and all apply, of course, to either or both change in stocks on hand or on order.

[1] The period has been selected without experimentation. In general, different series "need" different degrees of smoothing, but it was not feasible to arrive at these particularized techniques. Moreover the criterion of "need" is tricky when, as here, the subject under study is one for which quite short-term change is relevant. Ideally, I would like to remove choppiness caused by irrelevant influences, such as seasonal patterns in working days, weather, promotional occurrences, length of the business day, bunching of business. I would not like to remove choppiness that might

DURABLE GOODS MANUFACTURING

Conformity and Timing

The second curve of Chart 6 pictures the course of rates of change in materials ownership for manufacturers of durable goods. There were five clear cycles; a sixth one, the expansion that interrupted the decline following the Korean War, was not strong enough to select as a specific cycle, but does nevertheless warrant attention as a minor movement.

Cycles of ownership investment have a recurrent pattern—troughs occur no later than the middle of business cycle contractions. There is a fast upward movement as, first, the rate of decline slackens and, then (as the curve crosses the zero line), the rate of rise accelerates. Peaks in the rate of investment tend to occur within ten months after business expansion begins.[2] But though the rate of rise does not continue to accelerate, ownership itself continues to rise and at a rapid rate (though not at an increasing rate) for the periods of ten to eighteen months previously noted as characterizing the first spurt of expansion.

The net result is that the rate of change in ownership has an irregular pattern over business cycle expansion after the first spurt has slowed. The rise may continue for a while and then actually reverse, as was the case in the first postwar expansion and during the Korean period; it may continue, though at

a declining rate, and this may take place for a short or for a long period of time. These often long and irregular periods of declining rate of rise cause peaks in ownership investment to bear an irregular relation to the following peak in business. Table 18, lines 1 and 2, shows a median lead of 22 months and an average deviation from the median of 8 months; if the subcycle reference frame is used, the median lead is 13 months and the deviation almost as great.

The high volatility of outstanding orders means that it is the order segment that determines the basic characteristics of changes in ownership in the durable goods industries. Consequently, most of what has just been said concerning conformity and timing of changes in ownership applies to changes in outstandings alone. Table 18, line 4, shows that the timing in change of ownership and outstanding orders is virtually identical.

Changes in materials stocks lead turns in general business (Table 18, lines 6 and 7), though of course by shorter intervals than do outstandings. At troughs the average lead is very short indeed.

Rates of change in ownership or outstandings, like the data proper, lead turns in materials stocks. The median lead for all turns is four and five months respectively—eight months at peaks (lines 3 and 8 with signs reversed). Here, as in the case of the level of stocks and outstandings, the lead seems surprisingly long. Fluctuations in change in stocks

represent, for example, a tendency for certain months of the year to be characterized by unusually strong buying in good years and unusually weak buying in poor years.

I am saying, in other words, that hand-tailored smoothing is a complicated problem, and I have not undertaken it except in isolated cases. The five-month average seems to achieve enough smoothing to make it feasible to study the time series. Also it may be reasonably realistic in that business procedures as-

sociated with planning and review may average experience over a number of months and thus in effect perform a similar smoothing operation.

[2] The peak in investment took place seven months after the 1947 trough, six months after 1954, nine months after 1958, and ten months after the 1961 trough. The extraordinarily heavy speculative movement during the Korean episode was associated with a somewhat later peak—sixteen months after the trough in 1949.

CHART 6

Rates of Change * in Stocks and Unfilled Orders, Durable Goods Manufacturers, 1946–64

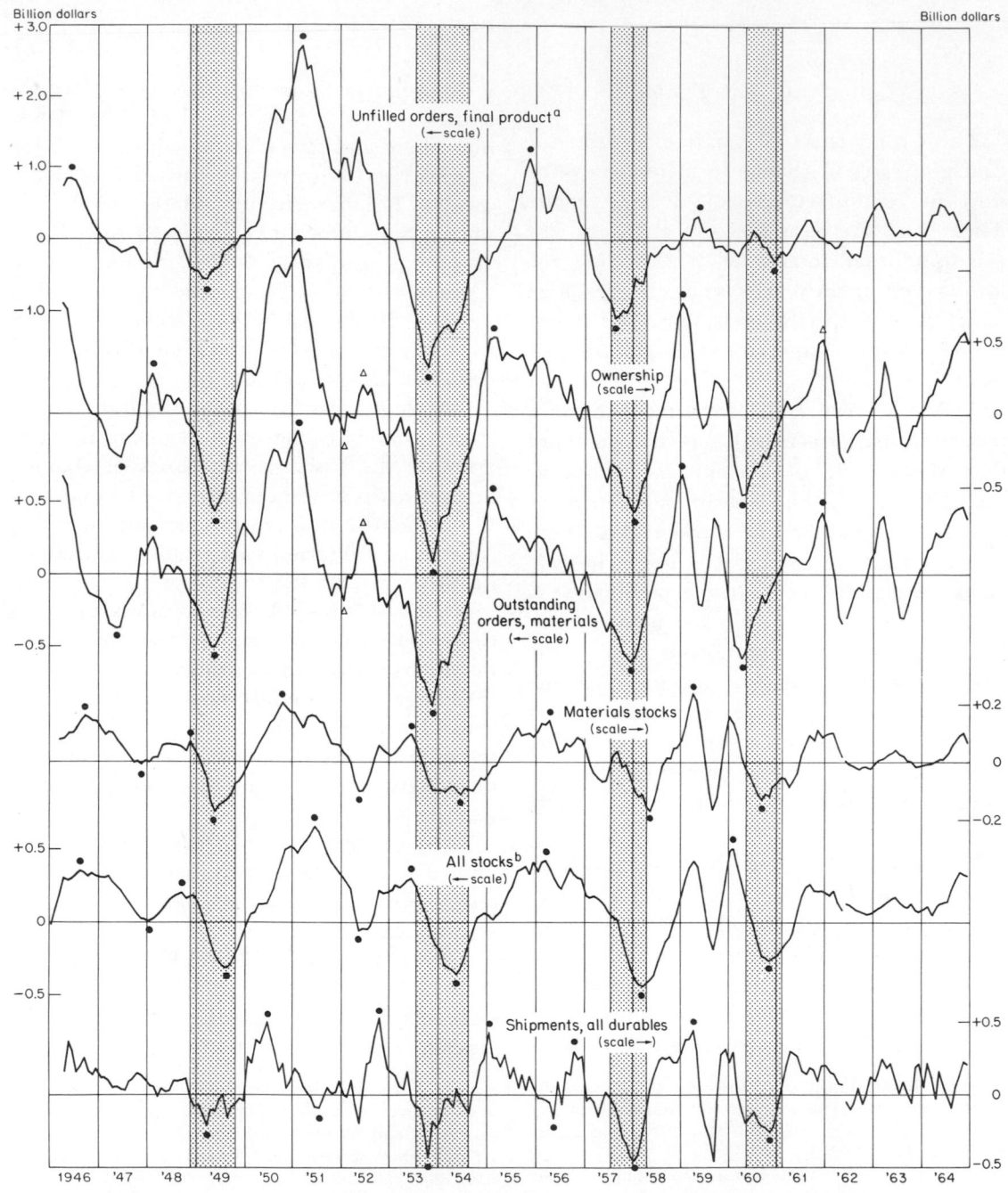

Note: Shaded areas represent business contractions. Specific cycle turns are marked by dots, additional minor turns are marked by triangles.

* Five-month centered moving average of monthly change.

a Final product industries are the machinery and transportation equipment industries.

b Finished, in process, and materials stocks of all durable goods manufacturers.

TABLE 18

Timing: Change in Stocks on Hand and on Order, Durable Goods Manufacturers, 1946–62

		Section A: Months Lead (–) or Lag (+) for Matched Turns[a] Chronology[b]											
Line	Reference Series[c]	P (1/47)	T (7/47)	P 11/48	T 10/49	P (2/51)	T (6/52)	P 7/53	T 8/54	P 7/57	T 4/58	P 5/60	T 2/61
	Specific Series: Change in Ownership												
1	Business cycles			−9	−5			−29	−9	−29	−3	−16[r]	−10[r]
2	Subcycles	⊕	−1	−9	−5	0	−5[r]	−13[r]	−9	−29	−3	−16[r]	−10[r]
3	Change materials stocks	⊕	−5	−9	0	+4	−4	−12	−7	−14	−4	−3	−5
4	Change in outstanding orders	⊙	+1	0	0	0	0	0	0	0	+1	0	0
5	Change shipments	⊙	Ω	Ω	+2	+8	+6	−4	+1	+1	0	−3	−7
	Specific Series: Change in Stocks, Materials												
6	Business cycles			0	−5			−1	−2	−15	+1	−13	−5
7	Subcycles	−4	+4	0	−5	−4	−1	−1	−2	−15	+1	−13	−5
8	Change in Outstanding orders	Ω	+6	+9	0	−4	+4	+12	+7	+14	+5	+3	+5
9	Change all stocks	+1	−2	+2	−3	−8	0	0	+1	+1	+2	−10	−2
10	Change shipments	Ω	Ω	Ω	+2	+4	+10	+8	+8	+15	+4	0	−2
11	Shipments	Ω	Ω	−1	−5	−5	−2	−1	−4	−9	+1	−2	−4
	Specific Series: Change in Outstanding Orders												
12	Business cycles			−9	−5			−29	−9	−29	−4	−16[r]	−10[r]
13	Subcycles	⊕	−2	−9	−5	0	−5[r]	−13[r]	−9	−29	−4	−16[r]	−10[r]
14	Change unf. orders final products	⊕	Ω	Ω	+2	−1	Ω	⊙	+1	−9	+4	−4	−8
15	Change shipments	Ω	Ω	Ω	+2	+8	+6	−4	+1	+1	−1	−3	−7
	Specific Series: Change in Unfilled Orders, Final Product												
16	Business cycles			−29	−7			−28	−10	−20	−8	−12	−3
17	Subcycles	−7	⊕	⊕	−7	+1	⊕	⊕	−10	−20	−8	−12	−3
	Specific Series: Change in All Stocks												
18	Business cycles			−2	−2			−1	−3	−16	−1	−3	−3
19	Subcycles	−5	+6	−2	−2	+4	−1	−1	−3	−16	−1	−3	−3
	Specific Series: Change in Shipments All Durables												
20	Business cycles			⊕	−7			−9	−10	−9	−3	−13	−3
21	Subcycles	⊕	⊕	⊕	−7	−8	−11	−9	−10	−9	−3	−13	−3

(continued)

TABLE 18 (concluded)

Line	Reference Series [c]	Number Matched −	+	0	Median [e] P	T	All	Average Deviation [f] P	T	All Turns Wt'd		Section C: Timing Adjustment [g]	% Mos. 7/46− 12/61

Specific Series: Change Ownership

1	Business cycles	8	0	0	−22.5	−7.0	−9.5	8.2	2.8	7.2	5.5	−9, −10	57
2	Subcycles	10	0	1	−12.7	−5.0	−7.7	7.3	3.3	5.8	5.1	−9	63
3	Change materials stocks	9	1	1	−8.0	−4.5	−3.7	5.6	1.5	3.9	3.4	−5	77
4	Change in outstanding orders	0	2	9	0	0	0	0	0.3	0.2	0.2	0	99
5	Change shipments	3	5	1	−1.0	+1.0	+0.7	4.0	3.0	3.5	3.4	+1, 0	73

Specific Series: Change Stocks, Materials

6	Business cycles	6	1	1	−7.0	−3.5	−3.5	6.7	2.2	4.5	4.5	−4, −5	63
7	Subcycles	9	2	1	−4.0	−1.5	−3.0	4.5	2.7	3.9	3.6	−3, −4	75
8	Change in outstanding orders	1	9	1	+8.0	+5.0	+5.3	5.6	1.5	3.7	3.4	+5	79
9	Change all stocks	5	5	2	+0.5	−1.0	0	3.7	1.7	2.7	2.6	−2 to +1	83
10	Change shipments	1	7	1	+11.5	+7.3	+8.7	6.5	4.3	4.9	5.3	+4, +5	68
11	Shipments	9	1	0	−2.7	−3.3	−3.0	2.5	1.7	2.2	2.1	−2, −3, −4	81

Specific Series: Change Outstanding Orders

12	Business cycles	8	0	0	−22.5	−7.0	−9.5	8.2	2.5	7.1	5.4	−9, −10	61
13	Subcycles	10	0	1	−12.7	−5.0	−7.7	7.3	2.2	5.7	4.5	−9	64
14	Change unf. orders, final product	4	3	0	−4.7	+1.5	−1.3	2.9	3.2	4.0	3.1	−1, 0	77
15	Change shipments	4	5	0	−1.0	+0.7	+0.7	4.0	3.3	3.6	3.6	+1, 0	72

Specific Series: Change Unfilled Orders, Final Product

| 16 | Business cycles | 8 | 0 | 0 | −24.0 | −7.5 | −11.0 | 6.2 | 2.0 | 7.6 | 4.1 | −11 | 58 |
| 17 | Subcycles | 7 | 1 | 0 | −9.5 | −7.5 | −7.5 | 6.5 | 2.0 | 4.2 | 4.2 | −7, −8 | 66 |

Specific Series: Change All Stocks

| 18 | Business cycles | 8 | 0 | 0 | −2.5 | −2.5 | −2.5 | 4.0 | 0.8 | 2.4 | 2.4 | −2, −3 | 75 |
| 19 | Subcycles | 10 | 2 | 0 | −2.5 | −1.5 | −2.0 | 4.2 | 2.0 | 3.1 | 3.1 | −2 | 80 |

Specific Series: Change Shipments All Durables

| 20 | Business cycles | 7 | 0 | 0 | −10.3 | −5.0 | −8.3 | 1.8 | 2.8 | 2.8 | 2.3 | −9 | 57 |
| 21 | Subcycles | 9 | 0 | 0 | −9.0 | −6.7 | −8.7 | 1.2 | 3.1 | 2.5 | 2.2 | −9 | 68 |

Notes to Table 18

[a]Specific series are matched with the indicated reference series (see note c) in accordance with the standard NBER rules. A double relaxation of rules is marked r; it applies to cases for well-conforming series in which two like turns are matched, though an unlike turn lies between them. The figure is underlined when subcycle chronology is the reference series, a minor cycle in the specific series has entered a comparison; or, when two individual series are compared, a minor cycle in either series has entered a comparison. When the business cycle chronology provides the reference, minor specific cycle turns are ignored. The meaning of other symbols is:

   ⊕ = Turn in the reference series does not appear in the specific series.

   ℛ = Turn in the specific series does not appear in the reference series.

   ⊙ = There is no turn in either series in neighborhood of the chronology date.

[b]Chronology dates are business cycle reference dates. In addition, four minor subcycle dates, enclosed in parentheses, are added to form a subcycle chronology.

[c]Reference series are of three sorts: (1) the business cycle chronology as shown in column heads, excluding the dates in parentheses; (2) the subcycle chronology as shown in all column heads; (3) particular series whose specific cycles and minor cycles constitute the reference dates for the comparison.

[d]The number of months during which the specific series is in like phase with the reference series is expressed as a percentage of the total number of months covered between dates as given.

[e]Median is the average timing of the center two or three turns.

[f]Average deviation from the median. The "weighted" (wt'd) average is the deviation from the median for peaks and for troughs separately, weighted by the number of turns.

[g]In determining months in like phase a timing adjustment is made which maximizes confluence. Before counting the months in phase, the specific series is in effect moved to the right to allow for a lead and to the left to allow for a lag if by so doing the percentage of months in like phase (as rounded) is increased. If the months in phase are as large or larger without an adjustment, this is indicated by a "timing adjustment" of 0.

In some cases we wish to know the percentage of months in phase on a synchronous basis, regardless of whether the percentage in phase is thereby maximized. If so, the "timing adjustment" is given as "none."

and outstandings have 79 per cent of the months in like phase after allowing for the five-month lead (line 8, Section C).

Amplitude

The swings in changes in ownership were typically quite substantial. The average specific cycle rise or fall—that is, the average algebraic difference between the monthly rate of rise at peaks and the rate of fall at troughs—was $1,338 million [3] (Table 19). This represented 6.5 per cent of the average level of ownership proper. It represents 11.8 per cent of the level of shipments of all durable goods manufacturers. The total swing from low to high and back again was, of course, about twice these figures.

expansion is, algebraically, the rate of rise at a peak minus the rate of fall at the previous trough. The fall during contraction is the rate of fall at a trough minus the rate of rise at the following peak.

Total average phase amplitude is the algebraic sum of rises minus falls divided by the number of phases. The figure is, therefore, one-half of the full cycle amplitude and, implicitly, positive for expansions and negative for contractions. The average amplitude per month is obtained by dividing total amplitude by the number of months from the first to the last turn covered.

[3] The figure is obtained in the following way. Standings are five-month averages of month-to-month change centered at months of turn. Rates of rise have a positive, and of fall a negative, sign. The rise during

TABLE 19

Average Specific Cycle Amplitude of Monthly Change in Stocks on Hand and on Order,
Durable Goods Manufactures, 1946-62

| | Date of First and Last Peak or Trough (1) | Amplitude Per Phase | | Amplitude Per Month, Rise or Fall[a] | | Average Level of Data Proper 1946-62 ($ million) (6) |
		($ million) (2)	% of Data Proper (Col. 2÷6) (3)	($ million) (4)	% of Data Proper (Col. 4÷6) (5)	
Ownership	T 6/47 to					
	P 12/61	1,338	6.54	69.2	.34	20,456
Materials stocks	P 9/46 to					
	P 11/61	267	3.85	17.6	.25	6,931
Outstanding orders	T 5/47 to					
	P 12/61	1,212	8.97	62.3	.46	13,508[b]
All stocks	P 8/46 to					
	P 9/61	633	2.68	42.0	.18	23,630
Unfilled orders, final Product	P 6/46 to					
	P 9/61	2,110	6.84	92.2	.30	30,842

[a]Peak or trough standings are five-month averages centered. Specific cycle fall during contraction is added to the rise during expansion, summed for all cycles, and divided by the number of months between initial and terminal turns. For further description see text, note 3.

[b]Shipments of durable goods manufacturers in the materials group averaged $5,382 mil. per month 1946-61. For outstanding orders, which are the unfilled sales orders of the same group, the amplitude per phase (col. 3) average 22.5 per cent of shipments, and per month (col. 5), 1.2 per cent.

Of the two components of ownership, changes in stocks on hand (curve 4) and changes of stocks on order (curve 3), the latter, Chart 6 suggests, fluctuates several times as vigorously as the former. (Note that changes in stocks are drawn on twice the scale of outstandings.) We see in Table 19 that change in materials stocks rose or fell during its specific cycles by an average of $17.6 million a month; the corresponding figure for outstandings was $62.3 million, three and a half times as large. It may be recalled that for the data proper outstandings were about four times as unstable as materials stocks (see Table 3)—roughly speaking, about the same as for rates of change. The far larger instability of outstandings is due in part to the higher level of outstandings proper (Table 19, column 4), but even on a relative basis they fluctuate twice as much (column 3).

The economic significance of cycles in inventory investment is a function, among other things, of the size of the swings relative to that of the flows that fill and empty the inventory pools; and a similar remark, though with "other things" playing a more important part, applies to change in outstandings orders. Shipments by manufacturers of durable goods *materials* may be used as a very rough indication of the size of one of these flows (the outlet).

Rises or falls per month during specific cycles in change in outstandings represented 1.2 per cent of the monthly level of shipments of materials producers; the amplitude per phase represented 22.5 per cent of the monthly level of shipments (see Table 19, note). Some notion of the meaning of these figures is suggested by the fact that the amplitude of specific cycles in materials shipments itself was about the same—1.4 per cent per month and 23.2 per cent per phase.

Other Comparisons

Parenthetically, I want to call attention to two additional relationships. The first concerns outstanding orders for materials and unfilled orders for final products, the third and top curves in Chart 6. Note, first, the precipitous rate at which unfilled orders for final products built up during the Korean episode and the 1955–56 expansion; the scale for the final products curve is two times that of materials outstanding. The shape as well as amplitude of the movements appear to differ. Materials show five well-developed movements and a minor additional one. (I ignore, as always, the strike episode in 1959.) Final products miss the two extra cycles; [4] their movements since 1958 have been minimal. For such movements as were shared by both rates-of-change series, the persistent lead of materials noted in the data proper seems to have disappeared. At peaks, rate of increase in outstanding orders for materials do seem to start down before those for final products; but at troughs, the rate of decline in outstandings tends to decelerate after that of final products (Table 18, line 14).[5]

[4] The hesitation in the rate of deceleration of final-product backlogs in 1952 may seem similar to the contemporaneous movement in materials outstandings. But note that final-product backlogs were rising heavily throughout the period, while materials outstandings actually fell (crossed the zero line) and then rose again.

[5] Retardation precedes turns in the data proper for unfilled orders for final products by unusually long intervals—nine to twenty-two months for the five comparisons that can be made—the median lead is thirteen months. For unfilled orders for materials, the range is two to eighteen months, with a median of six months for the twelve comparisons.

In spite of the long production period of many final products, the rate of change per month in these unfilled orders, though larger in dollar amounts, is smaller relative to unfilled orders proper than is the case for the relation of the rate of change in outstanding orders for materials to these data proper; rates of change, as a percentage of the data proper, are .3 and .5 respectively (Table 19, column 5).

The second parenthetical observation concerns the basic similarity between investment in all durable goods stocks and in durable stocks of materials (compare Chart 6, curves 4 and 5). Thomas Stanback has observed that the pattern of investment in goods in process and in finished stocks is very similar to that of materials alone. Comparing all stocks with those of materials only, our Table 18 (line 9) shows that 83 per cent of the months are in like phase, matched synchronously. This hints that if we could learn more about why stocks of materials change, in part, perhaps, via further understanding of the role of unfilled orders, the knowledge would help to illuminate the aggregate behavior of investment in total stocks. These fluctuations, of course, vary far more in absolute amount (though less as a percentage of the level of stocks) than do materials, which represent about 30 per cent of the total in book value.[6]

Stocks and Shipments

Analysis of management problems in Chapter 2 suggested that incremental relations between sales and stocks might, under several circumstances, tend to be constant when rela-

[6] The relative importance of materials stocks is underplayed by book-value figures. Stanback's figures, based on book value, are 30, 40, and 30 per cent for materials, in process, and finished stocks for durable goods manufacturing (*Postwar Cycles*, p. 25). But to convert the proportions to the number of weeks of shipments for which they constitute the supply, an allowance must be made for the value added to book value. If materials are taken to be 50 per cent of their finished value and in process 75 per cent, the adjusted proportions are 40, 40, 20.

tions between sales and stocks proper might not.

Because rates of change may be positive or negative, it is awkward to examine the degree of their relationship as we did for the data proper for which ratios could be used. Accordingly, it will suffice for the moment to ask the less exacting question: How much of the time do rates of change in shipments and in the several stockpiles rise or fall together and what are their characteristic sequences?

The bottom curve in Chart 6 shows monthly change in shipments of all durable goods manufacturers smoothed by a five-month centered average. Its turns inevitably lead those of the business cycle or subcycle chronology, beginning in 1949 (Table 18, lines 20 and 21). Before 1949, the rise in shipments tapered off slowly, so that rates of change underwent no cycles of their own. It is exceedingly interesting also that there appear to be no clear fluctuations in the rate of rise in shipments, 1961–64. For the nine turns matched with the subcycle chronology, leads averaged about nine months with quite moderate variability; indeed, at peaks average deviation was only 1.2 months.

If investment in stocks on hand responded to these monthly amounts of increase or decrease in shipments, they often did so quite slowly. The median lag was nine months (line 10). Changes in outstandings, on the other hand (line 15), turned sooner about as often as later than changes in shipment. The correspondence in terms of the percentage of months in like phase was poor, 72 per cent. Changes in ownership, of course, behaved in virtually the same way (line 5). In chapters 9 and 11, we return to these relationships for more careful scrutiny and explanation in terms of business objectives and achievements. In the meantime, one cannot help questioning whether they express a determined effort to keep stocks firmly linked to shipments, other things the same, and whether, if so, other things actually tend to be the same.

DEPARTMENT STORES

Conformity and Timing

Information for department stores about rates of change in stocks, outstanding orders, and ownership as a whole is shown in Chart 7. Change in ownership had five clear cycles. Peaks and troughs tended to lead the reference dates on the average by almost a year (Table 20, lines 1 and 2). Indeed, the peak in ownership investment occurred about a year after business contraction ended, not far from the times, previously observed, when the spurts in buying begin to recede.[7] There are no rules for the last two-thirds of the expansion phase of business cycles—ownership investment may drop to a trough and rise again (the first two expansions), or continue a retarding or irregular rate of rise.

Once again we see, this time for the rate of change, materials on order reaching peaks and troughs well ahead of those on hand (Table 20, line 9). The median lead is four months at peaks and troughs. The intervals again seem long in view of the fact that outstanding orders constituted only about one month's supply on the average. But in spite of this there appears to be a rather substantial similarity, after allowing for the average lead of four months, in the timing of fluctuation in the rates at which outstanding orders and stocks rise and fall. Eighty-three per cent of all months were in like phase.

Let me pause for a procedural note. Why is 83 per cent of months in like phase a

---

[7] The periods from business cycle trough to the following peak in change in ownership were eight months after the 1949 trough, fourteen months after 1954, and thirteen months after 1958.

CHART 7

*Rates of Change in Sales and Ownership and Its Parts,
Department Stores, 1946–63*

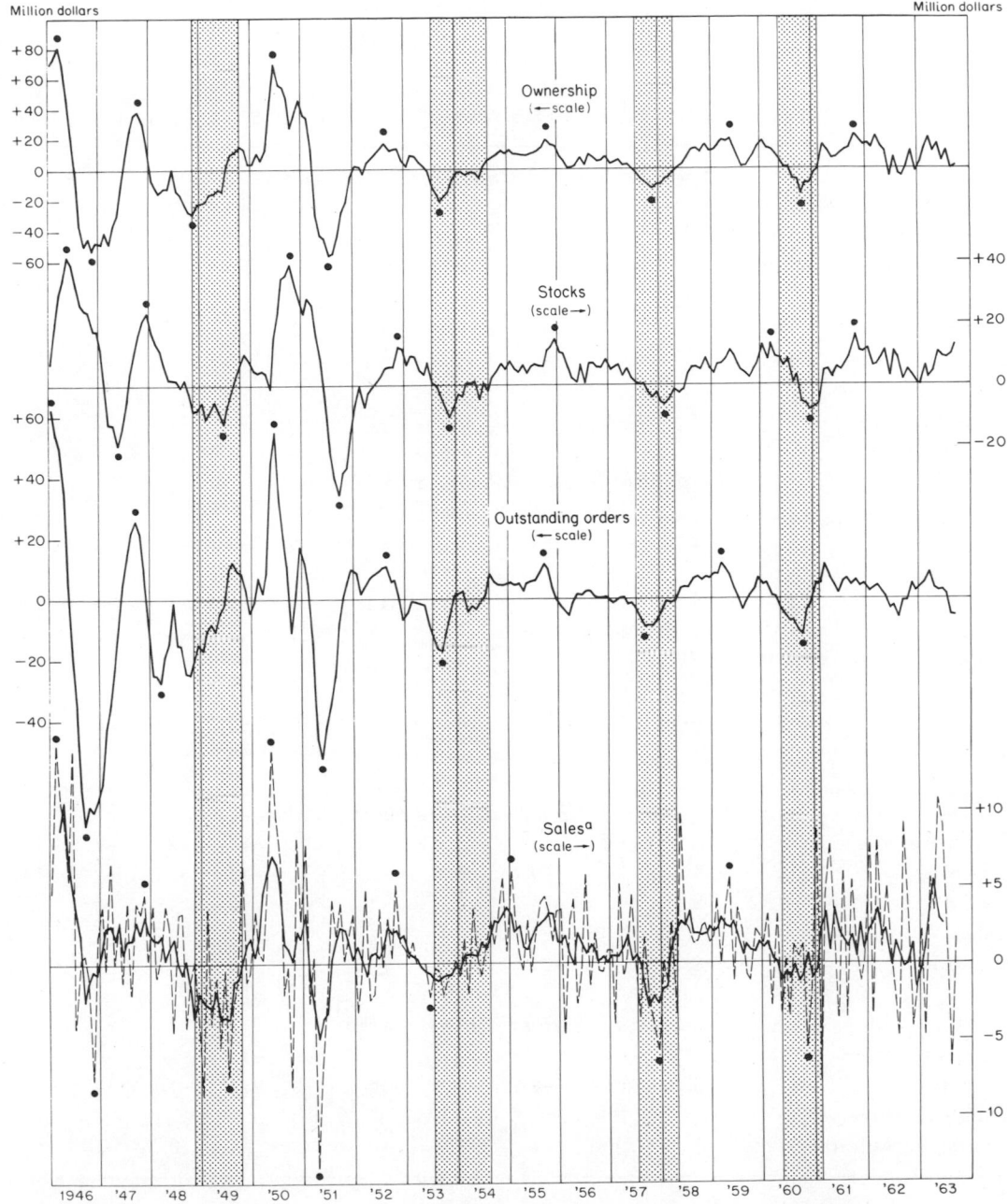

Note: Shaded areas represent business contractions. Specific cycle turns are marked by dots.
   a Dashed line is five-month centered average of month-to-month change in seasonally corrected monthly sales; turns are marked in these data. Solid line is a nine-month weighted average.

TABLE 20

Timing: Change in Stocks on Hand and on Order, Department Stores, 1946–62

Section A: Months Lead (–) or Lag (+) for Matched Turns[a]
Chronology[b]

Line	Reference Series[c]	P (1/47)	T (7/47)	P 11/48	T 10/49	P (2/51)	T (6/52)	P 7/53	T 8/54	P 7/57	T 4/58	P 5/60	T 2/61
	Specific Series: Change in Ownership												
1	Business cycles			−13[r]	−11[r]			−11	−11	−21	−5	−12	−4
2	Subcycles	−10[r]	−8[r]	−13[r]	−11[r]	−8	−11	−11	−11	−21	≈5	−12	−4
3	Change stocks	−2	−6	−2	−7	−4	−2	−3	−2	−2	−3	−10	−2
4	Change in outstanding orders	+2	+2	+1	+8	0	+2	0	0	+1	+2	+2	0
5	Change in sales	+1	0	−1	−8	+1	+3	−2	+3	+9	−1	0	−1
6	Change in ownership, durables	Ω	−7	−4	−6	−8	<u>−6</u>	<u>+2</u>	−2	+8	−2	+4	+6
	Specific Series: Change in Stocks												
7	Business cycles			−11	−4			−8	−9	−19	−2	−2	−2
8	Subcycles	−8	−2	−11	−4	−4	−9	−8	−9	−19	−2	≈2	≈2
9	Change in outstanding orders	+4	+8	+3	+15	+4	+4	+3	+2	+3	+5	+12	+2
10	Change in sales	+3	+6	+1	−1	+5	+5	+1	+5	+11	+2	+10	+1
11	Change in materials stocks, dur.	−4	−6	−11	+1	0	−8	−7	−7	−4	−3	+11	+3
12	Sales	Ω	Ω	−10	−1	−3	+5	−6	−2	−20	0	−1	−1
	Specific Series: Change in Outstanding Orders												
13	Business cycles			−14[r]	−19[r]			≈11	−11	−22	−7	−14	≈4
14	Subcycles	−12[r]	−10[r]	−14[r]	−19[r]	−8	−13	−11	−11	−22	−7	−14	≈4
15	Change in sales	−1	−2	−2	−16	+1	+1	−2	+3	+8	−3	−2	−1
16	Change outstanding orders, dur.	Ω	−8	−5	−14	−8	<u>−8</u>	<u>+2</u>	−2	+7	−3	+2	+6
	Specific Series: Change Sales												
17	Business cycles			−12	−3			−9[r]	−14[r]	−30	−4	−12	−3
18	Subcycles	−11[r]	−8[r]	≈12	−3	−9	−14	−9[r]	−14[r]	−30	−4	−12	−3
19	Change in shipments, durables	Ω	Ω	Ω	+4	−1	−3	0	−4	0	−1	+1	0

(continued)

TABLE 20 (concluded)

Section B: Average Time of Turns

Line	Reference Series[c]	Number Matched			Median[e]			Average Deviation[f]			Section C: Percentage of Months in Like Phase[d]	
										All Turns	Timing Adjustment[g]	% Mos. 7/46– 12/61
		−	+	0	P	T	All	P	T	Wt'd		

Specific Series: Change Ownership

1	Business cycles	8	0	0	−12.5	−8.0	−11.0	2.8	3.2	3.2	3.0	−11	76
2	Subcycles	12	0	0	−11.5	−9.5	−11.0	2.8	2.7	2.8	2.8	−11	82
3	Change in stocks	12	0	0	−2.5	−2.5	−2.5	1.8	1.7	1.8	1.8	−2	89
4	Change outstanding orders	0	8	4	+1.0	+2.0	+1.5	0.7	1.7	1.3	1.2	+2	91
5	Change sales	5	5	2	+0.5	−0.5	0	2.3	2.7	2.5	2.5	0	84
6	Change ownership, durables	7	4	0	+0.7	−4.0	−2.7	5.1	3.5	4.5	4.2	−2	74

Specific Series: Change Stocks

7	Business cycles	8	0	0	−9.5	−3.0	−6.0	5.0	2.2	4.6	3.6	−6	68
8	Subcycles	12	0	0	−8.0	−3.0	−6.0	4.0	2.7	4.0	3.3	−6	73
9	Change in outstanding orders	0	12	0	+3.5	+4.5	+4.0	1.8	3.3	2.6	2.6	+4	83
10	Change sales	1	11	0	+4.0	+3.5	+4.0	3.5	2.3	2.9	2.9	+4,+3	81
11	Change materials stocks, durables	8	3	1	−4.0	−4.5	−4.0	4.8	3.7	4.2	4.2	−4	73
12	Sales	8	1	1	−6.3	−0.7	−1.5	5.3	1.7	4.3	3.5	−1	71

Specific Series: Change Outstanding Orders

13	Business cycles	8	0	0	14.0	−9.0	−12.5	2.8	4.8	4.5	3.8	−12,−13	73
14	Subcycles	12	0	0	−13.0	−10.5	−11.5	3.2	3.7	3.6	3.4	−12,−13	77
15	Change sales	8	4	0	−1.5	−1.5	−1.5	2.3	4.0	3.2	3.2	−2	80
16	Change outstanding orders, dur.	7	4	0	−0.3	−5.5	−3.3	4.9	5.2	5.3	5.0	−3	69

Specific Series: Change Sales

17	Business cycles	8	0	0	−12.0	−3.5	−10.5	5.2	3.0	6.1	4.1	−10	66
18	Subcycles	12	0	0	−11.5	−6.0	−10.0	4.2	4.3	4.8	4.2	−10	69
19	Change shipments, durables	4	2	3	0	−1.3	−0.3	0.5	2.3	1.6	1.5	0	79

Notes: See Table 18.

"rather substantial similarity"? For data proper I have passed over confluence of this order. There is inevitably a substantial judgmental element in what does or does not seem noteworthy confluence. But two chief considerations influence the judgment. First the more phases a series has the harder it is to reach a given confluence score. Thus, here there are 12 turns compared over 186 months. An average deviation of only 2.6 months at each turn would account for the 17 per cent of the months which are out of phase, even if there were no unmatched phases. Had there been only eight turns matched, the corresponding per cent in phase would have been 89. Second a given percentage of months in phase is more noteworthy for series that do not move generally with the business tides than for those that do (see Chapter 9, note 2 below). Both considerations tend to imply that a given score for rates of change tends to be more impressive than the same score for data proper.

Amplitude

In spite of the relatively smooth course of retail sales, the swings in ownership investment were quite substantial. The figures are given in Table 21. The average rise or fall was plus or minus $70 million. This represented 4.1 per cent of the average level of ownership proper (column 3) and, incidentally, 16.3 per cent of the average level of sales or receipts. On a monthly basis the rate of rise or fall averaged $4.4 million, or .26 per cent of the average level of ownership proper. Contrast the latter with the corresponding figure of .34 per cent for durable goods manufacturing.

The very substantial character of these fluctuations is also indicated by their relation to the level of department store sales or receipts, which averaged, almost identically, $427 million a month from 1946 to 1962. Month-to-month change in ownership represented 1.03

TABLE 21

Average Specific Cycle Amplitude of Monthly Change in Stocks on Hand and on Order, Department Stores, 1946-62

	Date of First and Last Peak or Trough (1)	Amplitude of Rise or Fall					Average Level of Data Proper 1946-62 ($ million) (7)
		Per Phase		Per Month[a]		Per Month, % of Level of Receipts, 1946-62[b] (6)	
		($ million) (2)	% of Data Proper (col. 2 ÷ col. 7) (3)	($ million) (4)	% of Data Proper (col. 4÷7) (5)		
Ownership	P 3/46 to T 10/60	69.6	4.11	4.4	.26	1.03	1,694
Stocks	P 5/46 to T 12/60	38.7	3.25	2.4	.20	.57	1,191
Outstanding orders	P 1/46 to T 10/60	60.5	12.03	3.8	.75	.89	503

[a]Peak or trough standings are five-month averages centered. Specific cycle fall during contraction is added to the rise during expansion, summed for all cycles, and divided by the number of months between initial and terminal turns. For further description see text, note 3.

[b]Receipts average $427 million from 1946 to mid-1962. The figures in column 4 are divided by this figure to give the data in column 6.

per cent of the average level of receipts (column 6).

Of the two parts of investment in ownership, change in stocks and in outstandings both contributed materially to the pattern. The absolute size of fluctuations in dollar terms was larger for outstandings than for stocks. This was true of the rise or fall during the whole phase or on a monthly basis, for which it was $2.4 million for change in stocks and $3.8 million for outstandings. This per month fluctuation in rates of change in outstandings represents 158 per cent of those of stocks; the corresponding figure for the data proper was 118 per cent (Table 11). Since stocks were substantially larger than outstandings proper, this meant, as would be expected from what we observed in the previous chapter, that the rate of change in outstandings relative to outstandings proper was substantially higher than for stocks relative to stocks proper—.75 and .20 per cent respectively (column 5).

Stocks and Shipments

The rate at which department store sales rise or fall is shown in the bottom curve of Chart 7. The dotted line smooths the month-to-month change by means of a five-month centered average. The very sawtooth character of curve reflects the character of the underlying data—a series which is itself relatively insensitive to cyclical fluctuation, yet has a strong seasonal and perhaps random component. To make the material more manageable, I have added a second smoothing, a five-month average of the first average.[8] However, to preserve consistency with other data, the turns were kept as they had been marked in the series having the single smoothing.

Retail sales (Table 20, lines 17 and 18) reach their fastest rate of increase typically nine months to a year before business cycles or subcycles reach their peak. At troughs, turns are likewise early, though the intervals are quite irregular.

The maximum rate at which retailers increase or decrease their stocks on hand tends to occur about a third of a year after sales have reached their maximum rates of increase or decline, respectively. Eighty-one per cent of months are in like phase after allowing for a three- or four-month lag (line 10).

For change in ownership, however, a much prompter reaction to sales appears possible. Line 5 of the table shows timing which is synchronous on the average, with 84 per cent of the months in like phase. I state these facts baldly, though they obviously are rich in meaning. But we will be in a better position to extract it after the other facts are in.

SUMMARY

Rates of change in stocks measure the difference in the flow of goods into and out of a stockpile. If the inflow is greater than the outflow in a given month, the rate of change in stock between the beginning and end of the month is positive. The larger the excess of inflow, the larger the rate of increase of stock. Analogous but opposite remarks apply to an inflow that is smaller than the outflow and rates at which stocks decline. In this sense, then, rates of change provide a most appropriate measure of the impact on the economy of business behavior that causes stocks to rise or fall. Since the findings of this chapter have generally repeated those based on the data proper, they chiefly expand upon just how the behavior of ownership and its parts may be expected to influence the flows of goods in the economy. However, they also throw

[8] The double smoothing provides a graduation covering nine months. The center five months carry 76 per cent of the total weight.

some light on our other major preoccupation —why stocks behave as they do. A quick review is in order.

1. Specific major and minor cycles in change in ownership and its parts, outstandings and stocks, for durables and department stores all conform to each postwar cycle and minor cycle.

2. Change in ownership for both sorts of enterprise lead the turns in general business, especially at peaks; the median lead at all peaks (including the minor ones) is about a year, and at troughs half to three-quarters of a year. More or less the same statements apply to change in outstandings. Changes in stocks also anticipate turns in the business cycles or subcycle chronology; the median lead is longer for department stores than for durable good manufacturers—about six and three months respectively.

3. Investment in stocks on hand and on order ordinarily rises sharply during the first year or fifteen months of business expansion. Thus rates of change conform to the periods of thrust (if only because they were taken into account in delineating them).

In several ways, then, the stimulating impact of positive investment in ownership starts early. It begins in outstandings, which slacken their rate of decline while recession is in full swing; it is reinforced by stocks before general business starts to improve. Total ownership accelerates during the first year of expansion. This set of influences, in other words, seem to work behind the scenes to help turn the tides of business decline.

4. Because backlogs of final products often start to retard a long while before they begin to decline or to rise, rates of change in purchase orders for materials do not clearly lead rates of change in backlogs of sales orders, as was the case for the two sorts of unfilled orders proper. For orders proper, materials inevitably lead final products by three to nine months for the eight matched turns; rates of change lag almost as often as they lead.

5. For durable goods manufacturers, the relation between the two parts of ownership was characterized by the same long lead of change in outstandings relative to changes in stock that appeared for the data proper. But for department stores, the trough figures only were similar. At troughs the median leads of outstandings relative to stocks ranged from three to five months whether for durables or department stores, data proper or rates of change. At peaks the median leads, as registered for both sorts of enterprises and forms of data, was seven or eight months except for rates of change for department stores. Apparently, though stocks proper continued to rise for seven months on the average after outstandings turned down, merchants succeeded in getting the rate of change in stocks under control more swiftly; the interval averaged three and a half months. Nevertheless, for rates of change as well as for the data proper, the figures present the same puzzle. Why is the lead so long?

The question is the more insistent because rates of change seem to reaffirm the tendency observed in the data proper for considerable parallelism (after allowing for a lag in stock) of fluctuation in the two parts of ownership. This was clearly true of rates of change for department stores, though somewhat less so for durable goods manufacturers.

6. The amplitude of fluctuation in rates of change in ownership is such as to contribute materially to an increase in instability as demand moves from the final consumer to earlier stages of production. The specifics of this manifestation will be further developed in the next two chapters.

7. The far greater instability of investment in outstandings relative to that of investment in stocks for both materials goods manufacturers and department stores repeats our findings for the data proper. Expressed as a percentage of the average level of each stockpile, monthly instability of stocks is again about the same for the two sorts of enterprises. For

outstandings, first differences showed relative fluctuation somewhat larger for department stores than for durables. Perhaps the safer conclusion is simply that on the basis of both types of statistics these figures are surprisingly alike for the two sorts of enterprises.

8. Timing comparisons and similarity in movement of rates of change in "demand" on the one hand and in stocks on the other give a further dimension to the basic description of how stocks respond to changes in demand. The chapter has shown that, for department stores, change in ownership, which can be swiftly adjusted to desired levels, appears to be kept closely parallel to the rate of change in sales. For durable goods manufacturers, where it would seem that adjustment is potentially more facile, the empirical picture is somewhat ambiguous.

7. Stocks and Adjacent Flows, Department Stores

Patterns in the behavior of stock on hand and on order, and more particularly in rates of change in these stocks, carry implications which bear on how demand for final products is passed back to earlier stages of the production process. Does the behavior of stocks, generated by the selling, processing, and procurement problems of businessmen, cause the earlier stages to receive advice of changing levels of demand earlier or later than did the producer of the final product? Is the amplitude of fluctuation increased or decreased as it moves to earlier stages, and by how much? This chapter tries to answer these questions for department stores and their suppliers, and the following chapter deals with the durable goods industries. Changes in stocks are examined in relation to the associated flows of goods at successive stages.

But in pursuing these questions, which bear primarily on the impact of inventory investment on the economy, we shall wish to keep in mind that other group of questions that ask what the data on stocks and flows can suggest about the procurement and stock-carrying problems of business firms and how they solve them.

The reservoir, department store stocks, is filled by the flow of goods received at the stockroom and drained by the flow of sales to consumers. The monthly rate of change in stocks is receipts minus sales. For outstanding orders, the bounding flows are the inlet stream of new orders placed with suppliers, net of cancellation, and the outlet is receipts at the store. For ownership they are new orders and sales. It will be instructive to view the three sets of statistics together, which is done in Chart 8. Note that at an arithmetic level the association between a change in stock and its inlet stream is predisposed to a positive parallelism; for the outlet stream, the predisposition is to an inverse parallelism.

TIMING AND CONTOURS

Sales, New Orders, and Ownership

The third group of curves shows the streams that bound ownership of department stores—retail sales and net new orders placed with suppliers—each smoothed by a five-month moving average. New orders systematically precede turns in general business by about half a year and show the two extra cycles (lines 10 and 11, Table 22). Sales, as noted previously, tend to lead the turns in business, though only very slightly at peaks; they shared only one of the extra cycles, the Korean one (lines 1 and 2).

Peaks and troughs in the orders that department stores place with their suppliers typically precede those in department store sales to consumers. The lead is far greater at peaks (seven months) than at troughs (one month), as line 12, Table 22, indicates. All but one comparison at peaks is a four-month or longer lead, and at troughs the longest

CHART 8

Sales, Receipts, New Orders, and Ownership, Department Stores, 1946–63

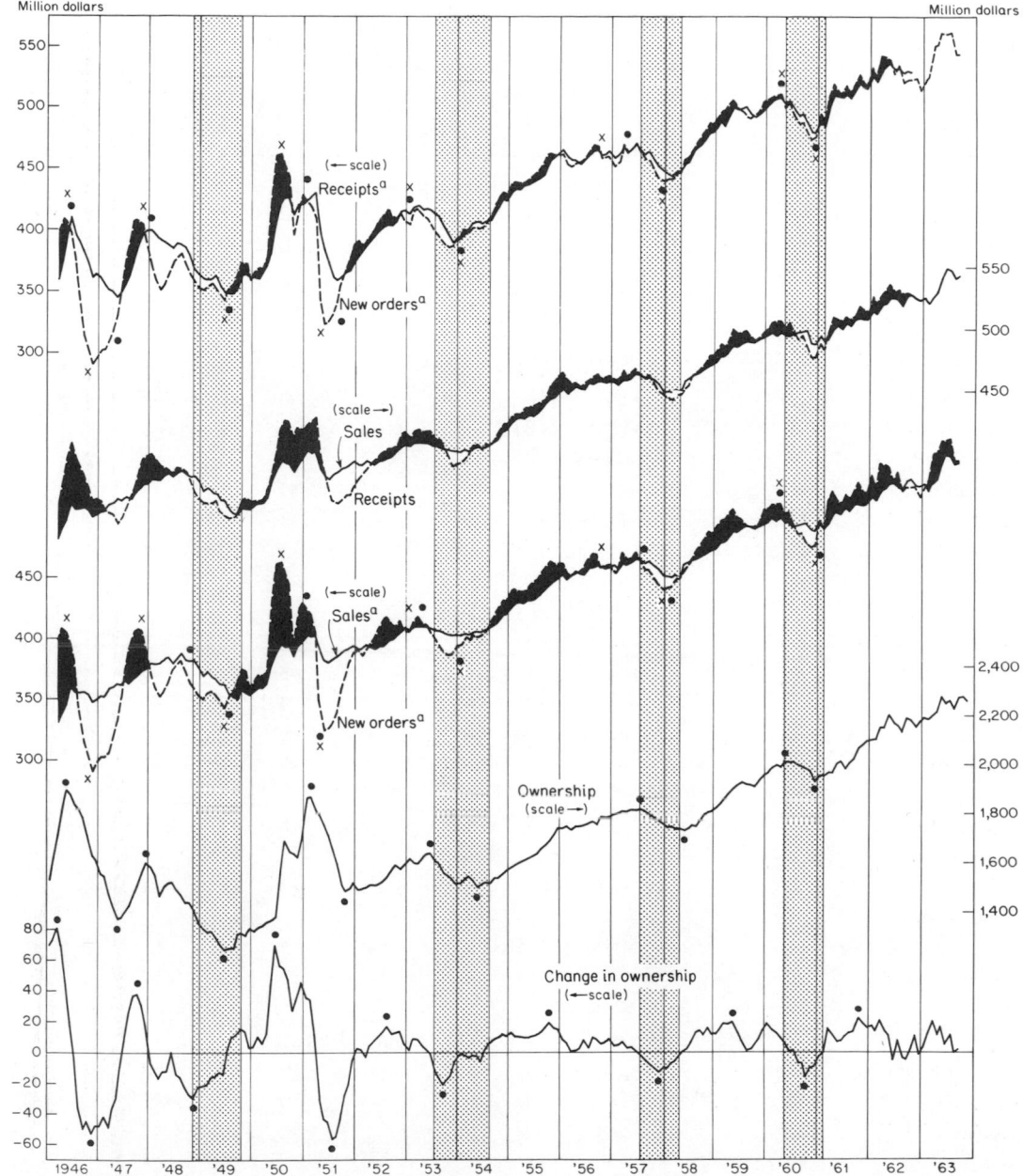

Note: Shaded areas represent business contractions. Specific turns are marked by X in new orders and by dots in sales, receipts, and ownership.

a Five-month moving average centered; turning points are marked for underlying monthly data.

TABLE 22

Timing: Stocks and Adjacent Flows, Department Stores, 1946–62

Section A: Months Lead (−) or Lag (+) for Matched Turns[a]
Chronology[b]

Line	Reference Series[c]	P (1/47)	T (7/47)	P 11/48	T 10/49	P (2/51)	T (6/52)	P 7/53	T 8/54	P 7/57	T 4/58	P 5/60	T 2/61
				Specific Series:	*Sales*								
1	Business cycles			−1	−3			−2	−7	+1	−2	−1	−1
2	Subcycles	⊕	⊕	−1	−3	−1	−14	−2	−7	+1	−2	−1	−1
3	Ownership	⊕	⊕	+10	+1	−1	−6	−1	−4	+1	−3	−1	+1
4	Stocks	⊕	⊕	−1	−1	−3	−13	−3	−7	+1	−6	−7	−2
				Specific Series:	*Receipts*								
5	Business cycles			−10	−3			−6	−7	−3	−4	−1	−2
6	Subcycles	−6	−1	−10	−3	−1	−9	−6	−7	−3	−4	−1	−2
7	Sales	Ω	Ω	−9	0	0	+5	−4	0	−4	−2	0	−1
8	Outstanding orders	+2	+1	+1	+1	0	0	+3	−4	+2	−3	0	0
9	Change in stocks	+2	+1	+1	+1	+3	0	+2	+2	+16	−2	+1	0
				Specific Series:	*New Orders*								
10	Business cycles			−12	−4			−6	−7	−9	−4	−1	−2
11	Subcycles	−8[r]	−8[r]	−12	−4	−7	−14	−6	−7	−9	−4	−1	−2
12	Sales	Ω	Ω	−11	−1	−6	0	−4	0	−10	−2	0	−1
13	Receipts	−2	−7	−2	−1	−6	−5	0	0	−6	0	0	0
14	Ownership	0	−6	−1	0	−7	−6	−5	−4	−9	−5	−1	0
15	Change ownership	+2	0	+1	+7	+1	−3	+5	+4	+12	+1	+11	+2
16	Outstanding orders	0	−6	−1	0	−6	−5	+3	−4	−4	−3	0	0
17	Change outstanding orders	+4	+2	+2	+15	+1	−1	+5	+4	+13	+3	+13	+2
18	Change stocks	0	−6	−1	0	−3	−5	+2	+2	+10	−2	+1	0
				Specific Series:	*New Orders, Trend Adjusted*								
19	Business cycles			−12	−4			−10	−7	−20	−4	−11	−2
20	Subcycles	−8[r]	−8[r]	−12	−4	−7	−14	−10	−7	−20	−4	−11	−2
21	Change ownership	+2	0	+1	+7	+1	−3	+1	+4	+1	+1	+1	+2
22	Change outstanding orders	+4	+2	+2	+15	+1	−1	+1	+4	+2	+3	+3	+2
23	Change sales	+3	0	0	−1	+2	0	−1	+7	+10	0	+1	+1

(continued)

TABLE 22 (concluded)

Section B: Average Timing of Turns

Line	Reference Series[c]	Number Matched			Median[e]			Average Deviation[f]		All Turns		Section C: Percentage of Months in Like Phase[d]	
		−	+	0	P	T	All	P	T		Wt'd	Timing Adjustment[g]	% Mos. 7/46– 12/61[d]
							Specific Series: Sales						
1	Business cycles	7	1	0	−1.0	−2.5	−1.5	0.8	1.8	1.5	1.2	−1, −2	92
2	Subcycles	9	1	0	−1.0	−4.0	−1.5	0.6	3.8	2.5	2.2	−1, −2	83
3	Ownership	6	4	0	−0.3	−2.0	−1.0	2.7	2.6	2.7	2.7	−1	80
4	Stocks	9	1	0	−2.3	−5.0	−3.0	2.1	3.6	3.0	2.9	−3	80
							Specific Series: Receipts						
5	Business cycles	8	0	0	−4.5	−3.5	−3.5	3.0	1.8	2.2	2.4	−3, −4	80
6	Subcycles	12	0	0	−4.5	−3.5	−3.5	2.8	2.3	2.6	2.6	−3, −4	83
7	Sales	5	1	4	−2.7	−0.3	−0.5	2.9	1.7	2.5	2.3	0, −1	81
8	Outstanding orders	2	6	4	+1.5	0	+0.5	1.0	1.5	1.4	1.2	0, +1	91
9	Change stocks	1	9	2	+2.0	+0.5	+1.0	2.8	1.0	2.1	1.9	+1	87
							Specific Series: New Orders						
10	Business cycles	8	0	0	−7.5	−4.0	−5.0	3.5	1.2	2.9	2.4	−4, −5	81
11	Subcycles	12	0	0	−7.5	−5.5	−7.0	2.5	3.2	2.8	2.8	−7	82
12	Sales	7	0	3	−6.7	−0.7	−1.5	3.5	0.7	3.1	2.1	−1, −2	81
13	Receipts	7	0	5	−2.0	−0.5	−1.5	2.0	2.2	2.2	2.1	−1, −2	86
14	Ownership	9	0	3	−3.0	−4.5	−4.5	3.2	2.2	2.7	2.7	−4, −5	83
15	Change ownership	1	10	1	+3.5	+1.5	+2.0	4.0	2.5	3.2	3.2	+2	79
16	Outstanding orders	7	1	4	−0.3	−3.5	−1.3	2.0	2.0	2.5	2.2	−1	84
17	Change outstanding orders	1	11	0	+4.5	+2.5	+3.5	4.0	3.2	3.8	3.6	+4	76
18	Change stocks	5	4	3	+0.5	−1.0	0	2.8	2.5	2.7	2.7	0	83
							Specific Series: New Orders, Trend Adjusted						
19	Business cycles	8	0	0	−11.5	−4.0	−8.5	2.8	1.2	4.5	2.0	−8, −9	73
20	Subcycles	12	0	0	−10.5	−5.5	−8.0	3.0	3.2	3.6	3.1	−8	77
21	Change ownership	1	10	1	+1.0	+1.5	+1.0	0.2	2.5	1.3	1.3	+1	91
22	Change outstanding orders	1	11	0	+2.0	+2.5	+2.0	0.8	3.2	2.0	2.0	+2	87
23	Change sales	2	6	4	+1.5	0	+0.5	2.5	1.5	2.2	2.0	0, +1	85

Notes to Table 22

[a]Specific series are matched with the indicated reference series (see note c) in accordance with the standard NBER rules. A double relaxation of rules is marked r; it applies to cases for well-conforming series in which two like turns are matched, though an unlike turn lies between them. The figure is underlined when subcycle chronology is the reference series, a minor cycle in the specific series has entered a comparison; or, when two individual series are compared, a minor cycle in either series has entered a comparison. When the business cycle chronology provides the reference, minor specific cycle turns are ignored. The meaning of other symbols is:

⊕ turn in the reference series does not appear in the specific series.
Ω turn in the specific series does not appear in the reference series.
⊙ there is no turn in either series in the neighborhood of the chronology date.

[b]Chronology dates are business cycle reference dates. In addition, four minor subcycle dates, enclosed in parentheses, are added to form a subcycle chronology.

[c]Reference series are of three sorts: (1) the business cycle chronology as shown in column heads, excluding the dates in parentheses; (2) the subcycle chronology as shown in all column heads; (3) particular series whose specific cycles and minor cycles constitute the reference dates for the comparison.

[d]The number of months during which the specific series is in like phase with the reference series is expressed as a percentage of the total number of months covered between dates as given.

[e]Median is the average timing of the center two or three turns.

[f]Average deviation from the median. The "weighted" (wt'd) average is the deviation from the median for peaks and for troughs separately, weighted by the number of turns.

[g]In determining months in like phase a timing adjustment is made which maximizes confluence. Before counting the months in phase, the specific series is in effect moved to the right to allow for a lead and to the left to allow for a lag if by so doing the percentage of months in like phase (as rounded) is increased. If the months in phase are as large or larger without an adjustment, this is indicated by a "timing adjustment" of 0.

In some cases we wish to know the percentage of months in phase on a synchronous basis, regardless of whether the percentage in phase is thereby maximized. If so, the "timing adjustment" is given as "none."

lead is two months. The characteristic lead is also displayed in Chart 8: the crosses mark the turns in orders and the dots those in sales. The dashed line always forms the upper boundary and the solid line the lower boundary of the blackened areas, the times when ownership is accumulating. Incidentally, the turns are marked in the series prior to the double smoothing to which the plotted lines have been subjected.

It is of special interest to note when and how the orders that retailers place with suppliers exceed their sales to consumers and vice versa. It is these crossovers that determine the direction of change in ownership. When orders exceed sales, consumer demand is in some sense augmented as it moves back to earlier stages of production; when they are less than sales, the reverse is the case. New orders, starting from a depressed level, begin to rise a bit earlier or at the same time as sales (Table 22, line 12). They soon catch up with sales and consequently ownership starts to rise (line 3). As prosperity develops, orders continue to rise and move promptly to a substantial excess over sales (the black areas in Chart 8 widen). But this does not last long without at least temporary interruption. In two cycles, the interruption was followed by a sharp drop in orders; in two others, the course of sales and orders was roughly parallel for a while. Before business expansion or consumer buying nears its peak, new orders start to recede from their currently high level. Their peaks lead those of sales by seven months, on the average (line 12). By the time sales begin to decline, new orders have been cut to the level of sales. As a result, ownership declines; and note please it does so within just one month of the peak of sales on all but one occasion (line 3). New orders then move rapidly to substantial deficiency early in recession.

The extent to which new orders placed with suppliers exceed or fall short of sales to consumers is a measure of the whip that backward transmission of demand generates. It is depicted by the width of the shaded or white areas that separate orders from sales. These differences, by definition the rate of change in ownership, are plotted up and down from the zero line and on a larger scale (bottom curve).[1] They are, of course, and the chart brings this out, heavily affected by the shapes of the banks in new orders and sales, as well as by their timing at turns. More particularly, since sales move serenely and new orders with far more agitation, the difference between the two series tends to parallel new orders. It therefore persistently leads sales, and also tends to lead new orders. Line 15 of Table 22 shows that change in ownership leads those of new orders at every turn but two. The average lead is 3.5 months at peaks in new orders and a bit less at troughs.

The time when the orders received by suppliers of department stores reach their peak and start to decline has important bearing on the process of cyclical fluctuation. Accordingly, it is interesting to know whether these turns, which are not, as we have seen, regularly or closely associated with sales are associated with changes in one or more of the stock series. Lines 15, 17, and 18 of the table show that changes in stock on hand seem to have the most systematic relationship; 83 per cent of the months are in like phase on a synchronous basis. But apparently the picture is confused by the upward trend in new orders associated, no doubt, with the upward trend in sales. Abstracting from this trend,[2] change in ownership (leading one month) and new orders are in phase 91 per cent of the months (line 21). The peaks in new orders occur almost precisely one month after those in change in ownership as recorded by a five-month centered average for end-of-month data. It would be synchronous with such an average based on beginning-month data.

Stocks and Outstandings and Their Bounding Flows

The relation between buying by retailers and buying by consumers, which results in changes in ownership, needs to be viewed in two segments: the relation between buying by retailers and their receipts of the merchandise, which results in changes in outstandings, the top pair of lines in Chart 8; and the relation between the receipt of merchandise and its sales to consumers, which results in changes in stocks, the second pair of lines. Judging from the top set of curves, new orders placed by retailers start to exceed current receipts of merchandise in the middle or last quarter of recessions; the excess begins to reverse after about a year of business expansion has passed. This is simply another way of calling attention to the early turns and brief thrusts of expansion in outstanding orders. The second set of curves shows that receipts start somewhat more tardily to exceed consumer buying—more nearly as contraction ends—and the excess persists well into the following contraction. The two sets of comparisons taken together seem to show how the bulge of excess procurement squeezes along in time. It starts in outstanding orders, moves to desired stocks, and ends, as expansion terminates (and here we interpolate possible motive), in undesired stock accumulations.

---

[1] In addition to the difference in scale, some lack of precise correspondence is due to the fact that new orders and sales, as shown in the interlaced curves, have been smoothed by a five-month moving average. Differences in seasonal corrections may also account for minor variations.

[2] A straight line was fitted visually on semilogarithmic paper. The trend is thus that of a uniform rate of change.

As in the case of change in ownership and the inlet stream, new orders, change in stock on hand likewise has a close timing association with its inlet stream, receipts. Looked at the other way, the turns in receipts reflect those of inventory investment one or two months earlier. Eighty-seven per cent of the months are in like phase after allowing for a one-month lead, but the figure does not do credit to the closeness of the association because of one very long lead (Table 22, line 9). All turns are matched, and of the twelve comparisons ten are within two months of one another.

Change in outstanding orders leads new orders, its inlet stream, quite substantially and does not have a close association with it (line 17). A trend correction for new orders, however, improves the association if a two-month lead is allowed for; 87 per cent of the months are then in like phase (line 22). Change in outstanding orders and receipts, its outlet stream, is predisposed to inverse association, but this is still poorer than is its direct association with new orders.

However, one interesting relation between outstandings and receipts does exist. It is between outstandings proper and receipts. Line 8 shows that 91 per cent of the months are in like phase either on a synchronous basis or with outstandings leading one month. This could perhaps reflect a vestibule effect. But there is another explanation that will be suggested later.

I do not know just what conclusions to draw from these relations between change in stocks and their inflow streams. If the trend adjustment is accepted as appropriate, they are close; change in stock and receipts are close in any event.[3] Of course, at a causal level, the similarities between the inflow series and the change in reservoirs for which sales are the outflow could, as noted earlier, express nothing more than an arithmetic of frenetic orders and relatively smooth sales.

But in any event it has further implication. We have seen that if new orders fluctuate, so will the rates of change in ownership. But consider the converse of this fact: retailers for whatever reason wish to increase or decrease a rate of change in stocks on hand, or the volume of goods on order. The orders they place with their suppliers tend to show an absolute increase or decrease, even if sales to consumers do not. A change in these sales orders received by retailers' suppliers may well influence their production schedules and perhaps communicate to the next stage, that of suppliers' suppliers.

AMPLITUDE

New orders placed by retailers are obviously far more cyclically unstable than are retail sales, the orders placed by consumers. This means that cyclical instability generates within the process whereby retailers decide how much to buy, given the amount that they sell. It is desirable to learn the quantitative importance of the amplification. But how can it be measured?

For the period 1946–61, the average specific cycle amplitude of retailers' orders was a rise or fall per month of ±1.38 per cent of the

[3] The trend adjustment here raises the question whether it ought not to be used for other comparisons. However, it is interesting that the trend adjustment has much stronger influence on the timing of peaks in new orders than in sales or receipts. The reason is doubtless the tendency for new orders to rise heavily in the early stages of expansion; further rise is therefore frequently supported chiefly by the trend increase. For sales the trend adjustment would reveal flat tops, but whether the dates of turns would change depends on the subtleties of the trend adjustment. For receipts, only the turn associated with the 1957 cycle peak would clearly be changed by a trend adjustment. Making the changes leaves change in stock in phase with receipts 93 per cent of the months after allowing for a one-month lag of receipt.

These facts have the provocative corollary that if trend adjustment had been made for all series, new orders would have had a stronger lead relative to sales and to receipts than now appears.

TABLE 23

Average Cycle Amplitude of Sales, Orders, and Receipts,
Department Stores, Cycle Relatives,[a] 1946-60

Date of First and Last Peak or Trough (1)	Total Per Phase			Per Month[b]		
	Rises (2)	Falls (3)	Both[c] (4)	Rises (5)	Falls (6)	Both[c] (7)
Specific Cycles						
1. Sales 7/49 to 1/61	13.0	−5.5	9.2	.46	−.84	.54
2. Receipts 6/47 to 12/60	18.4	−12.6	15.5	.85	−1.16	.96
3. New orders 10/46 to 12/60	28.3	−18.9	23.5	1.31	−1.52	1.38
Reference Cycles						
4. Sales 10/49 to 2/61	11.5	−.4	6.0	.33	−.04	.26
5. Receipts 10/49 to 2/61	11.9	−1.9	6.9	.34	−.18	.30
6. New orders 10/49 to 2/61	9.2	1.1	4.1	.26	.10	.18

[a]Source: Standard National Bureau business cycle analyses. Cycle relatives are amplitudes expressed as a percentage of the average standing of the series during each cycle.

[b]The averages are the sum of all rises (or falls) divided by the sum of all months of rising (or falling) phase.

[c]Sum of conforming minus nonconforming amplitude divided by the number of phases (column 4) or by the number of months from the initial to terminal turn (column 7).

average level of orders. The corresponding figure for sales was ±.54 per cent. Table 23 gives the figures in the last column. Thus sales were about 40 per cent as unstable as orders. The rate of change in ownership was somehow involved in this difference, but the arithmetic of the involvement is ambiguous unless orders and sales are compared for identical dates. Then, for each interval, the rise (or fall) in new orders is equal to the rise (or fall) in retail sales plus the positive (or negative) increase in the rate of change in ownership.[4] Table 24 summarizes various ways of marking off intervals that seem meaningful in the context of the process of vertical transmission of fluctuations. Subsequent tables indicate how the calculations were made. It has been convenient for this purpose to work with

dollar figures rather than with the cycle relatives. Specific cycle amplitudes averaged $1.75 million for sales and $3.53 million for orders (line 1, columns 9 and 10)—just about twice as much as sales (column 12).

One way to mark off significant periods is by a chronology of peaks and troughs of major business fluctuation. During this standard reference scheme, new orders rose and fell less on the average than did retail sales, ±$.88 million per month on the average compared with ±$1.35 million for retail sales, Table 24, line 2. The reason is that new orders turn early and therefore have lost altitude by the time the business peak occurs, and have gained it by the time the trough occurs.

Our notions of cyclical fluctuations and their chronology focus on the major economic activity of the nation. New orders anticipate activity and therefore exert their inflence in a cycle that casts its shadow before. The third

---

[4] This may be an increase in a positive rate, a decrease in a negative rate, or the algebraic sum of a positive rate minus a negative rate.

TABLE 24

Average Monthly Amplitude of Sales and Orders During Variously Selected Periods, Department Stores, 1947-61

Basis of Defining Phase	Rise During Expansion Phases[a]				Fall During Contraction Phases[a]				Rise or Fall, All Phases[a]			
	$ Millions per Month		Sales as % of Orders	Orders as % of Sales	$ Millions per Month		Sales as % of Orders	Orders as % of Sales	$ Millions per Month		Sales as % of Orders	Orders as % of Sales
	Sales	Orders			Sales	Orders			Sales	Orders		
	(1)	(2)	(3)	(4)	(5)	(6)	(7)	(8)	(9)	(10)	(11)	(12)
1. Specific cycles in each series	1.60	3.33	48	208	2.38	3.87	61	163	1.75	3.53	50	202
2. Reference cycles	1.46	1.24	118	85	1.10	0			1.35	.88	153	65
3. Reference cycles with 6-months lead	1.20	1.44	83	120	.40	.67	60	165	.97	1.22	80	125
4. Periods of thrust[b]	1.59	2.87	55	180								
5. Specific cycles in orders	1.63	3.33	49	204	.49	3.87	13	790	1.21	3.53	34	291
6. Selected periods of accelerating rise or fall in ownership[c]	2.54	5.83	44	230	1.50	5.50	27	367	2.37	5.78	41	244

[a]Amplitudes are based on standings calculated as five-month averages centered on first and last month of each phase. Averages are the sum of the rises during expansion phases (falls during contraction phases) divided by the number of months in all expansion (contraction) phases.

[b]"Periods of thrust" begin six months before business cycle troughs and continue to the first subcycle peak or hesitation. See Table 25.

[c]From Table 26. Expansion phases starting in the neighborhood of each business cycle trough; contraction phases starting in the neighborhood of each business cycle peak; 41 months of three expansion phases and 8 months of two contraction phases.

line of Table 24 assumes that the shadow is six months long and compares the amplitude of sales and new orders using this uniformly predated business cycle chronology. The monthly amplitude of orders is now somewhat greater than that of sales for each cycle, and it averages 125 per cent of it; that is, the orders received by suppliers add an additional whip of about 25 per cent to the average monthly fluctuation of retail sales during cycles starting or ending half a year before cyclical peaks or troughs. It is much greater during contraction (165 per cent) than during expansions (120 per cent).

But we have noted in many contexts that, characteristically, materials buying spurts during the early months of expansion and then levels off at least for a while. During these periods of first thrusts, new orders will reflect the spurts. The fourth line in the table measures the rise from six months prior to business cycle troughs to the end of the period dated (as described in earlier chapters) by using the minor turns of a subcycle chronology and adding two extra dates which seem to represent some general hesitation in business prosperity. During these periods, orders placed by department stores rose 180 per cent of the rise of their sales (Table 24, line 4, column 4). The details of how this figure is arrived at are presented in Table 25, and in columns 4 and 5 we see that 61 of the 105 months of expansion are included in the early thrust as defined. During these periods new orders rose at the rate of $2.87 million per month, whereas sales rose by $1.59 million per month (Table 25, columns 9 and 13, or Table 24, line 4, columns 1 and 2). Though in each case the rate of rise was substantially higher than during all the months of reference expansion (lines 2 or 3, Table 24), it was particularly so for new orders. Again, then, we see the picture of the heavy influence of the inventory-purchasing syndrome early in expansion and, as indicated in the previous paragraph, during contraction. The figures suggest orders of magnitude.

Another way of defining intervals of interest is by asking what portion of the notoriously large specific cycle fluctuation in orders is a direct reflection of contemporaneous fluctuation in consumer buying; the rest, by definition, is associated with change in ownership. Line 5 of Table 24 gives the summary figures which are shown cycle by cycle in Table 26. Department store orders rose or fell by $3.53 million per month on the average during their specific cycle phases. Between the identical calendar dates, retail sales rose or fell on the average by $1.21 million per month (Table 26, columns 6 and 7, bottom line, or Table 24, columns 9 and 10, line 5). Thus, of the total specific fluctuation in orders, 34 per cent directly reflected fluctuation in consumer buying and the rest, 66 per cent, fluctuation in the rate of change in ownership. In other words, the whip in new orders was almost three times that of sales (291 per cent), Table 26, column 8, bottom line. The other figures in columns 6 to 8 make a further suggestion: the whip for both expansion and contraction decreased over the interwar years that have been examined. The figures seem to indicate that most of the notable instability of new orders is a direct reflection not of contemporaneous instability in sales to the final consumer but of a tendency for retailers' buying to be either greater or less than their sales.

It would be useful to know how sellers and buyers respond to the associated changes in ownership. It seems inevitable that when there is a thirst for goods, reflected in a rise of ownership and at an accelerating rate, this would express and convey optimistic expectations. Corresponding remarks apply to the pessimistic implications of decline at an accelerating rate. Whether this is also the case after the rise or fall in ownership has slackened is perhaps more doubtful. Of particular interest are the months close to business cycle troughs when ownership starts to rise at an accelerating rate, or close to business cycle peaks when ownership starts to decline at an accelerating rate. At these times, the

TABLE 25

Amplitude During Reference Cycle Phases Predated Six Months and Periods of First Subcycle Expansion Sales and New Orders, Department Stores, 1946-62

| Reference Dates, Predated Six Months | | | Sales | | | | | | New Orders | | | | | |
Trough (1)	Peak (2)	Sub peak[a] (3)	Interval (months) Trough to: Peak (4)	Sub-peak (5)	Rise or Fall (−) ($ millions)[b] Total Phase Cycle (6)	Sub (7)	Per Month Cycle (6÷4) (8)	Sub (7÷5) (9)	Rise or Fall (−) ($ millions)[b] Total Phase Cycle (10)	Sub (11)	Per Month Cycle (12)	Sub (13)	New Orders As % of Sales Cycle (10÷6) (14)	Sub (11÷7) (15)
					Expansions									
4/49	1/53	2/51	45	22	38	33	0.84	1.50	52	67	1.16	3.05	136.8	203.0
2/54	1/57	12/55	35	22	56	46	1.60	2.09	52	61	1.49	2.77	92.9	132.6
10/57	11/59	3/59	25	17	32	18	1.28	1.06	47	47	1.88	2.76	146.9	261.1
Total			105	61	126	97			151	175				
Average[c]					42	32	1.20	1.59	50	58	1.44	2.87	119.8	180.4
					Contractions									
5/48	4/49		11		−17		−1.55		−10		−0.91		58.8	
1/53	2/54		13		−2		−0.15		−4		−0.31		200.0	
1/57	10/57		9		1		0.11		−3		−0.33		−300.0	
11/59	8/60		9		1		0.11		−11		−1.22		−1,100.0	
Total			42		−17				−28					
Average[c]					−4		−0.40		−7		−0.67		164.7	
					All Phases									
Total			147		143				179					
Average					20		±0.97		25		±1.22		125.2	

[a]For selection of dates see text.

[b]Standings are five-month averages of the data centered at the month of turn. Rises are standings at peak minus standings at previous trough; falls are standings at trough minus standings at previous peak.

[c]Total rise during expansion phases (falls during contraction phases) divided by the number of phases covered for average of phase amplitude (cols. 6, 7, 10, 11) and by number of months covered for average per month amplitude (cols. 8, 9, 12, 13).

general business climate would presumably be sensitive to whatever impact this set of influences might wield.

Table 27 puts the question to the data. The accelerating rises in ownership started close to business cycle troughs (note that most of the period of rise followed the cycle trough, column 5); they lasted twelve to sixteen months (column 3); unrelated episodes are in parenthesis. Accelerated decline likewise started virtually at the peaks but lasted only a few months, two to five (lower half of Table 27, columns 3–5). During the 41 months of accelerating rise in ownership, the rate of in-

TABLE 26

Amplitude of Sales and New Orders During Specific Cycles
of New Orders, Department Stores, 1946-60

Dates, Expansion in Orders		Interval (months)	Rise ($ millions)[a]				Total Phase
			Total Phase		Per Month		Orders as % of Sales
Trough	Peak		Sales	Orders	Sales	Orders	
(1)	(2)	(3)	(4)	(5)	(6)	(7)	(8)
			Expansions				
11/46[b]	10/47[b]	11	23	117	2.09	10.64	509
6/49	7/50	13	32	120	2.46	9.23	375
4/51	1/53	21	18	61	0.86	2.90	339
1/54	10/56	33	57	64	1.73	1.94	112
12/57	4/60	28	48	71	1.71	2.54	148
Total 10/47–4/60		95	155	316			
Average[c]			39	79	1.63	3.33	204[d]

Dates, Contraction in Orders		Interval (months)	Fall ($ millions)[a]				Total Phase
			Total Phase		Per Month		Orders as % of Sales
Peak	Trough		Sales	Orders	Sales	Orders	
(9)	(10)	(11)	(12)	(13)	(14)	(15)	(16)
			Contractions				
5/46[b]	11/46[b]	6	2	−115	0.33	−19.17	−5,750
10/47	6/49	20	−8	−66	−0.40	−3.30	825
7/50	4/51	9	−7	−118	−0.78	−13.11	1,686
1/53	1/54	12	−4	−10	−0.33	−0.83	250
10/56	12/57	14	−8	−19	−0.57	−1.36	200
Total 10/47–4/60		55	−27	−213			
Average			−7	−53	−0.49	−3.87	789[d]
			All Phases				
Total 10/47–4/60		150	182	529			
Average[c]			23	66	1.21	3.53	291[d]

[a]Five-month average centered at the month of peak minus five-month average centered at the month of trough. Thus rises have a positive and falls a negative sign.

[b]To make these calculations comparable with others in the series, these phases are omitted from the averages.

[c]Averages are total rise or fall divided by number of phases or total number of months.

[d]Average per phase for orders divided by sales.

TABLE 27

Amplitude of Sales and Orders During Selected Periods of Accelerating Rise or Fall in Ownership, Department Stores, 1947-61

		Duration (months)			Sales Change ($ millions)[b]		New Orders Change ($ millions)[b]		Change: Orders as % of Sales
			Relation to B.C. Trough[a]			Per Mo.		Per Mo.	
Start	End	Total	Before	After	Total	(6÷3)	Total	(8÷3)	(8÷6)
(1)	(2)	(3)	(4)	(5)	(6)	(7)	(8)	(9)	(10)
				Periods of Accelerating Rise					
(6/47)[d]	(10/47)	(4)	⊕	⊕	(+9)	(+2.25)	(+57)	(+14.25)	(633.3)
6/49	6/50	12	4	8	+25	+2.08	+120	+10.00	480.0
(11/51)	(8/52)	(9)	⊕	⊕	(+5)	(+0.56)	(+40)	(+4.44)	(800.0)
6/54	10/55	16	2	14	+40	+2.50	+61	+3.81	152.5
4/58	5/59	13	0	13	+39	+3.00	+58	+4.46	148.7
Total, Selected Periods[c]		41			+104		+239		
Average[d]					+35	+2.54	+80	+5.83	229.8
				Periods of Accelerating Fall					
			Relation to B.C. Peak[e]						
		Total	Before	After					
(12/47)	(11/48)	(11)	(11)	(0)	(+6)	(+0.55)	(−32)	(−2.91)	(−533.3)
(3/51)	(7/51)	(4)	⊕	⊕	(−18)	(−4.50)	(−75)	(−18.75)	(−416.7)
6/53	9/53	3	1	2	−3	−1.00	−16	−5.33	−533.3
6/57	11/57	5	1	4	−9	−1.80	−28	−5.60	−311.1
Total, Selected Periods[c]		8			−12		−44		
Average[d]					−6	−1.50	−22	−5.50	−366.7
				Periods of Rise And Fall					
Total, Selected Periods		49			116	2.37	283		
Average[d]					23	2.37	57	5.78	244.0

[a]The interval (column 3) is broken into the segments preceding and following the associated business cycle trough dates. The starting dates of the period (as per column 1) and the cycle trough dates, respectively, are: 6/49, 10/49, 6/54, 8/54; 4/58, 4/58.

[b]Five-month average centered at the month of peak minus five-month average centered at the month of trough. Thus rises have a positive and falls a negative sign.

[c]Selected for inclusion are those periods of rise that start close to business cycle troughs and those periods of fall that start close to business cycle peaks. Episodes for which figures are enclosed in parentheses do not conform to this principle. They are not included in the totals or averages but are shown for the purpose of comparison (contraction 12/47 to 11/48 was excluded because it was too early to be conforming).

[d]Averages are total rise or fall divided by number of phases or number of months.

[e]The total interval is broken into the segments preceding and following the associated business cycle peak dates. The starting dates of the period (as per column 1) and the cycle peak dates, respectively, are: 12/47, 11/48; 6/53, 7/53; 6/57, 7/57.

crease in new orders was exceedingly high, $5.83 million per month, much higher, of course, than for the whole stretch of specific cycles in new orders which averaged $3.53 million per month (Table 24, line 1). For retail sales the corresponding figures were far lower, $2.54 million, which was nevertheless much faster than the average specific cycle amplitude of $1.75 million per month (Table 24, line 1).

For these periods, then, which last for about a year after business troughs, and which also on occasions have given a second thrust later in expansion, orders shot way ahead of sales, though sales themselves were rising relatively swiftly. The average whip was 230 per cent. Reversing the comparison (Table 24, line 6, col. 3), 44 per cent of the fluctuation in new orders during these periods is directly associated with current sales. Accordingly, 56 per cent was associated with the rate of change in ownership and therefore in some sense a reflection of the inventory-purchasing complex.

SUMMARY

In conclusion, it seems clear that changes in stockpiles are strongly reflected in the contours of the stream that feeds them. This appears in the similarity of the timing of turns and the slight leads that change in stock tends to have. But the more significant manifestation, from the point of view of the impact of the "inventory cycle" on economic events, is the large increase in amplitude that occurs. Clearly retailers' stocking and procurement procedures amplify fluctuation in final demand as it moves toward their suppliers.

There is no single answer to how much amplification takes place. Perhaps the simplest measurement compares the intrinsic fluctuations in retailers' selling and buying; that of buying is over twice as large. But the strong lead in orders placed by retailers, relative to their sales to final consumers, means that the whip effect precedes the turns in business. Characteristically the time when the backward fillip to demand generated by buying procedures is greatest started close to the trough in business and continued for about a year. The depressant influence was greatest during months close to business cycle peaks and for a while thereafter. During these periods new orders placed with suppliers rose or fell almost two and a half times as rapidly as sales to consumers.

8. Stocks and Adjacent Flows, Durable Goods Manufacturers

The reservoir, manufacturers' stocks of purchased materials, is filled by the flow of goods received at the loading docks (receipts); it is drained by the flow of "raw" materials into the first stage of processing (utilization). For outstanding orders, the bounding flows are net new orders placed with suppliers as inlet and receipts as outlet. For ownership they are new orders and utilizations respectively. To picture the relation between the two bounding flows and the stock reservoir, it is necessary to have the triplicate of information for the same firms and in identical units. Unfortunately neither criterion can be met for materials ownership of all durable goods manufacturers.[1]

Only for one segment of ownership, changes in materials stocks on order, is a consistent triplet of information available. Hypothetically, the purchasers are manufacturers of all durable goods, particularly of the final products, machinery and transportation equipment. The stockpool is their outstanding purchase orders for materials; the inlet, their new purchase orders, and the outlet, their receipts of materials. Actually, the statistics are those submitted by the seller rather than the purchaser; they are sales orders, shipments, and backlogs of sales orders for primary metals, fabricated metals, and "other" durables industries.[2] At least this one segment of ownership, then, outstanding orders for materials, can be submitted to examination along with the flows that bound it. It constitutes, it will be recalled, the lion's share of total materials ownership.

TIMING AND CONTOURS

The upper set of the interlaced lines in Chart 9 shows the two flow series, new orders placed for and receipts of materials by durable goods manufacturers. New orders smoothed by a five months' average, is the dashed line which always lies above the blackened areas. The crosses mark the turns in the monthly data (not in the charted smoothed series).

New orders had a strong extra movement during the Korean War. The postwar phantom recession was evidenced only by a sharp flattening followed by a sharp rise which was not marked as a specific movement. As Table 28 shows, new orders systematically lead business cycle turns (lines 8 and 9). Receipts at first synchronize and later lead business cycles (lines 1 and 2). Their association with new orders (line 10) is that of a systematic lag which averages five months at peaks and two months at troughs. Allowing for an average lag of four months, 90 per cent of the months are in like phase.

New orders are cyclically more volatile than

---

[1] The difficulties derive from the fact that all information on orders and shipments concern the *sales* of reporting firms. The problems were discussed in Chapter 3, particularly notes 8 and 9. There is no information on utilization and production starts, nor can it be constructed from presently available data.

[2] The extent to which the actual and hypothetical requirements meet is considered in Chapter 3, note 8.

CHART 9

Receipts, Orders, and Change in Outstanding Orders, Durable Goods Manufacturers, 1946–64

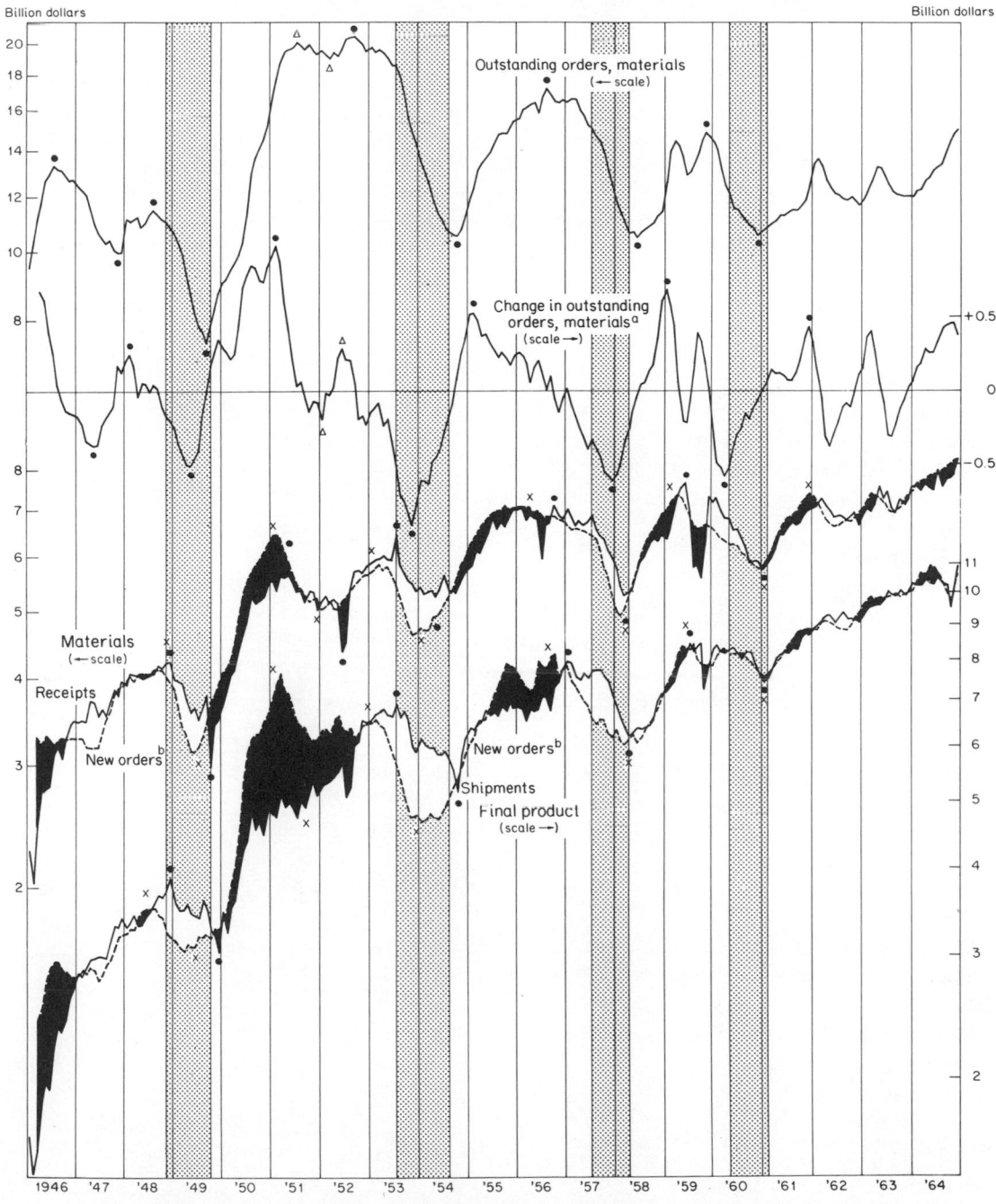

Note: Shaded areas represent business contractions. Specific cycle turns are marked by X and by dots in shipments, receipts, and ownership.

a Centered five-month average of month-to-month change.   b Five-month moving average centered; turning points are marked for underlying monthly data.

TABLE 28

Timing: Receipts and New Orders, Durable Goods Manufacturers, 1946–61

| | | Section A: Months Lead (−) or Lag (+) for Matched Turns[a] | | | | | | | | | | |
| | | Chronology[b] | | | | | | | | | | |
Line	Reference Series[c]	P (1/47)	T (7/47)	P 11/48	T 10/49	P (2/51)	T 6/52	P 7/53	T 8/54	P 7/57	T 4/58	P 5/60	T 2/61

Specific Series: Receipts, Materials*

Line	Reference Series	P (1/47)	T (7/47)	P 11/48	T 10/49	P (2/51)	T 6/52	P 7/53	T 8/54	P 7/57	T 4/58	P 5/60	T 2/61
1	Business cycles			+1	0			0	−3	−9	−1	−11	−1
2	Subcycles	⊕	⊕	+1	0	+3	0	0	−3	−9	−1	−11	−1
3	Outstanding orders, mat.	⊕	⊕	+4	+1	<u>−2</u>	<u>+3</u>	+10	−5	+2	−3	−5	+1
4	Change in outstanding orders	⊙	⊕	+10	+5	+3	<u>+5[r]</u>	<u>+13[r]</u>	+6	+20	+3	+5	+9
5	Change material stocks, all dur.	⊕	⊕	+1	+5	+7	+1	+1	−1	+6	−2	+2	+4
6	Shipments, final product†	⊙	⊙	0	−2	Ω	Ω	0	−5	−3	−1	−1	0
7	Change in outstanding orders, materials inverse	⊕	⊕	−5	−16	<u>−8</u>	<u>0</u>	−4	−9	−14	−10	−10	−11

Specific Series: New Orders, Materials*

Line	Reference Series	P (1/47)	T (7/47)	P 11/48	T 10/49	P (2/51)	T 6/52	P 7/53	T 8/54	P 7/57	T 4/58	P 5/60	T 2/61
8	Business cycles			0	−3			−6	−7	−15	−1	−15	−1
9	Subcycles	⊕	⊕	0	−3	−1	−6	−6	−7	−15	−1	−15	−1
10	Receipts, materials	⊙	⊙	−1	−3	−4	−6	−6	−4	−6	0	−4	0
11	New orders final product†	⊙	⊙	+5	+1	0	<u>+3</u>	<u>+1</u>	+1	−4	−1	−4	0
12	Shipments, final product†	⊙	⊙	−1	−5	Ω	Ω	−6	−9	−9	−1	−5	0
13	Change ownership	⊙	⊕	+9	+2	−1	<u>−1</u>	<u>+7</u>	+2	+14	+2	+1	+9
14	Change material stocks, all dur.	⊕	⊕	0	+2	+3	−5	−5	−5	0	−2	−2	+4
15	Change in outstanding orders, materials	⊙	⊕	+9	+2	−1	<u>−1</u>	<u>+7</u>	+2	+14	+3	+1	+9
16	Shipments, all durables	⊙	⊙	−1	−3	<u>−2</u>	<u>−7</u>	−6	−9	−9	−1	−4	0
17	Outstanding orders mat.	⊕	⊕	+3	−2	<u>−6</u>	<u>−3</u>	+4	−9	−4	−3	−9	+1

(continued)

TABLE 28 (concluded)

Section B: Average Timing of Turns

		Number Matched			Median[e]			Average Deviation[f]		All Turns		Section C: Percentage of Months in Like Phase[d]		
Line	Reference Series[c]	−	+	0	P	T	All	P	T	Wt'd	Timing Adjust-ment[g]	% Mos. 7/46– 12/61	% Mos. 1/48– 12/61

Specific Series: Receipts, Materials*

Line	Reference Series	−	+	0	P	T	All	P	T		Wt'd	Timing Adjustment	% Mos. 7/46–12/61	% Mos. 1/48–12/61
1	Business cycles	5	1	2	−4.5	−1.0	−1.0	5.2	0.8	3.0	3.0	−1	79	76
2	Subcycles	5	2	3	−2.7	−0.7	−0.5	5.3	0.9	2.9	3.1	0, −1	81	83
3	Outstanding orders, mat.	4	6	0	+1.3	−0.3	+1.0	4.3	2.7	3.4	3.5	+1	73	80
4	Change outstanding orders	0	10	0	+9.3	+5.3	+5.5	5.1	1.5	3.7	3.3	+5, +6	74	78
5	Change materials stocks, all dur.	2	8	0	+3.0	+1.3	+1.5	2.4	2.5	2.4	2.4	+1, +2	79	85
6	Shipments, final product†	5	0	3	−0.5	−1.5	−1.0	1.0	1.5	1.2	1.2	−1	88	86
7	Change in outstanding orders, materials inverse	9	0	1	−7.7	−10.0	−9.5	3.1	3.6	3.5	3.3	−9, −10	76	78

Specific Series: New Orders, Materials*

Line	Reference Series	−	+	0	P	T	All	P	T		Wt'd	Timing Adjustment	% Mos. 7/46–12/61	% Mos. 1/48–12/61
8	Business cycles	7	0	1	−10.5	−2.0	−4.5	6.0	2.0	4.8	4.0	−4, −5	74	71
9	Subcycles	9	0	1	−7.3	−2.7	−4.5	6.1	2.2	4.3	4.2	−4, −5	74	74
10	Receipts, mat.	8	0	2	−4.7	−2.3	−4.0	1.5	2.1	1.8	1.8	−4	90	89
11	New orders final product†	3	5	2	−1.0	+0.7	+0.5	3.0	1.1	2.0	2.3	0, +1	89	88
12	Shipments, final product†	7	0	1	−5.5	−3.0	−5.0	2.2	3.2	2.8	2.8	−5	82	80
13	Change ownership	2	8	0	+5.7	+2.0	+2.0	4.9	2.0	3.8	3.4	+2	73	77
14	Change materials stocks, all dur.	5	3	2	−0.7	−1.7	−1.0	2.1	3.3	2.8	2.7	−1, −2	77	83
15	Change in outstanding orders, materials	2	8	0	+5.7	+2.3	+2.5	4.9	2.3	3.9	3.6	+2	73	77
16	Shipments, all durables	9	0	1	−4.0	−3.7	−3.5	2.4	3.1	2.8	2.8	−3, −4	85	83
17	Outstanding orders mat.	7	3	0	−2.3	−2.7	−3.0	4.7	2.3	3.4	3.5	−3	73	80

Notes to Table 28

[a]Specific series are matched with the indicated reference series (see note c) in accordance with the standard NBER rules. A double relaxation of rules is marked r; it applies to cases for well-conforming series in which two like turns are matched, though an unlike turn lies between them. The figure is underlined when subcycle chronology is the reference series, a minor cycle in the specific series has entered a comparison; or, when two individual series are compared, a minor cycle in either series has entered a comparison. When the business cycle chronology provides the reference, minor specific cycle turns are ignored. The meaning of other symbols is:

⊕ turn in the reference series does not appear in the specific series.

℆ turn in the specific series does not appear in the reference series.

⊙ there is no turn in either series in the neighborhood of the chronology date.

[b]Chronology dates are business cycle reference dates. In addition, four minor subcycle dates, enclosed in parentheses, are added to form a subcycle chronology.

[c]Reference series are of three sorts: (1) the business cycle chronology as shown in column heads, excluding the dates in parentheses; (2) the subcycle chronology as shown in all column heads; (3) particular series whose specific cycles and minor cycles constitute the reference dates for the comparison.

[d]The number of months during which the specific series is in like phase with the reference series is expressed as a percentage of the total number of months covered between dates as given.

[e]Median is the average timing of the center two or three turns.

[f]Average deviation from the median. The "weighted" (wt'd) average is the deviation from the median for peaks and for troughs separately, weighted by the number of turns.

[g]In determining months in like phase a timing adjustment is made which maximizes confluence. Before counting the months in phase, the specific series is in effect moved to the right to allow for a lead and to the left to allow for a lag if by so doing the percentage of months in like phase (as rounded) is increased. If the months in phase are as large or larger without an adjustment, this is indicated by a "timing adjustment" of 0.

In some cases we wish to know the percentage of months in phase on a synchronous basis, regardless of whether the percentage in phase is thereby maximized. If so, the "timing adjustment" is given as "none."

*Receipts of or new orders for materials are actually shipments of or sales orders of the materials – producing durable goods industries.

†"Final products" refer to sales orders or shipments of machinery and transportation industries (final products).

receipts, and more because troughs are lower than because peaks are higher.[3]

New orders tend to fall below receipts beginning some months before the peak in business; they remain so throughout business recession. In the neighborhood of troughs, orders, having previously started to rise, begin to exceed receipts when, or shortly after, receipts themselves start to rise. Consequently the early thrusts in outstandings reflect the

faster rise of new orders when *both* receipts and orders are rising. The *cessation* of the first spurt in outstandings, on the other hand, does seem typically to be associated with an absolute fall in new orders. Corollary to these observations are those brought out in Chapter 4 concerning the strong lead of outstanding orders at business cycle peaks and closely synchronous behavior at troughs (Table 1, line 10 or 11).

The extent to which new orders are more unstable than receipts is traced by the second curve on Chart 9. It is the rate of change in outstandings.[4] Apparently the maximum rate

---

[3] It is an interesting question whether this rapid decline and depth of fall during recession may be related to cancellations. Unfortunately the matter has not, to my knowledge, been comprehensively studied. Statistics for cancellations are given for machine tools; these do not seem to show systematic clustering of cancellations around business troughs, though they do suggest a midcycle cluster in 1947 and 1951 (Moore (ed.), *Business Cycle Indicators*, pp. 450, 454).

[4] As in Chart 8, it represents the space between the new order and shipments curves with the difference measured up and down from zero. The measurement is approximate not merely because of the enlarged

of decline in outstandings tends to occur somewhat before the trough in new orders (Table 28, line 15). This means, as noted in an earlier chapter, that the rate of decline lessens while most economic events are still deteriorating. Conversely, the rate of rise reaches its maximum before new orders arrive at its first peak and when expansion is still young. Continued expansion may or may not result in a new lift in orders and an associated spurt in outstandings and their rate of change.

The rate of change in outstandings does not appear to have a systematic relation to the inflow or outflow series. Allowing for an average lead of two months, only 73 per cent of months are in like phase (line 15) with the inflow, new orders. Its relation to the outflow series, receipts, is unimpressive whether matched directly with a lead (line 4), or inversely (in accord with the arithmetic predisposition) with a long lag (line 7).

SALES AND PURCHASE ORDERS

It would be useful to trace the pattern of the sales orders of the same companies whose purchase orders we have just described. Such a comparison might indicate whether and in what form companies appear simply to pass on to their suppliers the pattern of the orders that they receive from their customers. This is, in effect, the sort of comparison that has been made for department stores.

Of course, we do not have the requisite information on sales orders for durable goods manufacturers. It would consist of the sales orders of producers of final products (which we do have) plus a part of the sales orders of materials manufacturers—the part that is not sold to producers of final products but to producers in the materials group. (This part is present in total durable goods orders but cannot be separated from the rest of the orders of the materials group.) Nevertheless, it may be useful to inspect for a moment the segment of the relevant total that can be isolated—those for manufacturers in the final products group. These sales orders can be viewed in association with shipments and change in backlogs (unfilled orders) for about the same companies. The second group of interlaced curves of Chart 9 display the two flow series.

scale, the smoothing for all of the three series, and differences in seasonal adjustments, but because orders and receipts are on a log scale and change in outstandings on an arithmetic scale.

The curves seem to suggest some very real parallelism between the sales and purchase data, and the visual judgment is supported in lines 6 and 11 of Table 28. Orders for materials lag those for final products in the early part, and lead after 1956; but even so, 89 per cent of months are in like phase on a synchronous basis. The two sets of shipments likewise have marked similarity in the timing of turns. But there is a clear difference in the progress of expansion. Shipments of materials increase vigorously during the first year or so of expansion, and then retard; in 1951 they even decreased for a while after the peak in the Korean boom had passed. Shipments of final products build up more gradually and persistently throughout their entire expansion phase. But a break with the past appeared after the 1959 peak. Then, shipments of final products declined very little; even new orders did not decline much before starting a slow steady climb. Materials on the other hand behaved in a more usual fashion.

The implications of these facts in terms of unfilled orders is displayed in the chart. To repeat, unfilled orders increase when the space between the lines is black, and the width of the black spaces shows the rate of increase; similar remarks apply to decreases and the white areas. The relatively even climb of shipments of final products in the face of early post-trough spurts in new orders generated huge backlogs not only at the time of the

Korean War but also, though more moderately, in 1946 and 1955–56.[5] This contrasts with the routinely far more agile response of receipts of materials to new orders. In the light of these precedents, it is particularly interesting to see the sharp break with the past that occurred in 1958, when virtually no build up of unfilled orders for final products took place, though materials outstanding seemed to behave in the usual fashion.

AMPLITUDE

In Chapter 6 specific cycles in the rate of change in unfilled materials orders were found to average $62.3 million a month, or about 1.1 per cent of the average level of shipments of materials. The significance attached to these figures in the context of vertical transmission of instability depends in part on how they compare with the severity of cyclical fluctuations in shipments and new orders. Accordingly, it will be useful to repeat the spate of measures reviewed in the previous chapter. However, here they have far more limited significance. For department stores, we could view a triad for which the bounding flows were purchases of consumers and purchases of the first commercial agent in the sequence. This difference bears on the way in which instability in consumer demand is augmented by economic processes.

[5] This chart shows the two sets of flow curves on a scale that reflects the *relative* size of fluctuations. It is on a logarithmic scale. The change in unfilled orders, shown by the width of the black and white spaces between the curves, is thus also scaled very roughly as a percentage of the level of each set of flow data which are not far from the same size. The two upper curves, on the other hand, the change in backlogs and materials orders, plotted up and down from a zero line, are scaled for visual similarity as required for Chart 6. Change in backlog is scaled down—if the scale for materials had been used, fluctuation would have been twice as large. Thus it is clear that the range of fluctuation in change in backlogs is much higher relative to shipments of final products than is change in outstandings relative to receipts of materials. This is indicated also by the wider areas of black and white (prior to 1958) for the bottom set of curves compared with the set for materials. Incidentally, the relation of rates of change in unfilled orders to the level of the data proper is quite another matter, since the average book value for unfilled orders of final products was about two and a quarter times that of materials.

For durables, we can compare only the materials received by durable goods manufacturers and the materials for which they currently place orders. The difference—change in outstanding orders—obviously has some bearing on the vertical generation of instability, though it is impossible to relate it to the broader context—the relation between sales and purchase orders for these firms. Nevertheless the narrow context is not without meaning, and the figures therefore require review.

Table 29 summarizes the group of calculations that correspond exactly to the calculations for department stores shown in Table 24; however we omit most of the supporting tables. Line 1 indicates (columns 9 and 10) that the average monthly specific cycle fluctuations in receipts is $72.9 million; for new orders it is $100.2 million, or 37 per cent higher. These figures express the intrinsic instability of each series. The problem is again to choose intervals, significant to the vertical transmission of fluctuation, during which rises and falls in orders and receipts and in changes in outstanding orders can be studied. The same alternatives for defining intervals are used here as previously.

During reference cycles, receipts fluctuate more than new orders and for much the same reasons that apply to department stores—new orders have a strong lead and are on their way down at reference peaks or up at troughs. Conversion of the reference chronology to one that hypothetically focuses on orders rather than outputs would involve earlier dating. Using the rough rule of thumb of a uniform six months' lead, new orders fluctuate more than receipts—about two-thirds again as much

TABLE 29

Per Month Amplitude of Receipts and Orders During Variously Selected Periods,
Materials Manufacturers, 1948-61

Basis of Defining "Phases"	Rise During Expansion Phases[a]				Fall During Contraction Phases[a]				Rises and Falls[a]			
	$ Millions Per Month		Receipts as % of Orders	Orders as % of Receipts	$ Millions Per Month		Receipts as % of Orders	Orders as % of Receipts	$ Millions Per Month		Receipts as % of Orders	Orders as % of Receipts
	Receipts	Orders			Receipts	Orders			Receipts	Orders		
	(1)	(2)	(3)	(4)	(5)	(6)	(7)	(8)	(9)	(10)	(11)	(12)
1. Specific cycles in each series	81.1	118.9	68	147	63.9	83.4	77	130	72.9	100.2	73	137
2. Reference cycles	48.1	37.4	128	78	78.3	49.1	159	62	56.7	40.8	139	72
3. Reference cycles with 6-month lead	35.0	49.4	71	141	33.5	76.4	44	228	34.5	57.1	60	165
4. Periods of thrust[b]	65.0	113.4	57	175								
5. Specific cycles in orders	75.0	118.9	63	159	45.3	83.4	54	184	59.5	100.2	59	172
6. Selected periods of accelerating rise or fall in outstandings[c]	105.3	165.6	64	157	22.2	91.6	24	413	64.2	129.1	50	201

[a]Amplitudes are based on standings calculated as five-month average centered on first and last month of each phase. Averages are the sum of rises during expansion phases divided by the sum of the months covered; for contractions, they are the sum of the falls during contraction phases divided by the sum of the months covered.

[b]For definition of periods of thrust see text.

[c]Expansion phases starting in the neighborhood of each business cycle trough; 42 months were covered in four phases. Contraction phases starting in the neighborhood of each business cycle peak; 41 months were covered in four contraction phases. See Table 30 for details.

(line 3, column 12). The whip is greater for contractions than for expansions (compare columns 4 and 8).

The characteristic early thrust in orders as contraction weakens is shown in line 4. Starting six months before the end of cyclical contraction and ending at the dates previously chosen to formalize the periods of thrust (61 months of the 105 months of reference expansion during the years 1948–61), orders rose three-quarters again as fast as did shipments (column 4).

One final question: What portion of total specific instability of orders was directly associated with receipts as opposed to changes in outstandings? Line 5, column 11, indicates that the answer is about 60 per cent. It is not too different for expansions and contractions.

This information is difficult to interpret, failing the companion piece of sales orders received and shipments by the firms whose purchase orders for, and receipts of, materials we view. For example, if these sales orders were complete counterparts, unit per unit, of the purchase orders, one might interpret the lesser fluctuation that characterizes receipts— that is, the materials shipments of suppliers— as a manifestation of some stabilization in vertical transmission of demand that was facilitated by the advance information that suppliers had received concerning what their customers would require. If, on the other hand, the sales orders were counterparts of materials received, something in the inventory-buying procedure would have passed back to suppliers information which, insofar as it influences production or other decisions, would have generated substantial additional instability.

In any event, it seems likely that the increasing or decreasing backlogs and the rate at which they change would in themselves have destabilizing attributes. At least, when backlogs are increasing at an increasing rate, this must convey a notion about developing market tensions and the possibility of impending shortages or price increases; conversely, when backlogs are decreasing at an increasing rate, buyers are likely to feel fortified in their ability to demand prompt delivery and favorable terms.

Table 30 details the calculations which are summarized in the last line of Table 29. In postwar years, periods of accelerating accumulation of backlogs by materials manufacturers occurred in the neighborhood of each cyclical trough. They appear as the widening areas of the first set of interlaced curves in Chart 9. They started one or two months before or after cyclical turns (upper section of column 4) and lasted five to eighteen months, averaging ten and a half months for four cycles (column 3). During these intervals, both new orders and receipts increased very rapidly— $165.6 million and $105.3 million per month respectively (Table 30, columns 9 and 7 or Table 29, line 6, columns 1 and 2). Nevertheless, the amplitude of receipts was only 64 per cent of the total increase in new orders; the other 36 per cent was therefore associated with increasing rate of accumulation of outstandings (Table 29, line 6, column 3).

The periods of accelerating decline, on the other hand, of which there were four averaging ten months each (Table 30, column 3, second section), tended to start well before the cyclical peaks in business (column 4). (Note where the white spaces between the curves in Chart 9 begin.) These were periods of rapid fall in new orders, but receipts declined relatively slightly or even increased. The rate at which receipts fell was a quarter of that of new orders (Table 30, line 6, column 7). Nevertheless, the decline in outstanding orders, backlogs of unfilled orders for the supplier, must itself imply weakness to come. For one thing, it changes the relative bargaining strength of buyer and seller. For another, it may carry needlessly pessimistic information insofar as firms with reduced backlogs order less materials and the firms that receive these orders are not in position to judge how much of the decline is associated with changes in the movement of goods and how much with reduction of backlogs.

SUMMARY, CHAPTERS 7 AND 8

This and the preceding chapter have examined the relation between changes in materials stocks on hand and on order and the flows of goods that constitute sales, receipts, or orders.

This triplicate of information helps to de-

TABLE 30

Amplitude of Receipts and Orders During Selected Periods of Accelerating Rise or Fall in Outstanding Orders, Materials Manufacturers, 1947/1961

Start (1)	End (2)	Duration (months) Total (3)	Relation to B.C. Trough[a] Before (4)	After (5)	Receipts Change (million dollars)[b] Total (6)	Per Mo. 6÷3 (7)	Orders Change (million dollars)[b] Total (8)	Per Mo. 8÷3 (9)	Change in Orders as % of Shipments 8÷6 (10)
Periods of Accelerating Rise									
(10/47)	(2/48)	(4)	⊕	⊕	(+246)	(+61.50)	(+258)	(+64.50)	(104.9)
8/49	2/51	18	2	16	+2,010	+111.67	+3,165	+175.83	157.5
(3/52)	(6/52)	(3)	⊕	⊕	(−261)	(−87.00)	(+14)	(+4.67)	(−5.4)
9/54	2/55	5		5	+461	+92.00	+958	+191.60	207.8
6/58	1/59	7		7	+876	+125.14	+1,230	+175.71	140.4
12/60	12/61	12	2	10	+1,076	+89.67	+1,604	+133.67	149.1
Total, Selected Periods[c]		42			+4,423		+6,957		
Averaged[d]		10.5			+1.106	+105.31	+1,739	+165.64	157.3

Periods of Accelerating Fall

Start	End	Total	Relation to B.C. Peak[e] Before	After	Total	Per Mo.	Total	Per Mo.	8÷6
9/48	5/49	8	2	6	−457	−57.12	−986	−123.25	215.8
(8/51)	(1/52)	(5)	⊕	⊕	(−167)	(−33.40)	(−388)	(−77.60)	(232.3)
9/52	11/53	14	10	4	(+113)	+8.07	−864	−61.71	—
9/56	12/57	15	10	5	−716	−47.73	−1,572	−104.80	219.6
12/59	4/60	4	4		+151	+37.75	−334	−83.50	—
Total, Selected Periods[c]		41			−909		−3,756		—
Averaged[d]		10.2			−227	−22.17	−939	−91.61	413.2

Periods of Rise And Fall[c]

Total, Selected Period		83			5,332		10,713		
Averaged[d]					666	64.24	1,339	129.07	200.9

[a]The interval (col. 3) is broken into the segments preceding and following the associated business cycle trough dates. The starting dates of the period and the cycle trough dates, respectively, are: 8/49, 10/49; 9/54; 8/54; 6/58, 4/58; 12/60, 2/61.

[b]Five-month average centered at the month of peak minus five-month average centered at the month of trough. Thus rises have a positive and falls a negative sign.

[c]Selected for inclusion are those periods of rise that start close to business cycle troughs and those periods of fall that start close to business cycle peaks. Episodes for which figures are enclosed in parentheses do not conform to this principle. They are not included in the totals or averages, but are shown for the purpose of comparison.

[e]The total interval is broken into the segments preceding and following the associated business cycle peak dates. The starting dates of the period and the cycle peak dates, respectively, are: 9/48, 11/48; 9/52, 7/53; 9/56, 7/57; 12/59, 5/60.

scribe how the rates at which stocks on hand or on order are changing tend to increase instability of demand as it moves from the final-product end of the economic process to earlier stages of processing. It will be useful to place the information for department stores developed in the previous chapter alongside of the more limited information for producers of durable materials reviewed here.

1. Orders that department stores place with suppliers tend to reach peaks 7 months on the average before those received from their customers, that is, the sales to final consumers. But they start increasing orders when, or only slightly before, sales start to improve. Durable goods producers, on the other hand, appear to have a generally synchronous relation on the average between their sales orders and purchase orders. One of the facts that must have a bearing on this difference is that buyers of machinery are often willing to wait while machines are being produced whereas consumers expect immediate deliveries.

Compared with consumer buying, the merchandise orders of department stores tend to have additional (or far more marked) extra cycles just after World War II and during the Korean crisis. Similar remarks apply to the relation between orders for materials placed by durable goods manufacturers and their receipt at the factory.

2. Ownership proper for department stores typically increases (or decreases) when both consumer buying and retailers' buying are increasing (or decreasing). For durable goods manufacturers, materials orders outstandings increase when orders for materials are increasing but receipts of materials may or may not be.

3. The amplification that rates of change in department stores' ownership of merchandise contributes to the backward transmission of demand is a composite of relatively early changes in outstandings, prolonged by somewhat later changes in stocks.

4. For department stores there seems to be rather pervasive correspondence between changes in stocks and the inlet stream into the stock reservoir. Monthly receipts follow a course markedly parallel and virtually synchronous to that of the rate of change in stocks. Likewise, new orders for materials parallel the rate of change in ownership after allowance for the upward trend in orders. These similarities may reflect nothing more than the arithmetic of a stock with a relatively smooth outlet and a fluctuating inlet stream. Even so, there are implications concerning the process of vertical transmission of fluctuation —if there is reason for buying or receipts to fluctuate, then so, and in a parallel fashion, must investment in ownership or stocks fluctuate; conversely, if there is reason for retailers' investment in ownership or stocks to fluctuate, then the orders received by their suppliers or shipments from them must bear the imprint. For business enterprises at this earlier stage, fluctuation in sales orders and their shipments, and no doubt also production, will be strongly influenced by the inventory and ownership objectives or buying problems of retailers as distinguished from the buying of consumers.

5. For durable goods manufacturers, change in outstandings does not parallel new materials orders. Could this imply that change in outstandings is, in a sense, the limp result of the pattern of orders, on the one hand, and of the capacity to fill them, on the other? If delivery terms change, so will the average periods that orders are "outstanding." This "capacity thesis" is examined in Chapter 10.

6. The role that changes in ownership play in the vertical transmission of instability depends in part on the size of the fillip that the inventory-purchase syndrome bestows on earlier, relative to later (more finished), stages. For department stores, changes in ownership double or triple the instability of consumer buying as it moves to the next earlier stage. Looked at the other way round, the instability of orders received by the suppliers of department stores is once or twice again that of orders received by department stores—

consumers' purchasing. This statement applies to periods defined in any one of several ways—when materials orders are at their specific highs or lows; when the rate of change in ownership may well have its greatest impact because it is rising or falling at an accelerating pace; during the unmatched periods when either sales or orders are at their own specific cycle highs or lows.

7. Instead of defining periods on the basis of highs and lows in the data under examination, we may do so using some more general scheme. The scheme of business cycle turns shows no evidence of augmented instability associated with department store buying—indeed, quite the reverse. This is caused by two characteristics of purchasing behavior that have appeared again and again—its tendency to lead; its tendency to spurt during the early months of expansion. These characteristics can be admitted into a widely based reference scheme by applying a uniform lead of six months at business cycle reference peaks and troughs and, for the expansion phase, looking only at the period between the predated troughs and the time when general hesitations in activity have been noted in other contexts. During these months, orders received by the suppliers of department stores are about four-fifths again as unstable as that of consumer buying; during contraction phases predated six months, they are two-thirds again as unstable.

9. For durable goods manufacturers, the instability of orders for materials can be compared only with that of their receipt by the purchaser. One cannot know to what extent the greater fluctuation of orders constitutes a net addition to fluctuation at earlier relative to later stages, since this would require both sales orders and purchase orders for the same firms. Nevertheless, for whatever it is worth, new orders for materials were about two-thirds again as unstable as shipments of them. The particulars vary with the periods for which comparisons are made. But in general, a substantial magnification in fluctuation appears to take place especially during the first years of expansion or contraction.

The observations contributed by the last two chapters combine with those of earlier chapters to sketch a picture of inventory fluctuation which suggests, as does an analysis of the business problem itself, that the management of stocks and of purchasing responds to many variables besides the level of sales. The rest of the book attempts to determine what factors may be largely responsible for the behavior that has been described and how their influence seems to interact, cumulate, and recede.

III. SEARCH FOR EXPLANATIONS

9. Causes of Fluctuation in Ownership: The Sales Link

The observations based on time series and described in the previous five chapters have relevance to two major groups of questions: the objectives, problems, and procedures that govern purchasing and inventories in business enterprises and their implications with respect to patterns of fluctuation; the impact of this behavior on economic fluctuation in the economy at large. This and the following two chapters explore and analyze the first group of considerations. Chapter 12 tackles the second group, though in a cursory fashion. The final chapter of the book asks how the interaction of the two sorts of processes—business conduct and aggregative impact—may be more adequately understood and effectively explored.

HYPOTHESES AND PROCEDURES

The actual behavior of stocks and ownership as displayed by the time series needs to be analyzed in terms of the business objectives and managerial problems that give rise to it. What these may be was discussed at the outset of the study. Several generalizations emerged. Though they require a great deal of further testing and specification, I want simply to use them here as a point of departure.

Generalizations About Factors That Influence Stocks

1. Stocks on order are an integral part of the stock management problem. Since purchasing or refraining from purchasing materials is the most direct and usual act by which a stock objective is achieved, stocks must be planned in terms of the time required for purchases to be delivered as well as in terms of the time required for processing and marketing operations to take place. Accordingly, if the behavior of stock is to be linked with the business procedures that give rise to it, it is necessary to focus on both stocks on hand and those on order—to focus, that is, on ownership as well as on each of its two parts.

The size of stocks on hand and on order, individually and collectively, is influenced by what is known and what is expected concerning the specifics of several sorts of business problems and the behavior of the several sorts of business costs.

2. The volume of sales is an important determinant of the volume of stocks that should be held on hand or on order. However, the ideal relationship is not that of a constant ratio. When sales rise, total stocks do not need to rise as much as proportionately; nor do they need to fall as much when sales fall. A proportionate change is required for the part of stocks that serve to sustain the period required for processing, whether the process involved is that of manufacture, of preparation of raw materials, or of delivery by the supplier to the purchasing company. But for the portion of total stocks that serve various sorts of insurance and efficiency functions, appropriate

variation is ordinarily substantially less than proportionate to sales.

3. Whatever the specific objective with respect to sales, there are bound to be disparities between actual and ideally desired stocks on hand and on order. Disparities of the "passive" variety tolerated or perhaps not recognized; if clearly "unintended," efforts to reverse them are made. They are of several sorts:

The disparity will reflect the relation between the sales that are expected at the time when orders have to be placed and the sales that actually occur. The disparity is likely to be less for total ownership than for either of its parts, since the inflow, new orders, can be readily adjusted to the outflow, sales. The upward adjustment can be made almost at will. The downward adjustment may be a bit more circumscribed, but nevertheless speedy compared with the adjustment of stock alone.

The disparity will reflect the procedures that it is worthwhile to institute for the purpose of defining, correcting, or even detecting undesired change in stock. These procedures have an opportunity cost in terms of management time and the exacerbation of other management problems. Simple ineptitude may cause large disparities.

The difference between actual stocks and their ideal sales-linked level will also reflect other factors that are intended to influence their size, factors mentioned in the following two paragraphs. It reflects also failures to foretell these other factors precisely.

4. Changes in stocks can reflect changes in cost both of stocks and of other ways of serving the management function that stocks serve. An example of the first is the changing cost of financing stock. This includes not merely the interest charges often examined in this context but also the opportunity cost of internal funds, which may have their own patterns of variation as funds from retained profits rise or fall. Examples of the second are: the higher cost, when factories are busy, of minimizing stocks by means of flexible production schedules; the lower cost of obsolescence

of stocks acquired to cover sales for which advance orders have been taken.

5. Changes in stocks on hand and on order can reflect changing conditions in or expectations concerning the markets in which materials are bought. Such conditions include the expected price of materials, speed and reliability of deliveries, and the adequacy of selections or the reliability with which quality specifications are met. Stocks on order typically reflect most of the initial impact of such change.

Methods of Study

The time series examined in Part II have displayed two basic characteristics that generalizations based on the firms-eye view of stocks suggest: the importance of stocks on order and their strong patterns of fluctuation; and a behavior that does not simply mirror sales. Evidence on these two general points appeared in all sorts of specific forms.

ECONOMETRICS TABLED

It would now be possible to take a further step and make some guesses about what sorts of things account for the behavior unexplained by the sales link. These hunches could be dignified by a formal hypothesis which then might be submitted for econometric test.

However, there are several reasons why it would be foolish at this point to follow this pedigreed procedure. For one thing, there is much more preliminary work to be done in order to weed out some and underscore others of the many factors that may, according to my basic view, play a part in causing fluctuations in ownership.

Further, the basic view is resistant to well-founded hypothesizing. On the one hand, it holds that a great many things can influence the size of stocks. On the other hand, it provides only a shaky a priori basis for selecting which are likely to be quantitatively important. For one thing, the judgment can at the present time be based only on normative considerations and not on sound knowledge about actual business behavior. For another, the judgment implies knowledge of the business conditions that prevailed during the period under study—how significantly what sorts of costs were actually expected to change in what way. As a result of this inability to arrive at a confident hypothesis by deduction, we need to coax the time series to go as far as they can to narrow down alternative explanations.

But even after this further specification has been completed, it is still not at all clear that econometric analysis of the time series presently available would advance the inquiry very far. In any event, it is not undertaken in this study.

There are two chief difficulties which in the context of our particular problems aggravate the perennial headaches associated with multivariate analysis of time series:

The Data. The statistics for durables manufacture are, as has been pointed out, inadequately matched. Directions of change are, I believe, fairly reliably indicated, but the volumes involved are not. Statistics in book-value terms increase the difficulty still further. In consequence, quantitative comparisons are very risky, both with respect to the relations of the various stockpiles to one another and with respect to each of their relations to shipments and orders. The difficulty of proper empirical representation is still more acute in connection with some of the other variables for which the theory calls: forecasts of sales, actual and expected change in replenishment time, expected materials prices, financing costs, and other opportunity costs such as that of flexible employment schedules.

Multidirectional Causal Relationships. Yet in spite of the indubitable deficiencies of available proxies for the independent variables, it is not at all clear whether the multivariate analysis would under- or overstate their true explanatory value. On the one hand, the causal relations at an aggregate level are multidirectional: the accumulation of inventories influence market expectations concerning de-

livery times and prices as well as vice versa; the level of sales influences the cost of financing, which influences the size of stocks, which influences the cost of financing, and so on.[1]

On the other hand, these multidirectional influences follow no prescribed temporal sequence. The association in time may be immediate as well as anticipatory or lagged. Consequently, the coefficient of whichever variable is designated "independent" will actually reflect a zigzag of cause and effect between independent and dependent parameters.

Finally, each of the broad aggregates is responsive to the general level and temper of business conditions. In consequence, some portion of the displayed association between independent and dependent variables reflects the association of each with general business conditions. This problem is, of course, intrinsic to any effort to impute causal connection on the basis of temporal parallelism. In a crude form I have, as indicated earlier, kept it in mind in judging whether, in a particular case, the percentage of months in like phase seems to suggest a "close" relationship. Other things the same, it does so more strongly when conformity of both series to reference chronology is poor than when it is good. For formal correlation analysis the problem can falsify both the regression coefficients as typically interpreted and the multiple and partial correlation coefficients. Techniques for subduing the difficulty are not, as far as I know, in use.[2]

---

[1] Equation systems are, of course, directed toward dealing with this problem, but the extent to which they succeed appears to be highly problematical. For one thing, prerequisite to success is adequate representation of all of the important causal elements.

[2] Consider a simple regression of Y on X. The measures of significance and correlation express in some form the proportion of the deviation of each of the y_1, y_2 . . . y_n from the average $\bar{y}$, which is explained by, on the one hand, some designated systematic association with corresponding x values and, on the other hand, left unexplained.

The deviation of the y's from their average reflects analytically distinct influences: (1) the impact on Y of general business conditions via their influence on demand, business mood, supply, finance, and so on; (2)

There is a third impediment to multivariate analysis which I can only mention very tentatively. The importance of expectations in the causal nexus with which we are concerned casts doubt on the appropriateness of linear models. The final chapter explores the question further.

A FLEXIBLE DIALOGUE

For these many reasons, then, I aim at modest and preliminary goals: to focus the empirical findings on the factors that influence inventory and purchasing procedures by means of a flexible dialogue between the statistical data and the logic of management problems and procedures. We aim to arrive at answers, admittedly tentative answers, which are as specific and precise as the data permit. I might add that I shall frequently go farther than the data permit. No investigator can adequately curb his prejudiced enthusiasms. This is one reason why "facts" are such relative things.

In the main, the statistics provide four handles by means of which one may attempt to draw the figures and the explanation of behavior together:

1. The over-all pattern of fluctuation of stocks and its gross correspondence with that of data to which it is hypothetically causally related.

2. The distinction between these relations in the case of stocks on hand and those on order; the logic of behavior calls for differences which evidence could confirm or deny.

3. The distinction between the relations among stocks and explanatory variables for department stores and for durable goods manufacturers; here again the logic of behavior calls for differences which the evidence could confirm or deny.

4. Finally, a distinction that lies outside of the main scope of this work, but one on which scattered light can be shed, concerns differences between other business expansions and the one starting in early 1961; until some time in 1964, this expansion was notably lacking in the usual buildup of optimistic market expectations, and this presumably would cause distinctive behavior of stocks on hand and on order.

In this chapter I concentrate on the association between sales and stocks, either on hand

the impact of X on Y; (3) the impact of other particular influences that fail to be represented in the equation or equation system; (4) a residual (theoretically unexplained) random element.

But each matching value of X and Y share in some degree influence 1. If so, the correlation and regression coefficients that are developed reflect not only the influence of X on Y (influence 2), but also the influence of general business conditions on *both* X and Y. Coefficients reflect only these influences if we can assume that there is no causal influence of Y on X, and no other independent influences correlated with X which have been omitted (influence 3). For broad economic aggregates, influence 1 can be large and consequently produce high measures of correlation, even if the "true" association between Y and X is quite small. For narrow aggregates, data for individual industries or geographic areas, the influence of general business conditions may be less strong (relative to the influences that are isolated) or they may simply be different—the general affairs of the industry or the region.

To correct for influence 1, it seems to be necessary to isolate that portion of the total standard deviation of Y's subject to the particular explanation which the

regression proffers. Conversely, it is necessary to specify that portion of the total deviation which is explicable without recourse to the particular explanation that the regression proffers, the portion reflecting the impact on Y and X of the general business climate. As a result of this impact, Y and X would have some specified chance of conforming in some specified degree to the time pattern traced by a group of series of a like order of generality. What this pattern may be could be determined in a number of ways. But the raw materials for the determination would seem to be a *bank of series of like order of generality*. From these one could evolve, by simulation or other methods, a generalized pattern and a probability distribution of the degree of divergence of individual series from the pattern.

This approach gives expression to a common-sense procedure that an analyst uses intuitively. He judges that a correlation of such and such is "pretty good" for "this type of data," whereas the same figure would be "not very impressive" for another set of time series. As suggested in the text, I have constantly resorted to this sort of framework in pointing to the percentage of months in like phase, which in the several and different contexts seems to me to suggest meaningful association.

or on order, and ask whether it explains the behavior of stock in terms either of a desired relationship or of one reflecting inevitable error and its correction. I conclude that a large amount of the behavior of stocks on hand and particularly of stocks on order remains to be explained after any reasonable association with sales has been taken into account. The residual is greater for durable goods manufacturing than for retailing. It is greater prior to 1961 than thereafter.

The next chapter turns to the residuals— the portion of the behavior of stocks on hand and on order that seems unexplained by the pattern of sales. We examine the evidence that suggests the role of market conditions and of expectations with respect to changes in delivery periods, prices, and backlogs of sales orders. Attention is also given to whether market expectations can be explained largely in terms of capacity limitations of suppliers.

Chapter 11 looks at how the two major influences—sales and market conditions—combine in shaping the unfolding history of changes in materials ownership and new orders for materials; it leads to modification of the usual formulations of the "acceleration principle."

THE SALES LINK

Stocks could not, of course, fail to have some sort of broad parallelism with sales, and Charts 2 and 4 have pictured this general association. The association must in part reflect basic business requirements which are too obvious to discuss. Interest attaches rather to the particular quantitative characteristics of the parallelism and its precision. What light can the time series throw on these matters? Measures of conformity and timing are reviewed in this section and quantitative relationships in the next.

Timing Relationships

Table 31 assembles previously presented measures of association between peaks and troughs and specific cycle peaks and troughs. In studying the location of turns alone, a gross simplification is imposed on the history of events: things may either improve or worsen, and nothing else. Moreover, since it is not always crystal clear just when the reversal takes place, there is often an arbitrary element in the designations. The moment when a series begins to descend, and therefore ceases to ascend, may be compared with the analogous moment in another series which may, not unreasonably, be causally related to it. If these particular moments (characterized by the fact that they are moments of reversal) tend systematically to, say, precede those of the first series, it seems reasonable to assume that other moments also would. In other words, a regression analysis which allowed for the lead would show a higher coefficient of correlation than one using synchronous or other timing. This is the logic of studying the specific cycle measures of timing and the percentage of months in phase.

For both department stores and durable goods manufacturers, stocks turn two or three months later than sales, on the average. Table 31, line 3, shows that, allowing for the three months' lag, 80 and 84 per cent of the months, respectively, are in like phase for the two sorts of enterprises.[3]

The figures suggest some minimal systematic association for both sorts of enterprises, and comparison of the visual contours in Charts 2 and 4, above, support this conclusion. However, its meaning in terms of direct causal association cannot be pushed very far, since both sales and stocks move with general busi-

[3] Since there is no specific cycle in department store sales prior to 1948, the retardation in the stock series is bound to be out of phase. Limiting the comparisons to January 1948 through December 1961, the percentage of months in phase for department stores is 82, and for durable goods manufacturers 83.

TABLE 31

Summary of Timing association of Sales and Stocks on Hand and on Order, Department Stores and Durable Goods Manufacturers, 1946-61

Table Line	Specific Series[a]	Reference Series[a]	Median Timing Lead (−) Lag (+) P	T	All	Timing Adjust.	% in Like Phase % of Months 7/46 to 12/61	1/48 to 12/61
							Department Stores	
1	Ownership	Sales	+0.3	+2.0	+1.0	+1	80	84
2	Change in owner-ship	Change in sales	+0.5	−0.5	0	0	84	
3	Stocks	Sales	+2.3	+5.0	+3.0	+3	80	82
4	Change in stocks	Change in sales	+4.0	+3.5	+4.0	+3, +4	81	
5	Change in stocks	Sales	−6.3	−0.7	−1.5	−1	71	74
6	Outstandings	Sales	−4.3	+1.3	−0.5	0	75	
7	Change in out-standings	Change in sales	−1.5	−1.5	−1.5	−2	80	
8	Sales	Subcycles	−1.0	−4.0	−1.5	−1	83	
9	Change in sales	Subcycles	−11.5	−6.0	−10.0	−10	66	
10	Ownership	Subcycles	−0.5	−2.5	−2.0	−2	82	
11	Stocks	Subcycles	+0.5	0	0	0	91	
12	Outstandings	Subcycles	−6.5	−2.5	−3.5	−4	81	

Table Line	Specific Series[a]	Reference Series[a]	Median Timing Lead (−) Lag (+) P	T	All	Timing Adjust.	% in Like Phase % of Months 7/46 to 12/61	1/48 to 12/61	Source Table Dept. Stores	Durables
							Durable Goods Manufacturing			
1	Ownership	Shipments	−1.5	−0.5	−0.5	−1, 0	72	75	15	6
2	Change in owner-ship	Change in ship-ments	−1.0	+1.0	+0.7	+1,0	76		20	18
3	Stocks	Shipments	+4.7	+3.0	+2.5	+2, +3	84	83	15	6
4	Change in stocks	Change in ship-ments	+11.5	+7.3	+9.3	+4, +5	70		20	18
5	Change in stocks	Shipments	−2.7	−3.3	−3.0	−2	81	87	20	18
6	Outstandings	Shipments	−1.7	−0.7	−1.0	−1	73	80	15	6
7	Change in out-standings	Change in ship-ments	−1.0	+0.7	+0.3	0, +1	72		20	18
8	Shipments	Subcycles	−1.7	+0.3	0	0	84		15	6
9	Change in ship-ments	Subcycles	−9.0	−6.7	−8.7	−9	68		20	18
10	Ownership	Subcycles	−4.0	+1.0	−1.5	−2	75		9	1
11	Stocks	Subcycles	+1.3	+3.7	+3.0	+3	82		9	1
12	Outstandings	Subcycles	−6.0	+0.5	−2.5	−3	74		9	1

[a]"Stocks" are stocks of purchased materials. Outstandings are, of course, outstanding purchase orders for materials. (The series is actually the unfilled sales orders of the primary metals, fabricated metals, and "other" durables goods industries.)

ness conditions (Table 31, lines 8 and 11). We cannot, therefore, rule out the possibility that such similarity as the two series show is the result of each of them moving in accord with the general tides of business. Other relationships serve to fill in this ambiguous picture.

Ownership is capable of prompt adjustment to intentions, and its behavior is therefore of interest. For durable goods, line 1 of the table indicates a very poor association between ownership and shipments; only 72 of the months are in like phase. And Charts 1 and 2, it will be recalled, revealed notably different shapes, as well as timing, of cycles in the two series. For department stores, on the other hand, ownership and sales are in like phase 80 per cent of the time after allowing for a one-month lag in ownership. If comparison is confined to the period after 1948, department stores are in phase 84 per cent and durable goods manufacturing 75 per cent of the time.

Rates of change in both sales and stocks provide further evidence concerning management objectives and their validation. It is possible for stocks and sales proper to be precisely in like phase and yet for first differences in the two series to be in opposite phase for a substantial part of the time. The relationship between cycles in rates of change and in data proper are diagramed below:

	Accelerating		Decelerating	
	Data Proper (a')	Change (a")	Data Proper (d')	Change (d")
1. Rising	↑	↑	↑	↑
2. Falling	↓	↓	↓	↓

Thus data proper for two series could both be rising; but if one was rising at an accelerating rate (box 1a'), and the other at a decelerating rate (box 1d"), the rates of change for the two series would be out of phase. Analogous remarks apply to falling phases. It is equally possible, of course, for phases in rates of change in two series to be matched and the

data proper out of phase for substantial intervals. This occurs in boxes 2a" and 1d" or 1a" and 2d". Finally, of course, phases for both data proper and rates of change for two series can be matched (the a' and a" boxes), thus indicating a more exacting parallelism than for either characteristic alone. Which of these several possibilities apply to the actual data and to what degree?

For department stores, Table 31 shows that change in stocks (inventory investment) was in like phase with change in sales 81 per cent of the months after allowing for a three- or four-month lag. The lag, like that of stocks with respect to sales proper, seems to reflect some of the difficulties of effectuating intentions. Note that it is not present for change in ownership, which, on a synchronous basis, is in phase with change in stock 84 per cent of the months (line 2). Reference to Table 20, line 5, indicates that twelve turns are matched, only two of which diverge by more than three months; seven turns are within plus or minus one month of one another. These figures then, and those for ownership proper, seem to reflect some very determined effort to keep stocks aligned with sales when alignment is sensitive not merely to directional change but to rates of change as well.

This double criterion is not exhibited for durable goods manufacturers. The alignment between rates of change in stocks of materials and in shipments (line 4) or in ownership and in shipments (line 2) has about the same average timing association as for department stores. But phase-by-phase correspondence is relatively sloppy; 70 per cent of the months are in like phase for change in stocks and 76 per cent for change in ownership. Apparently, when sales are rising or falling at declining rates, stocks do not usually follow suit.

Line 5 of Table 31 suggests what they may be doing, though perhaps not forcefully enough to carry much weight. For durable goods manufacturers, rates of change in stock tend to bear a fairly systematic relation to shipments proper. Allowing for a two-months lead in inventory investment, changes in stocks and shipments proper are in like phase 81 per cent of the whole period and 87 per cent beginning in 1948, whereas the corresponding figures for department stores are 68 and 71 per cent.

Do the figures for durables reflect a purposeful effort to maintain this association between inventory investment and shipments proper? If so, the logic would be obscure, but even the evidence does not speak for it, since change in ownership, for which validation of an objective is mechanically easy, has a very unsystematic association with shipments proper.[4] A second explanation might be in terms of adjustment lags. Hypothetically, the effort to increase stocks as sales rise at first succeeds only in the form of a retardation in the fall in stocks (box 1a' for sales and 2d'' for stocks). Only after the rise in sales starts to slow down do stocks manage to rise and at an accelerating rate (box 1d' for sales and 1a'' for stocks). An association of this sort is in accord with the evidence. However, note that in any event it could hardly result from a high management priority to enforce a precise average or incremental association between sales and stocks, in view particularly of the possibility of foreknowledge of requirements which advance orders for finished goods implies.

I conclude that the figures suggest a relatively strong sales link for department stores and a much weaker one for durable goods manufacturers. That this is a sensible finding seems implicit in the difference between the procurement problems of retail merchants and of manufacturers of durable goods.

For department stores, stock control is a central management concern. A large part of the capital of a retailer is invested in stocks. Moreover, a department store's customers make their selections primarily out of goods in stock; poor stocks mean lost sales. However, since at best the items that may be wanted are vast in number, the natural tendency for stocks to grow too large can only be kept in check by carefully devised stock-control methods and perpetual vigilance. A situation of this sort virtually demands a sharply defined stock objective, the enforcement of which carries high management priority.

For durable goods manufacturers, on the other hand, stocks of materials account for only a small part of total invested capital. A specific unit of material often has only a loose physical link to a specific finished article, since processing is sufficiently flexible to use it as an ingredient in any one of a number of finished items. Obviously, the penalty for a relaxed link of sales-to-materials stocks is far smaller than for department stores. At the same time, a durable goods manufacturer would technically be in a better position to keep shipments and materials strictly aligned than would a retailer. His customers are often willing to wait, whereas those of department stores are not. The advance knowledge of projected shipments that order backlogs provide can be the basis of materials buying capable of enforcing a stock objective: both the inflow to and the outflow from the stockpile, receipts and production starts, can be predetermined. Even the two- or three-month lag of stocks relative to shipments seems to evidence a weak sales-linked intention for manufacturers, whereas for retailers it could simply reflect the absence of the clairvoyant's capacity to foretell sales.

The examination of one sort of evidence, then, data on timing and confluence of fluctuations, seems to suggest the inevitable link of stocks or total ownership to sales. The association tends to be synchronous for ownership, whereas stocks lag about three months. But for department stores the figures seem to show a substantially tighter and more pervasive association than for materials stocks of durable

[4] Allowing for a five-month lead, 71 per cent of the months are in like phase.

goods manufacturers. That this would be the case seems implicit in the differences in the business operations that the two sorts of enterprises perform.

Quantitative Relationships

The evidence examined is of course most incomplete. For one thing, we have looked at relations between one of the factors that could influence stocks and sales, whereas there are necessarily other factors too; the joint impact of sales plus the others could easily obscure the effect of sales, other things the same. For another thing, our measures have been concerned not with either sales or stocks but, as mentioned at the start, a schematic representation of both—in effect, a sequence of triangles marked off by the low and high months of movements identified as specific cycles or minor cycles. The height of the peaks and troughs and the pattern of intervening months have been largely ignored. Ratios of stocks to sales provide a steppingstone around both limitations. It is necessary to try to take this further information into account.

MORE THAN PROPORTIONAL RISE OR FALL

One type of quantitative relationship between sales and stocks, one with a venerable analytic history in economics, is that of a constant average relationship. Yet we saw, on the one hand, in Chapter 2 that there is little reason to suppose that a close adherence to management rules, directed toward efficient servicing of sales, other things the same, would produce a constant ratio. The empirical data, on the other hand, showed that in fact stocks not only increased as much as sales but increased more during substantial periods of either business expansion or expansion in sales. And it seems reasonable to interpret this behavior as intended, at least in some loose sense, since when sales are rising, stocks are not likely to back up unexpectedly.

For department stores, the ratio of stocks on hand to sales rose in 59 per cent of the months during which sales themselves rose; for the ownership-sales ratio the corresponding figure was 68 per cent. For durable goods manufacturers, the comparable percentages were 44 and 37 respectively. Table 32 gives these figures.

The beginning of the more than proportional rise in stocks does not wait for the latest stages of expansion in sales but starts within a year of its commencement.[5]

Ownership started to rise faster than sales or shipments within eight months of the trough in the flow series or, for that matter, the trough in business cycles except for the long lag after the 1961 trough. A glance at Charts 3 and 5 will help to recall the appearance of these ratios.

During contractions in sales, a rise in the ratio might mean either that stocks could not be reduced at all or that they could not be reduced fast enough to keep pace with the fall in sales. And certainly either of these situations could well occur, however lamented by management. But a decline in the ratio—stocks falling faster than sales—would, like a rise during expansion, seem intended in the sense that it must result from efficacious purposeful procedures. Table 32 shows that stocks were falling faster than sales for only 40 per cent of the months for department stores and 36 per cent for manufacturers. Several months elapsed after the peak in sales before stocks started to fall, and several more before their rate of fall passed that of sales. The median lag for peaks in the ratio relative to those in sales was four months for department stores and nine for durables.[6] Certainly the lag represents a failure of control mechanisms, and it is interesting that again control is closer for department stores than for the manufacturers.

---

[5] An exception was a lag of fourteen months after the 1954 trough for the department store data referred to here and in the following paragraph. These and subsequently mentioned figures are from Table 8, lines 3, 7 and 13; and Table 17, lines 4, 9, and 14.

[6] Timing comparisons were given in Tables 17 and 8.

TABLE 32

Comparison Between Sales and the Stock-Sales Ratio
Department Stores and Durable Goods Manufacturers
1948-1961

Ratio	Sales Rising[a] % of months when ratio rose	Sales Falling[a] % of months when ratio fell
Department Stores		
Ownership-sales	68	66
Stock-sales	59	40
Outstanding-sales	59	83
Durable Goods Manufacturers		
Ownership-sales	37	88
Stock-sales	44	36
Outstandings-sales	47	83

Note: "Sales" signify sales of department stores or shipments of all durable goods manufacturers.

[a]All comparisons cover the months January 1948 to December 1961. Months of rise (fall) in sales or shipments are delineated by the location of specific or minor specific cycles and likewise for the ratios. Figures in column 1 were originally presented in Tables 7 and 16. Those in column 2 have not been previously given.

Ownership, on the other hand, was brought in line much faster, and the ratio declined during 66 and 88 per cent of contraction months respectively for department stores and durables. This high correspondence was associated with the fact that the ratio sometimes started to fall before sales reversed, and in no cases waited longer than three months for department stores and four or five months for durables.[7]

In general, then, such directional parallelism as we observed previously between stocks and sales had the further characteristic that

[7] Charts 3 and 5 bring out the fact that for durable goods the ownership-shipments ratio declined for substantially more months than it rose. This explains in part both the low conformity of the ratio with shipments during expansions and the high conformity during contractions.

stocks on hand and on order rise relatively more than sales during a substantial portion of the time that sales rise; an analogous statement applies to the fall in total ownership, though not to that of stocks alone.

HYPOTHETICALLY EFFICIENT SERVICE STOCK

If I am correct in thinking that, were all other factors to remain the same, the efficient sales link would not dictate increases or decreases of these magnitudes, then it must be concluded that other factors have not in fact remained the same. How great a part of the total fluctuation in stocks may result from the impact of these factors?

I know of no way to answer this question with confidence at the present time. We can neither simulate the typical management procedure for linking stocks to sales, other things the same (this requires knowledge of management conduct which we do not have) nor can we (as explained at the start of the chapter) resort to the time series, represent all relevant variables that affect the size of stocks including that of sales, and see how much of the total variance sales explain.

Nevertheless, I want to make three assumptions and see what they imply. I apply them to ownership and not to stocks alone. The choice is conditioned by the need to concentrate on *intended* behavior. The basic procedure is first to determine sales-linked stocks by applying some assumption about the character of the link between stocks and specific cycle fluctuation in sales, and second to compare the fluctuation in ownership so generated with the actual fluctuation during specific cycles in ownership. The difference is attributed to influences other than those of sales.

The picture is confused insofar as unintended change is caught up and displayed in the comparison, for unintended change can be generated by error in estimating either sales, market conditions, or any other relevant consideration. But unplanned stocks of both the passive and unintended sort distort the pattern of stock on hand far more, it seems reasonable to believe, than they do the pattern of total materials ownership. The timing associations as well as the logic point to this conclusion. For ownership, then, it seems permissible to consider the total *specific fluctuation in ownership* as more or less intended and compare it with the sales-linked part of this total as defined in terms of a specified relationship to the total *specific fluctuation in sales*.[8] The assumptions concerning the efficient sales-

stock link, other things assumed unchanged, are:

Assumption A. Efficient service requirements are defined as change in ownership which is proportional to the change in sales when the proportional relationship is specified by the low points in the actual relationship (the figure used is the average for specific cycle troughs in the ratio). This assumption presumably makes the sales-linked portion of change in ownership unrealistically high, and consequently the part requiring further explanation correspondingly too low. Nevertheless, for department stores, an average of three-quarters of the increase in ownership during each specific expansion is accounted for by this assumption, and accordingly one-quarter by factors other than sales. The cycle-by-cycle figures are given in Table 33, line 10a. For durable goods manufacturers, the corresponding hypothetical sales-linked portion of ownership developed in Table 34, also averages three-quarters of the total, and the percentage increases over the period (line 10a).[9] It accounts for *more* than the total during the 1958–59 expansion and during the first year of the expansion starting early in 1961 (Table 34, line 10a).

Assumptions B and C. Both share the basic assumption that the efficient sales-service link implies a constant *incremental* association, plus buffer stocks changing according to a square-root principle. The two assumptions differ only with respect to the size of the ratios that were used.

The incremental ratios that I have selected are in all cases smaller than the average ratio of ownership to sales over the years. For department stores, the average ratio was close to four months' supply. However, I have assumed (C) that if sales are expected to rise, ownership need rise no more than two times the size of the expected increase. I think of

---

[8] An alternative would be to confine examination to what occurred to ownership during specific cycles in sales only (that is, not those in ownership itself). But this automatically rules out the possibility of viewing the impact of factors whose incidence may not precisely parallel that of sales. In Chapter 11 we make a calculation of this sort because we ask this specific question.

[9] The increase would have been much more marked had not the downward trend in the ratios been recognized in the computation. See Table 34, note b.

TABLE 33

Hypothetical Sales-Linked Change in Ownership, Department Stores, 1948 to 1961

	P or Exp. 10/48	T or Cont. 7/49	P or Exp. 1/51	T or Cont. 4/51	P or Exp. 5/53	T or Cont. 1/54	P or Exp. 8/57	T or Cont. 2/58	P or Exp. 4/60	T or Cont. 1/61	Average P or Exp.	Average T or Cont.	Average All Phases
1. Sales, Specific Cycle Dates													
2. Standing at P&T (3 mo. av.), mil. $	385.3	351.7	416.5	371.5	408.7	400.3	465.7	445.7	497.3	481.7	+434.7	−410.2	
3. Change during cycle phase, mil. $		−33.6	64.8	−45.0	37.2	−8.4	65.3	−20.0	51.7	−15.6	+54.7	−24.5	±37.9
Hypothetically sales-linked change in ownership under three assumptions[a]													
4a. Assuming aver. ratio of 3.74, mil. $[b]		−125.6	+242.3	−168.3	+139.1	−31.4	+244.6	−74.8	+193.0	−58.3	+204.8	−91.7	±141.9
4b. Assuming incr. ratio of 1.5 mil. $ (line 3x1.5)		−50.4	97.2	−67.5	55.8	−12.6	98.0	−30.0	77.6	−23.4			
4c. Assuming incr. ratio of 2.0 mil. $ (line 3x2.0)		−67.2	129.6	−90.0	74.4	−16.8	130.6	−40.0	103.4	−31.2			
5. Buffer, 2.33 $\sqrt{D(T+N)}$ mil. $[c]		−2.7	5.4	−3.7	3.1	−0.7	5.2	−1.5	3.9	−1.2			
6b. Assuming ratio of 1.5 + buffer, mil. $ (line 4b+line 5)		−53.1	102.6	−71.2	58.9	−13.3	103.2	−31.5	81.5	−24.6	+86.5	−38.7	±60.0
6c. Assuming ratio of 2.0 + buffer, mil. $ (line 4c+line 5)		−69.9	135.0	−93.7	77.5	−17.5	135.8	−41.5	107.3	−32.4	+113.9	−51.0	±79.0
Actual ownership													
7. Specific cycle dates for ownership	12/47	6/49	2/51	10/51	6/53	5/54	7/57	5/58	5/60	12/60			
8. Standings at P&T (3 mo. av.) mil. $	1575.0	1255.0	1848.7	1495.7	1623.3	1510.3	1814.0	1735.0	2007.7	1953.3	+1773.7	−1589.9	
9. Change during cycle phase, mil. $		−320.0	593.7	−353.0	127.6	−113.0	303.7	−79.0	272.7	−54.4	+324.4	−183.9	±246.3

(continued)

TABLE 33 (concluded)

											Average		
	P or Exp. 10/48	T or Cont. 7/49	P or Exp. 1/51	T or Cont. 4/51	P or Exp. 5/53	T or Cont. 1/54	P or Exp. 8/57	T or Cont. 2/58	P or Exp. 4/60	T or Cont. 1/61	P or Exp.	T or Cont.	All Phases
Percentage relationship: hypothetically sales-linked change in ownership to actual change													
10a. Under assumption A (line 4a ÷ line 9)		39.2	40.8	47.7	109.0	27.8	80.5	94.7	70.8	107.2	75.3	63.3	68.6
10b. Under assumption B (line 6b ÷ line 9)		16.6	17.3	20.2	46.2	11.8	34.0	39.9	29.9	45.2	31.9	26.7	29.0
10c. Under assumption C (line 6c ÷ line 9)		21.8	22.7	26.5	60.7	15.5	44.7	52.5	39.3	59.6	41.9	35.2	38.1
Ratio, change in ownership to change in sales													
11. Actual (line 9 ÷ line 3)		9.52	9.16	7.84	3.43	13.45	4.65	3.95	5.27	3.49	5.63	7.65	6.75
12a. Under assumption A (line 4a+line 3)		3.74	3.74	3.74	3.71	3.74	3.75	3.74	3.73	3.74	3.74	3.74	3.74
12b. Under assumption B (line 6b ÷ line 3)[d]		1.58	1.58	1.58	1.58	1.58	1.58	1.58	1.58	1.58	1.58	1.58	1.58
12c. Under assumption C (line 6c ÷ line 3)[d]		2.08	2.08	2.08	2.08	2.08	2.08	2.08	2.08	2.08	2.08	2.08	2.08
Ratio, level of ownership to level of sales, actual and hypothetical (when change during expansion under three assumptions is added to actual trough standing)[e]													
13. Actual (line 8 ÷ line 2)	3.57	4.44	4.03	3.97	3.77	3.90	3.89	4.04	4.06		4.09	3.86	3.96
13a. Under assumption A	3.59		4.00		4.00		3.77		3.88		3.81		
13b. Under assumption B	3.26		3.80		3.80		3.46		3.85		3.59		
13c. Under assumption C	3.33		3.85		3.85		3.53		3.70		3.60		

Notes to Table 33

[a]Assumptions are (A) the ownership-sales ratio is constant and its level is averaged for the three major troughs; (B) the ratio of change in ownership to change in sales (incremental ratio) is constant at 1.5 months; sales plus allowance for insurance stock; (C) same as B, but an incremental ratio of 2 months' sales.

[b]The ratio of 3.74 is applied to the *standings* at peaks and troughs; rises and falls are calculated using these figures.

[c]The formula utilizing the Poisson distribution, at a level that permits stockouts 1 per cent of the time is 2.33 $D\sqrt{(T+N)}$. D is 1 month's sales, T (The replenishment period)

is assumed to be 1 month, and N (The order interval) 2 weeks; thus we solve for $2.33\sqrt{1.5(D)}$.

[d]Note that these ratios round to the same figure because line 5 represents so small a portion of the total and does not vary enough to change the number and the second decimal place.

[e]To illustrate: Trough standing of ownership, 6/49, from line 8 (1255.0) plus sales-linked rise in ownership, 7/49 to 1/51, from line 4a (242.3) = hypothetical standing under assumption A of 1497.3. This divided by sales from line 2 is $\frac{1497.3}{416.5}$ or 3.59.

---

this as consisting of about an extra six weeks' supply on hand and two weeks' on order.[10] Analogous remarks apply to falls. Assumption B cuts the incremental requirement to six weeks' supply. For durable goods manufacturers, the same figures were used—the B and C assumption is that change in sales require changes in materials ownership one and a half times and two times as large respectively. I picture the distribution for durables as consisting of two weeks on hand under both assumptions whereas four weeks and six weeks are held on order under B and C respectively. I am afraid that the C assumption is rather too large. To apply these relationships to the data, the ratios are cut in half to allow for value added in the sales dollar. The specifics of the calculation are given in notes to Tables 33 and 34. I shall not repeat them, since it is probably simpler to study the details of the calculation in connection with the figures themselves.

The logic that underlies selections is contained in Chapter 2. An incremental ratio that is substantially smaller than the average ratio implies that the level of total stocks is supported by a number of things which, on the one hand, it is not desirable to duplicate and, on the other hand, not worthwhile to eliminate—the history of previous purchases, some less successful than others, the need to

carry slow-moving items, the need in some cases to make long forward commitments, the cost of tailoring stock to precise requirements. I do not hold any special brief for the particular parameters that were chosen, and it might be interesting to try some further alternatives. But I think that the C lines at any rate define efficient sales-service requirements sufficiently liberally to provide a very conservative estimate of the portion of ownership that must be explained in terms of "other factors." [11]

---

[11] An alternative calculation, on which it may be useful to report, was tried and abandoned. The factors that determine the average, as distinguished from the incremental, association are, in one sense at least, also part of what may be thought of as an efficient sales-ownership relationship. They imply that higher levels of sales require higher levels of ownership. But the dynamics of the association would seem to involve long-term influences that settle back into these overall relationships rather than anything that needs to be, or indeed should be, an explicit management goal.

This line of thought suggests that a simulation of an efficient sales-ownership link might have two parts: (1) a trend part that takes account of an increase in ownership corresponding to the long-term trend in sales, (2) a cyclical part built on an incremental principle.

I made such calculations for expansions, but found that they came to grief when they were applied to contractions. For durable goods, a six-week incremental ratio was used to define the cyclical component of sales-linked change in ownership. Total sales-linked change—trend plus cycle—represented 51 per cent of the total actual increase in ownership. This figure is comparable to that of 58 per cent for the two-month incremental relationship alone (see text below). The corresponding figure for department stores, using a

---

[10] For convenience I have equated two weeks with half a month.

TABLE 34

Hypothetical Sales-Linked Change in Ownership, Durable Goods Manufacturers, 1948–1961

	P or Exp. 12/48	T or Cont. 10/49	P or Exp. 7/53	T or Cont. 10/54	P or Exp. 1/57	T or Cont. 4/58	P or Exp. 6/59	T or Cont. 1/61	4/62[a]	Average P or Exp.	Average T or Cont.	Average All Phases
1. Specific Cycle Dates for Shipments												
2. Standing at P&T (3 mo. av.), mil. $	7,860	6,736	12,794	10,889	14,758	11,615	15,557	13,370	16,377	12,742	10,653	
3. Change during cycle phase, mil. $		−1,124	+6,058	−1,905	+3,869	−3,143	+3,942	−2,187	+3,007	+4,623	−2,090	±3,175
Hypothetical sales-linked change in ownership under three assumptions[b]												
4a. Assuming aver. ratio with trend, mil. $[c]		−2,146	+8,547	−3,592	+4,816	−5,201	+4,976	−3,687	+3,344	+6,113	−3,357	±4,709
4b. Assuming incr. ratio of 1.5, mil. $[b] (line 3 x .75)		−843	+4,544	−1,429	+2,902	−2,357	+2,957	−1,640	+2,255	+3,468	−1,567	±2,382
4c. Assuming incr. ratio of 2.0, mil. $[b] (line 3 x 1.00)		−1,124	+6,058	−1,905	+3,869	−3,143	+3,942	−2,187	+3,007	+4,623	−2,090	±3,175
5. Buffer = to $2.33\sqrt{D(T+N)}$ mil. $[d]		−16[d]	+72	−21	+40	−30	+40	−21	+28	+51	−22	±34
6b. Assuming incr. ratio 1.5+buffer, mil. $ (line 4b+line 5)		−859	+4,616	−1,450	+2,942	−2,387	+2,999	−1,661	+2,283	+3,519	−1,589	±2,416
6c. Assuming incr. ratio 2.0+buffer, mil. $ (line 4c+line 5)		−1,140	+6,130	−1,926	+3,909	−3,173	+3,982	−2,208	+3,035	+4,674	−2,112	±3,210
Actual ownership												
7. Specific cycle dates for ownership	8/48	9/49	9/52	10/54	2/57	6/58	1/60	12/60	3/62[a]			
8. Standings at P&T (3 mos. av.) mil. $	16,874	12,533	27,703	17,376	25,341	18,277	22,983	18,750	21,953	23,225	16,734	
9. Change during cycle phase, mil. $		−4,341	+15,170	−10,327	+7,965	−7,064	+4,706	−4,233	+3,203	+9,280	−6,491	±7,687

(continued)

TABLE 34 (concluded)

	P or Exp. 12/48	T or Cont. 10/49	P or Exp. 7/53	T or Cont. 10/54	P or Exp. 1/57	T or Cont. 4/58	P or Exp. 6/59	T or Cont. 1/61	[a] 4/62	Average P or Exp.	Average T or Cont.	Average All Phases
Percentage of hypothetically sales-linked change in ownership of actual change												
10a. Under assumption A (line 4a ÷ line 9)		49.4	56.3	34.8	60.5	73.6	105.7	87.1	104.4	74.2	61.2	66.8
10b. Under assumption B (line 6b ÷ line 9)		19.8	30.4	14.0	36.3	33.8	63.7	39.2	71.3	43.5	26.7	33.9
10c. Under assumption C (line 6c ÷ line 9)		26.3	40.4	18.7	49.1	44.9	84.6	52.2	94.8	58.0	35.5	45.2
Ratio of change in ownership to change in sales												
11. Actual (line 9 ÷ line 3)		3.86	2.50	5.42	2.06	2.25	1.19	1.94	1.07	1.92	3.37	2.75
12a. Under assumption A (line 4a ÷ line 3)		1.91	1.41	1.89	1.24	1.65	1.26	1.69	1.11	1.30	1.79	1.58
12b. Under assumption B (line 6b ÷ line 3)		.76	.76	.76	.76	.76	.76	.76	.76	.76	.76	.76
12c. Under assumption C (line 6c ÷ line 3)		1.01	1.01	1.01	1.01	1.01	1.01	1.01	1.01	1.01	1.01	1.01
Ratio of level of ownership to level of sales, actual and hypothetical (change during expansion under three assumptions is added to actual trough standing)[e]												
13. Actual (line 8 ÷ line 2)	1.86	1.60	1.72	1.57	1.48	1.40	1.34	1.40	1.34	1.79	1.61	1.69
13a. Under assumption A[e]	2.17		1.50		1.49		1.35		1.35	1.65	1.55	
13b. Under assumption B[e]	1.35		1.38		1.37		1.28		1.28	1.35	1.37	
13c. Under assumption C[e]	1.46		1.44		1.43		1.33		1.33	1.46	1.44	

Notes to Table 34

[a]A high point in 1962, which does not constitute a specific cycle peak, provides an additional comparison. It is not included in the averages.

[b]Assumptions are: (A) An average ratio of ownership to shipments proper applies. The level of the ratio is indicated by its position at troughs. Since these are subject to a constant downward trend, values are read from a straight line on semi-log paper visually fitted to the 3 trough values. (B) An incremental ratio of change in ownership to change in shipments applies; the ratio is taken at 1.5 months; shipments (two weeks on hand and one month on order). But since value added is presumably about half of value of product, the equivalent book value of materials adjusted for value added is $\frac{1.5}{2}$ = .75 months; sales. (C) The ratio is taken at 2 months, sales; adjusted for value added, it is a ratio of 1.0.

[c]The ratios read from the trend line at each peak or trough month were applied to the standing of shipments. The ratios used (see note b) were, 12/48 1.79, 10/49 1.77, 7/53 1.60, 10/54 1.55, 1/57 1.47, 4/58 1.42, 6/59 1.38, 1/61 1.33, 4/62 1.29. Changes between these hypothetical hand-to-mouth levels of ownership constitute the entries in line 4a.

[d]The formula utilizing the Poisson distribution, $2.33\sqrt{D(T+N)}$, was applied under the assumption that the replenishment period, D,T was 6 weeks and, the order interval 2 weeks. Thus the variance allowance is for $2.33\sqrt{2}$ mo. shipments. Adjusting to allow for value added and the figure to 1 mo.; e.g., $2.33\sqrt{7,860} = 207$, $2.33\sqrt{6736} = 191$, change in buffer = 16.

[e]To illustrate: Trough study of ownership 9/49 from line 8 (12,533) plus sales-linked rise in ownership 10/49 to 7/53 from line 4a (4,544) = hypothetical standing under assumption A of 21,080. This divided by shipments 7/53 from line 2 is $\frac{21,080}{12,794}$ or 1.65.

The tables show that for assumption C the sales-linked portion of total actual specific cycle expansions in ownership is, hypothetically, 42 per cent and for durable goods 58 per cent. During contractions for either type of enterprise it was only 35 per cent (Tables 33 and 34, line 10c). As we have seen in several contexts, the sales-linked aspect played a larger relative part in the late fifties and in the sixties than in the earlier postwar years. This was particularly true of durable goods manufacturers. Indeed our calculations show that for the first year of the prosperity of the sixties (the only portion of the long expansion for which figures consistent with earlier years are available) virtually the entire change would

one-month incremental component, was 52 per cent (as compared with 42 per cent for the two-month incremental supply).

I abandoned these estimates because of their implication about the efficient relationship during *contractions*. The assumption that the trend rise in ownership should continue through contractions (and otherwise what is the meaning of a "trend"?) virtually ruled out an "efficient" sales-linked absolute *decline* in ownership, particularly for department stores. This does not seem at all sensible.

be attributed to the sales link under the C assumption. If the linked extrapolations (as charted) are used to extend the relationship, even the B assumption overexplains the entire actual change in ownership.

The same set of contrasts can be evaluated in somewhat different terms by examining the relations between ownership and sales that are implied. In the first place, note that the actual incremental ratios (the relation between specific cycle changes in ownership and in sales) are substantially larger than the average ratios (the relation between the level of ownership and the level of sales taken at peaks and troughs)—6.75 and 3.96 for department stores. For durable goods manufacturers the figures are 2.75 and 1.69, which, adjusted for value added, would be about 5.50 and 3.38 (last column, lines 11 and 13 in both tables). It is also noteworthy that the difference dwindles very markedly in the later years of the period under study.

Businessmen seem to speak and think primarily in terms of average ratios. It seems odd, therefore, that the marked differences between average and incremental ratios is not well publicized. It is possible that the reason is simply that unless attention is actually focused on the increments, it would be easy not to notice the disparity. The *average* ratios perhaps do not change enough as a result of the incremental change to call executive attention to discrepancies between plans and actuality. For example, would a ratio of 4.1 (4.0 if the Korean peak were excluded) at peaks in department store sales and ownership be noted as clearly different from the trough ratio of 3.9 (line 13)? For durable goods manufacturers, the same question applies to ratios in book-value terms of 1.8 and 1.6.[12]

I raise the question without knowing the answer. But if it is true that differences of this order do not flash blinking lights in management offices, perhaps the same line of thought would help to explain why actual incremental ratios can depart so far from those which represent efficient servicing of sales, other things the same. For department stores, the actual ratios at peaks in sales averaged 4.0 months of sales if the Korean episode is excluded, and the same figure applies to peaks in the ratio itself. If the incremental ratio had been constant at the trough average (assump-

tion A), the peak standings would have averaged 3.8. If the incremental ratio of 2 had been applied, the peak standings would have averaged 3.6 (summary columns, lines 13a–c). Do differences of this order present problems to managements? They may realize stock *can* be economized while business improves, but the need to do so may not seem urgent. For durable goods manufacturers the peak ratio actually experienced averaged 1.8, excluding Korea. At peaks the ratio averaged 1.5 under assumption A and 1.4 under assumption C.

I wish I could rephrase these questions to apply to stock on hand rather than to total materials ownership. But, as mentioned earlier, the unintended aspect of change in stocks leaves me baffled. In any event, the question that I raise is simply whether the implied change in ownership associated with factors other than change in sales is of an order of magnitude which is likely to worry executives trained in the constant-ratio rule of thumb. Most of the other influences with which this study is so particularly concerned can perhaps be sheltered under the generous umbrella of what passes for a constant-average ratio, tilted a bit this way in recognition of good times and that way in recognition of bad times. If so, it is an interesting arithmetic which can produce figures that appear unimportant at a micro-economic level, but have highly significant implications for the economy at large.

What, then, are some of these other factors that influence ownership?

---

[12] This question may mean that one ought to think in terms of the actual experienced ratios and *their* peak and trough differences. For the periods covered in the tables, the average standing of the ratios for department stores at their specific cycle peaks, excluding the Korean episode, was also 4.0; for troughs it was 3.7. For durables, the peak and trough ratios were 2.1 and 1.6 respectively; excluding the Korean episode, they were 1.8 and 1.6.

10. Causes of Fluctuation in Ownership: Market Conditions

That many sorts of factors other than an intended efficient association with sales can influence ownership has appeared and reappeared in the examination of the function that stocks serve in Part I. For one thing, targets are not met, so that changes in stocks reflect errors rather than intentions of any sort (except the intention not to pay the price of strict enforcement). The opportunity cost of flexibility in production or sales may have its impact on the uses to which stocks are put; these costs change in the course of business fluctuation and thereby change the desirable volume of stocks. The costs of stocks themselves can alter during business fluctuation, thus inducing changes in the size of stocks, other things the same. But the difficulty of giving these influences statistical form means that they must be largely ignored for the present. We are forced to look, not where ideally we would like to, but where the light is good. And the light shines, or at least glimmers, on market prospects.

Changing market prospects can be thought of as influencing primarily the *timing* of buying. Goods which in any event are expected to be needed at some particular time do not need to be bought at exactly that time minus a fixed interval—a uniform period required for their delivery and preparation. Instead they can be bought quite a bit earlier if there is reason to do so. On the other hand, they can be bought as close to the time when they are needed as possible; or since inventories can be drawn down, they may not for the time being be bought at all. The point is simply that there is what may be called a "period of option" with respect to the timing of buying. The way in which this option is exercised is influenced by market prospects.

REASONS FOR MARKET-ORIENTED SHIFTS IN THE TIMING OF BUYING

Changing conditions in the markets in which materials or merchandise are bought can affect the time when goods are purchased, goods which are in any event expected to be needed for resale or processing. Conditions in materials markets capable of influencing the timing of buying are doubtless of many sorts, but perhaps three dominate. They concern: (1) expected price of materials (this includes payment terms and free services as well as explicit price), (2) delivery periods and the buyers' confidence that deliveries will be made when promised, (3) quality, in general or with respect to particularized specifications, the range of selections, and the buyers' confidence that standards will be met. Though all of these matters can theoretically be reduced to a price differential, I believe that they are actually thought of by business as particular sorts of penalties or advantages, and therefore they are best considered separately.

If conditions change or are expected to change, how does the buyer behave? We can consider the question with respect to tightening markets without burdening the discussion with the counterpart of these statements covering slackening markets.

With respect to prices, it is anticipated rather than actual change which theoretically governs actions. Starting with a volume of stock which is efficient, assuming that prices and other market conditions are stable, the increase that is justified by an expectation of a stipulated rise in prices is a negative function of the cost of carrying the additional stock and a positive function of the expected *change* in price over the relevant period of anticipation, discounted for uncertainty. Extension in stock is justified as long as the positive advantage of further extension is greater than the associated cost. Thus the *level* of stock is governed by the *change* in prices. Since this point plays some part in later discussions, a brief illustration may be in order.

Suppose one month's supply is 100 units and it costs $9 to carry 100 units for one month. One month's supply is the normal physical requirement for efficient servicing of sales. Then, if prices are expected to increase 10 cents a unit over the next month, the purchase price of the 100 units would be $10 less if the goods were bought now than if they were bought one month later, when they would in any event be required. Since it would cost $9 to hold the extra supply, there would be a net saving of $1 and the advance purchase might be made if all costs were included and forecasts were, miraculously, believed to be certain. If, next month, prices were again expected to rise 10 cents, only the usual one month's supply could be purchased, since to do so would maintain the two months' level of stock with its attendant cost. If in the following month prices were expected to cease rising, there would be no buying since ownership should be reduced to the pre-rise one month's level because there would now be no offset to the $9 carrying cost of the extra month's stock. The level of price-linked stock, then, is a function of first differences in prices, other things, including uncertainty, the same.

Whether the identical logic applies to goods outstanding as well as to stocks on hand depends on whether there is a definable cost to holding goods on order. Certainly, since financing and storage costs typically do not commence until deliveries are received, the cost of holding goods on order is less, other things the same, than that of goods on hand. Perhaps the major cost of outstandings is that of risk—risk of buying goods that cannot be used at all or used as advantageously as some alternative. For these costs, whatever they are, the same logic would apply as previously sketched for stocks. Thus purchases to anticipate a rising price should ideally remain undelivered as long as feasible, since the cost of making a bet that prices will rise is thereby minimized. In any event, an increase in stocks on order is likely to involve, before long, at least some increase in stocks, and thereby blur the distinction.

If the buyer fears that his quality specifications will not be met, his defense again consists of *anticipation* of the event. Since quality deterioration is actually a de facto price increase, the response would be governed in the manner just described.

In connection with a change in delivery periods, either actual or expected change would presumably elicit a similar response. Goods on order would be increased to cover the same number of weeks' supply, but for the longer period—the new replenishment period. The delivery period is in effect a "process time," as discussed in Part I, and as explained there, stock which serves to bridge process time typically needs to increase proportionately to change in process time. In addition, the longer replenishment period demands somewhat greater insurance stocks on hand as well as on order. Thus ownership associated with this function would presumably increase slightly more than proportionately to a change in replenishment time, other things the same. This remark would apply to expected replenishment time, except that it might be discounted for uncertainty.

The previous paragraph assumes that there are no alternatives to the increase in delivery periods. But actually, of course, there are. Many sorts of materials may be purchased from the same, or more probably other, suppliers at a price high enough to command swift delivery. The price ordinarily is not simply a monetary one, since it may imply poorer service or other penalties. It seems likely, therefore, that if producers feel quite sure that delivery periods will lengthen, they will often prefer to purchase ahead, because the carrying cost, including risk, will often be less than the penalty of buying later for swift delivery.

However, often this preference cannot be exercised. For one thing, suppliers may not be willing to fill up their future plant capacity at current prices. They may worry that buying is unrealistically extended and therefore that orders will not remain firm or that returns and requests for delays and other concessions will develop. Perhaps the most usual reason for unwillingness to accept orders for longer delivery is simply that orders are already sufficient to plan future output efficiently over the convenient planning horizon. If the regular suppliers are not willing to write advance orders, goods must be picked up for prompt delivery elsewhere.

Purchases for prompt delivery also may constitute the part of response to expectations of lengthening replenishment periods since a transaction period needs to be covered. Materials are in a sense running away from the purchaser when delivery periods lengthen, and he may have to buy some ready supplies to sustain him while he catches the withdrawing ones.

These paragraphs imply that the response to the expectation that delivery periods will lengthen is very likely to be not only an increase in advance orders but also an increase

in purchases for immediate delivery, and consequently of materials stocks on hand. This is true even if we assume that expectations are held with assurance.

But, of course, expectations seldom are sure. For example, if purchasing agents are not very sure that markets will tighten, they may prefer not to extend commitments but to take a chance on having to pay premium prices for swift delivery *if and when* actual tightness develops. They exchange a sure cost of advance buying for a possible cost of a premium price.

In connection with the possibility of prices rising, uncertainty reduces the degree of extension that a purchaser would undertake. In connection with the possibility of a fall in prices or a shortening of delivery periods, uncertainty reduces the degree of retrenchment that is undertaken. In other words, in deciding by how much to alter his positions on the basis of judgments about market conditions, the expected gain is discounted for uncertainty and therefore the action taken is less than it would be were expectations sure.[1]

I have been discussing various manifestations of changes in market conditions and this implies the conceptual frame of "other things the same." But the introduction of uncertainty plays havoc with this handy conceptual tool. Over a period of months when business is expanding or contracting, the presence of uncertainty changes what is done; but uncertainty is itself changed by what is done. How then can one abstract from such change in order "to hold it the same"?

Two other factors that are likely to change concurrently with actual or expected market conditions are the cost of capital, which is relevant to stocks of goods on hand, and the cost of the risk of buying goods that are not needed,

[1] Price theory distinguishes between the character of risk premium for buyers and for sellers. It is assumed that buyers consider themselves more vulnerable to an error of underestimating a fall in price than of overestimating a rise; the opposite assymetry applies to a seller's reactions. See Oscar Lange, *Price Flexibility and Employment*, Bloomington, Ind., 1944, pp. 30, 31.

which is relevant to stocks either on hand or on order. This occurs, for example, when there is a change in the backlog of sales orders, "back orders" that a manufacturer has on hand. If materials are bought to cover an order which is on the books, the chances of buying materials that will not be used are minimal. For durable goods manufacturers these back orders are, as we have seen, both potentially large and highly variable. Their size, accordingly, can alter the risk cost of changes in outstanding purchase orders or stock on hand.

I have mentioned three major sorts of changes that can prompt a change in ownership position—actual or expected change in materials prices, in quality, or in replenishment time. *But it seems characteristic of market behavior that all of these changes tend to occur at the same time.* An individual buyer can, therefore, view his problems in any or all of these ways and still be *impelled to do the same thing at the same time.*

These notions about the factors that influence market prospects imply changes in purchasing behavior. Is there evidence that such changes actually occurred?

We want to examine the time series, first, to see whether there are indications that changes in market conditions appear to have been associated with changes in ownership. To do so requires that the impact of changing levels of sales of the company's product has been removed from the ownership statistics. Second, we want to try to learn which causal factors may, on the basis of the evidence, have played some part in the over-all changes in ownership that took place. Needless to say, the data can at best be suggestive.

Data for the durable goods industries are examined first and followed by the meager materials for department stores. The last section of the chapter addresses itself to the frequently asked question whether changing conditions of supply are primarily responsible for changing market expectations, and the role of capacity limitations is examined. These investigations, along with those of the previous chapter, prepare the way to tackle in the following chapter the slippery problem of the interrelations among the whole battery of influences that interact to create the inventory cycle.

OUTSTANDING ORDERS AND MARKET CONDITIONS

The most direct response to changing market conditions is the change in ownership of materials. The two parts, stocks and outstandings, can supplement or substitute for one another. But following the logic of the previous discussion, changes in stocks on order probably represent a lower-cost response than do changes in stocks on hand. Accordingly, outstandings may react more sensitively to changing conditions. In any event, evidence on the impact of market conditions afforded by stocks on order is not as confused by other matters (the level of sales or of production, and failure of expectations to come true) as is the evidence of stocks on hand. Consequently we examine the two parts of ownership separately and focus particularly on outstanding orders.

Cascaded Order Terms

Just how total outstanding orders change is complicated and it is necessary to understand it before looking at the evidence. Outstandings at any given time have typically been ordered at different times, not only because the interval between orders is usually shorter than an average delivery period, but because delivery periods themselves vary for groups of items on order.

Retailers, for example, will often order some portion of the expected requirements of style goods for the "season" at the time when lines are first shown by manufacturers. The proportion of these "preseason orders" may for some lines be as high as 70 per cent and for others as low as perhaps 30 per cent of the expected season's requirements. The proportion varies with types of merchandise and market conditions. Order terms for these purchases may be, say, two months or more. Other purchases will occur as requirements clarify and selling needs move closer. These "secondary orders" may, to pick an illustrative figure, be placed for delivery in four to six weeks. Finally, retailers' "fill-in orders" or "at-once orders" may reflect last-minute needs of several sorts. Manufacturers, on the other hand, may tend to order all of some sorts of materials and none of other sorts for relatively distant delivery, so that the range of order terms may tend to apply primarily to different materials and only secondarily to portions of the total requirements of each.

The Structure of Ownership

Procedures, in other words, differ widely. But in one way or another, a variety of delivery terms is likely to be usual for all materials outstanding at a given time. The range of these terms and their relative importance in total outstandings will shift as market conditions change. It will be useful to consider briefly just how these shifts, associated with the several sorts of conditions that affect outstandings, gradually envelop the totals of materials on order at given times. For this purpose an illustrative example is required.

AN ILLUSTRATIVE EXAMPLE

Consider the composition of ownership with respect to two aspects of each item bought: the time when it was ordered and the time when it is generally expected to move to production or selling floors. Ten units are bought each period and they are distributed with respect to delivery period in the following way: 3 units immediate, 5 units at end of two periods, 2 units at end of four periods.

In a retail store a distribution of this sort could mean that of the estimated requirements for the season, some 30 per cent was bought for immediate delivery, 20 per cent when lines were first shown, and 50 per cent at an intermediate time. In a manufacturing establishment it might represent the relative importance of various products characterized by different delivery conditions, though some of the cascaded aspect may also apply. The figures are merely illustrative of the point that some materials and some portion of most major materials are bought further ahead than others. "A period" can conveniently be visualized as two weeks.

Assume orders are placed at the beginning of a period; "immediate delivery" occurs at the end of the period (beginning of period

Structure of Ownership, Units

Time When Order Was Placed	Time When Use Occurs Number of Periods After Time 0							Total by Time Ordered	
Number of Periods Prior to Time 0	1 In Stock	2	3	4	5	6	7	Units	Per Cent
			On Order						
0			3		5		2	10	20.8
1		3		5		2		10	20.8
2	3		5		2			10	20.8
3		5		2				7	14.6
4	5		2					7	14.6
5		2						2	4.2
6	2							2	4.2
Total by units	10	10	10	7	7	2	2	48	100
Time used, per cent	20.8	20.8	20.8	14.6	14.6	4.2	4.2	100	

2). One period is required for preparation, so the earliest that these items which are purchased (time 0) can enter production is during period 3. Maintaining the same differential, those bought for delivery two periods hence arrive at the end of period 3, and so are ready for use during period 5; those bought for four-period delivery arrive at the end of period 5 and are ready for use during period 7.

Assuming there has been no change in this pattern of buying for seven periods, then the 48 units on hand and on order are analyzed, with respect to when they were bought, in the two right-hand columns. Thus 10 units, or 20.8 per cent of total ownership, were bought in each of the recent periods, whereas two units, or 4.2 per cent, were bought as long as six periods ago. The 48 units can also be analyzed with respect to when they are to be used, and the bottom two lines show that some goods presently on order will not be used, under the circumstances described, until seven periods hence. Each column shows when each item then sold or entering production was bought.

RESPONSE TO CHANGING SALES OR ORDER TERMS

If sales are presently expected to increase, the figures in the first line of the example will be increased, and it may well be that orders for immediate delivery (column 3, line 1) will be increased more. But if the new level of sales is expected to hold, longer-term orders (columns 5 and 7) would also rise. If expectations are realized, and the new level is maintained, other lines would be changed to cover the larger sales expectations, though now the usual *proportions* of orders of each term might be reconstituted. After sufficient time had elapsed for all of the table's lines to alter, the increase in outstandings should be approximately proportionate to the increase in sales (assuming that nothing else affecting procurement had changed). The proportionate relationship is a function of the fact that outstandings associated with delivery periods are largely "process-time stocks" as defined in Chapter 2.[2] However, note that if sales continue to rise (rather than simply to maintain the new level), outstandings will rise less than proportionately to sales unless the continuing increases are *anticipated* in advance orders.

If it is market expectations rather than sales volume that is expected to change, the relative weights of the several order terms are likely to shift. Thus materials covered in column 7 of line 1 might increase—more goods would be placed for delivery five periods hence. This could reflect (1) the unwillingness of suppliers to write orders for shorter terms, (2) purchasers' expectations that prices might rise, and the concomitant wish to fix prices sooner rather than later (3) the purchasers' fear that if one waited to place the usual three-period and one-period orders, the proper schedule of receipts could not be relied upon. This means that the number of units ordinarily purchased for advance delivery would be increased. It might even be that an order of still longer term would be placed—it would appear in the example in a new column 9 to the right of the present table.

However, if only the *relative* distribution of order terms changed, so that the new longer-term orders were placed at the expense of the new shorter-term ones, there would be a deficiency in receipts during the period when the shorter orders would ordinarily have been moving into stock. Since this is undesirable, perhaps the additional long-term orders often constitute an absolute increase in procurement. If so, outstandings would increase immediately and stocks would increase only when these longer-term orders started to reach their delivery dates.

This line of thought bears on the observations of earlier chapters that the lead of outstandings relative to stocks seemed longer than the length of the *average* period that goods remain on order could explain. The reason

[2] They would presumably increase slightly more than proportionately insofar as the need for insurance stocks rises somewhat with the volume of sales.

here suggested is that it is not so much the length of the average delivery period as the period characterizing that fraction of all materials ordered well in advance which is critical. For it is the latter that will determine when an increase in outstandings associated with changing market expectations is likely to affect the size of stocks on hand, other things the same. However, as usual, other things may well not be the same. Particularly, stocks may tend to be drawn down by unexpectedly high requirements for sales or production starts at just the times when heavier long-term orders are placed. If so, this would further contribute to the lead of outstandings relative to stocks. Suggestive evidence on this point appears in the last section of this chapter.

To summarize, four *analytic components* of change in the level of materials outstanding can be identified. Consider their application to an increase (comparable remarks apply to a decrease): (1) Sales plus the desired change in stocks on hand at all stations increase, and orders of each term increase proportionately. (2) The relative weight in all purchases of those of each order term shift in a fashion that increases the average period that goods remain outstanding.

Two other cases which are in a sense special instances of item 2 are worth separating out: (3) The delivery terms for major materials that must be bought ahead lengthen; that is, the terms of the longest-term orders of any consequence become longer than they previously were. (4) The delivery terms on the shortest orders of any consequence become longer than they previously were; that is, "at once" orders for some sorts of materials become in effect orders for two-week or thirty-day delivery.

Number of Months' Supply

Since market prospects are the subject under investigation, it is necessary to focus on those changes in outstandings that are associated with market conditions rather than with the changing levels of sales or production. To do so it is necessary to make some sort of an assumption about the influence of sales if market conditions were unchanging. Moreover, the influence of sales ought to be removed at a *low level* of market prospects— one that characterizes a buyers' market when purchasing is "hand-to-mouth." The assumption that I would like to make first, then, is the one previously made (Tables 33 and 34) in connection with ownership—that the impact of sales is given by a constant outstandings-sales ratio when that ratio is at its cyclical low. As indicated in the previous chapter, this is by no means an ideal solution, but it is less disagreeable in connection with outstandings, which have such a large element of "process-time stock," especially when business is slack, than with stocks on hand or even total ownership. In any event, it is the best that we can do.

DURABLE GOODS MANUFACTURERS

For durables, the trough level of the ratio averaged about .9 for the durable goods group; adjusted for value added in the sales dollar, it comes to about 1.8, or a bit short of eight weeks' supply. Accepting this relation between outstandings and shipment as the level that would be maintained if hand-to-mouth conditions persisted, then, were buying to stay on this basis, the outstandings-shipment ratio would be a horizontal line drawn at the .9 level.[3] If the basic hand-to-mouth level were assumed to conform to the downward trend in the ratio, this norm would be represented by a downward sloping line which was about at the 1.15 level in 1949 and the .75 level in 1962.[4]

---

[3] Strictly, this statement applies to a ratio dated a bit differently. Outstandings during the current months provide for shipments a sufficient number of weeks hence to allow for the completion of receipt and production. However, since the period shifts, it seems necessary to ignore the matter.

[4] The calculation is not very sensitive to the actual hand-to-mouth level that is picked. The ups and downs in the ratio, and thus the general contours of

Instead, Chart 10 shows, of course, that the ratio is actually a wavy line. We inquire whether the contours of the curve seem to reflect evidence of changing market conditions and if so what more can be learned of the sorts of conditions, sorts of responses, and associated factors.

Chart 10 compares the ratio, top curve, with several series that concern conditions in the metals markets. The second and third curves are based on a remarkable body of information collected by the Chicago Association of Purchasing Agents. It consists of answers to monthly questionnaires sent to two hundred companies, the large majority of which are manufacturers of durable goods.[5] Vendor performance, the second curve on the chart, focuses fairly sharply on the length of time required for materials to be received after they have been ordered. It is a cumulated diffusion index of the number of purchasing agents who report that the delivery period for major commodities is lengthening.[6] Thus it concentrates on what, at least to the buyer, ap-

pears to be a supplier-induced impact on his purchasing policy. Suppliers are delivering faster when the curve rises and slower when it falls. It probably focuses on the "analytic component" number 4—a change in the order term of advance deliveries.

The average term of purchase orders, the third curve, presumably combines this supplier-initiated characteristic of delivery periods with levels that might result from the purchasers' decision to buy farther ahead than usual for any one of the many reasons previously mentioned. But the reports doubtless focus on the major materials for which order terms change from time to time.[7] Thus the data probably cover not so much the "analytic component" number 2 as number 4 applied to a wider range of order terms. The terms averaged 2.2 months at peaks and 1.2 at troughs.

Both of these indicators of market conditions have the three and a half movements that characterize the ratio.[8] Table 35 gives measures of correspondence between the ratio and the two indicators of market conditions. For both, the proportion of months in like phase is high—88 months for the level of

---

non-sales-linked supply, remain unaltered if the hand-to-mouth position is designated as either higher or lower than the eight weeks' supply. Indeed the level might be realistically assumed to have a downward trend. This statement does not apply if the desired minimum is defined as an incremental association between sales and outstandings which differs from the average desired level. If the incremental association is less than the average, the average ratio will tend to decline when sales rise and vice versa.

[5] In 1961, an officer of the association was kind enough to supply the following figures concerning the number of firms in the sample:

Durable goods manufacturers	152
Non-durable or semi-durable goods manufacturers	39
Retailers	9

[6] The questionnaire asked whether deliveries made by vendors are "faster, slower, the same." A diffusion index was computed by adding the percentage reporting slower deliveries and one-half of the percentage reporting that they stayed the same.

This series, like all diffusion indexes, is roughly similar to a rate of change in data proper. (It differs from a rate of change in that each rise or fall is of identical size.) To glimpse what the data proper might have shown, the diffusion index was cumulated. Thus it portrays whether vendor performance is generally deteriorating (the curve rising) or improving (the curve falling).

[7] The series was constructed in the following way. One question on the Chicago Purchasing Agents questionnaire asks, "How far in advance must you buy in order to have principal materials on hand when needed: 0 to 30 days, 30 to 60 days, 60 to 90 days, 90 days or longer?" We constructed the index by using the percentage reporting each of the four delivery terms as weights for the average term included in the category. The average term was taken in the center of each 30 day period. Thus, 0 to 30 days was considered 15 days, or .5. The index, in other words, is a weighted-average delivery period in terms of months of supply.

[8] I refer to the movements terminating in 1949, for which the downward phase only is shown, the next two complete cycles, plus the movement starting in the beginning of 1959. Though outstandings recede in 1960 from the levels stimulated, at least in part, by the steel strike, the downward trend in the ratio and the ambiguity resulting from the shift in the statistical series mean that no terminal trough could be marked. Apparently the rise in outstandings at that time (see Chart 1) is not sufficiently greater, proportionately, than that of shipments to be clearly identified as a cycle in the ratio.

CHART 10

Ratio of Outstanding Materials Orders to Shipments Compared with Selected Series, Durable Goods Manufacturers, 1946–64

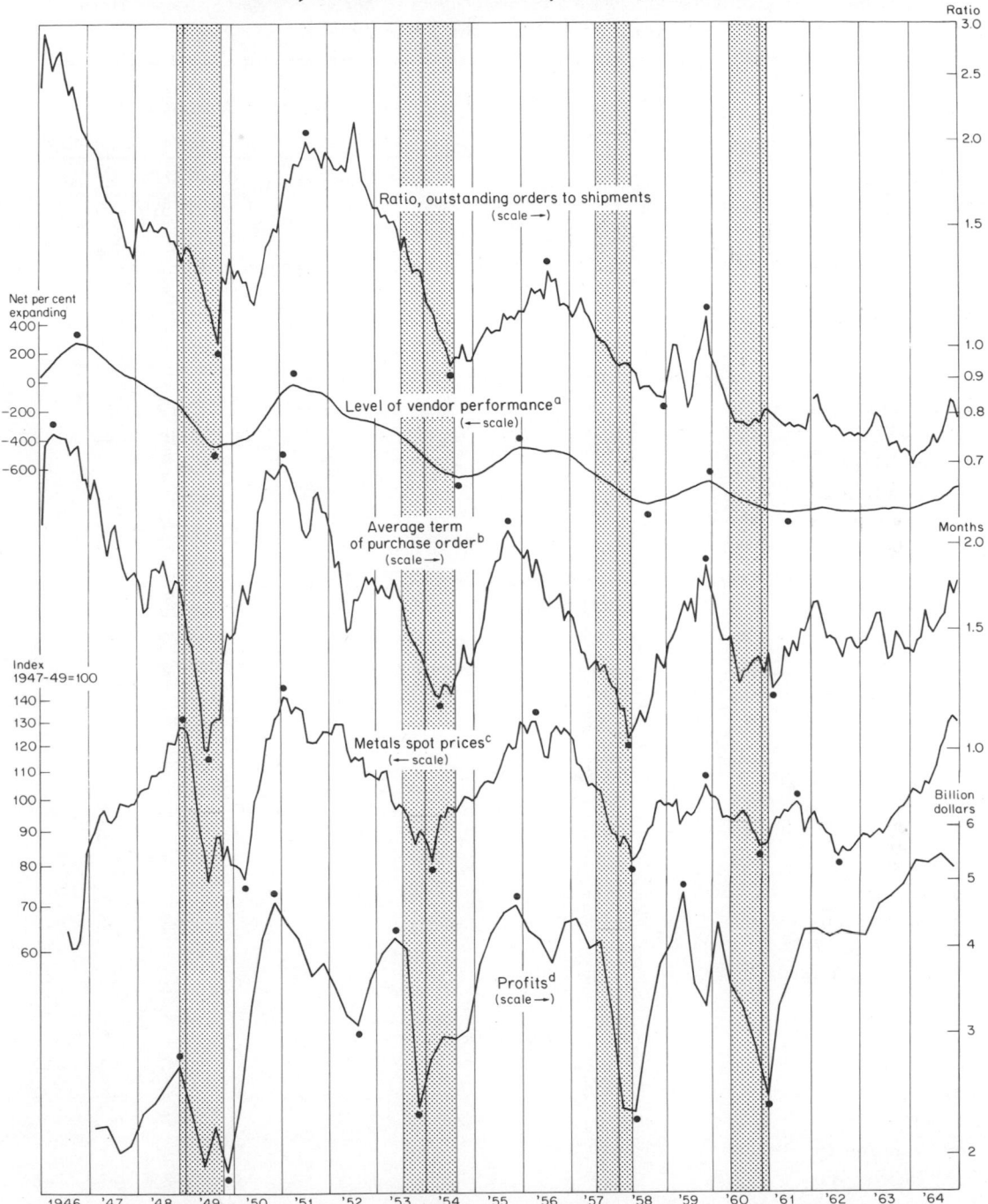

Note: Shaded areas represent business contractions. Specific cycle turns are marked by dots.
a Cumulated diffusion index, Chicago Purchasing Agents Association data. b Based on CPAA data, see text. c Index of spot-market prices of five metals. d Corporate profits before taxes, durable goods manufacturers, FTC, SEC data.

TABLE 35

Timing: Ratio of Outstandings Materials Orders to Shipments and Selected Data, Durable Goods Manufacturers, 1946–61

Section A: Months Lead (−) or Lag (+) for Matched Turns[a]
Chronology[b]

Line	Reference Series[c]	P (1/47)	T (7/47)	P 11/48	T 10/49	P (2/51)	T (6/52)	P 7/53	T 8/54	P 7/57	T 4/58	P 5/60	T 2/61
	Specific Series: Ratio of Materials Outstandings to Shipments, Durables												
1	Business cycles			⊕	−1			−24	−1	−12	+8	−6	⊕
2	Subcycles	⊕	⊕	⊕	−1	+5	⊕	⊕	−1	−12	+8	−6	⊕
	Specific Series: Level of Vendor Performance												
3	Business cycles			−25	−2			−27	+1	−19	+4	−5	+5
4	Subcycles	−3	⊕	⊕	−2	+2	⊕	⊕	+1	−19	+4	−5	+5
5	R: materials outstanding to shipments, dur.	Ω	⊙	⊙	−1	−3	⊙	⊙	+2	−7	−4	+1	Ω
	Specific Series: Average Term of Purchase Orders												
6	Business cycles			−31	−4			−30	−4	−22	−1	−5	+1
7	Subcycles	−9	⊕	⊕	−4	−1	⊕	⊕	−4	−22	−1	−5	+1
8	R: materials outstanding to shipments, dur.	Ω	⊙	⊙	−3	−6	⊙	⊙	−3	−10	−9	+1	Ω
	Specific Series: Metals, Spot Prices												
9	Business cycles			+1	+5			−30	−6	−15	0	−6	−2
10	Subcycles	⊕	−10	+1	+5	−1	⊕	⊕	−6	−15	0	−6	−2
11	R: materials outstanding to shipments dur.	⊙	Ω	Ω	+6	−6	⊙	⊙	−5	−3	−8	0	−3
12	Average term of purchase orders	⊕	Ω	+32[r]	+9	0	⊙	⊙	−2	+7	+1	−1	−3
	Specific Series: Corporate Profits												
13	Business cycles			0	−5			−2	−9	−20	+1	−12	0
14	Subcycles	⊕	⊕	0	−5	−3	+2	−2	−9	−20	+1	−12	0
15	R: materials outstanding to shipments, dur	⊙	⊙	Ω	−4	−8	Ω	Ω	−8	−8	−7	−6	Ω
16	Average term of purchase orders	⊕	⊙	+31[r]	−1	−2	Ω	Ω	−5	+2	+2	−7	−1

(continued)

TABLE 35 (concluded)

Section B: Average Timing of Turns

Line	Reference Series[c]	Number Matched −	+	0	Median[e] P	T	All	Average Deviation[f] P	T	All Turns	Wt'd	Timing Adjustment[g]	% Mos. 7/46–12/61	% Mos. 1/48–12/61
	Specific Series: Ratio of Materials Outstandings to Shipments, Durables													
1	Business cycles	5	1	0	−14.0	+2.0	−3.5	6.7	4.0	8.0	5.3	0	51	57
2	Subcycles	4	2	0	−4.3	+2.0	−1.0	6.2	4.0	5.2	5.1	0	63	60
	Specific Series: Level of Vendor Performance													
3	Business cycles	5	3	0	−22.0	+2.5	−3.5	7.0	2.5	10.5	4.8	−3,−4,−5	55	56
4	Subcycles	4	4	0	−4.0	+2.5	−0.5	5.8	2.5	5.1	4.1	0	62	62
5	R: materials outstanding to shipments, dur.	4	2	0	−3.0	−1.0	−2.0	2.7	2.0	2.7	2.3	−1,−2,−3	88	89
	Specific Series: Average Term of Purchase Orders													
6	Business cycles	7	1	0	−26.0	−2.5	−4.5	8.5	2.0	10.0	6.0	−4,−5	57	63
7	Subcycles	7	1	0	−7.0	−2.5	−4.0	6.2	2.0	4.4	4.1	−4	66	68
8	R: materials outstanding to shipments, dur.	5	1	0	−5.0	−5.0	−4.5	4.0	2.7	3.3	3.3	−3,−4,−5	87	86
	Specific Series: Metals, Spot Prices													
9	Business cycles	5	2	1	−10.5	−1.0	−4.0	10.0	3.2	7.6	6.5	−3,−4		64
10	Subcycles	6	2	1	−3.5	−2.7	−3.0	5.1	4.3	4.8	4.7	−3,−4		70
11	R: materials outstanding to shipments, dur.	5	1	1	−3.0	−4.0	−3.7	2.0	4.0	3.2	3.1	−3		74[h]
12	Average term of purchase orders	3	4	1	+3.5	−0.5	+0.5	10.0	3.8	6.9	6.9	0, +1	69	77[h]
	Specific Series: Corporate Profits													
13	Business cycles	5	1	2	−7.0	−2.5	−3.5	7.5	3.8	5.6	5.6	−6		60
14	Subcycles	6	2	2	−5.7	−1.3	−2.5	6.5	3.7	5.0	4.1	−6		66
15	R: materials outstanding to shipments, dur.	6	0	0	−7.3	−6.3	−7.5	0.9	1.5	1.2	1.2	−7,−8		83[h]
16	Average term of purchase orders	5	3	0	0	−1.0	−1.0	10.5	1.8	6.1	6.1	−1	70	77

Notes to Table 35

aSpecific series are matched with the indicated reference series (see note c) in accordance with the standard NBER rules. A double relaxation of rules is marked r; it applies to cases for well-conforming series in which two like turns are matched, though an unlike turn lies between them. The figure is underlined when subcycle chronology is the reference series, a minor cycle in the specific series has entered a comparison; or, when two individual series are compared, a minor cycle in either series has entered a comparison. When the business cycle chronology provides the reference, minor specific cycle turns are ignored. The meaning of other symbols is:

⊕ turn in the reference series does not appear in the specific series.

Ω turn in the specific series does not appear in the reference series.

☉ there is no turn in either series in the neighborhood of the chronology date.

bChronology dates are business cycle reference dates. In addition, four minor subcycle dates, enclosed in parentheses, are added to form a subcycle chronology.

cReference series are of three sorts: (1) the business cycle chronology as shown in column heads, excluding the dates in parentheses; (2) the subcycle chronology as shown in all column heads; (3) particular series whose specific cycles and minor cycles constitute the reference dates for the comparison.

dThe number of months during which the specific series is in like phase with the reference series is expressed as a percentage of the total number of months covered between dates as given.

eMedian is the average timing of the center two or three turns.

fAverage deviation from the median. The "weighted" (wt'd) average is the deviation from the median for peaks and for troughs separately, weighted by the number of turns.

gIn determining months in like phase a timing adjustment is made which maximizes confluence. Before counting the months in phase, the specific series is in effect moved to the right to allow for a lead and to the left to allow for a lag if by so doing the percentage of months in like phase (as rounded) is increased. If the months in phase are as large or larger without an adjustment, this is indicated by a "timing adjustment" of 0.

In some cases we wish to know the percentage of months in phase on a synchronous basis, regardless of whether the percentage in phase is thereby maximized. If so, the "timing adjustment" is given as "none."

hFor the period 1/49−12/61, the percentage of months during which line 11 was in phase was 80 per cent; line 12, 83 per cent; and line 15, 89 per cent.

---

vendor performance and 87 months for the order term.[9]

Outstandings continue to rise not only absolutely but relative to sales (the ratio rises) for about a quarter of a year after these two indicators of market conditions, particularly

the second, indicate some slackening in market tension. Analogously, at recessions, producers continue to decrease the volume of goods on hand and on order, both absolutely and relatively to sales, for a number of months after more purchasing agents report improved than report worsened performance. One can find several reasons for the lag, but they are all too problematical to propose as an explanation.[10]

[9] Again, the implications of the actual percentage of months in phase need to be evaluated in terms of the number of movements and the correspondence of both series to general business conditions. The first criterion would in this case discount the significance of the comparisons since the number of movements is small. The second would increase it since all three series have a very poor conformity to business cycles or subcycles (see the first two lines for each of the three measures in Table 35). As a result, any relation of the series to one another is not likely to be produced by their common relation to major business conditions.

[10] I think of the following possibilities. Purchasers may request postponement of deliveries at peaks and a hastening of them at troughs. The cessation of an increase in the longest delivery terms to which the CPA data relate does not necessarily, as explained in the previous section, mean that total outstandings will decrease, since an increase in orders of intermediate term can accompany and perhaps persist longer than the increasing terms of the longest of advanced orders;

The average order term also clearly exhibits the motif of early thrust previously noted in the materials-purchasing segment of the economy. From the time that order terms began to expand to when their expansion reached its maximum was 19, 17, and 20 months respectively in the three major postwar cycles. The increase appears to be continuous and steady during the rise, and likewise during the period of fall (though not quite as consistently so). The time series has an unusually triangular pattern.

Triangular patterns appear also in the outstandings-shipment ratio and elsewhere in market-oriented data. Time series do not as a rule rise or fall at a uniform rate right up to the time when they reverse their direction. Change ordinarily slows down before it reverses. The retardations, say at peaks, express either reduced participation of firms in the predominant pattern of change, or reduced amount of change by each participant, or both. The failure of data that focus on market expectation to exhibit the usual amounts of this reasonable behavior presents a puzzle which needs to be unraveled. The last chapter offers an explanation.

I conclude that the purchasing-agent data suggest that market extension is associated in part with the lengthening of delivery periods by suppliers, and that buyers, whether for this reason or others, purchase at least certain principal materials farther ahead than before.

Is it possible to find hints in these time series of motives for market extension other than that of the changed delivery periods which suppliers offer?

An expected rise in price would, as we have noted, provide one reason, and expectations may bear some relation to the actual spot-market price of metals.[11] After 1948, when most of the recovery from war-time controls

had doubtless been completed, prices seemed to bear a general family resemblance to the other market-oriented series. However, their measured correspondence to the ratio (Table 35, line 11) even beginning in 1949 shows just 80 per cent of the months in phase with the outstandings ratio. It is interesting to note for later reference that prices tend to lead the outstandings ratio. This is hard to explain in terms of expected prices, which should, according to the logic presented early in the chapter, lag, since first differences, not the data proper, should correspond with the level of outstandings.

The risk involved in extending market positions is due in part to the possibility of buying at the wrong price. But it is also due in part to the possibility of buying an article that will not be needed within a reasonable time, or even at all. This second risk is virtually eliminated if materials are bought for use in connection with finished product for which firm sales orders have been written. If so, outstandings might be larger if backlogs of sales orders were larger, other things the same. However the volume of unfilled orders for machinery and transportation equipment (consult Chart 1) appears to have little or no relation to the data under examination, nor does its conversion to months of sales alter this fact. However, as we shall see in a moment, unfilled sales orders do have a different sort of association with these data.

The bottom line of Chart 10 shows profits before taxes for corporations in the durable goods industries.[12] There appears to be a provocative similarity between profits and the rest of the events that have been described. But profits lead the outstandings-shipment

---

an analogous logic might apply to troughs. Unexpected change in sales may also play a part.

[11] The following commodities are included: lead, copper, scrap, steel ("heavy" and "Pittsburgh"), zinc, tin.

[12] Corporate profits before taxes, durable goods manufacturers, as computed in the Federal Trade Commission–Securities and Exchange Commission Series covering twelve durable goods industries. This series replaces one compiled at the National Bureau by Thor Hultgren which was used for all of our calculations. Turns are identical except that the trough in 1949 was in May rather than in November. Timing comparisons are based on the former date rather than on that of the series as charted.

ratio by at least six months; in this they join and exceed most of the other series that we have been examining. The lead is regular; the average deviation is only 1.2 months for the six turns that are matched. Beginning in 1949, 89 per cent of the months are in like phase after allowing for a lead of orders of some seven or eight months (line 15). If this visual similarity implies any causal relationship, it is doubtless of a complex sort. Stocks of materials on order and on hand rise in response in part to an additional volume of sales, and higher volume ordinarily means higher profits, too.

It may be that the volume of profits has some direct bearing on the willingness of a businessman to support the financing costs of inventories on hand, and the obligation implied in those on order. I hinted at the argument in Chapter 2: retained profits constitute a source of funds and some portions of these funds must be kept liquid against the demise of good times. Would not investment in inventories provide this liquidity, whereas investment in fixed capital would not? If so, the actual opportunity cost of financing the additional stock is not the standard earnings rate that all investment, including investment in inventories, is likely to be required to meet; this figure may be 15 to 25 per cent in the heavy industries. Instead, it is the opportunity cost of liquid funds, as set by the earnings rate of assets such as commercial paper or government bonds. Management rules do not discuss such matters, but it may nevertheless get around that the front office is willing to overlook inventory investment which is high by the usual standards.

DEPARTMENT STORES

For department stores, there is little pertinent information on market conditions with which to compare the ratio of outstanding orders to sales. Nevertheless, Chart 11 displays some relevant data and Table 36 gives matching measurements.

For one thing, the ratio has a persistent

lead relative to the business cycle or subcycle chronology. At peaks it averages nine months; at troughs three, and four of the six trough comparisons are leads of between two and four months (Table 36, line 2). Thus the department store ratio moves earlier than for the durable goods industry (line 8) and very systematically so. This may reflect the tendency for consumer buying to move early in the postwar years. But there is, of course, no reason why changes in market expectations, if indeed this is what the ratios reflect, should have identical patterns in markets as diverse as those for materials for durable goods industries on the one hand and for finished goods sold by department stores on the other. In any event, there are interesting similarities and differences between the outstandings-sales ratio for the two sets of enterprises.

Of particular interest is what they suggest about the periods of thrust that we have observed in other contexts. For durable goods, termination of these thrusts marks the beginning of a downturn that continues throughout the rest of expansion. For department stores a relatively level period (1959) or a fall followed by a subsequent rise (1947 and 1951) may follow after the first strong upward rise at the start of cyclical expansion. The extra movements correspond to those found in many economic series in 1947 and after the Korean boom. It is interesting, incidentally, that the business expansion starting in early 1961 was accompanied by increases in the number of months' sales covered by outstanding orders for department stores; whereas for durables, the increase in outstandings (which, note, did take place at exactly the same time—December 1960) was less than proportional to the rise in sales, so that the ratio continued to fall off.

Table 37 develops further characteristics of the ratios at the time of rapid expansion. If, for the sake of argument, we read the strong rises in outstandings-sales or shipment ratios as an indicator of increasing tensions in the relevant materials markets, the figures picture

CHART 11

Ratio of Outstanding Orders to Sales of Department Stores,
Compared with Selected Series, 1946–63

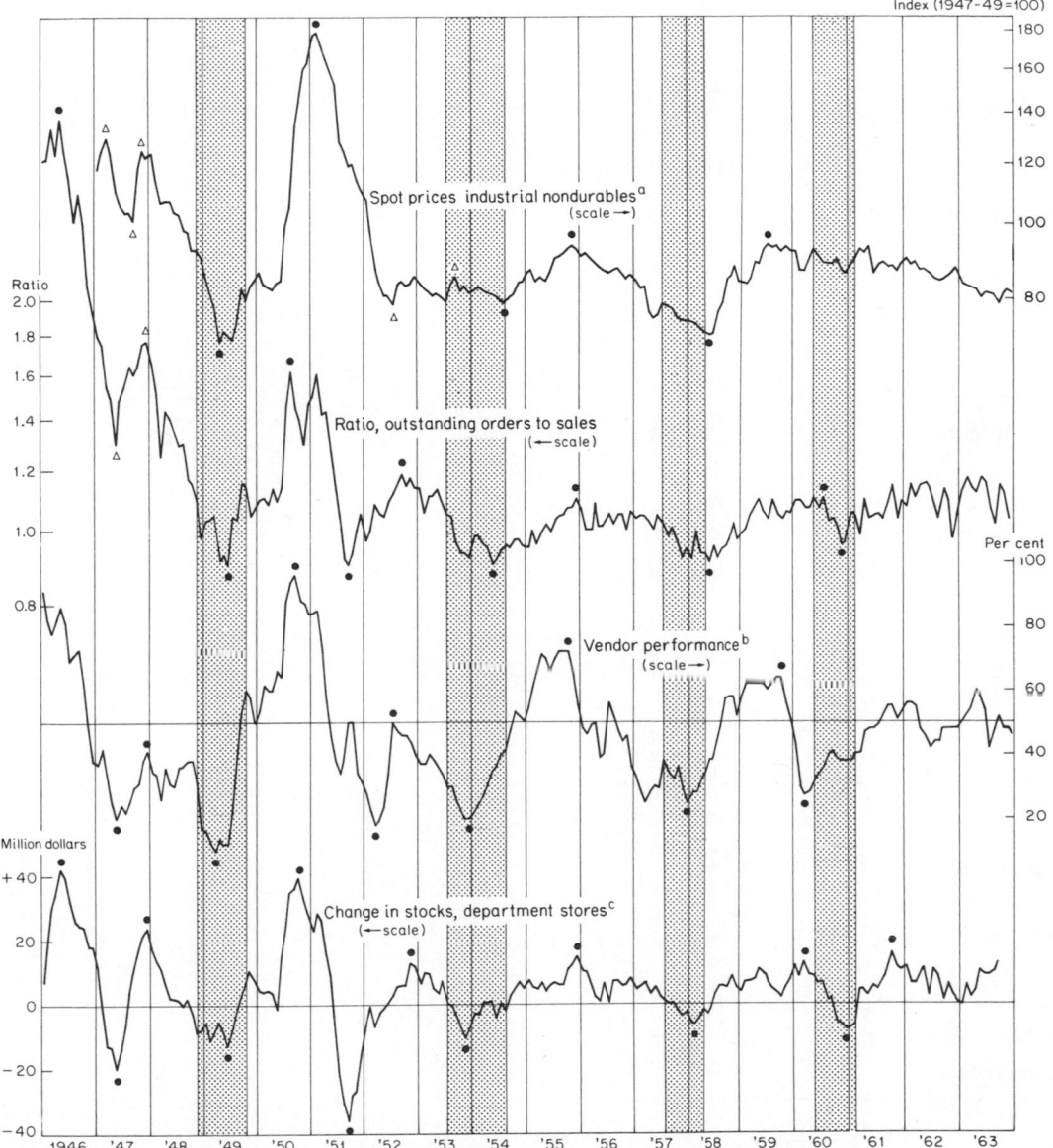

Note: Shaded areas represent business contractions. Specific cycle turns are marked by dots, additional minor turns by triangles.

a Index of spot prices of nine semidurable industrial commodities.

b Diffusion Index, Chicago Purchasing Agents Association.

c Five-month centered average of month-to-month change.

TABLE 36

Timing: Ratio of Outstanding Orders to Sales and Selected Data, Department Stores, 1946–61

		Section A: Months Lead (−) or Lag (+) for Matched Turns[a] Chronology[b]											
Line	Reference Series[c]	P (1/47)	T (7/47)	P 11/48	T 10/49	P (2/51)	T (6/52)	P 7/53	T 8/54	P 7/57	T 4/58	P 5/60	T 2/61

Specific Series: Ratio of Outstanding Orders to Sales

Line	Reference Series	P (1/47)	T (7/47)	P 11/48	T 10/49	P (2/51)	T (6/52)	P 7/53	T 8/54	P 7/57	T 4/58	P 5/60	T 2/61
1	Business cycles			−11	−4			−10	−3	−19	+1	+2	−3
2	Subcycles	−8	−2	−11	−4	−6	−9	−10	−3	−19	+1	+2	−3
3	Spot prices, semidurables	−10	−2	+1	+2	−6	−10	−12	−3	+1	0	+12	Ω
4	Level of vendor performance,	−5	Ω	Ω	−2	−8	Ω	Ω	−4	0	−3	+7	−8
5	Average term of purchase orders	+1	Ω	Ω	0	−5	Ω	Ω	+1	+3	+2	+7	−4
6	D. I. vendor performance[i]	Ω	0	0	+3	−1	−6	+2	+5	+2	+5	+9	+8
7	Change stocks dept. stores	−1	0	0	0	−2	0	−2	+6	0	+3	+4	−1
8	R: Materials outstanding to shipments, dur.	⊕	⊕	⊕	−3	−11	⊕	⊕	−2	−7	−7	−8	⊕

Specific Series: Change in Stocks

Line	Reference Series	P (1/47)	T (7/47)	P 11/48	T 10/49	P (2/51)	T (6/52)	P 7/53	T 8/54	P 7/57	T 4/58	P 5/60	T 2/61
9	Spot prices, semidurables	−10	−2	+1	+2	−4	−10	−10	−9	+1	−3	+5	Ω
10	Level of vendor performance,	−5	Ω	Ω	−2	−6	Ω	Ω	−10	0	−6	+3	−7
11	Average term of purchase orders,	+1	Ω	Ω	0	−3	Ω	Ω	−5	+3	−1	+3	−3
12	D. I. vendor performance[i]	Ω	0	0	+3	+1	−6	+4	−1	+2	+2	+5	+9

(continued)

TABLE 36 (concluded)

Section B: Average Timing of Turns

Line	Reference Series[c]	Number Matched			Median[e]			Average Deviation[f]				Section C: Percentage of Months in Like Phase[d]	
										All	Turns	Timing Adjust-ment[g]	% Mos. 7/46–
		−	+	0	P	T	All	P	T		Wt'd		12/61

Specific Series: Ratio of Outstanding Orders to Sales

Line	Reference Series[c]	−	+	0	P	T	All	P	T	Wt'd		Timing Adjust-ment[g]	% Mos. 7/46–12/61
1	Business cycles	6	2	0	−10.5	−3.0	−3.5	5.5	1.2	5.1	3.4	−3, −4	65
2	Subcycles	10	2	0	−9.0	−3.0	−5.0	4.7	2.0	4.5	3.3	−5	71
3	Spot prices, semidurables	6	4	1	−2.5	−1.7	−1.7	7.0	3.1	5.2	5.2	−2, −3	64[h]
4	Level of vendor performance,	6	1	1	−2.5	−3.5	−3.5	5.0	1.8	3.4	3.4	−3, −4	75
5	Average term of purchase orders,	2	5	1	+2.0	+0.5	+1.3	3.5	1.8	2.7	2.6	+1	79
6	D. I. vendor performance[i]	2	7	2	+1.7	+4.0	+2.3	2.5	3.5	3.2	3.0	+2	81
7	Change stocks dept. stores	4	3	5	−0.5	0	0	1.5	1.7	1.6	1.6	0	90
8	R: materials outstanding to shipments, dur.	6	0	0	−8.7	−4.0	−7.0	1.5	2.0	2.3	1.8	−7	79

Specific Series: Change in Stocks

Line	Reference Series[c]	−	+	0	P	T	All	P	T	Wt'd		Timing Adjust-ment[g]	% Mos. 7/46–12/61
9	Spot prices, semidurables	7	4	0	−1.5	−4.7	−3.0	5.2	4.1	4.5	4.7	−3	66[h]
10	Level of vendor performance,	6	1	1	−2.5	−6.5	−5.5	3.5	2.2	3.1	2.9	−5, −6	75
11	Average term of purchase orders,	4	3	1	+2.0	−2.0	−0.5	2.0	1.8	2.4	1.9	0, −1	79
12	D. I. vendor performance[i]	2	7	2	+2.3	+1.0	+1.7	1.6	3.5	2.7	2.7	+2	84

For notes a through g, see Table 35.

[h]Spot prices of semidurables were compared with each of the specific series for the time period 1/47–12/61.

[i]D. I. signifies diffusion index. For description see text footnote 6, above.

TABLE 37

Comparison of Timing and Duration for Periods of Thrust in Outstandings-
Sales Ratio, Department Stores and Durable Goods Manufacturers,
1946-65

Dates for Department Store Ratio		Timing: Durables Compared with Department Stores		Duration of Period	
Trough[a]	End of Thrust[b]	Trough[a] (1)	End of Thrust[b] (2)	Department Stores (3)	Durables (4)
5/47	12/47	unmatched		7	—
6/49	8/50	+3	+11	12	22
9/51	9/52	unmatched		12	—
5/54	12/55	+2	+7	19	24
5/58	5/59	+7	+6	12	11
11/60	5/62	unmatched	—	18	—
Average		+4.0	+8.0	13.3	19.0

Note: Ratio of outstanding orders to sales for department stores and ratio of outstanding materials orders to shipments for all durable goods manufacturers.

[a]Troughs are the specific cycle or subcycle trough dates.

[b]The termination date for department stores is the point at which the first continuous rise ceases or reverses; this is the date marked as the specific cycle or subcycle peak except for the last two movements. For durables it is in each case the specific cycle peak date.

a shingled overlay in the two markets. Suppliers of department stores feel the start of extension first—four months earlier on the average. (The last line shows that troughs in durables lag those in department stores by four months on the average.) But for suppliers of durable goods manufacturers extension persists longer (the peaks of the thrusts are eight months later on the average than those of department stores). Suppliers of department stores experience it more often—several episodes are unmatched. But the rises after major cyclical troughs, the movements shared by the two industries, can be of longer total duration in the durable goods than in the consumer supply fields (compare columns 3 and 4). It is interesting in this connection to remember that the percentage amplitude of rise during their expansion phases was virtually the same for the two ratios—peak standings on the average were 152 per cent of trough standings

for durables and 144 per cent for department stores. But of course, since the number of months' supply on order was far larger for durables, the absolute increase, in terms of weeks' supply, was also larger—over twice the size.[13] This is probably the more significant fact from the point of view of the market developments that are implied.

What the ratio suggests about market extension for department stores ought to be compared with information about the appropriate markets themselves, but unfortunately none seems readily available. A sensitive price index does not apply directly to finished consumer goods, but might have some indirect value as a reflection of tensions in those markets. The

[13] See Tables 7 and 16. The average week's supply on order for durable goods industries at troughs and peaks respectively was 8.2 and 12.5, an increase of 4.3 weeks during expansion. For department stores, the corresponding figures were 4.0, 5.7, and 1.7.

top line in Chart 11 is spot-market prices for nondurable industrial commodities, which, of course, are a poor representation of even the raw materials used in department store merchandise.[14] Perhaps all that can be said of this series is that it resembles retailers' advance buying more than would the metals price index of the previous chart. Nevertheless, though all turns are matched, the timing is very irregular and a very low percentage of months are in like phase (Table 36, line 3).

Firms reporting to the Chicago Purchasing Agents are chiefly manufacturers of durable goods. Nevertheless comparisons with the department store data are of interest. Indeed, line 4 of Table 36 shows that outstanding orders of department stores lead the level of vendor performance as the other timing figures imply, but correspondence is low. With the average term of purchase orders (line 5), its correspondence is a bit better, allowing for a lag of one month. But a somewhat closer association is evident with respect to the information that records not the level of vendor performance but its rate of change—the percentage of agents reporting that vendors' deliveries are deteriorating. This series, like virtually all first difference series, leads the level of performance. Eleven turns are matched and 81 per cent of months are in like phase after allowing for a two-month lag of the department store ratio. In Chart 11 (compare curves 2 and 3) the eye seems to support this measure of parallelism.

In view of the central need to have items on hand when customers may want them, part of retailers' defense against tightening markets is likely to be an effort to get goods delivered at once. The very high degree of correspondence (90 per cent of months are in like phase on a synchronous basis) of the outstandings ratio and the rate of change in stocks on hand, curve 4 of the chart (Table 36, line 7), could reflect this type of influence. It might also be reflected in the close association of inventory

investment with the rate of deterioration or improvement in vendor performance a month or so earlier (line 12). Eighty-four per cent of months are in like phase; eleven turns are matched, six of which are within two months of one another. At peaks the average deviation is only 1.6 months for the five comparisons.

In general there is little of consequence to go on, but the scraps that are available certainly do not deny the presence of market-directed considerations in retailers' buying. Also, market extension, as defined by the outstandings-sales ratio, occurs more often and typically a bit earlier than in the durable goods market. It has an exceedingly close counterpart in rates of change in stocks on hand.

Rates of Change in Outstandings

Rates of change are capable of enriching the meager information previously reviewed. For one thing, there are some additional series that can be introduced in this form. For another, comparisons of rates of change further specify information about correspondence yielded by data proper. Finally, and most important, it is possible that part of the process whereby a buying wave rises and falls operates through the impact of rates of change on the sensory apparatus of the market. Also, if adjustment to change in buying is sticky, high rates of change may occasion more response than low ones, other things the same; this line of thought finds application in the last chapter.

Once again, the most likely spot at which to see the reaction of buying to market conditions is in outstandings and rates of change in outstandings are particularly sensitive to market conditions. If more and more buyers fear that more suppliers will deliver more slowly or raise prices in one form or another, they will tend to place their orders for more goods farther ahead. In the aggregate buying is then likely to increase at an increasing rate.

In examining changes in outstandings it is

---

[14] The commodities included are burlap, cotton, hides, print cloth, rubber, tallow, wool tops, rosin.

just as well to include the response to changes in sales rather than to try to remove it by using ratios. It is clear by now that the sales influence is only one part of a complex picture, yet, since it may interact with the rest (and the next chapter shows that it does), it is better to include it than to take it out along with perhaps some other interaction effect.

Chart 12 displays an impressive parallelism between the rate at which outstanding orders for materials increase or decrease and the number of vendors that are reported to be making slower or faster deliveries. The two series share all the same movements and even the relative severity of each seems quite similar. The measures in Table 38, line 1, indicate that 82 per cent of the months are in like phase on a synchronous basis. There are eleven matched terms, eight of which are within two months of one another. Rates of change then support the other evidence suggesting that market extension takes place partly because suppliers require a longer time to make deliveries on at least some essential materials. However, the indication that this aspect tended to lead, which seemed implicit in the lead of the cumulative vendor performance index relative to the outstandings-shipments ratio, is weakened or rather qualified by the fact that, converted to rates of change, the association is not clearly different from synchronous. This is doubtless just another instance of how two phenomena can accelerate or decelerate at the same time, although the one does not actually reverse as swiftly as the other.

The association of outstandings and metals prices is deteriorated by differencing. This is caused at least in part by technical characteristics of the price series which may or may not have economic meaning: the data proper are unusually triangular in shape; therefore their first differences do not have the usual wavelike pattern, and selection of peaks and troughs is difficult and perhaps not meaningful. However, on the average, changes in outstandings are about synchronous with changes in prices. Thus, for whatever it is worth, these figures do not contradict the observation based on the data proper that timing association was not consistent with a causal link running from actual prices to expected prices to market expansion or contraction. This link would imply that prices lead because it is the rates of change in price and outstandings *proper* which would tend to be synchronous (or here second differences in prices and first differences in outstandings). The logic of this association was discussed at the start of the chapter.

The presence or absence of a backlog of sales orders can affect the risk cost of advance purchase of the materials required for the fabrication of the orders. Indeed, if a firm must write orders for future delivery at a predetermined price, it may be risky *not* to fix materials price (by immediate purchase) at the cost figured into the sales contract. Is there evidence that "backorders" affect the volumes of materials buying? The question may be examined by means of a series collected by the Purchasing Agents. Companies report whether the backlogs of the products the company sells are increasing or decreasing. This information for the same companies can be compared with the average term of purchase orders, the closest that the Purchasing Agents data come to changes in outstanding orders for materials. Eighty-six per cent of the months are in like phase (Table 38, line 8); of the eleven matched terms, seven are within two months of one another. However, it is interesting to find that changes in sales backlogs lag rather than lead changes in the average term of outstanding orders for materials (there is only one lead); the average lag is two months.

Further and somewhat conflicting evidence on the impact of unfilled sales orders of the machinery and transportation equipment industries with those of the materials-producing industries—hypothetically the outstanding materials orders of the first group (though with

CHART 12

*Changes in Outstanding Orders for Materials and Information
on Market Conditions, 1946–64*

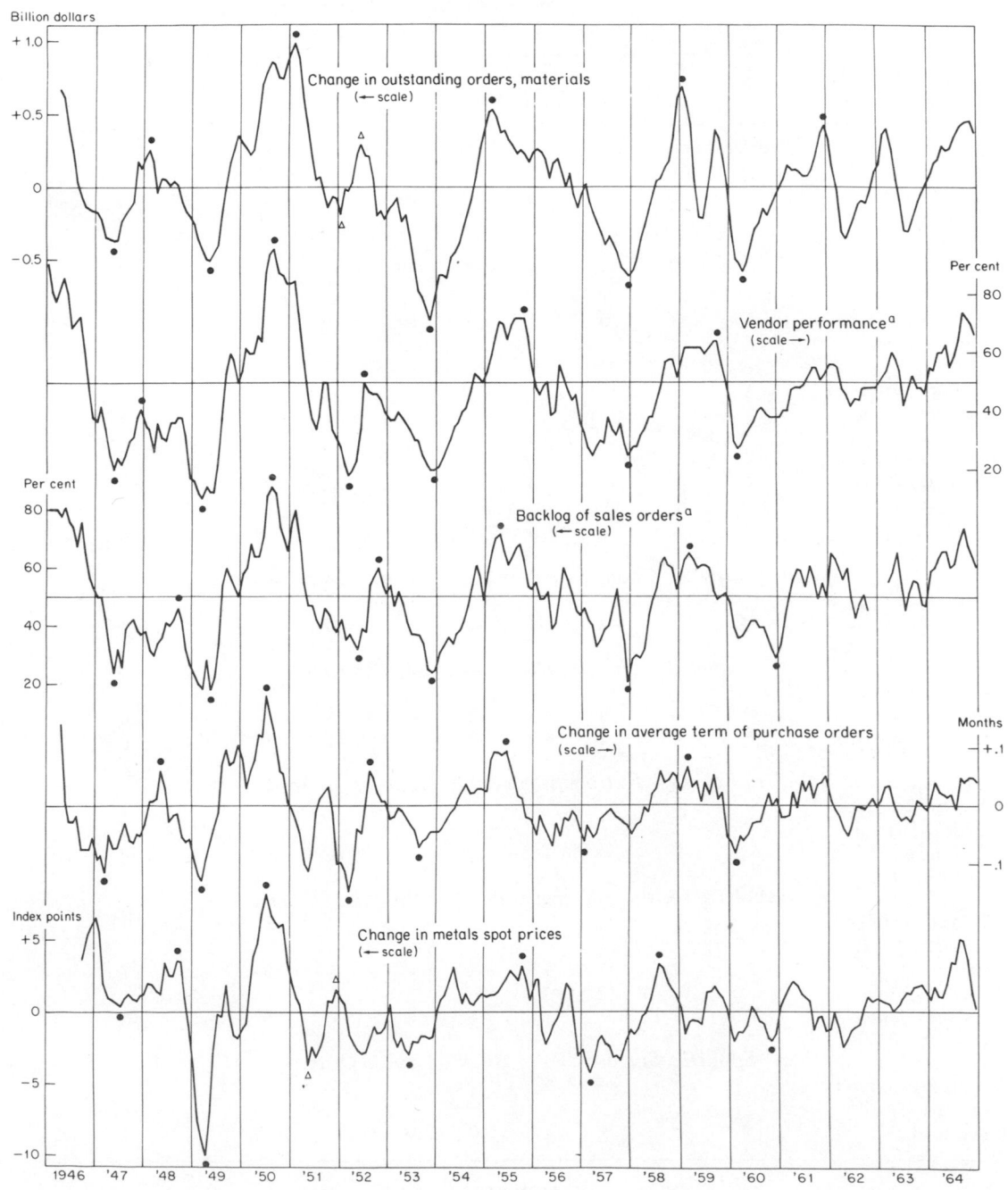

Billion dollars

Change in outstanding orders, materials
(← scale)

Per cent

Vendor performance[a]
(scale →)

Per cent

Backlog of sales orders[a]
(← scale)

Change in average term of purchase orders
(scale →)

Months

Index points

Change in metals spot prices
(← scale)

a Diffusion Index based on Chicago Purchasing Agents Association data.

TABLE 38

Timing: Changes in Outstanding Materials Orders and Selected Market Data,
Durable Goods Manufacturers, 1946–61

		Section A: Months Lead (−) or Lag (+) for Matched Turns[a] Chronology[b]											
Line	Reference Series[c]	P 1947	T 1947	P 1948	T 1949	P 1951	T 1952	P 1953	T 1954	P 1957	T 1958	P 1960	T 1961
	Specific Series: Change in Outstanding Orders, Materials												
1	D. I. vendor performance	⊙	0	+2	+2	+5	−2	−1	−1	−8	0	−9	+1
2	Change average term of purchase orders	⊙	+2	−3	+2	+7	−2	−2	+3	−4	+11	−2	+2
3	Change spot prices, metals	⊙	−2	−7	+1	+7	+8	+6	+5	−8	+9	−1	−7
4	Spot prices, metals	⊙	+8	−10	−10	+1	Ω	Ω	−3	−14	−4	−10	−8
5	Change unfilled orders, final product	⊕	Ω	Ω	+2	−1	Ω	Ω	+1	−9	+4	−4	−8
6	D. I. backlog sales orders	⊙	0	−7	0	+6	−4	−4	0	−2	0	−2	−8
7	Corporate profits	⊙	Ω	−9	0	+3	−7[r]	−11[r]	0	−9	−5	−4	−10
	Specific Series: Change in Average Term of Purchase Orders												
8	D. I. backlog sales orders	⊙	−2	−4	−2	−1	−2	−2	−3	+2	−11	0	−10
	Specific Series: D. I. Vendor Performance												
9	D. I. backlog sales orders	⊙	0	−9	−2	+1	−2	−3	+1	+6	0	+7	−9
10	D. I. production	⊕	Ω	−11[r]	+2	−1	+4	+3	0	−6	0	−8	+10
	Specific Series: Ratio Materials Outstanding to Shipments												
11	Change unfilled orders, final product	⊕	⊙	⊙	+6	+4	⊙	⊙	+9	+8	+16	+6	⊕
	Specific Series: Average Term of Purchase Orders												
12	Change unfilled orders, final product	−2	⊙	⊙	+3	−2	⊙	⊙	+6	−2	+7	+7	+3
13	D. I. backlog sales orders	Ω	⊕	⊕	+1	+5	⊕	⊕	+5	+5	+3	+9	+3
	Specific Series: D. I. Backlog Sales Orders												
14	Change unfilled orders, final product	⊕	Ω	Ω	+2	−7	Ω	Ω	+1	−7	+4	−2	0

(continued)

TABLE 38 (concluded)

Section B: Average Timing of Turns

| Line | Reference Series[c] | Number Matched | | | Median[e] | | | Average Deviation[f] | | All Turns | | Section C: Percentage of Months in Like Phase[d] | |
		−	+	0	P	T	All	P	T	All	Wt'd	Timing Adjustment[g]	% Mos. 7/46–12/61
	Specific Series: Change in Outstanding Orders, Materials												
1	D. I. vendor performance[h]	5	4	2	−2.3	0	−0.3	5.1	1.0	2.8	2.8	0, −1	82
2	Change average term of purchase orders	5	6	0	−2.3	+2.0	+0.7	2.5	2.3	3.6	2.4	0, +2	79
3	Change spot prices, metals[i]	5	6	0	−0.7	+3.0	+1.7	5.6	5.0	5.5	5.3	+1	68
4	Spot prices, metals[i]	7	2	0	−10.0	−5.0	−7.3	3.8	6.6	5.2	5.3	−8	77
5	Change unfilled orders, final product	4	3	0	−4.7	+1.5	−1.3	2.9	3.2	4.0	3.1	−1, 0	77
6	D. I. backlog sales orders[h]	6	1	4	−2.7	0	−1.3	2.7	2.0	2.9	2.5	−1, −2	83
7	Corporate profits	7	1	2	−7.3	−4.0	−6.0	4.1	3.6	4.0	3.9	−5, −6, −7	77
	Specific Series: Change in Average Term of Purchase Orders												
8	D. I. backlog sales orders[h]	9	1	1	−1.0	−2.5	−2.0	1.8	3.0	2.5	2.4	−2	86
	Specific Series: D. I. Vendor Performance[h]												
9	D. I. backlog sales orders[h]	5	4	2	+1.3	−1.0	−0.7	5.1	2.3	3.7	3.6	0	79
10	D. I. production[h]	4	4	2	−5.0	+2.0	0	4.4	2.8	4.5	3.6	0	70
	Specific Series: Ratio Materials Outstanding to Shipments												
11	Change unfilled orders, final product	0	6	0	+6.0	+10.3	+7.0	1.3	3.8	2.8	2.6	+6, +7, +8	84
	Specific Series: Average Term of Purchase Orders												
12	Change unfilled orders, final product	3	5	0	−2.0	+4.5	+3.0	2.2	1.8	3.2	2.0	+3	89
13	D. I. backlog sales orders[h]	0	7	0	+6.3	+3.0	+4.3	1.8	1.0	1.8	1.3	+4, +5	82
	Specific Series: D. I. Backlog Sales Orders[h]												
14	Change unfilled orders, final product	3	3	1	−5.3	+1.5	−0.3	2.2	1.2	3.3		0, −1	76

Notes to Table 38

NOTE: For notes a, d, e, f, see Table 35.

[b]Chronology dates are years when business cycle turns occur. They indicate the sequence and approximate time when the specific turns occur for which timing comparisons are given.

[c]Reference series are the series whose specific cycles plus minor cycles constitute

the reference dates with which matching cycles in the specific series are compared.

[h]D. I. signifies "Diffusion Index".

[i]Change in and level of spot prices of metals were compared with the change in outstanding orders materials for the time period 1/49–12/61.

serious impurities previously discussed). We have already noted that the data proper are poorly associated. Nor do the rates of change display an interesting confluence. Table 38, line 5, shows 77 per cent of the months in like phase on a synchronous basis: only seven turns are matched, and leads and lags are equally common. In Chart 6, where the two series were plotted, we saw that changes in backlogs do not have extra movements in 1947 and 1952; beginning in 1959 they had virtually no movements at all. This last characteristic brings to mind the ratio of outstanding materials orders to shipments, and further examination does indeed suggest other similarities. The rate at which back orders for final products built up or declined rose or fell on the average at least six months or more before the matched fluctuations in the ratio. Allowing for this lag, 84 per cent of the months were in like phase (Table 38, line 11).

All in all, the evidence bearing on the impact of backlogs of sales orders on materials buying is frustrating. For one thing the CPA data, which are highly pertinent, since they concern sales and purchase orders for the same companies, show close correspondence in, in effect, rates of change in the two sorts of unfilled orders; those for materials moved a bit sooner. The census data show an association between the level of purchase orders outstanding, expressed in terms of months of sales and the rate of change in sales orders of the heavy industries a good half a year earlier. The difference may conceivably be the result of the difference in the sorts of firms covered in the two sets of information; if so, this has some

economic meaning. But the possibility cannot be ruled out that difference results from technical characteristics of the CPA data.[15]

But I do not want to overemphasize the ambiguities of the evidence. The predominant impression is that of similarity. The empirical materials certainly are not inconsistent with the notion that a manufacturer is more likely to buy more materials farther ahead than usual at a time when backlogs for his own product are large, or that he is likely to return to a hand-to-mouth position when his customers are getting prompt deliveries.

[15] Concerning the problem of composition of the two sets of data, the CPA companies that report backlogs of sales orders are certainly not all members of the machinery and transportation equipment industries. Indeed, the proportion that are in some intermediate type of manufacture may well be large. For these, sales orders would be covered only as materials orders in the census data. This explanation seems consistent with the fact that when the two sets of statistics on change in unfilled sales orders are compared, the census series lags the other at the three peaks that can be matched (the average is five months) and leads slightly at the three troughs. This suggests a very long term for backlogs of orders in the heavy industries at peaks in business, and certainly this is sensible.

Concerning the problem of the technical character of the indexes, the CPA data for both sales and purchase orders are diffusion indexes of answers which themselves have no quantitative dimensions, but only a direction of change. It is possible that the *amount* of change tends to have a different pattern for sales and purchase orders. The census data are of course first differences of unfilled orders proper, which take the quantitative aspects of change into account.

A second possible technical basis for the high order of similarities for the CPA reports on sales and purchase orders outstanding could simply be that the same man, the purchasing agent, no doubt makes both reports. His judgment about what is happening to backlogs of sales orders may be colored by what he feels it necessary to do about buying—his own bailiwick.

CAPACITY LIMITATIONS

The Concept

All that has been learned about change in ownership of materials suggests that both buyer and seller participate in causing waves of market extension and contraction. This is dictated, in part, simply by the compound character of the phenomenon. It is dictated also by the fact that the cost of market extension is for the buyer an alternative to other ways of coping with the same problem; for the seller, rationing supply by selecting those customers who are willing to wait is an alternative to selecting those customers who are willing to pay a higher price.

However, it is perhaps also true that the entire phenomenon could be accounted for almost entirely in terms of delays in deliveries announced by suppliers, at times when the market could support them. This is an extreme statement and its truth or falsity is not important. A less extreme statement is clearly true: seller-instigated delays in delivery can be an important cause of market extension. How could a time series suggest the presence of this influence?

At first thought it might seem that the answer is simple—by a noteworthy parallelism between an index of percentage of capacity utilized and one depicting market extension. But a moment's thought disturbs the simplicity. Why should an increase in utilization from, say, 50 to 60 per cent have the same impact as an increase from 90 to 100 per cent? A more reasonable supposition may be that the increase from 50 to 60 per cent has no impact at all. This line of thought implies that a hypothetical perfect correspondence between time series on capacity utilization and materials outstanding could be something other than parallelism: extension might not start until utilization reached some minimum level. The association once underway might not be linear; rates of change might also be relevant.

A further difficulty concerns the degree to which capacity ceilings result from, on the one hand, growth in final demand, plus change in the stocks necessary to service it efficiently or, on the other hand, from growth of intermediate demand associated with the interplay between expectations and other short-term shifts in costs as visualized by buyers as well as sellers. Insofar as the first factors operate alone, capacity ceilings could be a chief cause of buying waves. Insofar as the second are also involved, they are at most only one of other contributing causes.

Obviously, then, it is not easy to specify precisely how evidence can inform on process. But in view of the character of the evidence, there is no reason to worry about the refinements. What, then, do the time series show? They show, in the first place, that they are most uncooperative. The basic difficulty is that the active element in estimates of percentage of capacity utilized is utilization. Utilization, ordinarily registered by an index of production, reflects the total level of demand whether for final sales or intermediate requirements of any sort. There is, therefore, no way to cleanse the picture of capacity limitations which are themselves the result of expected capacity limitations. The difficulty is accentuated by the fact that the data are annual. An interpolation for shorter time intervals virtually excludes any influence other than simply the current level of production.

The Data

Chart 13 presents the dilemma. The figures are those compiled by the Federal Reserve Board for the metals segment of "major materials." Capacity is based on engineering es-

CHART 13

Capacity and Output, Major Metals Materials, 1947–64

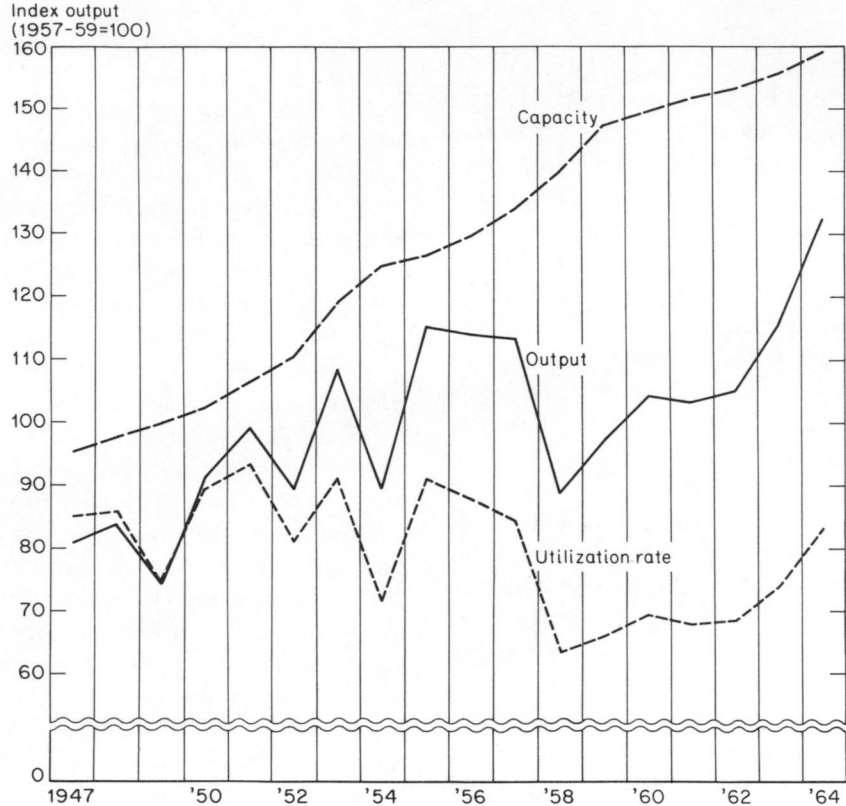

Source: Federal Reserve Board, Division of Research and Statistics.

timates.[16] The figures for 1962–64 exclude steel ingot capacity, reports on which were discontinued by the industry. All of the peaks in percentage of capacity utilized occurred in the same year as those of output. Thus the utilization series merely changes the trend of the output series from a rising slope to a level or declining slope (whether level or declining would depend on what inclusion of data for steel ingot capacity would do to the index).

A second group of information on plant utilization is reported by corporate officials in response to the McGraw-Hill Survey. It provides the basis for estimates of capacity

utilized in the durable materials industries, as they have been defined in this study, for 1954–62. After 1962 the steel reports are not available; accordingly, the index with iron and steel omitted is also shown.[17]

The McGraw-Hill materials industries index differs from the Federal Reserve Board major metals materials in several respects. For one thing, the former is dated December of each year and the latter covers the full year. For another thing, the coverage of the figures is, as I have described, different.

[16] The data are unpublished and I am indebted to Frank de Leeuw for making them available.

[17] The capacity estimates are published for the two-digit industries covered in our analysis for the durable goods materials group. I have combined them, using output weights.

CHART 14

Capacity Utilization Rates Compared with Outstanding
Orders and Order Terms, 1947–64

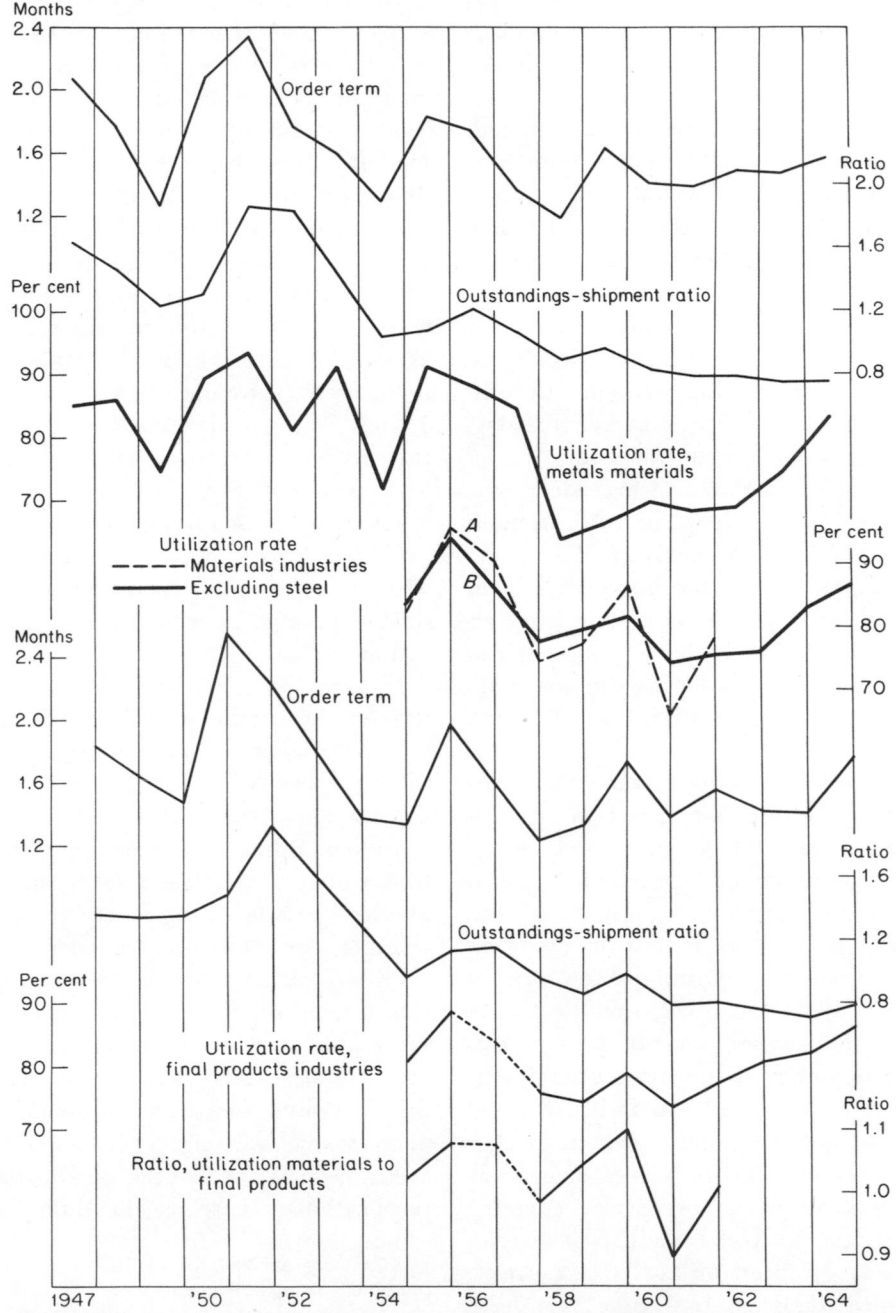

Notes: Order term is the Chicago Purchasing Agents Association Series on the average delivery term for purchase orders for major materials previously shown on a monthly basis. Curve 1 gives annual averages; curve 5 gives December figures.

Outstandings-shipment ratio is based on the Commerce data for durable goods materials manufacturers, previously shown on a monthly basis. Curve 2 gives annual averages; curve 6 gives December figures.

Utilization rate, metals materials. Curve 3 is FRB data as in Chart 13, curves 4A and 4B are McGraw-Hill data (see text).

Utilization rate, final products industries (curve 7), based on McGraw-Hill data (see text).

Ratio, curve 8, is curve 4A divided by curve 7.

Chart 14 shows both series, and there is no way of judging whether the difference in their course is due to conflict or to the technical differences. In any event, the two estimates of capacity utilized each drawn with a heavy line in the chart, may be compared with economic data which might be causally related. I choose outstanding orders and vendor performance, and they are shown above as annual averages (compare with curve 3) and below as December figures (compare with curves 4A and 4B).

Doubtless the annual figures are not adequate to display the subtleties of timing association. Nevertheless the troughs in outstandings seem to synchronize rather than lag, as they would if utilization rates did not influence buying until they had exceeded some trigger level. The dip in plant utilization in 1952 and its failure to peak in 1959 is no doubt associated with the long strikes in those years. Perhaps the most damaging aspect of the association is the very modest rise in outstandings in response to the sharp increase in capacity utilization in 1955 and 1956.

Rather more interesting is the visual correspondence with the average term of purchase orders (top or fifth curve), which incorporates the answers of purchasing agents to the question, "How far ahead must you buy in order to have principal materials on hand when needed?" Again, the low utilization rates in 1952 and 1959, doubtless associated with the strikes, do not have a corresponding tendency to improve vendor performance (cause the curve to fall). Allowing for this, there appears to be a general similarity in the direction and orders of magnitude of the movement in the two series—curves 1 and 3, or 5 and 4. And certainly, if activity in a plant starts to press on available capacity, customers are likely to find that they have to order farther ahead in order to have the product on time. Of all the factors influencing ownership that have been examined, the average order term is the one that should

most exactly transmit the impact of tight or slack supply conditions.

Of course, the figures say nothing about the sort of process that is involved in the deteriorating performance of vendors—whether, for example, it is associated with pressure from final demand or from a buildup in intermediate demand. One fragile piece of evidence on this point is afforded by a second segment of the McGraw-Hill data—an index covering the industries in our final products group (curve 7, Chart 14).[18] Though the average utilization rate in these industries is about the same as for the materials group, it fluctuates substantially less (compare curves 7 and 4A). The bottom curve, the ratio of the utilization rate of materials to that of final products, replicates much of the movement of its numerator. For whatever the figures are worth, they argue that something which happens as demand moves to earlier stages exacerbates variations in planned utilization.

However the basic difficulty sketched at the start of the chapter remains: it is hard to say how parallelism in market extension, or even in the speed with which vendors make deliveries, and capacity limitations should be interpreted. What is the meaning of the association which the statistics seem mildly to display? For one thing there is a question whether the timing is really appropriate as evidence of association. Why should order terms start to extend just when utilization rates first start to increase? At such times, there should be plenty of capacity to meet the increased demand; an analogous argument speaks for lags at peaks also. In any event, even if the association did have causal implications, there is no indication as to

[18] Capacity utilized in the following industries was combined using Federal Reserve Board production weights: machinery, electric machinery, autos and trucks and parts (except for December 1956), transportation equipment and aerospace. The auto group was not included in 1956 and therefore, as the dashed line in the chart indicates, the data for 1956–57 are not entirely comparable with the other years.

whether it resulted from a quasi-independent high level of utilization, from expectations of shortages and further actions which could be generated in the intermediate industries group, or from the two types of influence in combination. Perhaps all that can be safely said is that high utilization rates appear to have characterized some of the periods in the past when other signs of market extension were numerous and strong.

SUMMARY OF EVIDENCE

The question with which the chapter started— What are some of the factors other than sales that influence ownership?—has been answered largely in terms of a change in conditions in the market in which materials are bought, and in factors that influence the cost of taking these changes into account. Exclusion of other potential influences was forced by the absence of information on them. Even for the market-oriented group, the data permit no more than a highly impressionistic description. However, the time series that have been examined generally support the notion based on considerations of the functions that stocks serve in a business enterprise.

The following observations summarize the findings:

1. There does seem to appear in the aggregate data evidence that expectations about market conditions change very materially from time to time. (a) They undergo cyclical fluctuations which reach their high points some months prior to those in general business. (b) Their periods of most rapid rise occur quite early in expansion, participating very strongly in the phenomenon that I have called the first thrust of expansion. (c) A number of the series that reflect market conditions appear to rise very steadily during these periods and then reverse abruptly without the usual interval of retardation.

The logic of business problems prescribes that a number of factors are likely to participate in market-oriented fluctuation. The tables and charts that have been reviewed provide evidence that a number of these happenings are characterized by broadly similar patterns of change: backlogs of sales orders may accelerate or profits rise, thereby changing the costs associated with advance buying; suppliers may demand a longer delivery period, or prices may be expected to rise, thereby changing conditions or expectations concerning conditions in the materials market.

But though these influences are often likely to change together and consequently to act on materials procurement with united force, their patterns are far from identical. It is therefore instructive, by way of summary, to point to such differences in behavior as appear with sufficient persistence to seem potentially meaningful. The behavior will then be linked with its meaning as suggested by the analysis of market phenomena with which this chapter started.

Differences are exhibited in Table 39. There, all of the evidence bearing on each factor that may influence market conditions or expectations is compared with the evidence concerning levels of market positions and their rates of change.

2. Unfilled sales orders tend to lag outstanding orders for materials (lines 1 to 6). Defined in terms of rates of change, they lag by short intervals, particularly at peaks (section B). Defined in terms of levels of outstandings, the lag is clearer and somewhat longer, especially so at troughs (section A). The association shown in the purchasing agents' reports is quite close when rates of change are compared; however, as explained earlier, technical aspects of the data may overstate similarities. For the book-value information, confluence is low except when the rate of change in backlogs is compared with the level of materials that are outstanding about

TABLE 39

Average Timing of Market Factors Compared with Outstanding Materials Orders, Durable Goods Manufacturers, 1946-62

Series Reflecting Outstanding Materials Orders (reference series)	Series Reflecting Type of Market Factor and Series (specific series)	Basis of Comparisons										Source Table	Table Line
		A: Data Proper					B: Rates of Change						
		Timing[b]			Timing Adjustment	Months in Phase[a] %	Timing[b]			Timing Adjustment	Months in Phase[a] %		
		P	T	All			P	T	All				
Unfilled Sales Orders													
1. Outs. orders*	Unf. Orders, Fin. Prdt.*	+5	+5	+5	+4, +5	77						1	12
2. Chge. outs. orders*	Chge. Unf. Orders, Fin. Prdt.*						+5	−2	+1	0, +1	77	38	5
3. Chge. outs. orders*	Backlog Sales Ord., D. I.!						+3	0	+1	+1, +2	83	38	6
4a. Chge. av. term purch. ord.!	Backlog Sales Ord., D. I.!						+1	+2	+2	+2	86	38	8
4b. Vendor perform. D.I.!	Backlog Sales Ord., D. I.!						−1	+1	+1	0	79	38	9
Prices													
5. Chge. outstandings*	Chge. Metals Prices						+1	−3	−2	−1	68[c]	38	3
6. Ratio outs. to ship.*	Metals Prices	−3	−4	−4	−3	80[c]						35	11
Profits													
7. Ratio outs. to ship.*	Profits Dur. Gds. Mfrs.	−7	−6	−7	−7, −8	89[c]						35	15
Vendor Performance													
8. Chge. in outs.*	Vend. Perform., D. I.!						+2	0	0	0, +1	82	38	1
9. Ratio outs. to ship.*	Vend. Perform., Proper!	−3	−1	−2	−1 to −3	88						35	5
Av. Term of Purch. Order													
10. Chge. in outs.*	Chge. Av. Term!						+2	−2	−1	0, −2	79	38	2
11. Ratio outs. to ship.*	Av. Term! Purch. Ord.!	−5	−5	−5	−3 to −5	87						35	8

Notes to Table 39

!The series covered are the ones already familiar to the reader. However to aid in identifying them, those for which the source is the Census data for durable goods manufacturers are marked, and those for which the source is the Purchasing Agents Association of Chicago are marked!.

aThe period that is covered is 7/46 to 12/61; exception, see note c.

bNumber of months whereby market factor (Col. 2) lead (-) or lag (+), outstandings (Col. 1).

cRefers to the period 1/49–12/61. The timing for the rate of change in prices compared with the level of outstandings was: P, -12; T, -13; All, -12; 73 per cent of months in phase allowing for 12 or 13 month lead.

half a year later (Table 38, line 11). In general the picture is consistent with the notion that the presence of order backlogs tends, other things the same, to reduce the risk-cost of advance-materials ordering. However, the less than regular association, and the fact that extension of materials tends to precede that of finished products, indicates that other things are by no means the same. For one thing, we see that at least the backlog of sales orders needs to cease declining (or building up) at an increasing rate some months before procurement officers begin to extend (or contract) their orders outstanding. For retailers, since all sales tend to be for immediate delivery, the influence is entirely absent.

3. Profits, thought of as a source of funds, could also affect the costs that bear on procurement policy. Profits exhibit an impressive association with outstandings expressed in terms of months of sales about a half a year later. Eighty-nine per cent of months are in like phase. How can this association be explained? One possibility is that there is no direct causal link; instead we see merely parallelism in two sensitive representations of many things affecting sales and purchases. But there is a possibility that the confluence reflects a change in the opportunity cost of capital for firms that finance inventories largely with internal funds. The argument runs as follows: when internal funds are temporarily plentiful, businessmen are willing to invest the excess over normal supply of funds in assets that are relatively liquid (such as inventories or short-term financial obliga-

tions), but are unwilling to invest them in assets that will tie up the funds during times of possible future need. Thus the true opportunity cost of funds for inventories shifts from that of basic earning rates in the business to that of interest on liquid assets such as bonds or the like. As far as I know, the possibility of discontinuities of this sort has not been studied. It should be. For if there is anything to my argument, it would underscore the immunity possessed by some large firms, which finance stocks from internal funds, to efforts to restrict quasi-speculative inventory buying through monetary policy. For these firms, the argument would imply, not only would the restrictive monetary policy have little direct impact via a higher interest charge, but costs of funds for holding stocks could in effect actually be lower rather than higher (due to the shift in the appropriate opportunity cost) at just the times when credit stringency is developing.

4. Of the factors that bear on conditions in materials markets, sensitive prices are an obvious candidate. Prices tend to lead outstandings whether compared for department stores (Table 36, line 3) or for durables, whether as data proper or as rates of change (Table 39, lines 5 and 6). This is clearly not in accord with the causal explanation that moves from the actual rate of change in prices, through the expected rate of change in prices, to the desired level of ownership. The logic implies synchronous association between the rate of change in prices and the level of ownership. Instead, changes in

prices lead the level of ownership by about a year (Table 39, note c). The last chapter describes what a relationship of this sort might imply.

5. The time series also supply evidence concerning what earlier in this chapter I called the analytic components of increase or decrease in materials outstanding. The first component, outstandings associated with change in sales and sales-linked stocks, I have tried to remove by using ratios or first differences. But evidence on the others—changing delivery periods in the several categories (numbers 3 and 4), and changing weights in total outstandings of deliveries in each category (number 2)—is afforded by the body of data collected by purchasing agents concerning what they and their suppliers do—actions that affect these matters of delivery terms and their relative weights. This entirely independent source of information shows noteworthy correspondence to the level and rates of change in the book value of outstanding orders of materials.

The speed with which vendors offer to supply major materials ("vendor performance") accelerates or decelerates at much the same time as total orders outstanding (Table 39, line 8). Though there are minor differences, the same statement applies to rates of change in the average term of purchase orders (line 10). The first series is confined to changes in delivery periods—analytic component number 3; the second includes changing relative weights of advance and "at once" deliveries, component number 2.

The data proper have a different though quite systematic association (lines 9 and 11). The average term of purchase orders starts to decline and vendor performance starts to improve several months before the total volume of outstandings (expressed in months of sales) turns down; a like remark, toned down, applies to the trough comparison. The lag in outstandings may reflect, among other things, the tendency for orders bearing long delivery terms to remain outstanding after fewer new

orders of these terms are currently being written. In this sense, the explanation is analogous to that of the long lead of outstanding relative to stocks that was suggested earlier.

6. For department stores, such evidence of parallelism as the data afford does not justify an effort to distinguish the particulars of factors bearing on outstandings. Clearly, relevant data on market conditions are lacking. Nevertheless, in view of these deficiencies, there does seem to be an association worth noting between the level of outstandings expressed in terms of months' sales and the rate at which vendor performance was improving or deteriorating two months earlier. Eighty-one per cent of months were in phase (Table 36, line 6). The rate of change in stock also showed a close relation to this series with a two months' lag—84 per cent of the months were in phase (line 12). As we shall see in the next chapter, it is quite possible that the seasonal and other problems of retail stores mean that levels of outstandings and rates of change in stocks on hand reflect rates of change in market conditions.

7. These various particulars of timing association are interesting and bear on the dynamics of the process of inventory fluctuation. Individually, the bits of evidence are frail. Collectively, they seem to make a more reliable assertion: the rates of change in each of the variables that constitute market conditions tend to move, broadly speaking, within a few months of one another. Note the similarity of timing for all items in the second set of columns (section B), in which the rate of change in each market factor is compared with the rate of change in outstandings. This fact seems to underscore the interrelatedness of the compound phenomenon of fluctuation in ownership. Whether individual businessmen tend to change their market positions primarily because they expect prices to rise, deliveries to tighten, or other costs to change, they will all tend to do the same thing at the same time.

8. Is it possible to separate, at least collec-

tively, the group of factors affecting inter-mediate demand from those affecting the supply side of materials purchasing? A negative reply was developed in the last section of the chapter. Though there was evidence of some parallelism between the level of capacity utilization and the average term for which the materials remained outstanding, the fact of parallelism has an unclear causal interpretation. Certainly some of the more extreme episodes of advance buying occurred when utilization rates were high, but the waves seem to start and stop before the capacity thesis affords an explanation. Moreover, there seems no way to separate pressure on capacity ceilings that result from customers' concern over possible shortages from the pressure that would have resulted had this concern, and the buying that it stimulated, not existed. The time series are lines on a two dimensional surface. They are incapable of describing the crooked wormhole that events bore through the N-dimensional space.

Without doubt both expectations of shortages and actual levels of demand must be involved. But I would like to hazard a guess that their impacts are not simply additive. Pressure on capacity that is a function of the flow of products into final use tends to sensitize the economy to buying waves. Since it is reasonable to assume that plants are tooled up to handle at least the basic levels of previous final use, this pressure may result largely from the high rate of change in final use. When pressure of this sort exists, any further increase in demand (which may be due to changed expectations, or any of the other elements that are associated with changes in the timing of materials buying) will cause more serious pressure than it otherwise would. Further, rounds of cause and effect follow. If this is so, it raises some questions of public policy with respect to the desirability of encouraging manufacturers to maintain second-string idle capacity. It may be that tooling up so that profits are only adequate at high levels of plant utilization contributes to instability in the economy at large.

This chapter has tried to hold the influence of sales at arms' length while "other influences" are examined. Yet there is every reason to believe that these two groups of changes do not simply total their influences but change as they combine. Certainly it was not possible to think about the role of capacity limitation or any other piece of the total without recognizing the geometry of interplay between supply, demand, and expectations. Nor can we conclude the analysis of the dynamics of the inventory cycle without opening this troublesome and yet fascinating Pandora's box.

11. Fluctuation in Ownership and Inventory Models

The first of the two previous chapters concentrated on empirical evidence of the need to keep stocks aligned with sales, and the second on evidence of the need to time purchasing with an eye to conditions in the materials markets. This segmented approach, which in even more exaggerated form has characterized all of the empirical work in this book, must now be abandoned.

I want instead to attempt to read the data in the context of all of the factors that potentially influence stocks and their interrelationships. Also I want to project the implications of the procedures, which result in positive and negative inventory investment, in terms of their impact on the relation between selling and materials buying (a question that has occupied parts of Chapters 7 and 8). Integrated with the analysis of stocks and total ownership, this will afford a comparison between the findings of this study and other analyses of the amplifying and accelerating attributes of inventory investment. I find that when the several aspects of a model are specified for department stores, on the one hand, and durable goods manufacturers on the other hand, the amplifying and accelerating processes that result are rather different for the two sorts of enterprise.

TWO CONCEPTUAL PROBLEMS

The two objectives of this chapter each raise a conceptual problem that requires a moment's analysis. First, to examine the interrelationship of all of the factors that influence stocks, it is necessary to define and somehow cope with the failure to meet objectives and its manifestation—unintended stocks. Second, to analyze the relation between selling and buying, it is necessary to define selling: does it take place when sales orders are written or when the goods are shipped to customers?

Error and Inventory Objectives

The interrelations between the two influences on inventory fluctuation which the figures have highlighted, the sales link and market conditions, must be affected by any other influence that bears on the ownership of materials. Many of these have remained invisible in the data. They include a wide variety of opportunity costs, such as that of flexible production schedules, selling effort, and the executive time and other costs of formulating and enforcing precise inventory objectives.

But they also include downright error in the sense of more or less clearly formulated inventory objectives which are not met. The recognized error and resulting unintended inventory investment must be corrected in some way. Desired stocks are necessarily defined in terms of *future* demands, market expectations, and other factors; this implies predictions, and predictions are seldom accurate. Even when correction is firmly intended, it may take time to achieve; unintended or error stocks exist until the correction is effected.

The size of potential error depends on several matters—how well the target information can be predicted; the quality of the information system; the length of time between the target date and the time, in advance of that date, when action directed toward an achievement of intentions must be taken; the level of discipline in the organization; the possibility of piecemeal progressive correction.

If study focuses on stock on hand, error can be exceedingly troublesome. Its detection implies a virtually complete knowledge of intended inventory change, of the character of forecast, and of the machinery whereby objectives are acted upon. Yet without this information it is very difficult indeed to use empirical data to suggest what businessmen are trying to do and why; since they do not succeed in doing it, the data do not reveal it. The distributed-lag notion that has been used in econometric analysis tries to circumvent the difficulty. But, as suggested in Chapter 1, when calculations indicate that an inventory objective, as defined, is only half achieved in the course of the year, the dodge does not seem very effective.

Eventually it should be possible to learn enough to fill in more of the information that is essential to describing the path whereby action moves toward specifying and achieving inventory intention in various sorts of business enterprises. But in the meantime there is, I think, a different way around the difficulty. It is, of course, as indicated at the outset of this study, to include stocks on order as well as on hand.

If ownership turns out to be different than presently desired, the difference can be reversed. Desired ownership is partly defined by a set of desired relationships to a number of variables—sales, costs, and so on. Prediction of the ownership that will be optimal in the future implies a prediction of how the relevant variables will behave. Errors in these guesses are one source of discrepancy between actual and desired ownership. Difference may also result from a change in the relationship that is desired. But whatever the reason, new orders can correct promptly if the error is recognized and if it is deemed worthwhile to reverse it. Changes in the price of finished goods, sales pressure, and a number of other strategies may be brought into play. But certainly a most usual and important strategy is to modify the volume of new orders.

For errors of underestimation the correction can be virtually immediate; all that is required is an increase in new orders for materials. For errors of overestimation, correction may take a bit more time, since particular items may be overstocked by more than feasible reduction in new orders can immediately reverse. Even cancellation of orders may be unable to achieve the objective.

Of course the correction that orders effect may be less than optimal. Its first impact is on stock on order whereas one might prefer to change the amount of stocks actually on hand or, for that matter, in the process of production or finished. But as a rough approximation the level of total materials ownership may be regarded as hovering not too far from the desired level, if not month by month at least quarter by quarter.

Accordingly I make the assumption that unintended or "error stocks," in the restricted sense in which I have defined them, are sufficiently unimportant to neglect in statistics on materials ownership. The assumption relieves me of the embarrassing necessity of constructing a model which I do not know how to construct—one dealing with a detailed set of objectives, a time path of expectations and a time path of actions overlaid on one another as relevant information is generated.

However, and this is an important qualification, error of a more passive sort may be both present and large. I refer to ownership which on the one hand is different from what would presently be deemed ideal, but which on the other hand is not subject to explicit and high-priority correction. In other words, if the calculation is made, and it may not be made except as a visceral judgment, the opportunity costs of the sequence of procedures that would recognize and keep the error in check are too high. This passive unintended stock both on hand and on order is a no-man's land between stocks that conform to some formulated intention and stocks whose failure so to conform is, under the circumstances, worth the opportunity costs of identification and swift correction.

Orders and Shipments

The orientation of this study toward including materials stocks on order as well as those on hand was based on the belief that a basic aspect of management conceptualization and behavior was thereby duplicated. Procurement is oriented in terms of buying, which implicitly if not explicitly affects stock on hand as well as on order. Thus far I have largely ignored the question of whether there is a counterpart at the selling end of the business. The counterpart would assert that the basic conception of "demand" to which the sales-linked stock objective (or indeed any other stock objective) responded consisted of customers' orders rather than of shipments to customers (or production). Certainly this is a possibility that must be considered. My general conclusion is that it is more realistic to keep consideration of the stock-flow alignments focused on shipments, and to deal with the further impact of new sales orders in terms of the way in which they diverge from shipments; specifically, to deal with them in terms of the rate of change in unfilled orders, commonly called back orders or order backlogs.

This question has no operational implications in connection with the department store data, since customers' orders and sales are virtually identical. But in connection with the data for durable goods manufacturing, the difference can be quite significant and therefore it will be useful to take the detour necessary to spell out the whys and wherefores.

The basic reason is simply that there are costs associated with holding goods. Ideally, therefore, materials should be acquired just soon enough for them to arrive, with an acceptable likelihood and at an acceptable acquisition cost at the shipment (or processing) station at just the time when the work is scheduled to be performed. The time at which customers order an article is related to these scheduled times, but the relationship differs under at least four circumstances that need to be distinguished.

Variant 1. When the time between the writing of an order and the time when production of them must begin is long. The disparity can be due to delay in starting production because of backlogs already on the books. Or many months may be required actually to produce articles, and a scheduled flow of materials may be required throughout the processing period. Under either circumstance the efficient servicing of sales, other things the same, does not require that materials orders parallel sales orders; it requires rather that materials are ordered just on time to arrive with acceptable probability and at acceptable ordering costs at each production station as needed for production to get under way. However, as we have rehearsed all too often, many factors other than sales can influence procurement policy and argue in favor of buying before the efficient dates.

A firm order for the final product largely removes one set of risks which would otherwise attend advance acquisition—the risk of obsolescence, that is, of having purchased materials that will not be needed. Thus a backlog of sales orders provides a period of option during which materials can be bought ahead if it is judged desirable to do so at what is in effect a lower cost than if the backlog were not present.

Variant 2. When the purchasing may in large part be linked to a particular order as for variant 1, but the interval between the writing of an order and the start of production is short. In this case, materials purchasing and sales orders may have a systematic relationship, with orders leading by short intervals. The order in effect foretells shipment of the finished goods by the length of the production period, and helps thereby to effectuate sales-linked inventory objectives. Materials which are ordered at the time the sales order is written may arrive in time to be used in its fabrication, and if not they will at least replace the units of stock which were actually used.

Variant 3. When sales are customarily made from stock. This means that there is no necessary tie between a particular sale and a particular purchase of materials. Procurement is geared to the necessities of efficient production, efficient stock management, and expected shipments. In this case, then, sales orders and shipments of the company's product are virtually identical.

Variant 4. When only some sales are made from stock and some or all of such sales consist of goods that the purchaser orders to fill in depleted stocks. This portion of total sales may have a tendency to reach highs and lows ahead of the bulk of all other sales orders.[1] The pattern of these fill-in orders may forecast changes in total sales orders or shipments in the near future and thus serve to guide procurement toward realizing its inventory objective. But here the distinction is not between orders and shipments; it is between some portion of orders which are virtually identical to the same portion of shipments and different from the rest of orders, which in turn may be identical to shipments (variant 3) or different in one of the two ways described as variant 1 or 2.

In variants 1 and 2 there can be differences

[1] The reason for the lead is not material to the argument. It is implicit, I believe, in the tendency for forecasts to be based on current sales and for these forecasts to be the basis for advance orders. The advance orders will then be in error by the amount that sales have changed. These rates of change in sales tend to lead sales proper. (See R. P. Mack, *Consumption and Business Fluctuation*, pp. 105 and 243.)

between the time pattern of sales orders and shipments. For one thing, it is the pattern of shipments or, more particularly, production starts and other production stages that sets the requirements for materials that are needed to achieve physical efficiency in processing and shipments, other things the same. Second, variants 1 and 2 provide a good forecasting technique which makes it possible to enforce whatever shipments or production-linked inventory objectives may be held. In connection particularly with variant 1, though sometimes also with variant 2, advance knowledge of requirements reduces the risk and therefore the cost of altering the timing of buying with a view to future prices or market conditions—at least the wrong items will not be bought. Indeed it may be risky not to buy ahead in order to "fix materials prices" to correspond with the cost of materials as figured in the selling price.

In variants 3 and 4, orders and shipments are identical, but in the case of variant 4 one part of either shipments or orders can serve the function of aiding to forecast shipments and thereby to enforce a stock objective.

These observations imply the way in which demand should be conceptualized as it moves backward through a firm from its customers to its suppliers. The demand from the customer is best viewed in the first instance as shipments (or, where the data are available, as demand for materials at various critical stations such as the start of or other points in the process of production). Demand so defined gives rise to inventory objectives for goods both on hand and on order, and is therefore both directly and indirectly a basic determinant of the orders placed with suppliers. However, the pattern of sales orders can have an important further bearing on materials orders. For one thing, it can, via its role as a forecast of shipments, make it possible to enforce inventory objectives. Second, insofar as shipments and new sales orders differ, this difference is identified by the rate of change in back orders. The level of these back orders, and perhaps their rate of change, influences some of the cost of alternative materials purchasing and inventory schemes, and is therefore important to purchasing and inventory policy.

DEPARTMENT STORES

For department stores the data fall neatly into the ideal conceptual framework. Customers' orders are identical for all intents and purposes to department store sales and therefore unfilled sales orders are negligible. All inventory on hand and on order is presumably covered by the two sets of statistics. Orders placed for materials cover orders for all of the merchandise sold.

Dynamics of the Sales-Stock Link

The link of ownership to sales has appeared to be firm and relatively precise according to the picture presented in Chapter 9 and elsewhere. It is evidenced both by a marked parallelism between sales and ownership proper and also, a more sensitive test, between rates of change in the two series. The latter association is shown in curves 2 and 3 of Chart 15. Table 40, line 4, gives the individual timing comparisons. Seven of the twelve matched turns are virtually synchronous—within one month of one another—and only two differ by more than three months. Eighty-four per cent of the months are in like phase on a synchronous basis. To explain the association, the merchant may be pictured as judging whether and about how fast sales have been increasing (or decreasing) over the past few months and whether they are likely to in the immediate future. He then adjusts his buildup in stocks on hand and on order in an appropriate fashion.[2] If sales are expected to be higher by a given amount than at some reference date, stocks should also be higher by at least as much plus whatever stock cushion is needed and likewise if sales are lower. The adjustment consists of additions to and subtractions from new orders which would otherwise have been placed. (I am ignoring other adjustments, such as markdowns, which are also used.) The pattern of the adjustment would be that of the rate of change in sales, and its volume would depend on the character of the ownership-sales objective.

In actual practice, provisions are likely to have a shingled pattern. Advance orders are placed for some fraction of the expected season's requirements; expectations are based on corresponding periods of the previous year adjusted for special sales, weather, and other elements affecting last year's figure, and for trends over the intervening months. The adjustment can, in effect, mean that forecasts are virtually based on deseasonalized sales of previous months. Fill-in orders, placed as close to the time when they will be needed as speed of delivery permits, reflect more recent sales history. At-once orders, for immediate delivery, may provide a further form of adjustment. Both fill-in and at-once orders will reflect rates of change in sales, assuming that current or previous sales provide a common denominator of forecasting procedures.[3]

[2] The actual judgment is likely to compare the rate at which sales are "going ahead" relative to the corresponding months of the previous year; an ad hoc judgment may be made as to how appropriate the base months are. I have computed this set of ratios (using seasonally adjusted data, which are not appropriate), and differenced them, but they appear to be less well correlated with change in ownership than the moving average of recent change. This could mean that the ad hoc judgments which are made to adjust the formal calculations for recognized abnormalities are of some importance.

[3] The basis of these generalizations were discussed in connection with shoe retailing in my *Consumption and Business Fluctuations*, pp. 95–112. The sales-linked portion of buying was called "stable-market orders." For department stores as a whole, buying procedures were discussed in Ruth P. Mack and Victor Zarnowitz,

CHART 15

Changes in Sales Compared with Selected Series, Department Stores, 1946–63

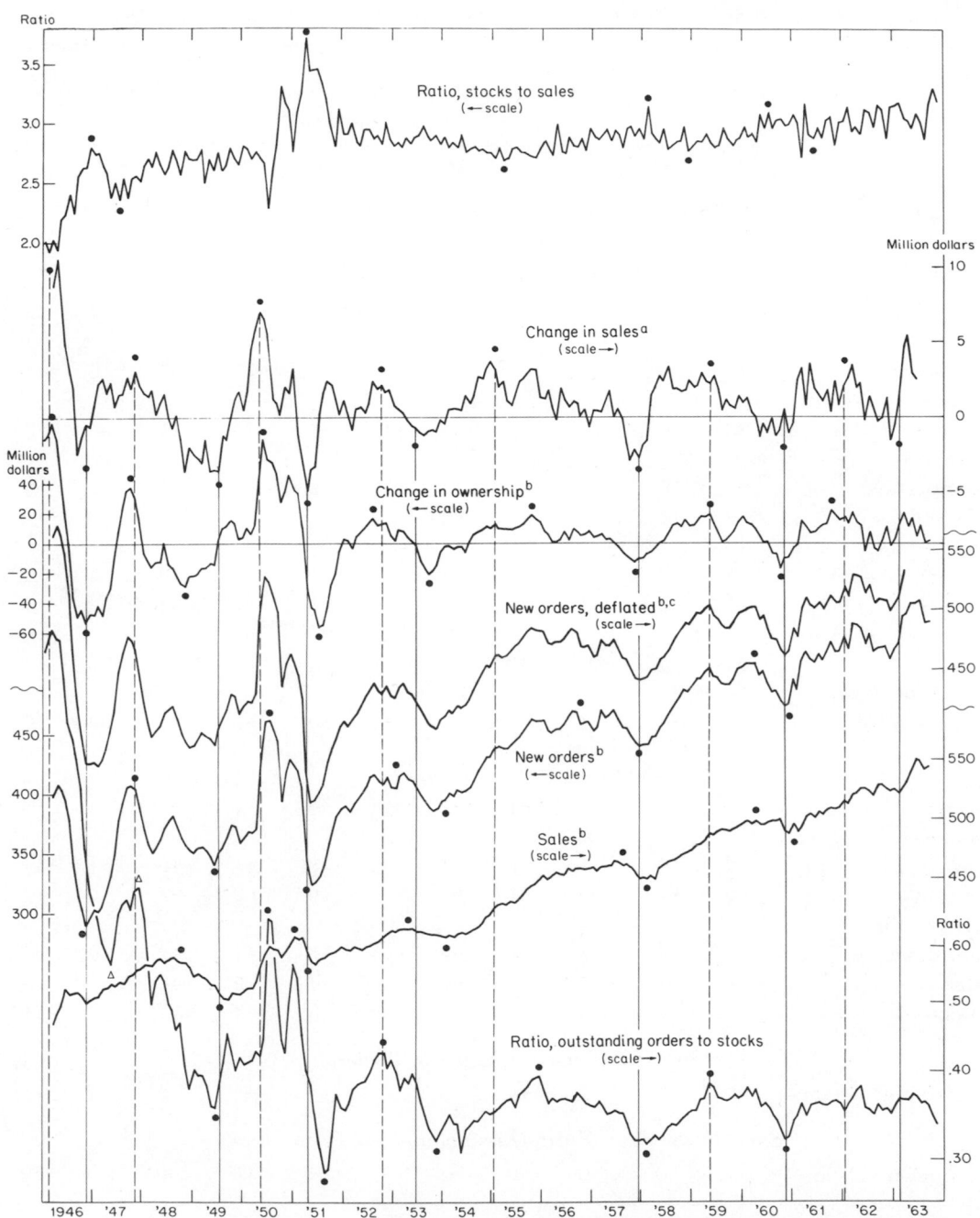

Note: Vertical dashed and solid lines mark, respectively, peaks and troughs in change in sales.
ᵃ Five-month average of five-month average; turns marked in the original five-month average prior to second smoothing.   ᵇ Five-month centered moving averages; turns marked in underlying monthly data except for change in ownership.   ᶜ New orders deflated by retail price index of commodities other than foods and autos, 1957–59 = 100.

TABLE 40

Timing: Change in Sales, Ownership, and New Orders, Department Stores, 1946–1962

Section A: Months Lead (−) or Lag (+) for Matched Turns[a]
Chronology[b]

Line	Reference Series[c]	P 1947	T 1947	P 1948	T 1949	P 1951	T 1952	P 1953	T 1954	P 1957	T 1958	P 1960	T 1961
	Specific Series: Change in Sales												
1	Subcycles	−11[r]	−8[r]	−12	−3	−9	−14	−9[r]	−14[r]	−30	−4	−12	−3
2	Ratio stocks to sales	−10[r]	−8[r]	Ⴚ	Ⴚ	−11	Ⴚ	Ⴚ	−21	−37	−12	−14	−7
3	Change in stocks, inverse	+6	+6	+19	+11	+6	+13	+7	+14	+24	+15	+8	+13
4	Change in ownership	−1	0	+1	+8	−1	−3	+2	−3	−9	+1	0	+1
5	New orders	−3	+1	0	+1	−2	0	−3	−7	−21	0	−11	−1
5a	New orders, trend corrected	−3	0	0	+1	−2	0	+1	−7	−10	0	−1	−1
6	Change in stocks	−3	−6	−1	+1	−5	−5	−1	−5	−11	−2	−10	−1
7	R: stocks to sales, inverse	−1	+4	Ⴚ	Ⴚ	0	Ⴚ	Ⴚ	−2	−2	+5	+4	+7
8	R: outstanding orders to stocks	−1	−6	−1	+1	−1	−4	0	−5	−11	−2	0	0
	Specific Series: New Orders												
9	Subcycles	−8[r]	−8[r]	−12	−4	−7	−14	−6	−7	−9	−4	−1	−2
10	Change in ownership	+2	0	+1	+7	+1	−3	+5	+4	+12	+1	+11	+2
11	Receipts	−2	−7	−2	−1	−6	−5	0	0	−6	0	0	0
12	D.I. vendor performance	Ⴚ	−6	−1	+3	−2	−11	+6	+1	+12	0	+6[r]	+9[r]
13	Sales	Ⴚ	Ⴚ	−11	−1	−6	0	−4	0	−10	−2	0	−1
13a	Change in sales	+3	−1	0	−1	+2	0	+3	+7	+21	0	+11	+1
	Specific Series: Change in Ownership												
14	Vendor performance	Ⴚ	−6	−2	−4	−3	−8	+1	−3	0	−1	−5	+7
	Specific Series: Ratio Outstanding Orders to Stocks												
15	Change in stocks	−2	0	0	0	−3	−1	−1	0	0	0	−10	−1

(continued)

TABLE 40 (concluded)

Section B: Average Timing of Turns

Line	Reference Series[c]	Number Matched −	+	0	Median[e] P	T	All	Average Deviation[f] P	T	All Turns Wt'd	Section C: Timing Adjustment[g]	% Mos. 7/46– 12/61	% Mos. 1/48– 12/61
	Specific Series: Change in Sales												
1	Subcycles	12	0	0	−11.5	−6.0	−10.0	4.2	4.3	4.8	4.2	−9,−10,−11	69	67
2	Ratio stocks to sales	8	0	0	−12.5	−10.0	−11.5	7.2	4.5	6.0	5.9	−11,−12	52	53
3	Change in stocks inverse	0	12	0	+7.5	+13.0	+12.0	5.3	2.0	4.5	3.7	+12,+13	68	71
4	Change in ownership	5	5	2	−0.5	+0.5	0	2.3	2.7	2.5	2.5	0	84	83
5	New orders	7	3	2	−3.0	0	−1.5	5.0	1.7	4.0	3.3	−1,−2	74	74
5a	New orders, trend corrected	6	2	4	−1.5	0	−0.5	2.5	1.5	2.2	2.0	−1,0	85	86
6	Change stocks	1	11	0	−4.0	−3.5	−4.0	3.5	2.3	2.9	2.9	−2 to −5	81	81
7	R: stocks to sales, inverse	3	4	1	−0.5	+4.5	+2.0	1.5	2.5	3.0	2.0	0,+2,+4	77	77
8	R: outstanding orders to stocks	8	1	3	−1.0	−3.0	−1.0	2.0	2.3	2.3	2.2	−1	85	86
	Specific Series: New Orders												
9	Subcycles	12	0	0	−7.5	−5.5	−7.0	2.5	3.2	2.8	2.8	−7	81	81
10	Change in ownership	1	10	1	+3.5	+1.5	+2.0	4.0	2.5	3.2	3.2	+2	79	79
11	Receipts	7	0	5	−2.0	−0.5	−1.5	2.0	2.2	2.2	2.1	−1,−2	86	88
12	D. I. vendor performance	4	6	1	+3.7	+0.5	+1.3	4.6	5.2	5.2	4.9	+1	69	72
13	Sales	7	0	3	−6.7	−0.7	−1.5	3.5	0.7	3.1	3.1	−1,−2	82	82
13a	Change in sales	7	3	2	−3.0	0	−1.5	5.0	1.7	4.0	3.3	−1,−2	74	74
	Specific Series: Change in Ownership												
14	Vendor performance	8	2	1	−1.7	−3.5	−2.7	1.9	3.5	2.8	2.8	−3	83	84
	Specific Series: Ratio Outstanding Orders to Stocks												
15	Change in stocks,	6	0	6	−1.5	0	−0.5	2.3	0.3	1.5	1.3	−1,0	91	91

Notes to Table 40

[a]Specific series are matched with the indicated reference series (see note c) in accordance with the standard NBER rules. A double relaxation of rules is marked r; it applies to cases for well-conforming series in which two like turns are matched, though an unlike turn lies between them. The figure is underlined when subcycle chronology is the reference series, a minor cycle in the specific series has entered a comparison; or, when two individual series are compared, a minor cycle in either series has entered a comparison. When the business cycle chronology provides the reference, minor specific cycle turns are ignored. The meaning of other symbols is:

⊕ turn in the reference series does not appear in the specific series.

Ω turn in the specific series does not appear in the reference series.

⊙ there is no turn in either series in the neighborhood of the chronology date.

[b]Chronology dates are years when business cycle turns occur. They indicate the sequence and approximate time when the specific turns occur for which timing comparisons are given.

[c]Reference series are the series whose specific cycles plus minor cycles constitute the reference dates with which matching cycles in the specific series are compared.

[d]The number of months during which the specific series is in like phase with the reference series is expressed as a percentage of the total number of months covered between dates as given.

[e]Median is the average timing of the center two or three turns.

[f]Average deviation from the median. The "weighted" (wt'd) average is the deviation from the median for peaks and for troughs separately, weighted by the number of turns.

[g]In determining months in like phase a timing adjustment is made which maximizes confluence. Before counting the months in phase, the specific series is in effect moved to the right to allow for a lead and to the left to allow for a lag if by so doing the percentage of months in like phase (as rounded) is increased. If the months in phase are as large or larger without an adjustment, this is indicated by a "timing adjustment" of 0.

In some cases we wish to know the percentage of months in phase on a synchronous basis, regardless of whether the percentage in phase is thereby maximized. If so, the "timing adjustment" is given as "none."

The fact that there is no systematic lag in change in ownership suggests that errors can be corrected within the month, either by at-once delivery of merchandise or by increasing or decreasing new orders relative to what they would otherwise have been. The responsibility of outstandings in effectuating intentions is suggested by the behavior of the ratio of stocks on order to stocks on hand; the ratio

constitutes the bottom line in Chart 15. By and large, outstandings become relatively larger when rates of change in sales are in rising phase—that is, when a decline slows or a rise accelerates—and outstandings become relatively smaller when a rise slows and a decline accelerates. In line 8 of Table 40 a comparison of change in sales and the outstandings-stock ratio reveals 85 per cent of months are in like phase after allowing for a one month's

"Cause and Consequence of Changes in Retailers' Buying," *American Economic Review,* March 1958, pp. 19–32. The formula used to represent the two portions of stable-market orders, advance buying and corrective orders, followed the general notions discussed in the text above.

Closely similar ideas are described in Richard M. Cyert and James G. March, *A Behavioral Theory of the Firm,* Englewood Cliffs, N.J., 1963. They made an intensive study of a department in a large retail department store and a less extensive study of about a dozen others. They believe that the decision process they report "could be generalized with trivial changes

to other departments in the same merchandizing group and could be generalized with relatively modest changes to most other departments outside the immediate group" (p. 129). They distinguish between advance orders and reorders. Advance orders consist of some percentage of the sales of the corresponding period of the previous year; reorders represent the rest of the last year's total plus "minimum amount of stock desired at all times" minus stock presently at hand "including stock ordered." Reorders cover the period that represents the minimum time that suppliers require to make deliveries.

lead of change in sales; twelve turns are matched, eight of which are within plus or minus two months of one another.

Though outstandings move sooner and more agilely than do stocks, it is notable that at least the rate of change in stocks is subject to a similarly rapid response. We noted this in the sharp parallelism between outstandings proper and the rate of change in stocks. It is visible here in the higher degree of correspondence between the rate of change in stocks and the outstandings-stock ratio (note that stocks proper are the denominator of the ratio): 91 per cent of the months are in like phase on a synchronous basis (Table 40, line 15).

These strong empirical associations seem to reflect what I have termed the shingled pattern of ordering. If current sales have been underestimated, retailers do two sorts of things: (1) They increase orders for at-once delivery; since these orders represent only a small part of total stocks (which in the aggregate are influenced by the level of sales), the influx of at-once orders influences primarily the rate at which stocks change. (2) They increase orders for longer term; since the base level of outstandings is relatively small, and the correction may be applied to requirements for several future months, the influx is likely to represent a sufficient portion of the total to determine its level rather than simply its rate of change.

If current sales have been overestimated, again, orders for both immediate and advance delivery will be affected. At-once orders will not need to cover shortages, and the usual complement of things that are better bought after all the news is in may tend to be smaller. Mark downs may help to turn stocks. The advance preseason orders will have covered a large enough portion of the season's requirements so that orders of intermediate term can be relatively low. Indeed, any excuse to cancel orders may be grasped. In addition, current buying for the *next* season may be more conservative.

These manifestations of effective effort to keep rates of change in sales and in ownership moving together seem to reflect the importance to successful retail store operation of precise inventory objectives enforced with determination.

Other Influences

But the association of ownership and sales that aggregate figures show differs in an important respect from what a simple physically efficient association with sales, other things the same, would imply: The adjustment is too large. Toward the end of Chapter 9 we tried to say how much too large changes in ownership may have been. The estimates were based on alternative assumptions about physically efficient ownership-sales relationships.

On the average, department store ownership equaled about four months' sales. Yet the increase and decrease in ownership during its specific cycle movements average $6\frac{1}{4}$ times the specific cycle increase and decrease in sales. Obviously change was more than proportional. Had it remained proportional at a hand-to-mouth level, cyclical fluctuation in ownership would have been $3\frac{1}{4}$ times that of sales. But the study of the purposes that stocks serve suggests that the efficient sales link tends to imply constant incremental rather than average relations at least in the short run. An incremental association of 2 would have meant, of course, that ownership rose and fell during cyclical phases just twice as much as did sales (a trifle more when buffer stock is allowed for).

An alternative way of expressing the problem the figures pose is to note that a constant average ratio, at hand-to-mouth levels, would have explained only about 70 per cent of actual change in ownership even if we assume that all specific change in ownership was somehow caused by the corresponding specific cycles in sales (Table 33, line 10a). If the incremental rather than average association had been the effective sales link, only 38 per cent of all change would have been attributable to cyclical changes in consumer demand (line 10c) even at the liberal incremental ratio of 2.

How can the rest of the fluctuation in ownership be accounted for? One possibility would be that it is unintended, though there is little reason to suppose that ownership (as distinguished from stocks on hand) would need to be seriously out of line for long. That it is not unintended in the sense that it moves up when sales move down or vice versa was indicated by the substantial confluence of the two series. Indeed, 88 per cent of the total specific cycle fluctuation in ownership occurred when sales were in like phase.[4] Apparently, then, the disproportionate volatility of ownership must be explained in terms of events that tend to parallel the direction of change in consumer demand.

Lack of appropriate data on conditions in the markets in which the wares carried by department stores are bought prevents adequate exploration of what some of these events might be. All that we can do is observe the not uninteresting parallelism between the quite inappropriate series, the rate at which vendors' performance (primarily in durable goods industries) deteriorates or improves, and the efforts of merchants to build up or draw down supplies, as reflected by the number of months' supply held on order or the rate of change of stocks on hand.

Interplay Between Demand and Market Considerations

Taken together, these conclusions require that the exaggerated association of change in ownership and in sales may be explained in

terms that account for a tight link to consumer buying and its rate of change, and yet allow for amplification on the one hand and other influences on the other hand.

Start with the individual store that has been "going ahead" by encouraging amounts (doing better than the corresponding period of the previous year). Buying must increase sufficiently to replace the merchandise sold and to take care of the normal needs for efficient servicing of sales. Good and improving profits provide funds for carrying the increase in stocks that this implies. Profits also provide funds for supporting further commitments at what may be felt to be low opportunity costs if there are reasons to buy more heavily. Will such reasons exist?

One reason may simply be the management rule of thumb which stipulates that the constant sales-stock ratio should be maintained. If this rule is in general currency in the store, the chances are that increasing sales make stocks look light; the incremental ratio is less than the average ratio, so that the average stock-sales ratio declines. Perhaps, if the increase of sales in the particular store is not part of a general increase in consumer buying, stocks would not be augmented in line with a constant average stock-sales ratio. Instead, management might simply rejoice in "improved stock turnover."

If, on the contrary, sales of most general merchandise stores are improving along with expanding consumer income and buying, a different set of occurrences is to be expected. Then stocks may increase not only by the amount of the turnover rule of thumb but by more. As more customers feel more affluent, several qualitative changes in sales are likely to occur which affect the size of stocks on hand and on order. For one thing, customers "trade up"; that is, they buy more heavily in the higher price lines. This may justify adding new higher price lines to the previous range, or it may simply suggest enriching assortments in the higher lines already carried; but in either case higher stocks are required. For an-

---

[4] The figure is an average of phase-by-phase ratios. The numerator for, say, an expansion phase is the rise in ownership between trough and peak dates for the specific cycle expansion in sales; the denominator is the rise in ownership during the matched specific cycle phase in ownership. Measures for a nonconforming cycle after the Korean peak were omitted.

other thing, customers may be more interested in high-style items and novelties, and this likewise tends to augment stocks. Affluence may also cause customers to become somewhat more interested in good service, including ample stocks, in contrast to low prices.

Not only customers but merchants, too, may be in an affluent mood and therefore receptive to changes in customers' preferences as they interpret them. But it is quite possible also that changes have occurred in cost structures. I have already mentioned the possibility that financing costs for stores that do not rely on commercial borrowing may actually decline. Salaries may have risen and availability of sales help declined; if so, it may seem advantageous to increase the efficiency of the sales force by carrying larger stocks.

These considerations explain why stocks rise when sales do and why, as the actual sales-ownership ratios indicate, they may rise more than the efficient sales-stock link would prescribe, other things the same.

There is another striking piece of evidence, on which these speculations touch at best somewhat feebly: the close association between the *rate of change* in sales and in ownership. The efficient-service function, since this involves a strong incremental association, would of course tend to produce the empirically observed parallelism between change in ownership (since ownership is presumably little influenced by the inevitable failures of forecasts) and changes in consumer buying. However, I rather doubt that the clarity of the incremental sales-ownership association can be explained without placing primary responsibility on the procedures for creating, perceiving, and correcting unintended change in stocks.

For department stores, unintended change must be present most of the time. Orders must be placed ahead of time in order to have goods on hand when needed. Orders must be placed on the basis of forecasts of sales. But forecasts are typically inexact because clairvoyance is, at best, rare, and retailers have no information on advance orders of their customers. There is, therefore, an inevitable discrepancy between most forecasts and actuality. The first impact is on stocks. But because successful store management depends on close control of stocks, they must be precisely planned. Also essential is machinery for perceiving discrepancy between plans and actuality. Accordingly, the errors of forecasts result in what I have called unintended, not passive, change in stocks, and steps are taken to correct the error. There are many ways of doing so, and here we consider only one of them, an important one, adjustments (which may be positive or negative) in new buying.

The pattern of the adjustment is determined by the character of the error. As explained earlier, the error tends to be something very close to first differences in sales with opposite sign. Correction of this discrepancy through alteration in new buying reverses the sign.

But the conventional shingled pattern of buying and its seasonal patterns may have a capacity to intensify the corrective factor. The first impact of, say, underestimation is likely to be in the "at-once" order; provisions are found to have been too low. New orders may need to be placed *both to make up for the earlier underprovision and to forestall like future mistakes.* If so, the correction would apply the current pattern of monthly or biweekly rate of change to expected sales of several order periods. Similarly, the fill-in order, anticipating sales of some weeks hence, may need to correct for underestimation of requirements when the preseason order was placed.

We have spoken thus far of the impact on stocks and buying of the level and rate of change in sales. These several influences could occasion a rise in stocks on hand and on order relative to the previous efficient-service requirements if there were no changes whatsoever in conditions in the markets in which merchandise was purchased.

However, these changes stimulate and are stimulated by actual and expected changes in the markets in which retailers buy. This interplay takes on increasing importance as our analysis proceeds. Combined with the fact that members of an industry have differing sensitivities to market-oriented change, it becomes the core of what is described in the last chapter as an ecological theory of fluctuation. It will therefore be useful to rehearse rather patiently how retailers are likely to proceed and to react. Much of the necessarily conjectural aspect of the analysis could be removed by appropriate investigations.

Some suppliers, those that have been lucky in developing popular numbers, will approach ceilings in productive capacity. If so, they probably will quote longer delivery periods and refuse to promise prompt fill-in orders at short notice. Perhaps they threaten that present prices apply to advance orders only, and they cannot guarantee that the same price will apply later on in the season. But whether or not these changes actually do take place, it is likely that retailers may fear that they will. If the changes actually do occur in connection with the merchandise on which fortune has smiled, fear that they will occur elsewhere is encouraged.

Seasonal patterns of buying may foster the development of market stringency or laxness. The preseason order covers requirements for some stipulated portion of the expected sales for a number of months—a "season" of perhaps a third of a year (durations differ for different seasons). There are advantages to placing orders early, but it is critically important not to buy more than will surely be used (after also allowing leeway for short-term buying intended to meet the unforeseeable whims in consumer buying). Consequently the preseason order must never exceed something short of the least that will be required.

When business improves, two things are likely to change. First, the estimate of the least that will be sold moves up; it is not impossible that the guess as to the least could move up even if the guess as to the most likely does not change.[5] Second, the advantage of placing orders early increases since failure to do so threatens poor selections, slower or unreliable deliveries, and even higher prices. Note that the retailer is *forced* to form a judgment about future conditions since he automatically takes some position—either a long or a short one—when he places his preseason order. Buyers, uncertain about what position to take, will be hungry for market news and prone to imitate what the recognized smart managements are doing.

I have been speaking of the impact of expectations about market conditions and consumer buying on retailers' preseason buying. But this buying itself must also have an impact on actual market conditions, as well as on further expectations about them. Actions based on expectations tend to be partially self-validating.

For one thing, conventional seasonal patterns, particularly the advance preseason order, may have a capacity to magnify the impact of changed expectations. The point is conjectural, but worth a moment's thought. The preseason order covers a portion of requirements for a number of months. If the portion is increased, the additional buying at the preseason date will apply to each of, say, four months which constitute the season. For example, assume that sales are expected to be $100 a month for four months, 40 per cent of which represents the usual preseason order, a total of $160. A shift in market evaluation which dictates 55 per cent advance coverage instead of 40 per cent implies an increase of $4 \times \$15$, or $60. This could constitute a very large absolute increase in business for companies receiving the orders; in one month, extra orders for 60 per cent of the monthly business are received. If sales are also expected to rise, the additional buying would of course be still larger. Thus if sales

[5] This is a fancy point. It implies that the shape of the probability distribution can change (kurtosis increase) with no change in its mean value.

were expected to be 10 per cent higher, the buying would be 55 per cent of $440, or $242, an increase of $82. Though these orders may actually be filled on a month-by-month pattern which is free of the bunched increase, I wonder whether the bunching of orders does not nevertheless influence market reactions. News of large absolute increases in orders received are more likely than news of small ones to spread around a market and influence opinion and even anticipatory actions of buyers and sellers.

Thus far we have considered influences that generate primarily from the side of demand. They provide ample reason for ownership to rise and fall with sales and with rates of change in sales. They explain also how, in both cases, response can be greater than required to enforce the efficient sales-stock link, other things the same.

But broadly expanding sales imply higher consumer income, and this in turn implies that business conditions in general tend to be good. If so, demand for, say, men's shirts by department stores competes with demand from other sorts of retailers. Firms supplying shirt manufacturers with materials are also experiencing increasing demand for other clothing and industrial materials. Demand from any or all of these sources may either support or initiate pressures on supply, which in turn cause fear of further pressure, action to forestall shortages, and thereby actual further pressure, and so on through rings of cause and effect.

Materials Orders of Department Stores and the Acceleration Principle

The argument may be summarized in terms of all the major factors that determine the pattern of materials buying for department stores and its relation to consumer buying.

1. *Provision for expected sales.* Merchandise that is expected to be sold must of course first be purchased. To do so, forecasting procedures are required in so far as goods are not ready for sale instantaneously upon the placement of an order for them, and in so far as goods on order are not perfect substitutes for goods on hand. Department store merchandise is ready for sale shortly after its arrival in the stores. However, substantial quantities of merchandise must be ordered many weeks or even months ahead of time, and for these, forecasts of requirements are necessary. Ignoring pertinent qualifications, this element of retailers' buying may be thought of as having, broadly, the pattern of earlier consumers' buying.

2. *Sales-linked stock.* As the level of sales change, stocks that service them must change roughly in proportion to the rate of change in sales.

The essence of propositions 1 and 2 form the law of "derived demand" as set forth many years ago by J. M. Clark.[6] The pattern of derived demand will depend, on the one hand, on the levels and shape of fluctuations in final demand, since this determines the pattern of rates of change and their relation to demand proper. On the other hand, it depends on the size and character of the capital ratio. The capital ratio refers in effect to what I have called the efficient-service requirement, other things the same.

Since rates of change tend to lead data proper, the new-capital requirement (increases or decreases in stocks) has the pattern of rates of change in sales and tends to lead sales proper. Because department stores require relatively large stocks, the capital ratio is large and this leading element is correspondingly emphasized. But the extent of the emphasis is moderated by the fact that the efficient-service requirement is not a constant average ratio but more nearly a constant incremental ratio and one which is less than the average. Thus far the analysis parallels that

6 John Maurice Clark, "Business Acceleration and the Law of Demand: A Technical Factor in Economic Cycles," *Journal of Political Economy*, March 1917, pp. 217–235 (reprinted in *Readings in Business Cycle Theory*, New York, 1944, pp. 235–260).

of J. M. Clark. The fact that we can inspect data on orders, which Clark could not, provides the wherewithal for a sharp demonstration of the Clarkian logic.

But we have found that demand as conveyed to retailers' suppliers is not merely derived demand in this simple sense. Factors in addition to the previous two are at work; they are:

3. *Changes in opportunity cost of stocks.* The desired stock-sales ratio reflects change in the cost of carrying stock relative to meeting management objectives in some other way. One form this can take results from the qualitative changes in demand associated with prosperity and recession and what this means concerning the selections that retailers want to offer customers. Another form is that of a trade-off for selling costs.

4. *Attention to the timing of buying.* Conditions in materials markets and expectations concerning them cause attention to the timing of buying—the decision concerning when expected requirements are purchased. These changes feed on actual conditions of supply such as levels of capacity, utilization, quoted delivery terms, and news of related markets; they feed on changes in demand; they feed on the interaction between these supply- and demand-oriented circumstances, and expectations concerning them, in a potential merry-go-round of cause and effect. I might add that John Maurice Clark made the points of this and the preceding paragraphs nearly fifty years ago.[7]

5. *Correction of error.* The high importance of stock control in retail stores implies not only sharp definition of requirements but prompt correction for failure to conform to the stipulations. Failure of total "in-sights" (total ownership) to conform will result from faulty prediction of sales. If sales of the past are the basis of prediction, correction will have the pattern of rates of change in sales. The required correction would presumably imply reversing the undesired change in stock resulting from the incorrect guess about what would be sold. Depending on just how objectives are formulated, it may also imply correction of service stock to a level appropriate to the actual rather than forecast level of sales. The pattern of these corrections will depend on the pattern of ordering. Thus a shingled

is something in which he is likely to economize when business is poor, and to be liberal when he can afford it." Clark goes on to say that in good times customers "would be less influenced by a slight saving in price, which can only be made sure of after close study of the qualities of the goods, than by an obvious superiority in quality of service and range of selection. When the buyer's mind swings in this direction the merchant is invited to respond in kind if he wishes to attract his share of the increase in business. . . . A time of general activity in business is a time when large stocks are good tactics commercially. One other fact which may make merchants more willing to invest in considerable stocks is that a time of growing demand for some one commodity, or a time of general increase in activity, are both times of rising prices for the intermediate products called for in the business affected. This makes these commodities a profitable investment so long as credit can be had on easy terms with which to enlarge one's holdings. Merchants tend to assure their future supplies by buying either outright or for future delivery" (*Ibid.*, p. 251).

"Taking all these things into consideration, one is justified in concluding that an increase in demand naturally tends toward an increased investment in dealers' stocks, which is, if anything, more than in proportion to the increase in sales, unless limited by (1) difficulty in getting added credit to carry the extra 'working capital,' (2) an extremely sharp rise in supply prices, (3) the fear that the prosperity is temporary, or (4) the inability of manufacturers to make deliveries (*Ibid.*, p. 252)."

I have quoted the discussion at some length because I have had the feeling upon rereading it that my book can be thought of as an effort to explore and extend these insights of J. M. Clark of about half a century back.

[7] "The chief reasons for keeping a stock are, first, to give the customer a wide selection of goods which he can actually inspect and, secondly, to give assurance of being able to fill large orders without delay. . . . Obviously, the larger the order, the greater the danger of being sold out, unless the stock is increased in a corresponding proportion, or something not too far short of it. (Note the last phrase.) The increase in demand would not seem to make it necessary to keep any wider range of goods in stock. But if we are thinking, not of what is necessary, but of what is profitable, we have a different situation" (Clark in *Readings in Business Cycle Theory*, p. 250).

"The size of stock is one element in the quality of service rendered by any dealer, which means that it

pattern of the sort described earlier implies a stepwise adjustment. It may also involve some magnification of error associated with highly seasonal sales and ordering; the question invites study.

I would like to defer the discussion of feedbacks which the model implies. They are discussed in both of the following chapters. But the reader must have noted that I may be storing up trouble for myself. On the one hand, feedbacks, and therefore multiplier effects, can take the form not only of income but also of expectational elements. On the other hand, my emphasis on orders, and the speed with which they can be delivered suggests that there is no justification for separating plans, actions, and corrections by formal periods. Lloyd Metzler's analysis of inventory cycles has featured the role of mistaken forecasts. But the dynamics that he emphasized moved from current income (which formed the basis of expected sales) to *subsequent* production, which, via the income payments that it generated, determined actual sales.[8] The errors that new orders are capable of reflecting do not involve this long and somewhat artificial causal chain. More of this later.

What then does the analysis suggest about the pattern of retailers' orders for merchandise compared to their final sales to consumers? Because of the need to forecast on the basis largely of past experience, and because of the high management priority accorded inventory control, paragraphs 1, 2 and 5 should dominate the recurrent picture. But this strong impact of rates of change superimposed on current levels of sales, which the large stocks and correction pattern imply, may tend to be further reinforced by the operation of the cost and market oriented aspects of the model, paragraphs 3, 4, and 5. Indeed, at times, elements generated on the side of supply or from other markets may visibly imprint their influence on total buying.

Chart 15 compares this hypothetical picture

with the actual one. At troughs, sales cease to fall very nearly at the same time that they reach their maximum rate of decline.[9] At troughs, then, either one of the demand-oriented influences—expected sales or demand for capital (change in stock)—will cause new orders to turn at about the same time. It seems reasonable therefore that the median timing of new orders compared with that of rate of change in sales was, except for the 1954 trough, plus or minus one month (Table 40, line 5).

At peaks, however, sales slowed their rate of rise well before they began to fall (compare Chart 15, curves 2 and 6). Change in ownership—an empirical receptacle for all the aspects of the model except point 1—turned within plus or minus two months of changes in sales at five of the six peaks. At three of these peaks, the magnification that change in sales underwent as a consequence of ownership objectives meant that the location of the turns in total materials orders was strongly influenced by the rate of change in sales; on these occasions orders turned no more than three months after the centered rate of change in sales. However the peak in new orders that occurred in 1956 and 1960 occurred many months after sales ceased to rise at an accelerating rate. Apparently the strong trend rise in sales kept the dollar value of new orders rising very gently after the factors embodied in the increasing rate of rise in ownership had started to decline (Table 40, lines 10 and 13a).

The model postulates that factors outside of the final demand-associated complex of events can also influence the pattern of backward transmission of fluctuation. Evidence of their influence on ownership has previously been discussed. But on new orders, the impact of price expectations, lengthening delivery periods, and the like does not take a form in which these influences are visible insofar as

---

[8] Lloyd Metzler, "Nature and Stability of Inventory Cycles," *Review of Economic Statistics*, August 1941.

[9] Five troughs can be matched. The timing of change in sales relative to sales proper is 0 for two of them, −2 in 1958 and 1961 and −7 in 1954.

they do not parallel changes in final demand. That much of the influence does follow this parallel course has been indicated by the measures of exaggerated amplitude of fluctu-

ation that have been presented: Retailers' buying has about two times the specific cycle amplitude of the fluctuations in consumer buying (see Table 24, line 1).

DURABLE GOODS MANUFACTURERS

The available data for durable goods fit poorly into the conceptual framework required for comprehensive analysis of fluctuations in ownership and its impact on the backward transmission of demand.

First, there are the all too familiar technical shortcomings of the data: the difficulty of using book-value figures to compare stocks and flows at various stages of processing; the fact that there is no way consistently to match, for the same companies, sales orders (or shipments or production) with inventories of materials on hand and on order and with orders placed for those materials (or receipts of them).

Second, we have studied only one of the three major sorts of stocks on hand—stocks of materials. The dynamics of change in materials stocks, and the backward transmission of demand as a whole, ought to cover the business alternatives concerned with whether to accumulate or draw down stocks at any stage of the productive process. The focus on the "raw" materials stage alone is a limitation that needs to be kept in mind.[10]

Finally, since the time pattern of customers' orders may differ substantially from that of shipments to them, "demand" confronts the problem discussed at the beginning of the chapter. Following the thinking there set forth, I shall focus on the association of stocks

and shipments and observe, as a second step, the impact of changes in unfilled sales orders.[11]

Indeed, for some purposes, particularly the examination of how stocks of materials on hand relate to the "need" for them, the most appropriate definition of demand might be production starts, rather than shipments of finished goods. However, there is no statistical information on this series of events. Shipments, then, will have to suffice.

The Sales Link—"Excess Stocks" and Materials Orders

In Chapter 9, the over-all movement of shipments and stocks of all durable goods manufacturers were seen to show substantial parallelism. However, their conformity to business cycles inhibits ascribing direct causal implication to the relationship, particularly since the more responsive stockpile—ownership—shows poor association with shipments (see Table 31).

Rates of change provide a more sensitive test. And Table 41, line 3, shows in detail that there is little apparent tendency for manu-

[10] Reference to the total stock-shipment ratio, the bottom curve of Chart 3, and to the rate of change of all stocks, the fifth curve of Chart 6, suggests that many statements concerning materials stocks may apply to total stocks. This would be still more likely to be the case if stocks were measured in terms of equivalent units of output, the most appropriate notion for examination of process, rather than in book-value terms. The latter underweights the importance of raw and, to a lesser extent, in-process stocks.

[11] This has some advantages also in terms of the technical difficulties of the data. Final products, defined as products of the machinery and transportation industries, fail to include the final products sold to firms in other industries, and thus include too little. On the other hand, final products, defined as products of all durable goods industries, include products that are intermediate and primary materials as well, and thus include too much. It has been judged the lesser disadvantage to include too much in dealing with shipments, and too little when dealing with outstanding orders. For the latter it is important not to cover as cause the very changes in outstanding orders for materials which, as effect, is a major focus of interest in this book.

TABLE 41

Timing: Change in Demand and in Stocks on Hand and on Order, Durable Goods Manufacturers, 1946–61

Line	Reference Series[c]	Section A: Months Lead (−) or Lag (+) for Matched Turns[a] Chronology[b]											
		P 1947	T 1947	P 1948	T 1949	P 1951	T 1952	P 1953	T 1954	P 1957	T 1958	P 1960	T 1961
	Specific Series: Change in Shipments, All Durables												
1	Subcycles	⊕	⊕	⊕	−7	−8	−11	−9	−10	−9	−3	−13	−3
2	Change ownership	⊙	⊕	⊕	−2	−8	−6	+4	−1	−1	0	+3	+7
3	Change stocks, materials	⊕	⊕	⊕	−2	−4	−10	−8	−8	−15	−4	0	+2
4	Change in outstandings	⊙	⊕	⊕	−2	−8	−6	−4	−1	−1	+1	+3	+7
5	New orders, materials	⊙	⊙	⊕	−4	−7	−5	−3	−3	−15	−2	+2	−2
6	Change new orders, materials	⊙	⊙	⊕	+1	0	+2	+4	0	0	+3	+9	+16
7	Change production, all dur.	⊕	⊙	⊙	−2	−2	−12	0	−2	−3	+1	+2	−2
8	New orders, mat. deflated	⊙	⊕	⊕	−4	−7	−8	−3	−3	−5	−2	+2	−2
	Specific Series: Ratio: Material Stocks to Shipments, All Durables, Inverted												
9	Subcycles	−5	+1	−8	−8	−6	−6	−5	−9	−24	−1	−13	−1
10	Change shipments	Ω	Ω	Ω	−1	+2	+5	+4	+1	+6	+2	0	+2
11	Change ownership	Ω	+2	+1	−3	−6	−1	+8	0	+5	+2	+3	+9
12	Change stocks, materials	−1	−3	−8	−3	−2	−5	−4	−7	−9	−2	0	+4
13	Change outstandings	Ω	+3	+1	−3	−6	−1	+8	0	+5	+3	+3	+9
14	New orders, materials	Ω	Ω	−8	−5	−5	0	+1	−2	−9	0	+2	0
15	New orders, mat. deflated	Ω	+3	−3	−5	−5	−3	+1	−2	+1	0	+2	0
16	Change outstanding orders, final product	+2	⊕	⊕	−1	−7	⊕	⊕	+1	−4	+7	−1	+1
17	D.I. vendor performance	Ω	+3	+3	−1	−1	−3	+7	−1	−3	+3	−6	+10
18	Corporate profits	Ω	Ω	−8	−3	−3	−8	−3	0	−4	−2	−1	−1
	Specific Series: New Order, Materials												
19	Subcycles	⊕	⊕	0	−3	−1	−6	−6	−7	−15	−1	−15	−1
20	Change outstanding orders, materials	⊙	⊕	+9	+2	−1	−1	+7	+2	+14	+3	+1	+9
21	Change stocks, materials	⊕	⊕	0	+2	+3	−5	−5	−5	0	−2	−2	+4
22	Shipments, all durables	⊙	⊙	−1	−3	−2	−7	−6	−9	−9	−1	−4	0
23	Shipments, final product	⊙	⊙	−1	−5	Ω	Ω	−6	−9	−9	−1	−5	0

(continued)

TABLE 41 (concluded)

		Section B: Average Timing of Turns								Section C: Percentage of Months in Like Phase[d]		
		Number Matched			Median[e]			Average Deviation[f]			Timing Adjust-ment[g]	% Mos. 7/46– 12/61	% Mos. 1/48– 12/61
										All Turns			
Line	Reference Series[c]	−	+	0	P	T	All	P	T	Wt'd			
		Specific Series: Change Shipments, All Durables											
1	Subcycles	9	0	0	−9.0	−6.7	−8.7	1.2	3.1	2.5	2.3	−9	68	71
2	Change ownership	5	3	1	+1.0	−1.0	−0.7	4.0	3.0	3.5	3.4	−1	73	73
3	Change stocks, materials	7	1	1	−11.5	−7.3	−8.7	6.5	4.3	4.9	5.3	−4, −5	68	67
4	Change in out- standings	5	4	0	+1.0	−0.7	−0.3	4.0	3.3	3.7	3.6	−1	72	73
5	New orders, materials	8	1	0	−5.0	−3.0	−3.3	5.2	1.0	2.9	2.9	−3	68	73
6	Change new orders, materials	0	6	3	+2.0	+2.0	+2.0	3.2	3.6	3.4	3.4	+2	75	77
7	Change produc- tion, all dur.	6	2	1	−1.0	−2.0	−2.0	1.8	2.6	2.2	2.2	−2	81	82
8	New orders, mat. deflated	8	1	0	−4.0	−3.0	−3.3	2.8	1.6	2.1	2.1	−3	76	81
		Specific Series: Ratio: Material Stocks to Shipments, All Durables, Inverted											
9	Subcycles	11	1	0	−7.0	−3.5	−6.0	4.8	3.7	4.2	4.2	−6	73	74
10	Change in shipments	1	7	1	+3.0	+1.7	+2.0	2.0	1.5	1.7	1.7	+2	82	85
11	Change in ownership	3	7	1	+3.0	+1.0	+1.7	3.6	2.8	3.3	3.2	+2	80	78
12	Change stocks, materials	10	1	1	−3.0	−3.0	−3.0	3.0	2.3	2.7	2.7	−3	82	82
13	Change in outstandings	3	7	1	+3.0	+1.5	+2.3	2.8	3.2	3.4	3.0	+3	80	78
14	New orders, materials	5	2	3	−4.0	−0.7	−1.0	4.2	1.5	3.2	2.9	−1,0	76	81
15	New orders, mat. deflated	5	4	2	−0.3	−1.0	−0.7	2.5	2.2	2.3	2.3	0	86	87
16	Change in out- standing orders, final product	4	4	0	+0.5	+1.0	0	3.8	2.0	3.0	2.9	0,+1	76	77
17	D. I. vendor performance	6	5	0	−0.3	+1.0	+0.3	3.9	3.5	3.8	3.7	0	77	76
18	Corporate profits	9	0	1	−3.3	−2.0	−3.0	1.6	2.0	1.9	1.8	−3	83	89
		Specific Series: New Order, Materials											
19	Subcycles	9	0	1	−7.3	−3.3	−4.5	6.0	2.3	4.3	4.2	−4, −5	74	74
20	Change out- standing orders, materials	2	8	0	+5.7	+2.3	+2.5	4.9	2.3	3.9	3.6	+2, +3	73	77
21	Change stocks, materials	5	3	2	−0.7	−1.7	−1.0	2.1	3.3	2.8	2.7	−1, −2	77	83
22	Shipments, all durables	9	0	1	−4.0	−3.7	−3.5	2.4	3.1	2.8	2.8	−3, −4	85	83
23	Shipments, final product	7	0	1	−5.5	−3.0	−5.0	2.2	3.2	2.8	2.8	−5	82	80

For notes see Table 40, notes a through g.

facturers to enforce an incremental association. Even after allowing for a lag of four or five months for inventory investment relative to change in shipments, only 69 per cent of the months are in like phase.

There seems little reason to ascribe the lag and poor correspondence to unavoidable error. In view of the foreknowledge of shipments that new sales orders provide for fabricators of heavy machinery, stocks certainly could be kept more closely associated with shipments if there were reason to do so and to pay the cost of doing so. Besides, the association is also poor between change in shipments and change in ownership for which a target size could presumably be enforced simply by modifying current ordering. Line 2 of the table shows only 73 per cent of months in like phase after allowing for a one-month lag of change in ownership.

However, needless to say, a company does not ignore the level of shipments in designing the level of stocks, nor can the speed with which shipments rise or fall be ignored. Disparities that are "too large" must be defined at least in operating terms. Do the figures point to any such definition?

A relaxed type of association is suggested by the fact that since 1948, though not before, there seems to be a tendency for a fall in shipment to have been preceded by a retardation in at least the rate at which stocks rise; similarly an upturn in sales was preceded by a slower rate of fall in stocks (Chart 16, the association between curves 3 and 6). But it is hard to describe the operational meaning of this association. What it could mean seems to be suggested in a more comprehensible way by the stock-shipments ratio. It is shown as the second curve in Chart 16. I would like to think of the curve as the locus of "excess stocks." This notion starts with the thought that there is some ideal association between shipments and stocks of materials required to service shipments efficiently. To illustrate, assume that it is one month's supply (.5 months for the book-value data assuming

value added is 50 per cent of the shipment price). Then, by definition, when the ratio is above a line drawn at .5, "excess stocks" are positive; and when below it, they are negative, that is, deficiency exists. Since the ratio seldom fell below .5, stocks were never too low according to this definition but only too large in varying degrees.[12]

Comparison between the two top curves of Chart 16 suggests that the rate of change in sales and the stock-shipments ratio are inversely correlated. Table 41, line 10, indicates that, allowing for a two-month lead of change in shipments, the two series are in opposite phase 82 per cent of the months, 85 per cent from 1948 on. Of course, sales are in the denominator of the ratio and therefore even the rate of change in sales might, because of the arithmetic, have a tendency to be inversely related to it. But changes in stocks, the numerator (third curve), have an inverse association also; 82 per cent of the months are in opposite phase with stock investment lagging three months (Table 41, line 12).

The typical relationships can be described in these terms. Both stocks and shipments are rising, and stocks more slowly than shipments (the ratio is falling). But producers find the rise in their shipments slowing down a bit. Though they may start to reduce materials buying, stocks, nevertheless, rise *relative* to shipments—excess stocks, as defined by the ratio, begin to build up (trough in the ratio). Before long, shipments may start to fall, but

12 What the desirable level actually is needs to be empirically determined. But for so complex an aggregate as all durable goods producers, the question is perhaps not too interesting. If the proper figure is higher than .5, what I refer to as small excess stocks would be a stock deficiency. The contours of the curve would be unchanged. If the desirable stock-sales ratio were more nearly a fixed incremental than fixed average ratio, and the incremental ratio differed from the averages, the contours may change. I have computed a series assuming a fixed incremental ratio of .5. Had this series been used instead of the one based on a constant average ratio, the argument that follows would be unchanged. Experiments suggest that this would also have been true had the incremental ratio been .33 instead of .5.

CHART 16

Ratio of Materials Stocks to Shipments Compared with Selected Series, 1946–64

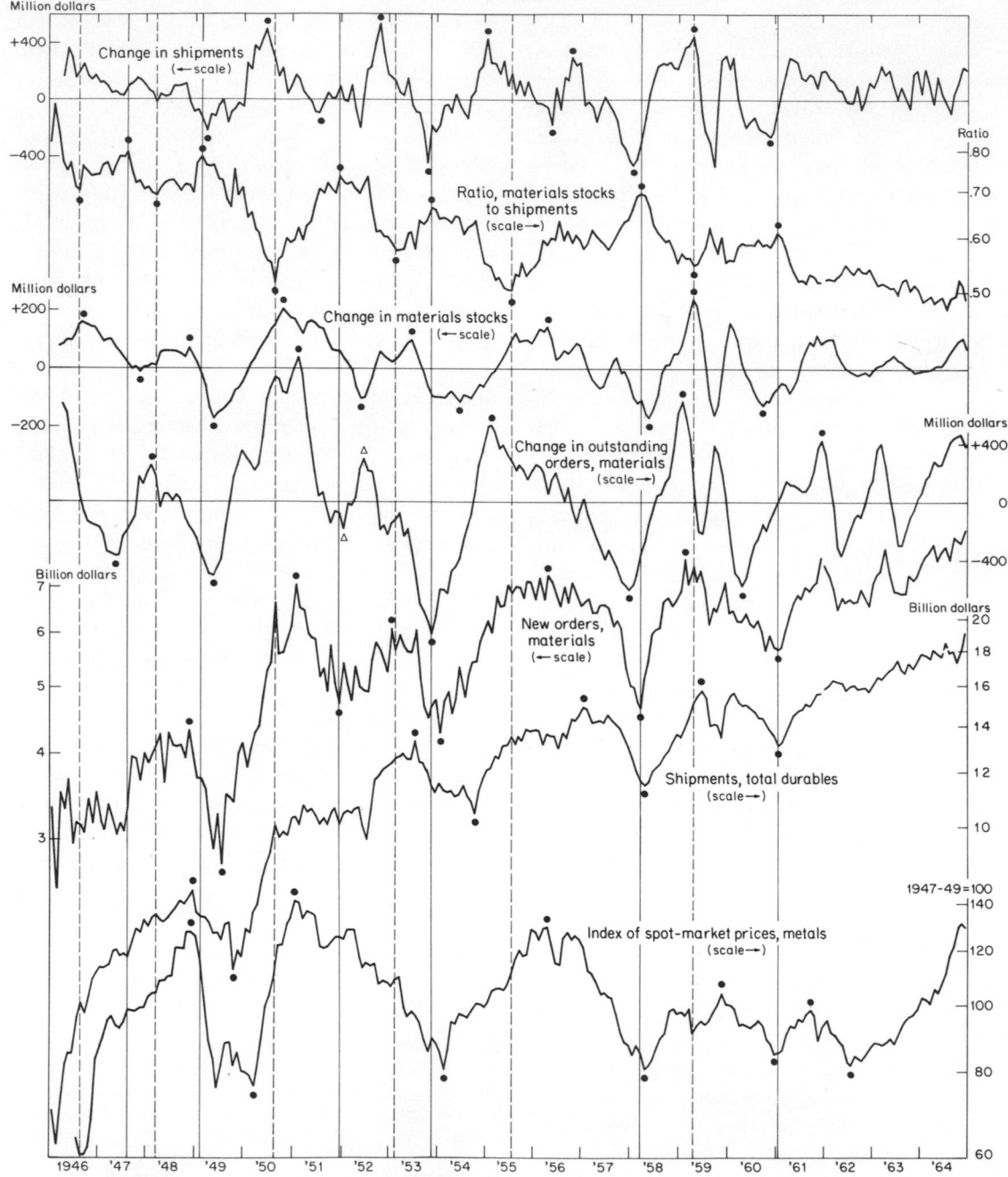

Note: Dashed lines mark the troughs and solid lines the peaks in ratio of materials stocks to shipments.

the cumulation of "excess stocks" continues either because stocks continue to rise or, falling, do so more slowly than shipments. As the fall in shipments starts to retard, retrenchment in stocks has a chance to catch up; the ratio reaches a peak and reverses as stocks start to decline faster than sales. As sales begin to rise, this *relative* reduction in stocks continues either because they have not started to rise or because they do so at a slower rate than do sales. This persists as long as sales continue to rise at an accelerating rate. But soon after they cease to do so, excess stocks cease to decline and start once again to build up.

This description does not seem to me to suggest a sharp inventory objective which is incapable of prompt enforcement. For one thing, the fact that orders are often on the books many months before shipments need to be made, or even production begun, suggest that stocks *could* have been acquired at just the most efficient time. But even if this had not been the case, why would it not be possible to enforce a stock objective by ordering materials from jobbers, or other manufacturers, paying if necessary a premium price for prompt delivery? If, on the other hand, stocks are too high, suppliers could have been asked to postpone deliveries. It seems reasonable to suppose that these things are not done for the reason that they are not worth doing. It is advantageous neither to formulate a stock objective with so strong an emphasis on alignment with shipments nor to pay the cost of monitoring and enforcing it.

The picture is rather that of a soft stock objective—a link of stocks to sales consisting, figuratively, of a set of elastic bands that pull stock in some prescribed direction, but give ground in response to pulls exerted by other management considerations.

Needless to say, many other considerations are present. The movement of the stock-shipments ratio reflects the impact of these factors at the point where materials stocks on hand have been affected. Some of the factors may have a fairly direct and prompt impact on stocks; for example, the combination of un-certainty about delivery conditions and ample funds may cause a buildup, via orders for fast delivery, of stocks on hand as insurance against possible shortages. But other factors, focusing on outstandings, will influence stocks on hand only after a considerable interval; classic examples are anticipatory orders with long delivery periods, or those intended to forestall an expected rise in price. Finally, the pattern of withdrawals from stockpiles, and failures to anticipate these, must also be listed among the factors that influence the size of materials stocks. Actions focusing both on outstandings and on the pattern of withdrawals from stock will cause current stock objectives to be blurred by the impact on stocks of actions undertaken at some earlier time which have, in a sense, committed the stock reservoirs to receipts or drains that tend to oppose the present direction in which the rubber bands are pulling.

This interpretation emphasizes the possibility that an intention to validate a sales-stock link may be so overlaid with other current objectives, and the residue of earlier ones, that it could not be seen in aggregative data; at least not without a complicated and correct conceptual model, good data of an unusual sort, and, of course, multivariate analysis.

But if efforts to enforce sales-linked objectives would be visible at all in the gross figures, they might be expected to be clearest at the point where the instrument of control is used. The act of ordering materials is the chief instrument, and accordingly we examine the patterns of ordering in the hope of identifying action intended to correct excess or deficiency in sales-linked stocks. Outstanding orders for materials and their rates of change also show the results of these actions. But since current actions are only one of the things that affect their size (see the analysis at the start of Chapter 10), it is more useful to concentrate on the flow of new orders for materials.[13]

[13] In line with these thoughts, as Table 41, line 13, indicates, change in outstandings tends to turn earlier than the ratio matched inversely, and to have poor positive conformity with the rate of change in shipments (line 4).

The fifth curve in Chart 16 is new-orders for materials. (It is actually the sales orders of the materials-producing durable goods industries.) The generally inverse association with the stock-shipments ratio is clear enough. The peaks and troughs in orders are generally close to the dotted and solid lines drawn through the troughs and peaks in the ratio. Table 41, line 14, indicates that the association is about synchronous on the average. However, the over-all correspondence, matched inversely, is only 81 per cent of months in like phase, starting in 1948. But the particulars of the individual turns suggest a more meaningful connection. For one thing, six of the ten matched turns are within plus or minus two months of one another. For another thing, the longer leads can be explained in terms of market behavior. At the peak of the ratio in 1949 (excess stocks hypothetically had reached their low), metals prices were falling rapidly, and this could account for the continued fall in new orders. Producers wanted to wait before resuming buying, in view of the weakness which the rapid fall in prices signified. At the three peaks in orders in 1948, 1950, and 1956, the lead of the ratio seems explicable in terms of strong movements in prices. The periods of delay between the beginning of excess stocks (trough in the ratio) and the peak in orders were quite precisely the periods of rapid rises in prices to unusual highs. Compare them with the bottom curve in the chart. Presumably the optimism and increasing market stringency that this implies caused producers to buy more materials than they otherwise would. "More" turned out to mean enough to keep new orders rising. In 1956, new orders turned down and the ratio up at virtually the same time; and metals prices were low and level.

For durables as for department stores, the process generates materials orders which reach peaks and troughs before those of shipments of the finished goods in which the materials are used. Inspect curves 5 and 6 in Chart 16. Table 41, in lines 22 and 23, calculates that new materials orders lead shipments at all turns except one synchronous one. For all durable goods shipments (which cover more ground than we want) the median lead was three or four months and the correspondence was high; 85 per cent of the months were in like phase. For shipments of the final-products industries only (which covers less ground than we want), the median lead was five months and the correspondence a bit lower.

I have explained the relation between excess stocks and materials orders in terms of usual and special conditions at particular times. The net result is a strong lead in orders relative to shipments. But I want to suggest a revision of this explanation, which has been based entirely on book-value figures, because of the ambiguity that prices imply in this context. The strict logic of the argument that links "excess" stocks to buying calls for a relation between physical quantities. The ratio, our measures of excess stocks, approaches this, since there is at least some degree of similarity of the prices of numerator and denominator. To make valid comparisons, new orders should be deflated for the price element in book-value figures. When this is done, the lag of new orders relative to troughs in the ratio in 1948 and 1956 disappears, though the descent is slow after the peak. The only substantial lags that remain occur at the time of the acute fall in prices in early 1949 and rise in 1950. For the rest, materials orders rise as excess stocks build up and fall as excess stocks disappear. The two series can be compared at the top of Chart 17; the ratio, curve 2, has been inverted in this chart, so that direct rather than inverted association with new orders is to be expected. Eighty-six per cent of months adhere to this pattern on a synchronous basis (Table 41, line 15).

In pointing to the unusual regularity of this association, one should not lose sight of its logical and empirical link to the rate at which shipments change. The difficulty of catching up with acceleration in shipments is the reason for the inverse movement of the ratio. The rate of change in shipments can be compared directly with materials orders in the context of the simple accelerator mechanism of the kind which seemed to apply to the buying of retailers. Using the deflated new-order series, beginning in 1948, 81 per cent of months were in like phase with centered change in sales leading by three months; alternatively this may be regarded as a synchronous association with change in sales during the previous five months (Table 41, line 8). The longer leads at peaks occurred in 1950 and 1955, when market conditions were tightening rapidly, and at least one of the two longer leads at troughs occurred in 1949, when markets were strongly deflationary. The rise in new orders in 1947 was not present in the rate of change in sales, and the latter rose in 1956 while new orders continued to fall. I stress the ratio as an intermediate causal link because of its most impressive empirical attributes (of which there are more to come), and because the logic of its operation seems to me to correspond realistically to business perceptions and techniques.

But without learning more about how objectives are formulated and enforced, it is foolish to push any particular association very far. These basic facts seem to stand out: (1) Materials orders clearly turn consistently earlier than shipments of finished products. (2) The lead is strongly associated with some sort of sales-linked inventory objective, albeit one constructed of lastex. (3) The fact that it is made of lastex, and that all sorts of other factors cause it to stretch and retract, makes one hesitant about calling the association another clear example of the impact of derived demand having the usual acceleration attributes. It has the empirical manifestations—the lead and greater amplitude. But to what extent is the sales-link causally responsible?

Other Influences and Their Link with Shipments

The answer must in the first place comprehend the amplitude of change, and here I need to shift back to ownership. Even for department stores, unplanned changes in stocks (primarily presumably of an unintended sort) made it undesirable to focus on change in stocks for empirical observation of the causal link to sales. For durable goods manufacturers, passive as well as unintended change in stock appears to be important. Changes in ownership can presumably be more deliberate. Of course, the very absence of sharp parallelism between change in ownership and in shipments means that the amplitude of change in ownership will reflect other influences than that of the sales link; nevertheless, magnitudes are of interest. It is useful to ask to what extent the magnitude of change exceeds what an efficient sales-link might demand.

Table 34 spoke to this point. There we saw (line 13) that on the average about 3.4 months' supply was on hand and on order; [14] however, the incremental association, the ratio of the specific cycle increase in ownership to that of sales, was equivalent to about 5.5 months' supply (line 11). If the ratio had remained at a hand-to-mouth level, the incremental association would have represented 3.2 months' supply, whereas a constant incremental relation of 2, or more likely 1.5, months would seem to define the efficient sales link more realistically, assuming nothing else changed.

The calculations can be interpreted in terms of the proportion of total specific cycle change in ownership that the several varieties of sales links explain. Apparently the constant hand-to-mouth average relation covered about two-thirds of the total, whereas the incremental association of 2 accounted for 45 per cent, and an association of 1.5 for about a third (lines 10a, c and b).

The large cyclical rises and falls in ownership relative to that of shipments must represent the impact of other elements that bear on the patterns of procurement. But here, as for department stores, we cannot even start

[14] The book value of ownership averaged 1.69 times shipments. Assuming value added represents 50 per cent of the value of product, this represents about 3.4 months' supply.

to measure their joint impact by looking at the times when shipments could not be responsible because ownership was moving in a contrary direction. Only 14 per cent of the total rise and fall in ownership occurred when ownership and shipments were in opposite subcyclical phases.[15] In general these figures tell about the same sort of story as did the corresponding ones for department stores; there is more change in ownership than the sales link justifies, most of which nevertheless is confluent with cycles in sales.

However, the explanation for durable goods manufacturing must, I believe, be cast less in terms of problems of forecasting and correction of errors, and more in terms of shifts in market conditions. Because shipments, ownership, and market conditions all, broadly, move up and down with general business conditions, they also move up and down with one another. However we can, I think, go somewhat farther by way of identifying the impact of market conditions and its relationship to shipments than this statement suggests.

For one thing, we saw in Chapter 10 that a number of factors indicative of changing costs and market conditions seemed to have patterns corresponding to changing materials ownership of durable goods manufacturers after the influence of shipments had been subdued by differencing or expressing outstandings in terms of months of shipment. It seems clear, in other words, that these factors are there and influential.

For another thing, we saw in Chart 16 that the influence of shipments on buying seems to have at least two forms. The first reflects the obvious need to replace the materials shipped out in the form of finished goods, and, further, to maintain stocks at some appropriate level. Whether this need takes the form of a constant average or incremental relationship is perhaps not too important at the moment. The second is a rather elastic influence

impersonated by the stock-sales ratio which reflects a cumulation of discrepancies from the average level of replacement needs. When the discrepancies are negative they stimulate more buying, and when positive less buying. Though these discrepancies themselves may reflect short-term rates of change in shipments, they may have the capacity to reveal aspects of the interplay between short-term demand and market conditions, the presence of which is so tantalizingly difficult to photograph. Chart 17 seems to suggest this liaison apparatus at work.

The stock-sales ratio is depicted in the second curve of the chart. It has been drawn so that its inverse impact can be viewed as a direct one.[16] Below it are drawn each of the major factors that the previous analysis has indicated show an association with the phenomenon of market fluctuation. The particular forms included in this chart are based on the findings of Chapter 10. They are intended to maximize the general picture of parallelism. Timing measures were given in Table 41.

In general the chart conveys the basic notion that all of these phenomena may belong to the same family of events. It suggests a few of the family characteristics:

First, we see in the top two curves the impressive correspondence previously noted between the periods when the ratio showed that deficiencies were building up or declining and those when the physical volume of new orders for materials were increasing and decreasing respectively.

Second, the chart suggests that periods of increasing deficiencies and rising new orders for materials were usually times when a number of other things were also taking place: more vendors were lengthening their delivery periods; more producers were themselves piling up sales orders for future delivery; in the aggregate, these occurrences were decreasing at a declining rate or increasing at an increas-

[15] For a description of the measure see note 4, above.

[16] The scale also has been increased so that, moving upward on the chart, the figures start at about .80 and ascend to about .50.

CHART 17

Ratio of Materials Stocks to Shipments Compared with Selected Series,
Durable Goods Manufacturers, 1946–64

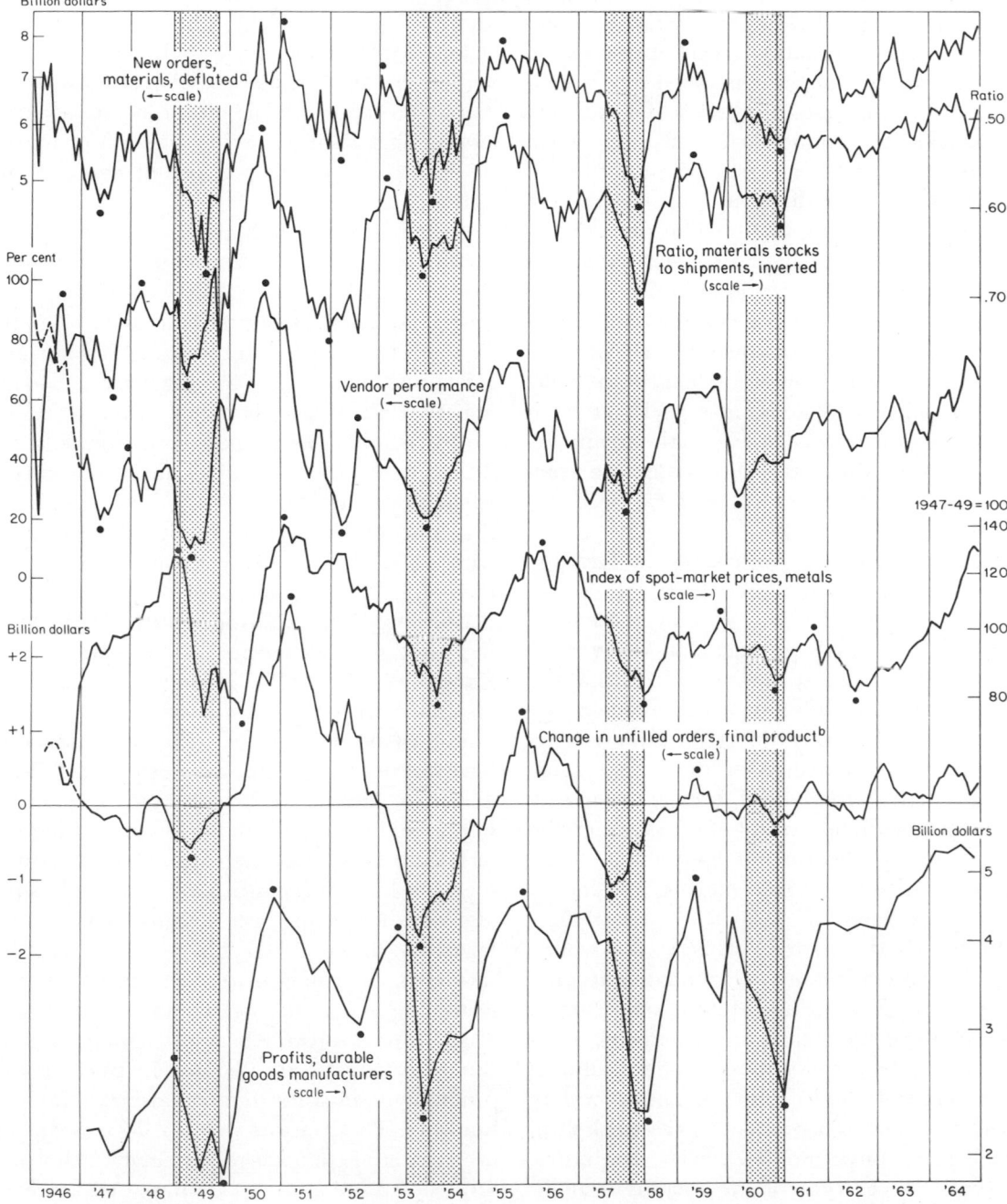

Note: Shaded areas represent business contractions.
a Deflated by wholesale price index for metals and metal products, 1957–59 = 100.
b Five-month centered moving average of month-to-month change.

ing rate. Two other things were occurring at most of the times: profits and the price of metals were rising. Consider the meaning of each briefly in turn.

Lengthening delivery periods for materials (third curve) probably reflect pressure on plant capacity. Pressure may take the form of a rate of increase in orders which it is uneconomical to produce at the rates at which orders are written, or it may take the form of levels of demand that put pressure on the physical capacity of plants. The data on capacity reviewed in Chapter 10 were consistent with the latter interpretation, among others. In the company of the changes visualized in Chart 17, we are prompted to ask whether the pressure on capacity, and associated delays in delivery periods, may itself result in part from the spurts in materials buying resulting from the interplay among the complex set of influences that we have been discussing.

An increasing rate of change in backlogs of sales orders (curve 5) means, of course, that new sales orders are growing relative to shipments of final products. In accordance with the argument at the start of this chapter, this may be thought of as a qualitative change in demand. Advance orders for materials required to manufacture products for which advance sales orders have been written may be placed with far less of the risk otherwise attendant on advance purchase of materials. Indeed, failure to cover may be considered risky.

Profits (bottom curve) provide the wherewithal for financing heavier commitments and, I have argued, sometimes at lower opportunity cost than average return on investment. They also stimulate optimistic expectations and actions. Table 41, line 18, shows a notably close association between profits and the stock-shipments ratio three months earlier. Beginning in 1948, 89 per cent of the months were in like phase.

How the prices of basic metals are involved in the complex of events is difficult to say.

One obvious causal connection—one moving from actual change in prices to expected change in prices to changed levels of inventories that should be held—is ruled out by the timing association. This point was developed in Chapter 10. I shall suggest a different sort of possible causal relationship in the final chapter. In the meantime, it is worth noting that their behavior may reflect result as well as cause—the pressure of demand on prices.

Some particulars of how these market-linked factors interact with the sales-linked elements are suggested by their behavior during the several episodes. The usual pattern may simply be that of mutual reinforcement. However, in a few cases divergences are suggested. In 1949 and 1951–52, excess stocks had ceased to build up five months before new orders picked up. These were, as indicated earlier, both times when prices were falling drastically; perhaps this, and other market conditions associated with it, tended to delay the resumption in buying.

Conversely, the continued increase in buying after the deficiencies at the time of the Korean War boom had started to decline was associated with a continued rise in prices and a level of output that was checked no doubt by capacity limitations in many firms. Producers of heavy equipment and armament were certainly among those whose backlog of unfilled orders were rising and at an accelerating rate. But materials producers as well were also slow in meeting orders, as the vendor performance index shows. Thus, expectation of shortages, or rising prices, caused more advance buying, which caused more shortages. High profits provided ample funds which could be temporarily invested in stocks both profitably and with due regard for future liquidity. These factors were strong enough to keep materials purchasing rising, even though shipments were no longer rising at an accelerating rate and the effort to reverse the growing deficiency in stock on hand had met with success. Much the same sequence of statements apply to mid-1955, except that in this case the continued buoyancy of market factors served not to postpone the peak in new orders but to greatly dampen the decline compared with what the sale-linked set of factors would otherwise have ordained.

The years following the business trough in early 1961 are particularly interesting, since they differ from the earlier period in a number of ways which seem internally consistent. In the first place, when recovery set in in early 1961, shipments rose only gradually and at a rate which underwent relatively little acceleration. After mid-1961, the stock-sales ratio likewise continued to record only a most gradual increase in stock deficiency.

In line with this unusual start, on the side of demand, of a prosperous period, there seems likewise to have been little stimulation of buying from the market-oriented elements. Orders for final products declined only slightly in the previous recession and increased only slowly and steadily during the expansion that followed. As a result, backlogs moved very gradually upward and their rate of increase was free of cyclical shapes. Capacity utilization was generally low, and "worsening" of vendor performance leveled off in 1961 and did not rise further until 1964. Profits increased, but the motive to invest them in inventories was absent. Sensitive metals prices fluctuated only very mildly until toward the end of 1963.

Possibly the new scientific methods of inventory management also played some part in preventing the usual spurts in materials buying. Of particular relevance is the possibility that better information and control techniques has reduced unintended stocks. But it is most hazardous, I believe, to heavily underscore this element in the complex of interrelated events. For one thing, most of the work on data processing for inventory management applies to finished stocks rather than purchased materials. But more important, the usual post-trough spurt in forward buying did not take place. The outstanding-sales, or own-

ership-sales, ratios slipped consistently downward after their peak in later 1959 until well into 1964 (see Chart 2). The ratio of stocks to sales recorded neither excess nor deficiencies; it oscillated around the level of .50, or, adjusted for value added, one month's supply. These facts are consistent with materials buying that is confined to requirements for actual production plus a true sales-linked inventory demand. And certainly a tendency of this sort would have been reasonable in view of the absence of the usual acceleration of final demand and the low level of utilization of the vast new plant capacity that had built up over the past five years or more. As we all know as this book goes to press, the situation did not last.

Acceleration Model for Durable Goods Manufacturers

The picture that the time-series sketch seems to imply that though a model of materials inventory for durable goods manufacture and for department stores would cover the same major elements, these elements would assume different forms and have different relative importance in the two types of enterprises. I shall state the particulars baldly; they are actually fields of investigation.

1. *Provision for expected shipments.* Unlike department stores, durable goods manufacturers often have some foreknowledge of requirements. As the discussion early in this chapter indicated, sales orders can provide (though in different ways for different sorts of firms) the basis of some very good guesses about what materials will be needed, and in ample time to purchase them.[17] In so far as

[17] A recent investigation by Michael Lovell provides provocative information on this point. ("Sales Anticipations, Planned Inventory Investment, and Realizations," in *Determinants of Investment Behavior*, Robert Ferber (ed.), New York, NBER, 1967.) When the statistics on sales anticipations now collected by the Office of Business Economics were used in explaining inventories, the addition of outstanding sales orders does not improve the result. Lovell notes that "this rather

this is the case, new orders for materials can actually precede shipments of finished goods and related production requirements.

2. *Sales-linked stock.* As shipments change, stocks must change in line with efficient service requirements, thereby implying something like a constant incremental ratio which is smaller than the average ratio. But an objective of this sort with respect to most durable goods materials is unlikely to carry the same management priority as does a corresponding objective for merchandise stocks of department stores.

3. *Changes in opportunity cost of stock.* Prosperity-linked changes in costs are likely to reduce the opportunity costs of stocks on hand and on order. This can occur by means of changes that reduce the cost of carrying stock, e.g., larger backlogs of sales orders which reduce risk, larger prosperity profits which, in so far as they need to be kept liquid, provide low-cost financing for stocks. It can occur by means of higher cost of alternatives to stock, such as high hire or overtime cost of flexible production schedules.

4. *Attention to the timing of buying.* Durable goods manufacturers must give considerable attention to just when they buy materials which they expect to require. On the one hand, conditions in materials markets are subject to substantial change capable of making it expensive to buy at the wrong times. On the other hand, manufacturers may often be able to extend or contract market positions in materials without much risk at least of buying goods that will not be needed.

5. *Correction of error.* Attribute 1 of the model implies that errors in forecasting sales will not have the systematic relation to rates of change that seemed to apply to department stores. Indeed, for many firms, error in procurement associated primarily with errors in

surprising result may well be explained by the possibility that in earlier studies unfilled orders were serving as a proxy for anticipated sales volume. . . ." This could mean that anticipations were themselves based in important part on the behavior of backlogs.

forecasts of shipments may be relatively minor. Attribute 4, on the other hand, implies that other factors influencing procurement will often be faultily foretold—market changes are volatile. Also, conditions which were correctly foretold at the time when buying was done may change, and thus cause ownership to be presently too large or too small and accordingly require correction. In part, this correction will involve materials outstanding, since it is in the goods-on-order segment that much of the first import of market-oriented buying falls. But as orders are delivered, stocks on hand are affected, and accordingly their volume too may be judged too large or too small. Note, however, that all of these characteristics involve a good deal of ambiguity about when ownership is too large or too small. If so, the correction of error is likely to be less a matter of enforcement of some precise norm than of resistance to the extent of departures from the norm. Thus, as stocks diverge from their normal relationship to shipments, either because of changes in utilizations, in buying, or in the pattern whereby outstandings are delivered, pressures to reverse the discrepancies build up and are acted upon.

Basic Characteristics of the Model

The models that I have sketched incorporate much that is familiar. They reassert, particularly, some of the basic thinking and findings of Franco Modigliani and his collaborators, Charles Holt, Kalman Cohen and others.[18] The emphasis I have placed on the

[18] A summary of a good bit of this work may be found in Charles C. Holt and F. Modigliani, "Firm Cost Structures and the Dynamic Responses of Inventories, Production, Work Force, and Orders to Sales Fluctuations," in *Inventory Fluctuations and Economic Stabilization, Part II*, materials prepared for the Joint Economic Committee, 1961 (87th Congress, 1st Session). See also Charles C. Holt, F. Modigliani, J. F. Math, and H. A. Simon, *Planning Production Inventories and Work Force*, Englewood Cliffs, N.J., 1960.

relevance of changing costs and opportunity costs of stocks is paralleled by their analysis of the impact of changes in production volume and in levels of factory activity. For "warehouse stocks," they believe that these elements are largely absent because of the relative costlessness of shifting the variations in demand to suppliers. This sort of thinking implies that different models are required for some sorts of enterprises than for others—a notion that in a different form appears very strongly in the two models I have presented. These similarities are reassuring since we have all approached the study of inventory behavior by addressing ourselves to the functions that stocks serve in individual enterprises and to the cost structures that are relevant to efficient management.

Nevertheless, the work reported in the foregoing chapters does suggest certain emphases which differ enough from other work to have substantial implications.

For one thing, full attention to opportunity costs implies that the behavior of stock will be different not only for the various sorts of stockpiles, a notion developed by Moses Abramovitz long ago, but also for different sorts of businesses. This is sharply demonstrated by the very different behavior of materials stocks in department stores and in durable goods manufacture (both a "warehouse" variety).

A second matter of emphasis is far richer in analytic consequences. The germinal notion is the serious attention to materials ordering as distinguished from materials receipts. This brings to the fore three sets of considerations: First, the large changes in orders outstanding that can result from changes in actual or expected market conditions. Changes in outstandings leave an imprint on stocks. Moreover, since leadtimes have strong cyclical patterns, cyclical fluctuation in stocks will tend to be larger than it would be if this set of influences were absent. Incidently, this last remark applies also to many of the other

changes in cost structures, which likewise have conforming cyclical patterns.

The second set of considerations concerns the speed and relative costlessness with which corrective action can be taken in the form of adjusted new orders when stocks or total materials ownership departs from desired levels. In consequence one cannot be satisfied to interpret sales-stock relationships in terms of distributed lags, a common device in econometric analysis. For ownership, the association is, we find, actually synchronous. This line of thought implies that if one must concentrate on stock rather than ownership it is essential to envision the particulars of forecasting, ordering (including the cascade of orders of different term), and enforcement techniques and priorities. However it may often be more informative to make the analysis in two groups: first explain ownership and second explain the flow of outstandings into stock.

The third set of consequences generated by my emphasis on orders is more subtle and more important. Orders placed for materials are orders received by suppliers. The information conveyed by the order and the associated expectations can touch off actions which have "multiplier effects" but without the usual time lags. They can coincide with or precede, as well as follow, the initial inventory investment, a subject taken up in the following chapter.

Finally, the emphasis on how expectations about supply conditions affect demand and vice versa, necessary implications of market-prospect-oriented buying, raises questions concerning how demand-and-supply conditions, and expectations concerning each, interact. Obviously these interactions must constitute an important part of an inventory model for durable goods manufacturing. However, as with the department store model, the feedback elements cannot be specified until some remaining questions are considered. Market information is rapidly conveyed; it can be acted upon almost immediately; the impact of these actions on markets, and on suppliers, and thus on the further information that is conveyed and further expectations aroused, is likewise swift. *Why, then, are the contours we have examined not that of a sharp rise, a sharp fall, followed by perhaps a period of dol-* *drum?* I shall propose an answer to this question in the last chapter. But first it is necessary to review the impact of these inventory and buying waves on economic fluctuations at large.

12. Inventory-Purchase Cycles and Business Cycles

The previous three chapters have analyzed the processes that appear to generate fluctuations within the complex of events central to purchasing and stock-carrying functions. Thus they concern primarily the first of the two sets of problems mentioned at the outset—the dynamics of inventory fluctuation viewed as a syndrome of causally interrelated phenomena. This chapter focuses on the second set of problems: how stocks and associated activities participate in economic instability.

The central fact about the objectives, problems, perceptions, and techniques associated with stock carrying and purchasing is that they tend to produce fluctuation in stocks on hand and on order and in their rates of change. But most other aspects of economic life are also subject to fluctuation, and to these instabilities inventory movements have the usual double relationship. On the one hand, they are influenced by fluctuations that are, at least in the first instance, external to the "inventory cycle." For example, we have previously explored how changes in levels and in rates of change in final demand, in planned utilization and various other shifts in costs and in market conditions, impinge on the process whereby stocks rise and fall. On the other hand, the levels of stocks on hand and on order, and particularly the rates at which they change, impinge on other aspects of the economy (including the ones just mentioned) and the manner in which they fluctuate.

The specifics of the impact differ, of course, for each aspect, and therefore cannot be examined here. It will, however, be instructive to make use of a general framework for business fluctuation and describe how the events primarily associated with the inventory-purchase complex join the configuration. I discuss first the timing of the events central to inventory-purchase movements, and second the amplitude of their impact on earlier as contrasted with later stages of production. The last section surveys how the inventory-purchase syndrome plays into the process whereby the forces of contraction cumulate and moderate, how expansion sets in, develops, and recedes.

BUSINESS CYCLE PATTERNS OF INVENTORY WAVES

Since World War II, many economists have felt that fluctuations in stocks have played a more dominant role in business fluctuation at large than previously had been the case. The reason is rather that other sources of instability have moderated than that inventories are becoming more unruly. It is not surprising, then, to find a high order of conformity to the National Bureau business cycle reference chronology of the activities involved in purchasing and inventory fluctuation.

Three Characteristics

Conformity: Table 42 gives reference cycle timing measures for the five series most cen-

TABLE 42

Average Business Cycle Reference Timing of Materials Stocks and Purchasing, Durable Goods Manufacturers and Department Stores, 1948-62[a]

	Median Leads (−) Or Lags (+), Months				Number Of Matched Turns					
	At Peaks		At Troughs		Dur. Mfrs.			Dept. Stores		
	Dur. Mfrs. (1)	Dept. Stores (2)	Dur. Mfrs. (3)	Dept. Stores (4)	−	+	0 (5)	−	+	0 (6)
1. Change in outstanding orders	−22.5	*−14.0*	−7.0	*−9.0*	8	0	0	*8*	*0*	*0*
2. Change in ownership	−22.5	*−12.5*	−7.0	*−8.0*	8	0	0	*8*	*0*	*0*
3. Change in stocks	−7.0	*−9.5*	−3.5	*−3.0*	6	1	1	*8*	*0*	*0*
4. Materials orders	−10.5	*−7.5*	−2.0	*−4.0*	7	0	1	*8*	*0*	*0*
5. Materials receipts	−4.5	*−4.5*	−1.0	*−3.5*	5	1	2	*8*	*0*	*0*
6. Outstanding orders	−8.0	*−7.0*	+0.5	*−2.5*	8	0	0	*8*	*0*	*0*
7. Ownership	−4.5	*−0.5*	+0.5	*−2.5*	6	2	0	*5*	*1*	*2*
8. Stocks	+0.5	*+0.5*	+4.0	*+0.5*	1	6	1	*1*	*4*	*3*
Average lines 1−5	−13.4	*−9.6*	−4.1	*−5.5*						
Average all lines	−9.9	*−6.9*	−1.9	*−4.0*						

	Skipped Reference Turns		Number of Extra Turns		Early Peak As High Or Higher Than Second Peak			
					in 1947		in 1951	
	Dur. Mfrs. (7)	Dept. Stores (8)	Dur. Mfrs. (9)	Dept. Stores (10)	Dur. Mfrs.	Dept. Stores (11)	Dur. Mfrs.	Dept. Stores (12)
1. Change in outstanding orders	0	*0*	2[b]	*4*	Yes	*Yes*	Yes	*Yes*
2. Change in ownership	0	*0*	1[b]	*4*	Yes	*Yes*	Yes	*Yes*
3. Change in stocks	0	*0*	4	*4*	Yes	*Yes*	Yes	*Yes*
4. Materials orders	0	*0*	2	*4*	No	*Yes*	Yes	*Yes*
5. Materials receipts	0	*0*	2	*4*	No	*Yes*	No	*Yes*
6. Outstanding orders	0	*0*	2[b]	*4*	Yes	*Yes*	No	*Yes*
7. Ownership	0	*0*	2	*4*	Yes	*Yes*	No	*Yes*
8. Stocks	0	*0*	0[b]	*4*	No	*No*	No	*Yes*

[a]For source tables, see corresponding lines of Table 43.
[b]In addition there were two extra minor specific cycle turns.

trally involved in inventory cycles and their impact on the economy. They are rates of change in ownership and in its two parts, and orders for materials and their shipment to the purchaser. The level of the three stockpiles is also shown in the table. For both durable goods manufacturers and department stores, all reference turns during the period examined (there were eight marked) were invariably matched by corresponding specific cycle turns.

Leads: Virtually all turns for the five series lead the business cycle chronology. For the two sorts of enterprises, eighty individual timing comparisons were made; two of these were lags, four synchronous,[1] and seventy-four leads. For outstandings proper, leads are also universal. Only for stocks proper are lags common. Average leads tended to be long, and longer at peaks than at troughs. The difference was far more marked for the durable goods industries than for department stores.

Extra Cycles: The table summarizes a further characteristic of the series. They tend to have additional specific cycle turns at one or both of the times when hesitations or minor reversals in business cycles have been noted. I refer to the two brief recessions which interrupted, on the one hand, the rise to the 1948 business peak and, on the other hand, interrupted the rise to the peak in 1953 after the first impact of the Korean War. Columns 9 and 10 of Table 42 show that department store inventory and purchase data all had these four specific subcycle phases. The durable goods inventory data usually had them, though often marked as a minor movement, whereas the book value of orders and shipments rose uninterruptedly during the first years of postwar demand, though it dipped after Korea. In general, then, for this whole group of activities, two of the three periods of business cycle expansion between 1946 and 1961 were interrupted by temporary setbacks.[2]

Indeed, the earlier of the two peaks in each of the interrupted business expansion phases was for the department store data, with one exception, uniformly as high or higher than the second, the one associated with the peak in general business.

The characteristic interruptions also have implications with respect to techniques of analysis. By using the subcycle reference scheme, more comparisons can be made, and the timing of individual turns becomes less erratic. These measures, summarized in Table 43, show again the almost universal presence of leads for the ownership investment data (columns 7 and 8) and likewise for materials orders. The tendency for average leads to be longer (or lags shorter) at peaks than at troughs is indicated (without the disruption of the very long leads relative to the business cycle turn in 1953).

Similarities and Differences in Timing for the Two Groups of Enterprises

By and large one is struck by the similarities in the timing comparisons for department stores and durable goods manufacturers. However, Table 43 does reveal, on closer examination, that for department stores median leads at troughs are invariably longer, or lags shorter, than for durables. This is perhaps no surprise in view of the tendency for retail sales to recover promptly during the postwar cycles.[3]

However, the similarities and differences in timing of events associated with the merchandise buying of department stores and with the materials buying of durable goods manufacturers deserve more careful study, for they bear on the important problem of whether

---

[1] The individual timing comparisons are given in the source tables for each line of Table 42.

[2] There appears also to have been an interruption at the turn of the year 1961–62, but, as previously explained, my figures need a thorough overhauling in order to deal reliably with this period.

[3] Compare lines 1 and 2 in Tables 6 and 15.

TABLE 43

Average Subcycle Reference Timing of Materials Stocks and Purchasing, Durable Goods Manufacturers and Department Stores, 1946-62

		Median Leads (−) Or Lags (+), Months					
		Peaks		Troughs		All Turns	
Series		Dur. Mfrs. (1)	Dept. Stores (2)	Dur. Mfrs. (3)	Dept. Stores (4)	Dur. Mfrs. (5)	Dept. Stores (6)
Dept. Stores	Durables						
Change in Ownership							
Outstandings	Outstandings	−12.7	*−13.0*	−5.0	*−10.5*	−7.7	*−11.5*
Ownership	Ownership	−12.7	*−11.5*	−5.0	*−9.5*	−7.7	*−11.0*
Stocks	Stocks	−4.0	*−8.0*	−1.5	*−3.0*	−3.0	*−6.0*
Purchase Data							
Merch. Orders	Materials Orders	−7.3	*−7.5*	−2.7	*−5.5*	−4.5	*−7.0*
Merch. Receipts	Materials Receipts	−2.7	*−4.5*	−0.7	*−3.5*	−0.5	*−3.5*
Stock Proper							
Outstandings	Outstandings	−6.0	*−6.5*	+0.5	*−2.5*	−2.5	*−3.5*
Ownership	Ownership	−4.0	*−0.5*	+1.0	*−2.5*	−1.5	*−2.0*
Stocks	Stocks	+1.3	*+0.5*	+3.7	*0*	+3.0	*0*
Average lines 1−5		−7.9	*−8.9*	−3.0	*−6.4*	−4.7	*−7.8*
Average all lines		−6.0	*−6.4*	−1.2	*−4.6*	−3.0	*−5.6*

		Number Of Matched Turns						Skipped Reference Turns		Source Tables			
		Dur. Mfrs.			Dept. Stores			Dur. Mfrs.	Dept. Stores	Dur. Mfrs.		Dept. Stores	
		−	+	0	−	+	0			Table	Line	Table	Line
		(7)			(8)			(9)	(10)	(11)		(12)	
Change in Ownership													
Outstandings	Outstandings	10	0	1	*12*	*0*	*0*	1	*0*	18	13	*20*	*14*
Ownership	Ownership	10	0	1	*12*	*0*	*0*	1	*0*	18	2	*20*	*2*
Stocks	Stocks	9	2	1	*12*	*0*	*0*	0	*0*	18	7	*20*	*8*
Purchase Data													
Merch. Orders	Materials Orders	9	0	1	*12*	*0*	*0*	2	*0*	28	9	*22*	*11*
Merch. Receipts	Materials Receipts	5	2	3	*12*	*0*	*0*	2	*0*	28	2	*22*	*6*
Stock Proper													
Outstandings	Outstandings	8	4	0	*12*	*0*	*0*	0	*0*	1	11	*9*	*11*
Ownership	Ownership	7	3	0	*8*	*1*	*3*	2	*0*	1	2	*9*	*2*
Stocks	Stocks	1	8	1	*3*	*5*	*4*	2	*0*	1	6	*9*	*6*

there is a tendency for inventory-purchase cycles to occur at the same time in diverse markets. Table 44 explores the question in terms of direct comparisons between department stores and durable goods manufacturers for the various stock and flow data, grouped in pairs, on as nearly a comparable basis as can be contrived.

The first eight lines refer to the same pairs of series for which the reference timing was given in Tables 42 and 43. The direct comparisons show, of course, the same tendency for department store stocks or outstandings, and their rates of change, to reach troughs ahead of those of durable goods manufacturers. Moreover, for rates of change, the average leads of three or four months are very consistent: average deviation ranged between 1.4 and 2.0 months for the three inventory investment series. Lines 11 and 12 indicate that one reason for the lead may be that, at troughs, department stores' sales also lead shipments of all durable goods manufacturers or those in the heavy industries. But the need for very close control of merchandise stocks doubtless also plays a part.

We saw in the previous tables that actions associated with the inventory-purchase syndrome caused department store merchandise orders to lead at cyclical turns as much or more than did the materials orders of durable goods manufacturers. Apparently, at only two of the ten matched turns (line 4) did the purchase orders of department stores turn later than those of durable goods manufacturers. The tendency for department store inventory investment and buying to turn early even relative to the most sensitive durable goods manufacturers' stocks, those of purchased materials, offers food for thought.

But perhaps even more interesting than the lead itself is the regularity of the association for the two sorts of enterprises. The series that represent the most direct influence of stocks on the economy as a whole are the rates of change in the stock aggregates, materials orders, and (via their influence on inventory

fluctuation) the rates of change in shipments (sales). Of these, the timing for the inventory investment and order data have already been discussed. For change in shipments (lines 13 and 14), the table shows a surprisingly close correspondence when the rates of change in department store sales are compared with either shipments of all durable goods manufacturers or those of the heavy industries only. Allowing for a lead of between two and zero months, 79–81 per cent of the months were in like phase for the whole period or, because of differences in the immediate postwar behavior, 83–86 per cent for the period beginning in 1948. Peaks occur at virtually the same time, the average deviation for the four matched peaks are .5 and .2 months respectively. For the five matched troughs, none are more than four months apart. Note that the timing is not nearly as similar for the data proper (lines 11 and 12), though the absence of turns in either series in the early years boosts the months in phase for the period as a whole (not for the post-January 1948 segment).

I might add, in view of the common assumption that differencing reduces collinearity, that it is common for comparable data for any of the stock and flow series for the two sorts of enterprises to have more months in phase when converted to rates of change than for the data proper.[4]

---

[4] The percentage of months in phase was compared for department stores and durable goods manufacturers as shown by first differences and by data proper in three stock series given in lines 1 to 3 and 6 to 8 of Table 44, and for the flow series for which the data proper are given in lines 9, 11, 4, 10 and 12. (The matching rates of change are given in the table only for lines 11 and 12.) This gave sixteen comparisons—eight pairs for percentage of months in phase for data proper and for their first differences; using the two periods, 7/46 to 12/61 and 1/48 to 12/61, produced sixteen pairs. Of these sixteen, the months in phase for department stores and durables were higher for first differences in thirteen cases, the same in one, and smaller in two. Timing also tends to be more nearly synchronous for the first differences in six of the eight pairs, the same in one, and longer in one.

I have not systematically examined whether, when other sorts of comparisons are made, the parallelism is

TABLE 44

Timing: Selected Series, Department Stores Compared with Comparable Data for Durable Goods Manufacturers, 1946–61

		Section A: Months Lead (–) or Lag (+) for Matched Turns[a] Chronology[b]											
		P	T	P	T	P	T	P	T	P	T	P	T
Line	Reference Series, Durables[c]	1947	1947	1948	1949	1951	1952	1953	1954	1957	1958	1960	1961
	Specific Series: Change in Ownership, Dept. Stores												
1	Outstandings	–2	–6	–8	–3	–6	–6	+1	–5	+6	–3	+5	0
2	Ownership	–7	–6	–8	–3	Ω	Ω	+9	–5	+5	–1	+4	0
3	Stocks	Ω	Ω	–3	–5	–11	–2	0	–4	+5	0	+6	–3
	Specific Series: Purchasing, Dept. Stores												
4	Materials, orders	Ω	Ω	–12	–1	–6	–8	0	0	+6	–3	+14	–1
5	Materials, receipts	Ω	Ω	–11	–3	–4	–9	–6	–4	+6	–3	+10	–1
	Specific Series: Stock Proper, Dept. Stores												
6	Outstandings	Ω	–8	–5	–14	–8	–8	+2	–2	+7	–3	+2	+6
7	Ownership	Ω	–7	–4	–6	–8	–6	+2	–2	+8	–2	+4	+6
8	Stocks	–4	–6	–11	+1	0	–8	–7	–7	–4	–3	+11	+3
	Specific Series: Demand, Dept. Stores												
9	Orders, final product	⊙	⊙	+4	+1	0	–5	+5	+1	+12	–2	+10	0
10	Orders, all dur.	⊙	⊙	+4	0	0	–5	+4	+1	+20	0	+10	Ω
11	Shipments, final product	⊙	⊙	–2	–5	Ω	Ω	–2	–9	+7	–2	+9	0
12	Shipments, all durables	⊙	⊙	–2	–3	–2	–15	–2	–9	+7	–2	+10	0
	Specific Series: Change in Sales, Dept. Stores												
13	Change shipments, final product	Ω	Ω	Ω	+4	–1	–2	0	–4	0	–2	0	–1
14	Change shipments, all durables	Ω	Ω	Ω	+4	–1	–3	0	–4	0	–1	+1	0

(continued)

TABLE 44 (concluded)

Section B: Average Timing of Turns

Line	Reference Series, Durables[c]	Number Matched			Median[e]			Average Deviation[f]		All Turns	Section C: Percentage of Months in Like Phase[d]		
		-	+	0	P	T	All	P	T	Wt'd	Timing Adjust-ment[g]	% Mos. 7/46– 12/61	% Mos. 1/48– 12/61
	Specific Series: Change in Ownership, Dept. Stores												
1	Outstandings	8	3	1	-0.5	-4.0	-3.0	4.7	1.8	3.4 3.2	-3	78	78
2	Ownership	6	3	1	+0.7	-3.0	-2.0	6.5	2.0	4.6 4.2	-1, -2	71	75
3	Stocks	6	2	2	+0.7	-3.0	-2.5	5.1	1.4	3.5 3.3	-2	77	79
	Specific Series: Purchasing, Dept. Stores												
4	Materials, orders	6	2	2	0	-1.7	-1.0	7.6	2.1	4.9 4.9	-1	72	71
5	Materials, receipts	8	2	0	-1.3	-3.3	-3.5	7.1	1.9	4.3 4.5	-3, -4	71	74
	Specific Series: Stock Proper, Dept. Stores												
6	Outstandings	7	4	0	-0.3	-5.5	-3.3	4.9	5.2	5.3 5.0	-2, -3	69	69
7	Ownership	7	4	0	+0.7	-4.0	-2.7	5.1	3.5	4.5 4.2	-2	74	74
8	Stocks	8	3	1	-4.0	-4.5	-4.0	4.8	3.7	4.2 4.2	-4	73	71
	Specific Series: Demand[h], Dept. Stores												
9	Orders, final product	2	6	2	+6.3	-0.3	+1.0	3.9	1.9	3.8 2.9	+1	80	77
10	Orders, all dur.	1	5	3	+6.0	0	+1.7	5.6	1.5	4.9 3.8	+1	71	68
11	Shipments, final product	5	2	1	+2.5	-3.5	-2.0	5.0	3.0	4.0 4.0	-2	81	79
12	Shipments, all durables	7	2	1	+1.0	-4.7	-2.0	4.8	4.7	4.4 4.8	-2	76	74
	Specific Series: Change in Sales[h], Dept. Stores												
13	Change shipments, final product	5	1	3	0	-1.7	-0.7	0.2	1.9	1.5 1.1	-1	81	86
14	Change shipments, all durables	4	2	3	0	-1.3	-0.3	0.5	2.3	1.6 1.5	0	79	84

Notes to Table 44

[a]Specific series are data for department stores. They are matched against the reference frame of the corresponding series for durable goods manufacturers in accordance with the standard NBER rules. A double relaxation of rules is marked r; it applies to cases for well-conforming series in which two like turns are matched, though an unlike turn lies between them. The figure is underlined when subcycle chronology is the reference series, a minor cycle in the specific series has entered a comparison; or, when two individual series are compared, a minor cycle in either series has entered a comparison. When the business cycle chronology provides the reference, minor specific cycle turns are ignored. The meaning of other symbols are:

⊕ turn in the reference series does not appear in the specific series.

৪ turn in the specific series does not appear in the reference series.

⊙ there is no turn in either series in the neighborhood of the chronology date.

[b]Chronology gives the approximate time when the specific turns in the reference series occurred.

[c]Each line compares the specified data for department stores (the specific series) with the data for durable goods manufacturers (the reference series). Also, see note f.

[d]The number of months during which the specific series is in like phase with the reference series is expressed as a percentage of the total number of months covered between dates as given.

[e]Median is the average timing of the center two or three turns.

[f]Average deviation from the median. The "weighted"(wt'd) average is the deviation from the median for peaks and for troughs separately, weighted by the number of turns.

[g]In determining months in like phase, a timing adjustment is made which maximizes confluence. Before counting the months in phase, the specific series is in effect moved to the right to allow for a lead and to the left to allow for a lag if by so doing the percentage of months in like phase (as rounded) is increased. If the months in phase are as large or larger without an adjustment, this is indicated by a "timing adjustment" of 0.

[h]The specific series for all comparisons is retail sales of department stores since this is both orders for and shipments of final product. The reference series for final products is, for line 9, orders for the machinery and transportation equipment industries and, for lines 11 and 13, shipments for those industries. Lines 10, 12, and 14 apply to all durable goods manufacturers.

BACKWARD TRANSMISSION OF FLUCTUATION

The rate of change in a stock and its relation to the flows that fill or empty the stock reservoir determine whether fluctuation in final demand is magnified or subdued at earlier levels of the economy. The potential acceleration or magnification can affect flows of information, such as orders; or flows of goods, such as shipments; or flows of activity and associated income, such as those which production implies. Each pair of flows may be studied in association with change in the appropriate stock (on hand or on order). What evidence is readily available bearing on the character of this backward transmission of fluctuation?

also greater for rates of change than for data proper. For example, instead of pairing two sorts of enterprises, one might compare flows variously defined (e.g., orders and shipments) or at various stages (e.g., shipments for final product and for materials). However, the few comparisons that were made did not necessarily show percentage of months in phase higher for these other sorts of relationships when represented by rates of change than by data proper, as was the case for the comparisons between the two sorts of enterprises.

Clearly, however, it is not correct to assume for the purpose of econometric analysis that differencing systematically reduces collinearity. It typically does so, of course, insofar as sawtooth irregularities are amplified; but if these are smoothed, cyclical collinearity among various first-difference series may be greater rather than less than for data proper.

Retail Sales and Two Stages of Production, Consumer Durables

One piece of evidence was examined in Chapter 7—the relation between orders placed by department stores and sales to final consumers. (The latter can be thought of as either orders by or shipments to consumers.) We saw that orders placed by retailers for merchandise lead retail sales by an average of seven months at peaks and were nearly syn-

chronous at troughs (Table 22, line 12). Retailers' suppliers, in other words, feel the downturn of business substantially earlier than do retailers. Thus demand, defined as orders, accelerates at peaks as it moves backward. It also is greatly magnified. Specific fluctuations in new orders for merchandise were about twice as strong as those of retail sales, the orders of consumers (see Table 23 or Table 24, line 1).

There is no way of isolating the firms that

CHART 18

Retail Sales and Two Stages of Production, Consumer Durable Goods, 1947–64

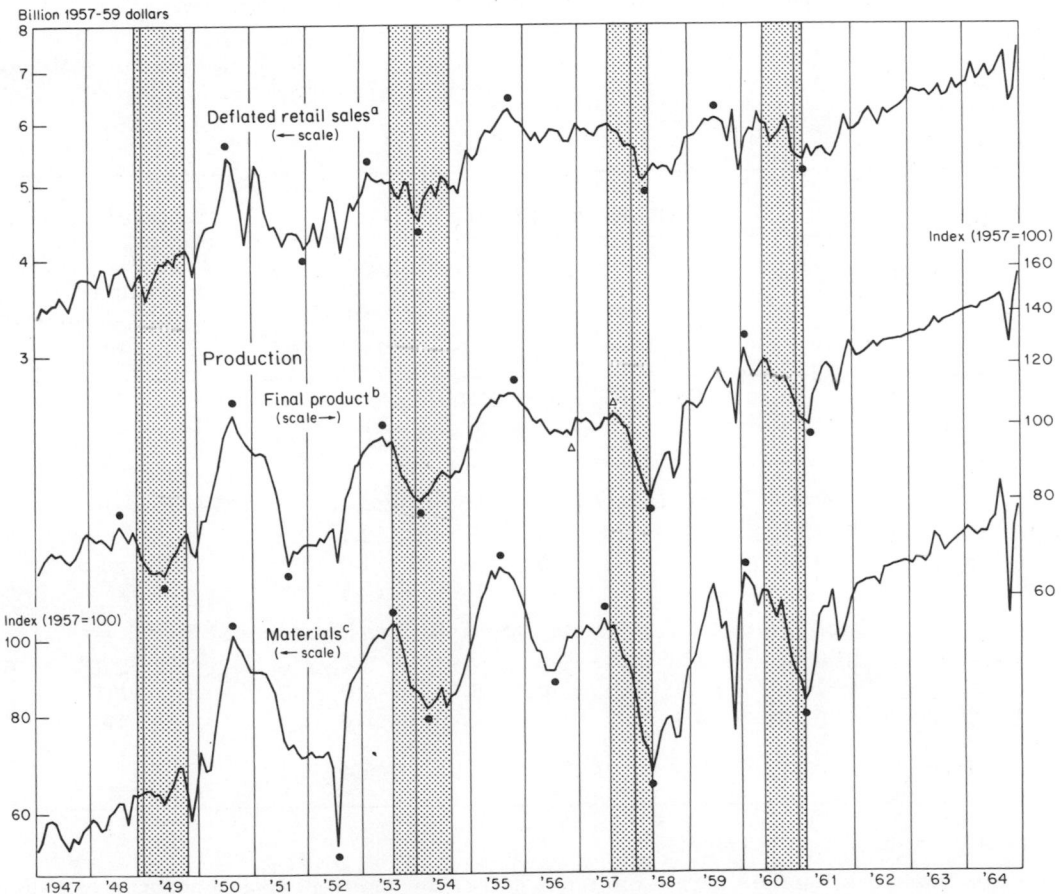

Note: Shaded areas represent business contractions. Specific cycle turns are marked by dots, additional minor turns by triangles.

a Retail sales of durable goods stores deflated by retail price of durable goods (1957–59 = 100).
b Production of automotive and home goods, FRB data.   c Consumer durable materials, FRB data.

TABLE 45

Timing: Retail Sales and Two Stages of Production, Consumer Durable Goods, 1947–1961

Section A: Months Lead (–) or Lag (+) for Matched Turns[a]
Chronology[b]

Line	Reference Series[c]	P (1/47)	T (7/47)	P 11/48	T 10/49	P (2/51)	T (6/52)	P 7/53	T 8/54	P 7/57	T 4/58	P 5/60	T 2/61
	Specific Series: Retail Sales												
1	Business cycles			⊕	⊕			−5	−7	−22	−1	−11	0
2	Subcycles	⊕	⊕	⊕	⊕	−7	−6	−5	−7	−22	−1	−11	0
	Specific Series: Production, Final Product (Automotive & Home Goods)												
3	Business cycles			−4	−5			−2	−7	−21	0	−4	+1
4	Subcycles	⊕	⊕	−4	−5	−6	−10	−2	−7	−21	0	−4	+1
5	Retail sales	⊙	⊙	Ω	Ω	+1	−4	+3	0	+1	+1	+7	+1
	Specific Series: Production, Materials, Consumer Durables												
6	Business cycles			⊕	⊕			0	−5	−24[r]	0	−4	0
7	Subcycles	⊕	⊕	⊕	⊕	−6	+1	0	−5	−24[r]	0	−4	0
8	Retail sales	⊙	⊙	⊙	⊙	+1	+7	+5	+2	−2	+1	+7	0
9	Production, final product	⊙	⊙	⊕	⊕	0	+11	+2	+2	−3	0	0	−1

		Section B: Average Timing of Turns								Section C: Percentage of Months in Like Phase[d]	
		Number Matched			Median[e]			Average Deviation[f]			Timing Adjust-ment[g]	% Mos. 7/46– 12/61
										All Turns		
Line	Reference Series[c]	−	+	0	P	T	All	P	T	Wt'd		
	Specific Series: Retail Sales											
1	Business cycles	5	0	1	−12.7	−2.7	−6.0	6.2	2.9	5.7	−6, −7	64
2	Subcycles	7	0	1	−9.0	−3.5	−6.5	5.2	3.0	4.4	−6, −7	73
	Specific Series: Production, Final Product (Automotive & Home Goods)											
3	Business cycles	5	2	1	−3.0	−2.5	−3.0	1.8	3.2	2.5	−3, −4	75
4	Subcycles	8	1	1	−4.7	−4.0	−4.6	4.3	3.8	4.0	−4, −5	76
5	Retail Sales	1	6	1	+2.0	+0.5	+1.0	2.0	1.5	1.8	+1	86
	Specific Series: Production, Materials, Consumer Durables											
6	Business cycles	3	0	3	−9.3	−1.7	−2.0	9.8	2.2	5.5	−1, −2, 0	62
7	Subcycles	4	1	3	−5.0	0	−2.0	6.5	1.5	5.0	−1, −2, 0	70
8	Retail sales	1	6	1	+3.0	+1.5	+1.5	3.2	2.0	2.6	+1, +2	88
9	Production, final product	2	3	3	0	+1.0	0	1.2	3.5	2.4	0	83

For notes a, c through g, see Table 44.

[b]Chronology dates are business cycle reference dates. In addition, four minor subcycle dates, enclosed in parentheses, are added to form a subcycle chronology.

supply department stores so as to examine orders received and placed in the next earlier stage; accordingly, this chain of events moves out of sight.

However, three stages can be compared for home goods (including major appliances) and automobiles. Chart 18 depicts the physical quantities of goods moving to consumers, and goods completing production at the finished stage and at the materials stage.[5] Matching information for orders is not available.[6] Thus we can examine flows of activity, but not flows of the associated information.

Table 45, line 5, shows that retail sales in constant dollars tended to turn rather consistently a bit earlier than did production of the finished goods. For the next earlier stage there was no further acceleration, though retail sales also led materials for consumer durables by an average of one or two months (line 8).

Amplitude of fluctuation was magnified at earlier stages—the average specific phase amplitude for production of finished consumer durables was two-thirds again as large as that of retail sales (Table 46, line 4, columns 1 to 3). The amplitude of materials production was well over twice as large (line 5), and the figure would doubtless be larger had the

appropriate portion of the output of primary metals been included (see footnote 5).

Chart 18 shows that there were spurts in consumer buying, starting when business as a whole reached troughs, and continuing for a year, more or less. Their cessation constitutes in each case a specific cycle peak. The dates seem to conform fairly well to those of the early thrusts that the inventory-purchase data have exhibited. These thrusts in consumer buying have their counterparts in more than proportional thrusts in the output of the finished goods and materials used in their manufacture. The magnification on a per-month basis is slightly greater for the thrusts than for all expansion months (compare, Table 46, columns 5 and 4, lines 4 and 5).

The magnification of contractions is still larger (column 6), but this could reflect no more than the arithmetic of the differential impact of an upward trend on series with different cyclical characteristics.[7] Even so, it suggests that an upward trend tends to cause the backward transmission of demand to intensify drops in output relatively more than rises in output.

These figures, like the ownership and stock data, suggest that magnification exceeds the requirements of efficient servicing of sales, other things the same. To illustrate, a calculation can be made assuming, for example, that the efficient stock-sales relationship consisted of an incremental stock-sales ratio of 2. The stockpile concerned would implicitly be that of stocks of retail stores plus finished stocks of manufacturers of the finished articles. The average rise of retail sales during expansion

[5] Retail sales are deflated by the retail price index for consumer durables. The production series are those developed by the Federal Reserve Board. The index for consumer materials production does not include the output of primary metals producers.

[6] Automobile companies do not report unfilled orders, and the company basis of reporting does not make it possible to isolate orders for major consumer appliances. The new divisional reports take an important step in this direction and may make it feasible to examine for later years the patterns of sales orders for at least the final product stage. However, the new tabulations do not separate producers supplying materials to the finished consumer durables industries from those supplying them to the producer durables industries.

[7] Consider three series. All have phases of two-year duration and upward trends of one index point a year. Series A has a cylical component of two index points a year, series B one of four points, and series C one of eight points.

| Series | Standings | | | Rise or Fall | | Amplitude as % of Series A | |
	Trough	Peak	Trough	Expansion	Contraction	Expansion	Contraction
A	100	106	104	6	2	100	100
B	100	110	104	10	6	167	300
C	100	118	104	18	14	300	700

TABLE 46

Average Amplitude of Specific Cycle Fluctuation, Retail Sales and
Two Stages of Production, Consumer Durable Goods, 1949–1961

	Average Phase Amplitude Cycle Relatives[a]			Per Month Amplitude Cycle Relatives[a]		
	Expansion (1)	Contraction (2)	All Phases (3)	Expansion (4)	Thrust (5)	Contraction (6)
1. Retail sales, consumer durables constant prices	21.0	11.7	16.3	1.23	1.27	.61
2. Production, final product: automobile and home goods	32.6	21.0	26.8	1.75	2.04	1.57
3. Production materials, consumer durables[b]	39.3	31.5	35.4	2.55	2.71	1.80
4. % final product to retail sales (line 2 ÷ line 1)	155	179	164	142	161	257
5. % materials to retail sales (line 3 ÷ line 1)	187	269	217	207	213	295
6. % materials to final products (line 3 ÷ line 2)	121	150	132	146	133	115

[a]Expressed as relatives of the average peak and trough standings for each phase. Standings are five-month averages centered at month of turn. Averages cover four expansion and four contraction phases starting with the trough in 1949 and ending with a peak in 1961. For retail sales there was no specific trough that corresponded to the business cycle trough in 1949; therefore the contraction point in that year was used instead.

[b]A specific cycle phase with a trough in 1956 and peak in 1957 was ignored in order to keep the measured comparable for the three series.

was 21.0 per cent of its average level (Table 46, column 1), and production of final products would presumably also need to increase in the same proportion as well as enough to accommodate the additions to stocks that are required. Stocks, we assume, must increase each month by twice the monthly increment in sales—1.23 index points (column 4). Assuming for the moment a triangular course of sales, this means that production would have had to rise during expansion by 21.0 index points plus 2.46 points, or 23.5. This figure may be a bit low,[8] but contrast it with the

8 The pattern of sales is not triangular, and therefore its rate of change (and, by the same token, the stock increments each month) is, at its maximum rate, larger than 1.23. But the maximum rate of change in sales does not typically occur at the same time that sales proper reaches its peak, so that the combined

actual figure of 32.6. For contractions, the difference that must be explained in terms of factors other than the efficient sales link is far larger still.

Durable Goods Manufacturing, Two Stages of Production, Shipments and Orders

For the range of commodities with which we have been concerned there is no other readily available sequence of aggregate data showing sales to final users and earlier stages of the economic processes that the goods undergo. However, two of the intermediate stages can be viewed for all durable goods.

Judging from the consumer durable sequence, most of the magnification took place between the retail and final processing stage (compare Table 48, lines 4 and 6). There is, I believe, a reason for this which is implicit in the difference in the acceleration process for manufacturers and for department stores, as described in the previous chapter. But first let us examine the character of the relation between the two manufacturing stages.

In Chart 19 the final-products industries, machinery and transportation equipment, are compared with all of the rest of the durables group industries which hypothetically make materials or parts used by the former group. Needless to say, the hypothesis is a long way from the truth, though the production data come much closer to it than do the others.[9] Table 47 shows that in terms of physical volume of output, final products and materials have no systematic tendency to lead or lag one another (line 5). A similar statement applies to new orders for the two groups, although

the timing relationship was considerably closer than for production (line 13). For shipments, materials tended to lead by short and quite regular intervals (line 8). Broadly speaking, then, the two stages move together on the average.

The amplitude of matching specific cycle fluctuations in the two groups of industries are compared in Table 48. The magnification of fluctuation as demand moves to the materials stage seems quite strong in the production data. On the average, materials undergo specific cycle phases with almost half again as much amplitude as that of final products (line 7, column 3). The per-month amplitude during the periods of thrust is substantially larger than for expansions as a whole, and more so for materials than for final production (compare columns 4 and 5, lines 1 and 2). Indeed, for materials, 86 per cent of the entire rise during expansions took place in the three relatively short early periods.

When the relationships are viewed in terms of shipments at book value, the magnification for expansion as a whole disappears, though it remains for the period of thrust (line 8). New orders do not portray any of these several characteristics.

I do not know how seriously to take these figures. Technical difficulties might well account for disparities in the story of backward transmission as told by the shipments compared with the production data.[10] But for orders the differences are strong enough to demand respect. Moreover, the analysis of process that has been presented seems consistent with the statistical evidence.

---

impact is less than the total rise in sales (replacement demand) plus the maximum rate of rise in sales times 2 (inventory investment requirement).

[9] The production indexes, which are compiled by the Federal Reserve Board, are based on establishment data, whereas the OBE-Census figures for shipments and orders are, as previously explained, based on corporate reports. Also, in the FRB production indexes, industry breakdowns are finer and construction materials are excluded from the materials group.

[10] The underlying data for shipments and new orders are corporate reports, and this is, of course, far too gross a reporting unit to provide the appropriate industrial distinctions between materials and finished products. For example, in the transportation equipment industries, the automotive group includes auto parts, and corporate reports include much more. The establishment data of the production statistics are more nearly capable of the required separations, including the exclusion of construction materials. The book-value attributes of the shipments and order data raise further problems.

CHART 19

Production, Shipments, and Orders, Final Products and Materials,
Durable Goods Manufacturers, 1946–64

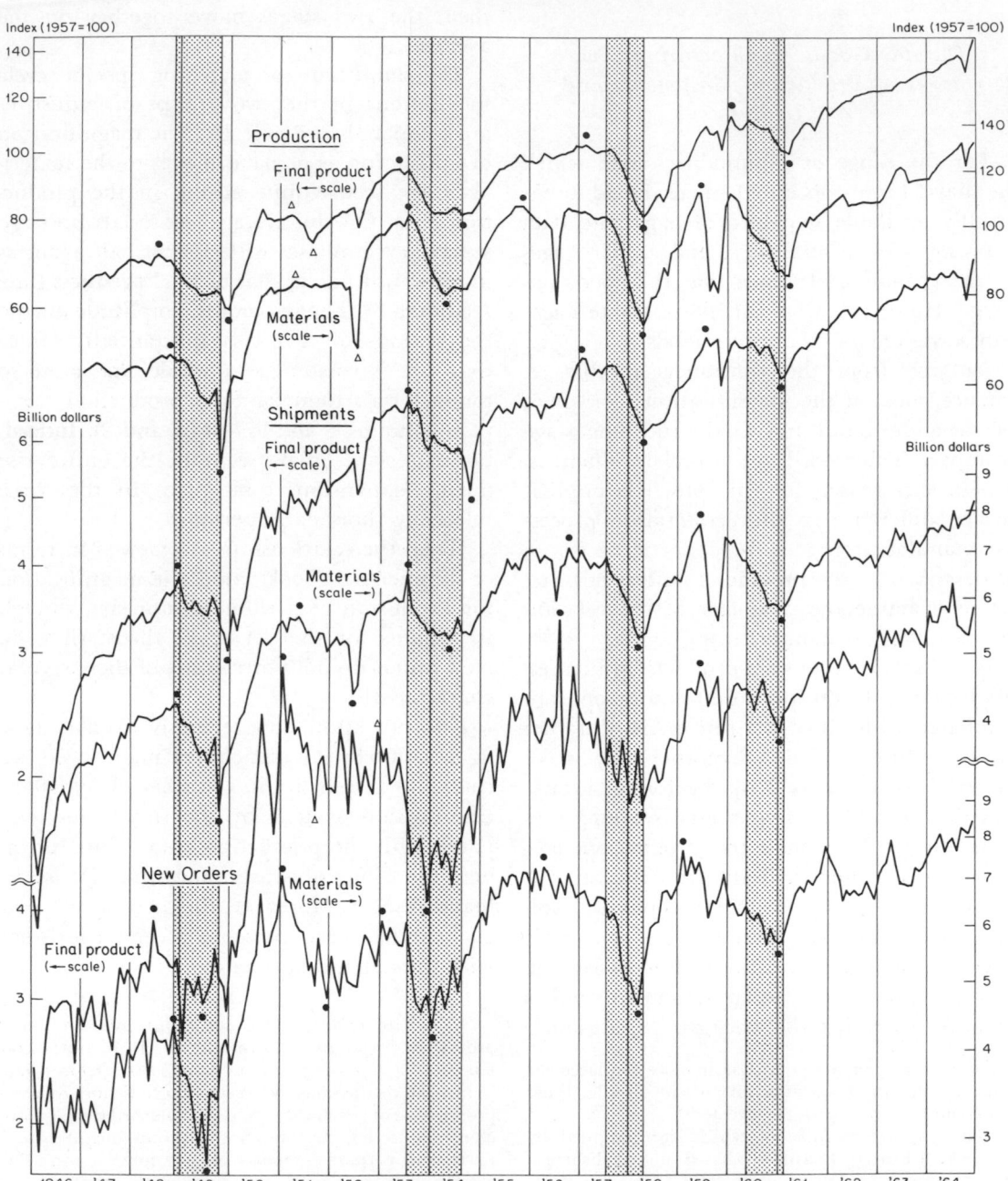

Note: Shaded areas represent business contractions. Specific cycle turns are marked by dots, additional minor turns by triangles.

TABLE 47

Timing: Production, Shipments, and Orders, Final Products and Materials, Durable Goods Manufacturers, 1946–1961

Line	Reference Series[c]	P (1/47)	T (7/47)	P 11/48	T 10/49	P (2/51)	T (6/52)	P 7/53	T 8/54	P 7/57	T 4/58	P 5/60	T 2/61
	Section A: Months Lead (−) or Lag (+) for Matched Turns[a] Chronology[b]												
	Specific Series: Production, Materials												
1	Business cycles			−1	0			0	−4	−20	0	−11	+1
2	Subcycles	⊕	⊕	−1	0	+2	+1	0	−4	−20	0	−11	+1
	Specific Series: Production, Final Product												
3	Business cycles			−4	+2			−2	0	−5	0	−4	+1
4	Subcycles	⊕	⊕	−4	+2	+1	−10	−2	0	−5	0	−4	+1
5	Production, materials	⊙	⊙	−3	+2	−1	−11	−2	+4	+15	0	+7	0
	Specific Series: Shipments, Final Product												
6	Business cycles			+1	+2			0	+2	−6	0	−10	−1
7	Subcycles	⊕	⊕	+1	+2	⊕	⊕	0	+2	−6	0	−10	−1
8	Shipments materials	⊙	⊙	0	+2	⊗	⊗	0	+5	+3	+1	+1	0
9	New orders, final product	⊙	⊙	+6	+6	⊕	⊕	+7	+10	+5	0	+1	0
10	Production, final product	⊙	⊙	+5	0	⊕	⊕	+2	+2	−1	0	−6	−2
	Specific Series: Orders, Final Product												
11	Business cycles			−5	−4			−7	−8	−11	0	−11	−1
12	Subcycles	⊕	⊕	−5	−4	−1	−9	−7	−8	−11	0	−11	−1
13	Orders, materials	⊙	⊙	−5	−1	0	−3	−1	−1	+4	+1	+4	0
	Specific Series: Shipments, Materials												
14	New orders, materials	⊙	⊙	+1	+3	+4	+6	+6	+4	+6	0	+4	0
15	Production, materials	⊙	⊙	+2	0	+1	−1	0	+1	+11	−1	0	−2

(continued)

TABLE 47 (concluded)

| | | Section B: Average Timing of Turns | | | | | | | | | Section C: Percentage of Months in Like Phase[d] | |
| | | Number Matched | | | Median[e] | | | Average Deviation[f] | | All Turns | | |
Line	Reference Series[c]	−	+	0	P	T	All	P	T	Wt'd	Timing Adjust-ment[g]	% Mos. 7/46– 12/61
	Specific Series: Production, Materials											
1	Business cycles	4	1	3	−6.0	0	−0.5	7.5	1.2	4.6	3.9	−1, 0	72
2	Subcycles	4	3	3	−4.0	+0.3	0	7.2	1.3	4.0	4.2	0	75
	Specific Series: Production, Final Product											
3	Business cycles	4	2	2	−4.0	+0.5	−1.0	0.8	0.8	2.2	0.8	−1, −2, 0	88
4	Subcycles	5	3	2	−3.3	+0.3	−1.0	1.7	2.7	2.9	2.2	−1, −2, 0	81
5	Production, materials	4	4	2	+1.3	+0.7	0	5.9	3.5	4.5	4.7	0	76
	Specific Series: Shipments, Final Product											
6	Business cycles	3	3	2	−3.0	+1.0	0	4.2	1.2	2.8	2.8	0	88
7	Subcycles	3	3	2	−3.0	+1.0	0	4.2	1.2	2.8	2.8	0	76
8	Shipments, materials	0	5	3	+0.5	+1.5	+1.0	1.0	1.5	1.2	1.2	+1	88
9	New orders, final product	0	6	2	+5.5	+3.0	+5.5	1.8	4.0	2.9	2.9	+5	83
10	Production, final product	3	3	2	+0.5	0	0	3.5	1.0	2.2	2.2	0	88
	Specific Series: Orders, Final Product											
11	Business cycles	7	0	1	−9.0	−2.5	−6.0	2.5	2.8	3.4	2.6	−5, −6, −7	81
12	Subcycles	9	0	1	−7.7	−4.3	−6.0	3.3	3.3	3.5	3.3	−5, −6, −7	78
13	Orders, materials	5	3	2	+1.0	−0.7	−0.5	3.0	1.1	2.0	2.0	0	89
	Specific Series: Shipments, Materials											
14	New orders, materials	0	8	2	+4.7	+2.3	+4.0	1.5	2.1	1.8	1.8	+4	90
15	Production, materials	3	4	3	+1.0	−0.7	0	2.6	0.9	1.9	1.7	0	90

For notes a to g see Table 44.

TABLE 48

*Average Amplitude of Specific Cycle Fluctuation, Final Products and
Materials, Durable Goods Manufacturers, 1949—1961*

	Average Phase Amplitude Cycle Relatives[a]			Per Month Amplitude Cycle Relatives			Amplitude of Thrust as Percentage of Total Expansion Amplitude
	Expansion (1)	Contraction (2)	All Phases (3)	Expansion (4)	Thrust (5)	Contraction (6)	(7)
Production							
1. Final product	29.6	12.9	20.1	.99	1.43	.87	67.0
2. Materials	38.8	21.5	28.9	1.60	2.08	1.43	86.1
Shipments							
3. Final product	41.8	13.7	25.7	1.69	1.68	.94	55.7
4. Materials	34.0	17.0	24.3	1.23	2.02	1.25	94.1
Orders							
5. Final product	51.9	20.9	34.2	2.58	2.79	.95	95.5
6. Materials	47.6	27.2	35.9	2.81	2.78	1.54	101.1
Percentage of Materials to Final Product							
7. Production (line 2 ÷ line 1)	131	167	144	162	145	164	
8. Shipments (line 4 ÷ line 3)	81	124	95	73	120	133	
9. Orders (line 6 ÷ line 5)	92	130	105	109	100	162	
Percentage of Orders to Shipments							
10. Final product (line 5 ÷ line 3)	124	153	133	153	166	101	
11. Materials (line 6 ÷ line 4)	140	160	148	228	138	123	

[a]Expressed as relatives of the average peak and trough standings for each phase. Standings are five-month averages centered at month of turn. Averages cover four contractions and three expansions starting in 1948 and ending in 1961.

Assume that manufacturers of finished products receive sales orders which have cyclical fluctuations of a stipulated sort. Their shipment will tend to lag orders, particularly at peaks, when positions are extended; they will also tend to have a narrower range of fluctuation. The reason for this pattern in the case of products distributed by retailers was outlined in the acceleration model for department stores in the previous chapter. For heavy equipment sold to final users, an important part of the work of the machinery and transportation equipment industries, a lead of sales orders must result from the long periods required to complete production; concerning the amplitude of the early thrust, one can only guess that users have selected "a good time to buy" and flashed a go-ahead signal for plans which are already virtually ready to go, and indeed may have been so for some time.

But these sales orders, when received by the manufacturer of final products, constitute forecasting instruments of considerable power. For made-to-order heavy equipment, the character of the forecast is obvious—the order is prerequisite to the start of production which may take months if not years to complete. Other ways in which orders provide forecasts of requirements were discussed at the start of Chapter 11. In any event, as a consequence of this foreknowledge, producers are in a position to place orders with suppliers in a fashion calculated to validate whatever inventory objective for materials they choose (providing suppliers will cooperate). There are a wide number of alternatives, as we have seen, depending on what changes, other than the change in expected sales, are deemed to have occurred or to be likely to occur.

For example, if physical service efficiency were the only consideration, these manufacturers would presumably purchase in a pattern which would cause materials to be available at the time they were needed for production, plus whatever change in stock was required for efficient service. If there were no reason to expect delays in deliveries of materials or changes in prices, this pattern ought to look more like that of shipments (actually something between that and production starts) than like the pattern of new sales orders.

On the other hand, if there was reason to buy ahead of the actual production needs—reason such as fear of slow deliveries, poor selections, rising prices, and so on—the pattern of materials orders could duplicate that of sales orders or have even more amplitude. A pattern of materials orders of this sort implies the presence of market expectations that

parallel sales and evidence examined in the previous chapter suggested that that parallelism may be common. Table 47, line 13, shows that orders for the two groups of industries, hypothetically sales and purchase orders of the final-products group, tend to reach peaks and troughs at much the same time. Six of the ten matched turns are within one month of one another; study of Chart 19 reinforces the picture of confluence.

In the context of backward transmission of fluctuation, this discussion makes two points. First, fluctuations in materials orders, which parallel sales orders and fluctuate more than a simple service function implies, bespeak the presence of expected or actual market-oriented materials buying which tends to parallel fluctuations in final demand. The general parallelism, and approximately equal amplitude of fluctuation, of orders for materials and for final products is explicable in these terms, in view of the far smaller amplitude of shipments for the two types of enterprises.

The second point is a corollary of the first. Once sales orders take on two characteristics —forecasting competence, and fluctuations which are wide relative to those of shipments —no further magnification of *orders* in additional backward sequences is essential to further magnification or even acceleration in *shipments or production*. This could result simply from a tendency for firms at earlier stages to match their shipments (or production) more closely to the pattern of their sales orders than is the case for firms at the more finished stages.

The evidence has suggested that the double characteristic of materials orders—market orientation and sales-forecasting competence— could very well be formed at the final marketing stage—that of retailers' purchase of merchandise or industries' purchase of heavy equipment for their own use.

How the physical flows actually do behave and what sort of acceleration actually does or does not occur is a function of the particulars, quantitatively defined, in each situation. Just what these are is an intriguing question, the investigation of which requires more trustworthy data for economic sequences than are available.[11]

The matter deserves study, for my argument implies that the pattern of acceleration is not prescribed by time-consuming sequences in flows of goods and changes in stocks, with lag building on lag and amplification on amplification. Instead, the potentially almost instantaneous transmission of orders can provide a common stem of information upon which the pattern of physical operations sprouts at each stage in whatever form is dictated by the particular economic and physical problems that characterize the stage.

THE INVENTORY-PURCHASE SEQUENCE IN BUSINESS CYCLES

I have considered an inventory cycle in terms of a sequence of causally related events resulting in changes in stock on order as well as on hand. Relative to the usual formulation, this construction changes the "system" to which inventory fluctuations belong.

On the one hand, it changes the emphasis: it throws attention toward actions that govern the size of stocks at the stage where the *inflow* into the stockpile is governed—the point where materials are purchased. This perhaps tends to underplay (but it in no sense needs to) the traditional interest in actions at the outflow stage—price changes which adjust stocks by speeding or inhibiting the outflow, sales. On the other hand, the system to which inventory fluctuation belongs is defined to include the placing of orders for materials and the factors that govern their size, rather than, simply, the receipt of merchandise. Changes in the size of materials orders affect expectations, market conditions, prices; changes in orders carry information, and soon affect shipments, production, and consequently stock on hand and also income flows. Accordingly, the inventory-purchase "system" reaches out to include more directly a wider group of events sooner than does the inventory cycle more conventionally conceived.

It will be useful to place the critical events associated with the inventory-purchase cycle in the framework of general economic fluctuation. This will serve to summarize the part of this investigation which asks how inventory-centered events participate in economic instability. I use the convention of average or typical sequences, thereby impoverishing description in the interest of comprehensibility.

Decline and Its Cessation

Recession is about half over. Series central to the inventory syndrome are shown in Table 49, where their troughs are matched with the previous business cycle reference peaks. Thus, in the "P" columns we ask how soon after business has started to decline each of the series begins to improve. Obviously the question is only relevant to the systematically

[11] Study of Chart 19 and of a work table on the basis of which Table 48 was constructed shows much variety in the phase-by-phase relationship for orders of the final-products and of the materials industries. If one had confidence in the comparability of the data, these differences and similarities would be most interesting to explore. For these very inadequate data, suffice it to note that the average deviation of phase amplitudes of new orders for materials industries is much smaller than for those of final products—an index of 10.1 in cycle relatives (the average phase amplitude was 35.9) as contrasted with an index of 17.6 for final products (the average amplitude was 34.2). For shipments, on the other hand, average deviation was virtually the same—between 8 and 9 in cycle relatives for both materials and final products. The amplitude of materials orders tends, in a rough sort of way, to be large relative to that of final products for phases when absolute amplitudes for both groups of industries are relatively small. This accords with previously reported observations based on outstandings-sales ratios and rates of change in ownership which suggested that materials markets seem more routinely sensitive to changes in the volume of activity than do final-products markets. The post-1960 behavior was a particular case in point.

TABLE 49

Timing of Troughs and Peaks of Selected Series at Business Cycle Reference Peaks and Troughs[a], 1948–1961

| | | \multicolumn{8}{c}{Months Lead (−) Or Lag (+) Of Specific Peak (Or Trough) Compared To Reference Trough (Or Peak)} | \multicolumn{3}{c}{Median Timing} |
| | | P | T | P | T | P | T | P | T | | T | |
Line	Reference Dates: Duration of Following Reference Phase:	11/48 11	10/49 45	7/53 13	8/54 35	7/57 9	4/58 25	5/60 9	2/61	P	Excl. 1961	Incl. 1961
	Change in Sales											
1.	Dept. stores	+8	+7	−1	+5	+5	+13	+6	+11[e]	+5.5	+8.3	+9.0
2.	Durables, shipments	+4	+8	+3	+5	+6	+12	+6	+2[e]	+5.0	+8.3	+6.5
3.	Durables, R: (inverted) materials stocks to shipments	+3	+10	+4	+11	+8	+12	+8	+6[e]	+6.0	+11.0	+10.5
	Change in Outstandings for Materials											
4.	Dept. stores		+8	+2	+13	+2	+11	+5	+6[e]	+3.0	+10.7	+9.5
5.	Durables, materials	+6	+16	+4	+6	+5	+9	−1	+10	+4.5	+10.3	+9.5
6.	Unfilled orders, final products	+4	+17	+3	+15	+1	+13	+7	⊕	+3.5	+15.0	
	Change in Ownership											
7.	Dept. stores	0	+8	+2	+14	+4	+13	+5	+8	+3.0	+11.7	+10.5
8.	Durables, materials	+6	+16	+4	+6	+6	+9	−1	+10	+5.0	+10.3	+9.5
	Change in Stocks											
9.	Dept. stores	+7	+12	+4	+16	+7	+23	+7	+8	+7.0	+17.0	+14.0
10.	Durables, materials	+6	+12	+11	+20	+10[r]	+12[r]	+4	+9	+8.0	+14.7	+12.0

(continued)

TABLE 49 (concluded)

		Months Lead (−) Or Lag (+) Of Specific Peak (Or Trough) Compared To Reference Trough (Or Peak)								Median Timing		
		P	T	P	T	P	T	P	T		T	
Line	Reference Dates:	11/48	10/49	7/53	8/54	7/57	4/58	5/60	2/61	P	Excl. 1961	Incl. 1961
	Duration of Following Reference Phase:	11	45	13	35	9	25	9				
	New Orders, Materials											
11.	Dept. stores	+7	+9	+6	+26	+5	+24	+7	+15[e]	+6.5	+19.7	+19.5
12.	Dept. stores, trend adjusted	+7	+9	+6	+15	+5	+14	+7	+15[e]	+6.5	+12.7	+14.5
13.	Durables	+8	+15	+6	+20	+8	+10	+8	+10[e]	+8.0	+15.0	+12.5
14.	Durables, deflated	+8	+15	+6	+10	+8	+10	+8	+10[e]	+8.0	+11.7	+10.0
	Market Conditions											
	Purchase orders											
15.	Change average term	+4	+9	+1	+10	−6	+11	−3	+10[e]	−1.0	+10.0	+10.0
16.	Average term proper	+7	+15	+9	+13	+8	+20	+10[r]	+12[e]	+8.5	+16.0	+14.0
17.	Vendor performance D. I.	+4	+11	+5	+14	+5	+18	−2	+12[e]	+4.5	+14.3	+13.0
18.	Spot prices, metals	+16[r]	+15[r]	+7	+20	+9[r]	+19	+7	+7	+8.0	+18.0	+17.0
19.	Corp. profits, durables	+6	+13	+4	+15	+10[r]	+13	+9[r]	+12[e]	+7.5	+13.7	+13.0
	Outstandings-Sales Ratio											
20.	Dept. stores	+7	+10	+10	+16	+10[r]	+27[rb]	+6	+15[e]	+8.5	+17.7[b]	+15.5[b]
21.	Durables	+10	+21	+12	+23	+17[r]	+19	⊕	⊕	+13.0	+21.0	
	Final Products, Shipments or New Orders											
22.	Dept. store sales	+8	+15	+6	+36[r]	+7	+24	+8	⊕	+7.5	+25.0	
23.	Orders, dur.	+7	+15	+5	+24	+9[r]	+14	+8	⊕	+7.5	+17.7	
24.	Shipments, dur.	+13[r]	+45[r]	+15[r]	+29[r]	+9[r]	+15[r]	+8	⊕	+11.0	+29.7	

Notes to Table 49

Timing comparisons under relaxed rules: "r" signifies a like reference turn has preceded the unlike reference turn for which the specific comparison is given. In other words, on a direct basis, the turn lagged rather than led the reference scheme. "e" refers to an extra turn marked at the cessation of the first rise following the business cycle trough of February 1961 when a specific cycle peak has not been located at that point. The points are included whenever a clear leveling or drop in activity seems evident; many if not most of the points would not qualify as candidates

for specific major or even minor turns. In any event, the change in the data beginning in 1962 inhibits accurate comparison with the rest of the series.

[a] A specific trough is matched with the previous business cycle reference peak, and similarly a specific peak is matched with the previous trough.

[b] The ratio for department stores virtually ceased to rise twelve months after the 4/58 trough. Replacing the +27 by the +12 figure, the trough averages for turns excluding 2/61 are 13.5; including it, they are 12.7.

"leading" series, and only these are covered in the table.[12]

Materials buying has been curtailed in response to falling demand by customers of both department stores and durable goods manufacturers (lines 11 and 13). Materials held on order have also been reduced for some time; indeed, curtailments had started before recession set in and the rate at which they are falling has already slowed up a bit (lines 4 and 5). Stocks on hand are declining and at an accelerating rate (lines 9 and 10). But sales are typically falling as fast or faster, so that the number of months' sales that stocks represent has usually not started to decline (see Charts 3 and 5). Sensitive prices are plummeting. Deliveries are moving toward a hand-to-mouth basis.

In spite of all these dreary occurrences, several things soon begin to modify the situation, even at this early stage when contraction is on the average about a half a year old. For one thing, the deterioration in aggregate sales to consumers or in shipments of durable goods manufacturers to industrial customers has begun to slow up (lines 1 and 2). And we have just seen that this influence occurs at close to the same time in retail sales and in durable goods shipments (Table 44, lines 13 and 14).

A deceleration in aggregate decline is likely

to imply two sorts of occurrences: the amount of decline for enterprises whose sales are falling becomes smaller; more enterprises begin to experience a rise. In either case the downward spiral of buying is subjected to modifying influences.

In the first case, the processes at work were discussed at length in the previous chapter. In a word, for department stores, the firm and precise stock objective, and the tendency for current sales to provide the basis of the sales forecast, tend, as retardation sets in, to cause buying frequently to underestimate demand and therefore to require upward revision. For manufacturers, the leavening influence may work through the tendency for "excess stocks" to decline and consequently to soften the efforts to reduce stocks further.

In the second case, the response to deceleration is in a sense exaggerated by the fact of an actual increase in sales. Increases in sales must be frequent, since sales proper is close to its trough. For department stores, lows occurred between six and eight months after the previous business cycle peak (line 22). For durables, at least new orders for final products, the output of machinery and transportation equipment industries reached lows between five and nine months after the previous peak (line 23). Though the sales orders of these goods with long production periods have an ambiguous relation to materials procurement, it is nevertheless interest-

---

[12] For the method of dealing with exceptions, see Table 49, note a, paragraph on timing comparisons under relaxed rules.

ing to see that they reach their lows close to the same time as consumer buying at department stores.

Changes tending to stimulate buying also take place in materials markets. The number of suppliers offering swifter deliveries has been increasing for some time, so that now fast delivery is the rule. This is evidenced by the fact that the average term of purchase orders is approaching its lowest level (line 16). Prices of materials are likewise in the neighborhood of cyclical lows (line 18). These slack market conditions are not a reason for buying in anticipation of needs, but they certainly do not inhibit the response of purchasing agents to current operating requirements when the need occurs.

Furthermore, reduction of materials stocks on hand and on order no longer provides an easy substitute for new buying. The rate of decline in total ownership has been declining for a month or so (lines 7 and 8), and even disinvestment in stocks on hand has started to slow up (lines 9 and 10).

The basic picture, then, reveals mixed experience; but a gradual increase in the experience of rises relative to falls in materials buying. The rises can result from an increase in purchasing by consumers or orders for heavy machinery; or they can result from correction of underprocurement, or from particular instances of optimistic expectations, or fears of shortages. The falls can result from declines in movement of goods to consumers, with the wish to curtail extended market positions in goods on order and on hand. The diffusion of falls in buying is waning, and of rises waxing, until the rises are more numerous than the falls. In consequence, materials buying proper starts to rise.

For both department stores and durable goods manufacturers the trough in materials buying (lines 11 and 13) occurred on all occasions no less than five months and no more than eight months after the previous peak in business.

At this point, then, in the late phases of contraction, prices are low, sellers are hungry, buyers are cautious, spirits are depressed, but orders start to rise.

Expansion's First Thrust

Orders rise very rapidly for a number of months. The phenomenon of the upward thrust has appeared at every level of this study. It characterizes consumer buying in department stores, and in a far more extreme form it characterizes the buying of merchandise by department stores. It characterizes orders for machinery and transportation equipment. It characterizes about equally the orders for materials placed by these enterprises; and this is the more notable since the buyer of heavy equipment *must* anticipate his receipt of the equipment by orders placed many months or even semesters in advance, whereas no such necessity prompts the equally strong rise in materials orders.

Materials outstanding rise not only absolutely but in terms of the number of months' sales covered, those of department stores somewhat sooner than those of durable goods manufacturers (lines 20 and 21). Stocks also rise before long. And the similarity in the cycles in outstandings and stocks supports the logic of a causal connection between extensions in stock on order and on hand.[13] Before long (for both sorts of enterprises the period averages about half a year after prosperity begins) materials stocks also begin to rise faster than shipments.

Conditions in materials markets encourage the eagerness of buyers: spot-market prices rise; vendor performance begins to deteriorate; the average term of purchase orders increases. Thus various parts of the inventory-purchase complex stimulate and support one another in a cumulative round of cause and effect. As buying spurts upward, events and expectations stimulate behavior that affects markets and output, which in turn stimulates

[13] See Chapter 5, summary paragraph 13, and Chapter 6, summary paragraph 5, and supporting discussions.

further expectations and related behavior. Cumulation, in other words, takes place at the level of information, expectations, and associated action in the fashion discussed in the previous chapter.

It takes place also at the level of actions which affect output, which in turn affects income and consequent spending along the lines suggested in income-multiplier notions of the conventional sort.

In view of the potential interplay of these several autocumulating elements, the mystery as I see it is why the upward surge is so strong, lasts for the particular period that it does (a bit over a year on the average), and ceases so abruptly while prosperity is still in sway.

The duration of the periods of thrust was defined in Chapter 4 on several bases. For department stores and for the durable goods industries, outstanding purchase orders provided the criterion: thrusts covered, as that chapter stated, "the months when, in the course of its first specific cycle rise in reference expansion, the rate of rise in outstandings has reached its maximum and declined to the half-way mark between its maximum and zero." For a generalized set of dates, the peaks of the minor cycles of the subcycle chronology were used and supplemented by two additional points in 1955 and 1959, when declines or retardations in numerous series had previously been observed. These durations are reviewed in columns 2–4 of Table 50. Omitting the two extreme entries, they range from between 16 and 11 months, they average 14 months, which is two-fifths of the average period of the three expansions—35 months.

As the thrust subsides, many manifestations associated with the inventory-purchase complex tend to snub the economic expansions. Table 50 assembles some of these facts in convenient form. Outstanding orders and total ownership by definition no longer increase as rapidly as before, and thereby the speed with which orders outrun shipments slows down. The slower pace of extension appears in fewer reports of lengthening order terms. It is soon followed by, or perhaps evidenced in, more reports of improvement in vendor performance (column 5). Other developments include shortening average order terms (column 6), falling corporate profits in durable goods industries (column 7), and, a bit later, falling spot-market prices of metal (column 8).

The slower rate of extension is of sufficient quantitative importance to cause the aggregate level of orders for materials to begin to slow down very markedly about the same time as the thrusts terminate. Physical volume of new orders for durable goods materials actually declined at this early point in the long postwar expansions (column 11). And the declines are also apparent in trend-corrected orders for department stores (column 12).

A decline in new orders need not, of course, have a counterpart in decline in output. For one thing, inventory investment in stocks of all sorts may still be accelerating, though investment in department store stocks and durable materials has about reached its peak (columns 9 and 10). Nevertheless, as Charts 18 and 19 indicate, declines or flat areas did typically appear in the production or shipments of durable goods materials. Shipments to department stores by their suppliers, like the orders placed, fell sharply in 1951 and flattened at the end of 1955. Apparently the hesitation reflected in the flows of information embodied in new orders had counterparts in the flows of goods and income.

Continued Expansion

However, other forces capable of lifting activity were sufficiently rugged to outlast the impact of these depressant influences. Many illustrations spring to mind in connection with aspects of the economy other than those connected with the inventory data examined in this book. A prime example is the ground swell of consumer buying of foods and services

TABLE 50

Lag Relative to Reference Cycle Troughs of Termination of Period of Thrust and of Peaks in Specific Cycles in Selected Data, 1947 to 1962, Months

Business Cycle Reference Trough	Duration of:				Lag Relative to Reference Trough:			
	Refer-ence Expan-sion	Period of Thrust[a]			D.I. Vendor Per-formance	Av. Term of Pur-chase Order	Profits Dur. Mfrs.	Spot Mkt. Metals Prices
		Chron-ology	Dur. Mfrs.	Dept. Stores				
	(1)	(2)	(3)	(4)	(5)	(6)	(7)	(8)
October 1949	45	16	18	16	11	15	13	15
August 1954	35	16	10	16	14	13	15	20
April 1958	25	11	11	15	18	20	13	19
February 1961[c]			12	13	12	12	12	7
Average for three phases		14	13	16	14	16	13	18

Business Cycle Reference Trough	Lag Relative to Reference Trough:									
	Inventory Investment		Materials Orders				Final Prdt. Orders[b]		Final Prdt. Shipments[b]	
	Dur. Mate-rials	Dept. Stores	Dur. Mfrs. De-flated	Dept. Stores Trend Adj.	Dur. Mfrs.	Dept. Stores	Dur. Mfrs.	Dept. Store Sales	Dur. Mfrs.	Dept. Store Sales
	(9)	(10)	(11)	(12)	(13)	(14)	(15)	(16)	(17)	(18)
October 1949	12	12	15	9	15	9	15	15	45	15
August 1954	20	16	10	15	20	26	24	36	29	36
April 1958	12	23	10	14	10	24	14	24	15	24
February 1961[c]	9	8	10	15	10	15	⊕	⊕	⊕	⊕
Average for three phases	15	17	12	13	15	20	18	25	30	25

[a]Figures in columns 2 to 4 are from Tables 4, 5, and 14 respectively.

[b]For department stores, both orders and shipments of final products are their "sales". For durable goods manufacturers they are the new sales orders and shipments of the machinery and transportation equipment industries.

[c]All figures in this line are highly tentative, as previously explained; slighter movements than would be selected as specific troughs have frequently been identified here.

and of the structures and services provided by governments. But even in the area of department store sales and durable goods manufacturing, the movement of final products continued to rise. Sales of department stores continued uninterruptedly upward for an average of twenty-five months during the three expansions. Moreover, it showed no significant hesitation in early 1962 (see Chart 8). Shipments of final products in the heavy industries continued to rise throughout most of the long expansion; the average period was thirty months. A similar remark applies, with one qualification, to the volume of production (see Chart 19).[14] Here, too, it is interesting that there was little suggestion of hesitation in early 1962. These hardy trends in both 1952 and 1956 reactivated the procurement sectors of the economy and produced a second round of boosts in buying and investment in materials on hand and on order.

However, the latter episodes were somewhat different from the first in that the market-oriented elements seemed weaker relative to the need for simply replenishing the supply of materials on hand and materials flowing into new production or sales. Charts 6, 7, 10, and 11 speak to these points and are worth a moment's review. It is particularly interesting, in view of the traditional emphasis

on declines in profits as harbingers of cyclical reversal, that in the durable goods industries, in each of the three complete business cycle expansions pictured, profits did not regain the highs reached at the end of the first year of expansion. It is interesting also that the recent experience constitutes a sharp exception (see Chart 17).

But such peaks as were attained as a result of a second lift in the materials-inventory syndrome occurred well before the peaks in business. Summary figures were given in Table 45. In this period of half a year or a year prior to the time when declines in general business started, and on into the early months of contraction, a declining rate of investment in stocks both on hand and on order and other market-oriented phenomena contributed to eventual pessimistic expectations and reduction in output.

SUMMARY

Events associated with materials purchasing tend to reverse their impact on the economy before general business reaches peaks or troughs. Rates of change in materials stocks proper lead by short intervals; those in stock outstanding by longer ones.

The pattern of output that is implied causes fluctuation at earlier stages to be stronger than at the later stages, those close to the consumer. The *amplification* is greater than the efficient servicing of sales would seem to require. However, there is no consistent tendency for the *timing* of turns in production to differ at successive stages of manufacture.

The information conveyed by new orders undergoes a major amplification between the buying of consumers and of retailers—the orders received by manufacturers of finished

goods that supply retailers. We cannot picture what further amplification may result as these producers place orders for materials. However, for all durables the amplification in new orders from one manufacturing stage to the next does not stand out: the orders for final products (machinery and transportation equipment) do not seem to have clearly less cyclical amplitude than do those for durable goods materials (unlike the amplitude of production for the two stages).

The major acceleration in new orders—the earlier turns—also takes place between consumers' and retailers' buying. But this anticipatory capability of distributors' orders, well maintained at earlier stages, makes it possible for production starts to increase or decrease at much the same time throughout a sequence of vertical stages in the preparation of goods. Finished production may lag when the production process is lengthy.

The force exerted by the inventory-pur-

[14] Production hesitated sufficiently after the Korean War boom to have a minor turn marked at that time (see Chart 19). However, new highs were being reached by early 1952.

chase complex differs at various stages of business cycles:

1. Prior to business cycle peaks and during the early months of contraction, its influence is depressant.

2. Midway in the brief business contractions that have characterized the postwar economy, its leavening influence sets in. This influence gains force during late contraction and still more so during the first year of expansion. Then it is sharply subdued.

3. During the rest of expansion its course varies. It tends to be depressant while the readjustments following the cessation of the buying surge take place. But in 1951–52, 1955–56, and again in 1962 the economic situation was strong enough to overcome these elements of hesitation and reactivate further investment in merchandise or materials. However, the market expansion which characterized the second round of episodes appears to have been more moderate than the first, though the 1964–66 situation has turned out to be an exception in which the usual sequence has been reversed.

This pattern reflects in part the complex ways in which the conditions in the economy at large affect stocks on hand and on order and how they change. For one thing, not only the level but, very significantly, the rates of change in final demand influence the appropriate service level of stocks. And note that rates of change in demand tend to be sharp at the two times when the influence of the inventory syndrome is strong—paragraphs 1 and 2 above. For another thing, these changes in demand, given the perceptions, objectives, and techniques available to businessmen, produce problems in enforcing objectives which imply further fluctuations in stocks on hand and on order.

Finally, changes take place in the relative costs of carrying stocks on hand, and also on order, compared with other ways of serving the business ends which stocks serve. These changes, particularly those associated with market conditions and available funds, imply further shifts in ownership position. The specifics of these several impacts on stock and their resultant patterns of fluctuation were discussed in Chapter 10.

Let me underscore again the importance of rates of change in this entire group of events. It means that the influences originate in what Arthur F. Burns has called the "unseen cycle" of diffusion, in contrast to the "seen cycle" in aggregates proper. Diffusion involves the dispersion of increases and decreases in individual business units. It involves also dispersion of retardations and accelerations in these units.

The participation of stocks in business fluctuation involves also an opposite stream of causality—one that concerns the impact of the inventory-purchase syndrome on the economy. The impact takes place at two levels.

The first level involves flows of information which influence the plans producers make, the expectations with which they live, the tone and substance of their negotiations with customers and suppliers. What happens at this level sends off further messages. The process can produce what one might call an expectations multiplier. Occurrences at the level of flows of information and expectation are a second type of "unseen cycle" which, like the cycle of diffusion, is counterpoint and often causally antecedent to the themes of the "seen" cycle.

The second level involves flows of output and associated income—that is, the actions upon which aggregative economics has focused. Positive inventory investment generates income which is not absorbed in the purchase of the goods produced. This additional income, spent and respent, stimulates productive activity and further income, in line with multiplier influences of the traditional sort.

The two levels—that of information or expectation and of production or income flows—often supplement one another. Thus information leading to the expectation that markets may tighten can motivate an increase in stock. Often they mute one another. Thus a rise in stock that occurs because sales were lower than expected conveys pessimistic expectations which in turn depress subsequent buying and production.[15] All too obviously, then, the two worlds—the world of information, of expectations, and the world of income and output, of action—interact.

[15] This notion has been expressed in the context of unintended and intended inventory investment. See, for example, Ragnar Nurkse, "The Cyclical Pattern of Inventory Investment," *Quarterly Journal of Economics,* August, 1952.

13. Toward a Theory of Inventory Behavior

In urgent need of being written, bit by bit, is the story of how flows of information take place, whereof they consist, how they influence expectations, how they are interpreted in actions, and how actions affecting income and product are translated back into information and expectations is a story.

IMPLICATIONS CONCERNING ECONOMIC CHANGE

It is, of course, a difficult story even to embark upon. For this there are several reasons. One concerns the character of the two worlds and of their relationship to one another. In a sense the two are one: information and action are, like mind and matter, part of the same corpus. Few actions do not rest on information and are not in turn converted to a "signal." But in another sense they are part of a continuum, one end of which is scraps of information and the other end of which is a concrete act. The continuum can stretch, for example, from an isolated and possibly irrelevant observation of a sentence in a trade journal to a response in terms of newly rolled steel sheet spinning onto its giant spools, or from a notation in a secret-service file that a cargo ship was sighted here, not there, to young men creeping over a beachhead. Dead center between the two ends of the continuum lies the command.

The Role of Orders

The command is identical to action if it is always precisely converted into action. Thus if new orders, which are in essence pieces of information, are never canceled and always delivered precisely as written, they are for all intents and purposes simply predated acts—shipments. In actuality, orders are sometimes canceled, postponed, or delivered late. Nevertheless the correspondence is close enough so that new orders cannot provide an explanation of shipments. They are too nearly simply an earlier version of the same thing. This is the difficulty to which I pointed in Chapter 1 when alluding to the serious deficiencies in current explanations of stocks in which orders, or changes in unfilled orders, play such a powerful causative part. In this book, orders have been cast partly in the role of effect rather than cause, since one definition of stocks includes stock on order. In a sense, then, a borderline member of the world of information, outstanding purchase orders, has been joined to the physical world of action and things.

The construct belongs fully to neither world. To picture output and income flows, ownership must be cracked apart and stock on hand alone isolated. To study the flow of information at a causal level, it is necessary to go behind the order to see what caused it. But in spite of these deficiencies, the half-breed has talents of its own—a power to display and convey information: On the one hand, ownership has a different speed of change and process of change than has stock on hand. On the other hand, it reflects information and expectations very sensitively and in a particular sort of way. Both characteristics demand recognition in the theory of inventory cycles.

As to the speed and process of change, two different manifestations are important. For one thing, the fact that orders swiftly embody intentions means that, particularly for department stores, intentions, and therefore the theory behind action, are readily visible in ownership though obscure in stocks. This is a convenience rather than a new ingredient.

But the order, and its inherent fluidity, condition the characteristics of vertical linkages in the economy. If only shipments or stocks are examined, the transmission of fluctuation associated with sales-linked stock objectives ought, it would seem, to move backward through the economy with sequential anticipatory leads and increasing amplitudes of fluctuation. But if we concentrate on flows of information instead, notably orders, the retailers' buying and producers' buying of raw materials can be linked with the speed of light, or at worst the time required for three telephone calls. The previous chapter expanded briefly on this point. It explains, I believe, a phenomenon that has troubled students for many years—the fact that though the logic of the acceleration principle calls for progressive acceleration (in timing as well as volume) as demand moves stepwise to earlier stages, empirical evidence fails to show it.[1]

The second attribute of ownership or outstanding materials orders, that of reflecting information and experience very sensitively, involves not so much the particular stock construct as it does a way of viewing the entire problem of procurement. It elevates the world of information to a place in the analysis

where it cannot for one moment be forgotten.

At the microeconomic level, emphasis on information means that, on the one hand, the notion of process is analyzed in terms of the information that the businessman uses and the expectations that he formulates. In the case of the procurement process, this emphasizes the part that expectations about market conditions can play in the timing of buying. It emphasizes possible changes in opportunity costs, including qualitative changes in customers' requirements. It emphasizes and particularizes the informational role of new sales orders.

But at a macroeconomic level, too, the emphasis on information and expectations has interesting implications which I want to develop. One reason for trying to think through some of these implications is a negative one: the speed with which information in general, and orders in particular, travel undercuts the basic assumption of "period analysis" as a complete explanation of inventory cycles. "The only indispensable assumption in the theory of the inventory cycle is that businessmen do not immediately adapt their production plan to a change in sales."[2] But insofar as orders constitute the adjustment, it can be virtually immediate. Moreover, insofar as expectations about market conditions are the reason for the adjustment, it is not unlikely that many people would want to adjust in the same way at very nearly the same time. If so, the inventory cycle could undergo a series of explosions or, if there were ceilings to response, a sawtooth rattle. There must be some way to explain the fact that time series do not show either peculiarity.

An Ecological Process

Accordingly, it may be useful to reflect on the patterns of interaction between information and action and what these interactions

---

[1] In lecture notes written thirty or forty years ago, Wesley C. Mitchell lingered over this problem. He explained it very tentatively in terms of inventory objectives conceived as fairly broad bands rather than as precise ratios. Many subsequent students have ignored the problem.

[2] Lloyd Metzler, "Factors Governing the Length of Inventory Cycles," *Review of Economics and Statistics,* January 1947, p. 11.

imply about the course of economic change. Biology has a word for it: "Ecology" concerns ". . . the relations between living organisms and their environment." [3] The focus seems directly applicable to economics when living organisms are restricted to man, and environment to the portion (largely though not exclusively economic) which influences economic behavior.

The way has been prepared for studies of the ecology of economic processes by the work of Herbert Simon. He has developed the notion that though man is "intendedly rational" in the sense attributed to Economic Man, the best that can actually be achieved is "satisfying," not "maximizing" or even "optimizing," behavior. Divergence from optimization is caused in part by shortcomings of available information and man's capacity to manipulate it. This implies that satisfying is at best slovenly optimizing fraught with uncertainty. But two characteristics are more fundamental in their implications: (1) Perception is necessarily selective; we appreciate, perceive, and even see not a total situation but the part of it for which we are in some sense ready. (2) That which is deemed "satisfactory," and which serves consequently as a proximate goal, changes as events prove the goal accessible or inaccessible.[4] If these two simple notions are taken seriously, and they are founded on widely held psychological ideas, the course of aggregate economic change will typically follow a different course from that implied by "optimizing" behavior.

The point of view demands an analysis that attends to the way in which a man sees, appreciates and thinks (on the basis of the information accessible to him) and the way a man acts (given his appreciations, expectations, customs, and what he wishes to achieve). Moving to an aggregative level, the analysis must attend to how the thinking and the acting of many men influence that of one another. Finally, at the aggregate level, the cross-influence must be encompassed: the influence of thinking on acting and of acting on thought, that is, on information and expectations, and particularly the assurance with which expectations are entertained. The simplest way to spell out these ideas is in terms of a model in which information and expectations, along with actual economic conditions, play their appropriate parts.

Note what these objectives and conceptions imply about the essential character of an aggregative model: it must be constructed out of pieces that display the behavior of individuals creating and responding to a situation which involves the behavior of other individuals in an economic environment. Man is a social animal; he is affected in his thinking, feeling, and acting by his perceptions of the thinking, feeling, and acting of other men. If an acting-reacting sequence gets under way, there is no reason at all to assume that individuals will react to the situation and to one another in a fashion that can be described in terms of linear aggregate behavior. Indeed, there is every reason to expect some sort of geometry of interaction, and it may "explode" or approach ceilings. However, there is no possible way to prejudge the particular aggregate function that will be found to apply, even if it were mathematically feasible to use it. The point is simply that the *coefficients* of response and feedback can themselves change as time goes on. How they will change can only be evaluated by constructing the social process in microanalytic terms. Happily, this is a job that computers are very able and willing to take on.

Not only the logic of information systems but also the empirical studies of previous chapters seem to present puzzles that invite a better explanation than the aggregative ap-

[3] *Webster's New World Dictonary of the American Language,* College Edition, 1959.
[4] Most of Herbert Simon's voluminous writings deal with these ideas at some level. But if a single reference is desired, I recommend Chapter 14 in *Models of Man, Social and Rational,* New York, 1957, "A Behavioral Model of Rational Choice." The article was reprinted from *Quarterly Journal of Economics,* February 1955.

proach readily affords. Chief among these is the phenomenon of thrust. Why does ownership of materials, for department store retailers as well as for durable goods manufacturers, appear, at an aggregate level, to build up abruptly as contraction ends and to exhibit the curious pattern of a uniform rate of change which abruptly ceases though other things continue to climb? A second minor puzzle is the character of the timing association between changes in sensitive prices and stocks or ownership; though a relationship seems present, ownership moves too late to be motivated primarily by anticipation of the rate of change in prices.

These empirical puzzles are joined by a theoretical one: The importance of expectations in governing the timing of buying and the speed with which information can be conveyed and responded to in terms of orders seem capable of causing abrupt spurts in buying followed by an equally abrupt plummet to a hand-to-mouth position. But the time series show gradual build ups and declines.

Why? The models outlined in Chapter 11 left this question unanswered.

Clearly an explanation must focus on those parts of the inventory-purchase complex most sensitive to changing expectations. Since we need to supply a missing piece of the compound process of inventory fluctuation, it will be useful to use the device of a model.

It concerns the influence of market prospects. But it will be useful to focus on only one aspect of all the factors that influence positive or negative buying associated with actual or expected changes in market condition—delivery conditions, assortments, quality, materials prices. Only the last, materials prices (other things the same), will be examined. This is not by any means the most influential of the group; delivery conditions are doubtless the most important single factor. But expectations about prices have some expositional advantages. As a matter of fact, some of the other elements slip in too, in spite of stern efforts to exclude them.

AN ECOLOGICAL MODEL OF PRICE-TIMED BUYING

Price-timed buying can be a positive or a negative quantity. It is the increment or decrement to materials orders consequent to the fact that materials prices are, or have recently been, expected to change. It concerns primarily when, in view of expected change in prices, materials will be purchased which are in any event expected to be required. If we assume as a first approximation that the flow of goods into production (or, for retailers, goods shipped to consumers) is not affected by price-timed buying, then cumulated price-timed buying is price-timed ownership. Viewed the other way round, price-timed buying effectuates desired *changes* in price-timed ownership.

From the point of view of a purchaser, the more price-timed ownership that can be kept on order (rather than on hand), the better,

assuming that the price is fixed at the time orders are placed and that there is no doubt whether goods will be delivered on schedule.[5] Materials on hand involve financing, insurance, and storage costs of which materials on order are free. However, uncertainty about delivery schedules may make it desirable to take delivery on some anticipatory purchases. In any event, delivery schedules seldom give perfect expression to the ideal separation of buying and shipments. For both reasons,

[5] Prices are not always fixed at the time the order is written. Steel producers have typically set prices at the time of shipment. (A break in the ranks by Wheeling Steel was reported in *The New York Times* of November 4, 1965.) Some products of the fats and oils industry have been priced in a similar way. These stipulations on the part of the seller force the buyer to, in effect, pay the full costs (storage, insurance, full risk, financing) for any price-timed buying he may wish to undertake.

stocks on hand will usually reflect some price-timed buying, often of an earlier date. Should the larger (or smaller) stocks no longer be desired, a compensating adjustment of new buying can adjust total price-timed ownership approximately to the level appropriate to the present situation. It is reasonable, therefore, to assume that the impact of price-timed buying is represented by changes in *ownership* without specifying which part of ownership—the part on hand or on order—is involved.

The model is built from three sorts of components: (1) structural characteristics of the industry and its member firms, (2) behavioral characteristics that define how actions resulting in price-timed buying are generated and governed, (3) market responses in terms of prices, delivery periods, and levels of plant and resource utilization. The only lags or leads that are admitted are those which seem to represent the time actually required for specified processes to take place.

Structural Assumptions

Two sorts of differences are resident in the structure of a firm and of an industry with respect to the potential advantage of price-timed buying. First, within any firm, potential advantage from further buying is a function of the level to which price-timed ownership has previously been extended. Second, the various firms in an industry differ with respect to their interest in—that is, in their proclivity to gain from—price-timed buying.

POTENTIAL COSTS AND BENEFITS OF PRICE-TIMED BUYING

That differences of both sorts are embedded in the normal structure of business situations can be seen by a moment's attention to the potential costs and benefits associated with price-timed buying. The benefit of price-timed buying is paying less for materials; the costs are those of carrying additional goods. It is advantageous to undertake positive price-timed buying so long as the expected increase in prices per unit, discounted for uncertainty, during a specified period of time is greater than the additions to carrying costs over the same period, other things the same. The discussion early in Chapter 10 spelled out the arithmetic of this statement. It implies that the *level* of price-timed ownership is a function of the expected *rate of change* in prices, discounted for uncertainty, other things the same.

In Chapter 10 this discussion is part of an analysis of other factors that bear on market-oriented buying and they imply that other things are not likely to remain the same. Indeed, in uncertain situations many changes tend to support one another. Thus an expected increase in replenishment period makes it advantageous to do price-timed buying on the basis of an expectation of a given price change which is less sure than would otherwise be required to justify it. The same remark applies to a change in back orders; if finished goods are sold at a price that is based on *present* costs of materials, the sale can be "covered" by materials purchases without many of the risks that would normally attend price-timed buying.[6] These thoughts re-emphasize the artificiality of a model that focuses on only one part of a process which *necessarily* moves as a whole. Since this thought is a constant irritant, let me then enter this blanket demurrer and cease bothering the reader by something that ceaselessly bothers me. Actually, as I indicate later, the model could be changed without much difficulty to cover the entire phenomenon of market-oriented purchasing. However, it can best be constructed in the first instance with the focus on price alone.

Optimum ownership associated with expec-

---

[6] It may be alleged that the normal procedure should be to cover, and that the notion of price-timed buying ought to apply to the failure to cover. Perhaps. But the critical point is that if prices were confidently expected to decline (and there was no problem about getting the materials later), a purchasing agent would *not* cover.

tations of change in prices is the point at which the following marginal equality is attained:

$$\text{Price-timed ownership in terms of months of expected sales} = \frac{\text{Per cent price change per month per unit}}{\text{Per cent marginal carrying costs per month per unit}}$$

In actuality, the price change in the formula is of necessity the expected change and it is, in effect, discounted for uncertainty. Carrying costs which have previously been discussed include storage, insurance, financing, physical depreciation, and obsolescence. The formula states that if, for example, the price of some material was *confidently* expected to rise 3 per cent per month, and carrying costs were confidently estimated at 18 per cent of selling price a year or 1½ per cent per month, it would be worthwhile to extend ownership by a two months' supply relative to the ownership appropriate to stationary buying prices.

As long as the expected rate of rise in prices (adjusted for uncertainty) remains the same, no further price-timed ownership (and consequently no price-timed buying) is warranted. If the expected rate declines price-timed buying turns negative as ownership declines. If the rise in prices is expected to accelerate further, the level of price-timed ownership would presumably increase. However, this statement is qualified by the first assumption, below.

Of course expectations about prices, or anything else, are virtually never sure. Accordingly, the right-hand side of the equation is reduced by an uncertainty discount. This means that price-timed ownership is always less than would be appropriate to sure expectations. An increase in assurance concerning an expected rate of rise in prices would, then, operate in about the same way as an increase in the expected rate of rise, as described in the previous paragraph. Conversely, increasing assurance about falls is equivalent to a faster drop, other things the same.

ASSUMPTION: INCREASING COST OF OWNERSHIP

As the number of weeks covered by advance purchases increases, the carrying costs of stock increase, at first gradually and eventually abruptly. I state this in the form of an assumption, though there is some empirical evidence to support it.[7]

The possibility of physical depreciation may sometimes increase with increasing ownership, but the major reason for the escalation is the risk of obsolescence. The longer ahead that requirements must be forecast, the more time there is for anticipated events to prove the forecast wrong. This is especially so in a seasonal business when an advance position crosses the months of a seasonal peak. For one thing, at the seasonal peak, advance positions cover sales for a big month rather than for a normal one. For another thing, many aspects of demand may be relatively stable within a season and changeable between seasons. The seasonal peaks therefore will often mark the point of rapidly increasing risk, which constitutes a virtual ceiling to advance commitments.

A second escalation of risk involves a guess about price itself. The longer the advance commitment, the longer prices must continue to behave at least in the anticipated fashion if the purchase is to be justified. Though errors are subject to correction by secondary negative or positive buying, it may not be feasible for the correction to be complete.

ASSUMPTION: HILL-SHAPED DISTRIBUTION OF PROCLIVITY TO GAIN

The potential advantage in shifting ownership position in line with expectations about materials prices will differ for various materials that an enterprise purchases and for the same materials in different enterprises. I would like to refer to the degree of potential advantage as the "proclivity to gain from

---

[7] See Franco Modigliani and F. E. Hohn, "Production Planning over Time and the Nature of the Expectation and Planning Horizon," *Econometrica*, January 1955, pp. 46–66.

price-timed buying." As mentioned at the close of Chapter 2, differences in sensitivity to any factor that influences stocks is a logical necessity if the advantage to be derived from stocks is a function of many costs and benefits of specific kinds. Though businesses share broad characteristics, they do not share precise cost structures in the sense of identical relative importance of various sorts of costs and benefits. These things depend on the particulars of management talents, customers' needs and expectations, financial resources, plant and production setup, and so on. However, it will be useful to enlarge on the specifics of these implications of the earlier analysis. What then determines the proclivity to gain from price-timed buying?

Proclivity will be affected by the potential gross gain from a correct guess about prices, the potential cost of carrying stocks, and the interest of management in the guessing game itself. In other words, it will be affected by any influence on the numerator or denominator of the equation of a few pages back, and by, in effect, the subjective utility of the calculation. Without attempting to be comprehensive, some of the more important characteristics falling in each of the three categories follow.

A high proclivity is associated with the size of the impact on profits of likely changes in prices. This depends on several business characteristics, other things the same.

1. *Volatile buying prices.* If prices change very little, a correct forecast can result at best in only small advantage.
2. *Low value-added relative to the cost of materials.* The impact on profits of guessing right about a given change in buying prices is greater when materials prices represent a large portion, and value-added a correspondingly small portion, of the value of the product.
3. *Cost of information.* If few rather than many materials are used, it becomes more worthwhile to spend time studying the probable course of prices. Other factors

that influence the relative cost of information are also relevant.

4. *A high turnover of working capital.* Profitability is a function of the relation of earnings to capital and is therefore reflected in capital-earnings ratios. Therefore the significance of a given earnings-sales ratio depends on the relation of sales to capitalization. A high turnover of working capital will tend to emphasize the significance of buying at the right price, other things the same.
5. *Relation of selling prices to materials prices.* If selling prices are set for a substantial period of time, the producer may have a *period of option* as to when materials are bought. This is an invitation to consider the probable changes in prices. A rather different situation, which can likewise intensify the need for advance buying, is that in which *selling prices are highly competitive* and likely to reflect the successful anticipation of changes in materials prices on the part of a few important competitors.
6. *Other opportunities to outdo competitors' efficiency.* Sure ways of effective competition are likely to be more popular than unsure ways, and in some industries, and particularly for some businesses, efficiency in factory or sales management provides a strong competitive tool. When this tool is weak, recourse to the more risky one of price-timed buying becomes more essential to effective competition.

A high proclivity is inversely associated with the impact of carrying charges, and this depends on:

7. *The possibility of stipulating when goods are to be received independently of when they are ordered.* When this can be done with confidence, the cost of price-timed ownership is reduced by confining it largely to stock on order.
8. *Low carrying costs.* Insofar as price anticipation does eventuate in related

changes in stocks, low carrying costs reduce the impact of such changes.

9. *Predictable requirements which reduce the risk of obsolescence*. Obsolescence can take the form of goods that cannot be used at all, used only after a write-down, or used inefficiently. Durable raw materials, many simple processed materials, or standard basic goods not subject to fickle demand are relatively resistant to these dangers. The presence of firm sales orders also tends to eliminate this additional risk for other sorts of materials.

A high proclivity adheres also to particular sorts of management structure and talent:

10. *Personnel*. Good judgment about price change requires that people able to make such judgments are available and authorized to make them. This requires a management structure that recognizes, provides, and rewards this type of talent. Top management talent tends to be located in purchasing operations where the factors previously mentioned contribute to a high proclivity to gain.

11. *Management philosophy*. The personality and sentiment of top management can be sympathetic or resistant to price-timed buying to which a "speculative" onus may be attached.

The proclivity to benefit from price-timed buying is a net result of all appropriate attributes in their business setting. Proclivities will differ by type of material and in firms characterized by different management problems and structure. Thus a given proclivity can be assigned to an enterprise-commodity unit.

The frequency distribution of the proclivity to benefit from price-timed buying will depend on the joint frequency distribution of all of the attributes that make for a high (or low) proclivity. What shape is the distribution likely to have?

Consider any one of the attributes making for a relatively high proclivity to gain from price-timed buying. Some commodities in some firms in a given industry will be rich in the attribute; other commodities in the same firm or in other firms in the same industry will be poor in it; but the very rich and the very poor will usually be infrequent compared with those possessing it in moderation.

For example, materials costs can be high relative to value added (item 2 above). Thus the cost of leather for a manufacturer of popular-priced men's shoes is likely to constitute a large proportion of value added, because manufacturing operations are highly mechanized and efficiently managed. At the other end of the frequency distribution, a manufacturer of high-priced women's shoes will find materials costs buried under the very large cost of many hand operations and elaborate distribution techniques. In between (consider calf leathers only) [8] lie the bulk of companies, with more men's shoe manufacturers at the high-proclivity end and women's shoe manufacturers at the low-proclivity end, and a substantial overlap somewhere in the central portion of the range where frequencies are high.

An analogous type of distribution would apply to other of the characteristics listed. Thus, a low risk of obsolescence of purchased sole and brown side leather, featured in popular priced men's shoes, would imply a high proclivity (item 9 above); the multifinished leathers characteristic of many sorts of women's shoes would place such firms at the low end of the distribution. Again, it seems reasonable to expect some humping around the central area of the array.

If we think of each enterprise-commodity unit as having a rank position from one to ten for each characteristic, then the unit's proclivity rating would be some sort of a weighted sum of the several ratings for each character-

---

[8] Calf and cattle hide might be considered part of the same commodity group, whereas kid and other leathers are excluded as having quite different conditions of supply.

istic. The weights would represent relative importance of the characteristic in the net proclivity to gain.

Just what these distributions would look like for a given industry cannot be determined a priori. Certainly there are fewer enterprise commodity units with extremely high proclivities than with moderate ones. At some point, as proclivity ratings decline, it seems likely that the number having a given rating would typically drop off. The distribution would not be symmetrical, however, but skewed toward the low proclivity end. Critical to my argument is the basic wedge shape and the further thought that it would at least flatten. Actually it seems likely to me that it would usually decline at the low-proclivity end of the array. It seems safe to assume that these minimal requirements would be met.

In other words, for the purpose of this analysis we must abandon the notion of the "representative firm" and think instead of the hill-shaped firm, or industry, or group of industries, or economy. The representative situation is precisely not a median or some sort of *average* condition but the basic character of the *distribution* of conditions.

STRUCTURAL ASSUMPTIONS AND PRICE-TIMED OWNERSHIP

The essence of the two assumptions is shown in Figure 4. The top figure portrays the assumption of increasing costs and shows how, as increasing rates of change in materials prices are expected, and guesses are held with increasing assurance, the amount of price-timed ownership increases and reaches a ceiling beyond which there tends to be no inducement to adventure further. The lower figure shows the hill-shaped frequency distribution of enter-price-commodity units in an industry. Concerning the shape of the distribution, I can only say that, pending empirical study, it seems to me to be a reasonable one.

The implication of the two structural assumptions can be displayed first under the highly artificial assumption that expectations

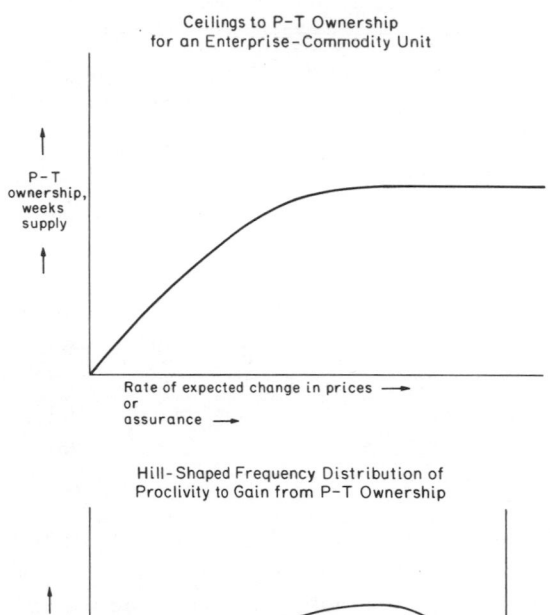

FIGURE 4

Potential Gain from Price-Timed Ownership

about prices are held with certainty and that there also is no uncertainty about sales or anything else capable of influencing expected costs or benefits from price-timed buying. Under these circumstances the level of ownership associated with expectations of higher and higher rates of change in prices would increase without limit and the ceilings of Figure 4 would not apply. A tabular example will illustrate the point.

Exhibit 3 assumes that the proclivities for one hundred different enterprise-commodity units range from a maximum rating of A to a minimum rating of E: the distribution of enterprise-commodity units among firms is, from A to E, 4, 22, 40, 28, 6, as shown in the top line of each of the first five columns.

EXHIBIT 3

Price-Timed Ownership and Buying, Assuming No Uncertainty,

(tons)

Expected Monthly Rate of Rise in Price	Ownership at Each Rate of Price Rise						Buying at Sequential Rates of Price Rise
	Proclivity Group					All Groups	
	A	B	C	D	E		
1/2	4					4	4
1	8	22				30	26
1 1/2	12	44	40			96	66
2	16	66	80	28		190	94
2 1/2	20	88	120	56	6	290	100
3	24	110	160	84	12	390	100
3 1/2	28	132	200	112	18	490	100

Assume further that an expected rise of the basic raw-material price of one-half of 1 per cent per month makes it worthwhile for the A group to undertake price-timed ownership sufficient to cover requirements for the sales of an additional month; for this an extra ton of materials per enterprise-commodity unit is needed. A rise of 1 per cent causes the B group to extend its ownership by a month's supply. But at that rate of price increase, the A group would extend its buying for an additional month. In each case one ton of materials is involved.

As, for each group, prices reach the rate that justifies some price-timed ownership, the amount appears in the first line of each column. But at each successive rate of rise in prices, enterprise-commodity units for which some price-timed ownership had been justified at the previous rate now should extend their position further. The appropriate levels of ownership are shown in the sequential lines for each column, that is, for each proclivity group. Aggregate ownership at each rate of price change is the sum for the five groups shown in the next-to-last column.

Additions to price-timed ownership are achieved by means of price-timed buying. This buying can be thought of as of two sorts: "initial price-timed buying," which lifts price-timed ownership from zero to the first positive figure—the difference between zero and the first lines in each column; "secondary price-timed buying," which lifts ownership to further levels appropriate to faster rates of price increase—the difference between all other lines in the table. Total price-timed buying is the sum of primary and secondary buying. It is shown in the last column of the table under the particular assumption that prices accelerated in the fashion represented by the sequential lines of the table. But of course this sequence is only one of the many patterns of change which could take place. In general price-timed buying simply effectuates the difference between the ownership appropriate to the present expected rate of change in prices and that appropriate to the previously expected rate of change. Consequently, the amount of price-timed buying at a given time depends upon the actual course of the change in prices.

This description has made a totally unrealistc assumption about the absence of uncertainty. Actually, uncertainty causes extension of ownership to involve increasing costs

EXHIBIT 4

Structural Assumptions and Price-Timed Ownership and Buying,
(tons)

Expected Monthly Rate of Rise in Price	Ownership at Each Rate of Price Rise						Buying at Sequential Rates of Price Rise
	Proclivity Group					All Groups	
	A	B	C	D	E		
1/2	4.0					4.0	4.0
1	7.6	22.0				29.6	25.6
1 1/2	10.4	41.8	40.0			92.2	62.6
2	12.4	57.2	76.0	28.0		173.6	81.4
2 1/2	13.6	68.2	104.0	53.2	6.0	245.0	71.4
3	13.6	74.8	124.0	72.8	11.4	296.6	51.6
3 1/2	13.6	74.8	136.0	86.8	15.6	326.8	30.2
4	13.6	74.8	136.0	96.2	18.6	339.2	12.4
4 1/2	13.6	74.8	136.0	96.2	20.4	341.0	1.8
5	13.6	74.8	136.0	96.2	20.4	341.0	0

and decreasing benefits in line with the two structural assumptions.

To illustrate, suppose that each repetition of secondary buying for a proclivity group is associated with cutting the addition to price-timed ownership under certainty by first 10 per cent and then 20 per cent of the units—30 per cent the second time. By the third time 50 per cent is lost, and 70 per cent the fourth time. By the fifth time the ceiling has been reached for all. In Exhibit 4 the figures of Exhibit 3 are changed in accordance with this principle.[9] Now aggregate ownership itself ceases to rise after the bottom proclivity group has reached its ownership ceilings. If prices had changed in accordance with successive

lines of the table, price-timed buying would be zero at that point (last column). However, it would have started to decline long before, when the decreases in secondary buying started to be larger than the increases in primary buying.

The exhibit illustrates the implications of realistic structural assumptions under entirely artificial behavioral assumptions. The latter must now be replaced by more sensible ones.

Behavioral Assumptions

The behavior on which attention centers is *price-timed buying*. By definition, it occurs in association with a change in price-timed ownership.

The amount of price-timed ownership that a firm wishes to hold depends in the first place on its position with respect to the two structural assumptions: (1) the current level of ownership—the lower the level relative to the ceiling levels, the less strong need reasons be to activate a specified amount of owner-

[9] For example, in column A, price-timed ownership under certainty, Exhibit 3, increases by four tons as the expected rate of price rise increases as shown in successive lines. Under uncertainty, Exhibit 4, we assume that four tons is cut by 10 per cent for the first round of secondary buying; thus price-timed ownership is $4 + .90 \times 4 = 7.6$. In the second round of secondary buying the increment of four is cut by 30 per cent, thus price-timed ownership is $7.6 + .70 \times 4 = 10.4$, etc.

ship; (2) the proclivity to gain from price-timed ownership—the higher the proclivity, the less strong need reasons be to activate a specified amount of ownership.

TWO LAGS

Administrative Response Lags. The placing of an order requires that an authorized purchaser make a telephone call, confirmed by an airmail letter. Authorization for routine purchases is not likely to be administratively cumbersome. It is ordinarily delegated in advance to some appropriate person. Authorization for further purchases associated with price expectations may be required to go through channels, but, in view of the presence of some leeway in most budgets, it may not actually need to wait upon confirmation. In general, then, the response lag to an increase in price-timed ownership is negligible. (Contrast this with the lag appropriate to purchases of durable capital goods.) Decreases in ownership, on the other hand, may require somewhat longer before negative price-timed buying can reduce ownership to the desired level. The maximum rate of reduction, even if there is no new buying at all, is the current volume of sales, item by item.

Learning Lag. Changes in price-timed ownership occur as a response to learning, and learning is a time consuming process. Information must be collected and inspected; it must be attended to in the sense of entering the field of perception; it must be appreciated and evaluated in terms of appropriate action.

All of these things take time and therefore give rise to a "learning lag." However, with one exception, the lag for price-timed buying is probably not long. The evidence bearing on the probable course of prices and on changes in business costs or competitors' behavior is swiftly come by. Appreciation and evaluation tend to focus on the purchasing agent's office and thus do not involve cumbersome interpersonal procedures. The excep-

tion to the potentially short learning lag lies in the process whereby assurance develops. This involves what may be thought of as a depth dimension for each of the components of learning mentioned in the previous paragraph, with particular emphasis on the last group. My point is that uncertainty must affect the learning process as well as being reflected in a final evaluation such as I discuss in the next two sections. Insofar as it does affect the learning process, it will tend to draw it out.

PRICE EXPECTATIONS AND CHANGES IN COSTS

The reason for and focus of price-timed buying is, of course, a belief about the future course of prices. The basic character of a belief about prices can be interpreted as a series of possible rates of change with likelihoods associated with each hypothetical occurrence. The complete array can be expressed in terms of an average value. Statistical decision theory formulates the average, the "expected value," as the average of all possible values weighted by their subjectively assigned probability of occurrence. But there are a number of other methods of selecting a central value.[10] Actually, most people probably deal with the future without any such mental gymnastics. Perhaps they consider, as Shackle has claimed, only two values, "focus gain" and "focus loss." [11] Perhaps they make a best guess and think also about how likely it is to turn out right. Perhaps the best guess takes

[10] For a classic formulation of statistical decision, see L. J. Savage, *The Foundations of Statistics,* New York, 1954. An excellent short summary of other decision rules is given in Irwin D. Bross, *Design for Decision,* New York, 1953, pp. 102–117.

[11] The notion is presented in *Expectation in Economics,* by G. L. S. Shackle, 2nd ed., Cambridge, 1952. An excellent short statement by Shackle appears in *Uncertainty and Business Decisions,* edited by C. F. Carter, G. P. Meredith, and G. L. S. Shackle, 2nd ed., Liverpool, 1957, pp. 94–104; see also G. Patrick Meredith, pp. 38–41, and the frontispiece, the three-dimensional diagram of the "model of the Shackle function."

the form simply of "Will prices rise, fall, or do neither?" No doubt different people think in different ways and even at different times.

The advantage associated with price-timed ownership also depends on carrying costs. Thus the amount that is undertaken will be influenced by changes which affect these costs. Previous chapters have pointed to the impact of the volume of back orders or *de facto* financing costs. What competitors are doing likewise influences the need to take a position. For one thing, it is often thought important to "buy along with the trade," since it is more dangerous to be short if competitors are long in supplies and less dangerous to take a long position (expecting prices to rise) if competitors also are long.

ASSURANCE

We have been speaking of expectations about changes in prices and costs. Expectations are hardly ever single-valued. An expected event may happen or not happen; more usually it may happen in one of many ways. Assume, to illustrate, that "expectations" take the form of a probability distribution. Thus, a purchasing agent may believe, explicitly or subconsciously, that there are 2 chances out of 10 that prices will fall, 3 that they will stay the same, and 5 that they will rise. Accordingly he believes, with some lack of conviction, that prices will rise. His assurance in this expectation would increase were his probability weights to shift to, say, 1, 2 and 7. He would feel more justified in buying more materials ahead when the distribution of weights has humped in this fashion than when it was flatter.

Or consider an example involving more specific expectations. Suppose that a purchaser thinks that five values for percentage change in prices are possible—minus 1, 0, plus .5, plus 1, plus 2. Say that if he feels relatively sure about his evaluations, they carry for him the probability ratios of .05, .10, .70, .10, .05, respectively. Then the "expected

value" is plus .5 per cent change.[12] But if he feels unsure, the probability ratios might be more like .40, 0, .20, 0, .40. The "expected value" is still plus .5, but the utility of price-timed buying, and therefore the amount that will be undertaken, is likely to have been reduced by the consciousness that there are four chances out of ten that the price will go down, not up.

However, it would seem that assurance, and consequently the action to which the opinion gives rise, can also increase as a result of changes of a somewhat different sort. Since these further processes are likely to have a significant bearing on how assurance waxes and wanes in an interrelated market, I want to describe them. Unfortunately, the matter has not been much explored and is controversial, and therefore the argument must be developed at some length. However, it is entirely possible to follow the model I present by interpreting change in assurance in the conventional fashion, simply as flattening or humping of a probability distribution—and skipping or rejecting the argument concerning "assurance" which follows. It concerns four additional ways in which the impact of assurance can be conceptualized.

First there is what William Fellner has called "slanting," or Donald Ellsberg "ambiguity." [13] The notion postulates that, feeling

[12] The calculation of expected value (e.v.) is:

Expected price change, per cent	−1.0	0	+.5	+1.0	+2.0	Sum
Probability weights	.05	.10	.70	.10	.05	1.0
Prices, weighted (line 1 × 2)	−.05	0	+.35	+.10	+.10	+.5

[13] William Fellner, "Distortion of Subjective Probabilities as a Reaction to Uncertainty," *Quarterly Journal of Economics*, November 1961, pp. 670–690, and Donald Ellsberg in the same volume. Fellner describes the correction factor for uncertainty in these terms, "Instead of postulating that individuals maximize the mathematical expectation of utility it is, at least for some processes, based on psychological weights that are in the nature of *distorted* probabilities" (p. 676). He has developed this basic idea in a recent book,

unsure of the evidence, perhaps even of the relevance of the evidence, the decision maker is aware that his opinion is poorly founded and unstable. This sort of feeling is not entirely captured in a flattening in a probability distribution for it also involves a fuzziness about the whole matter. Presumably, he will put fewer chips on a fuzzy and, admittedly, potentially unsound judgment than on a better one.

A second way of thinking about the impact of assurance on action is based on the psychology of perception. People do not simply know something or not know it. Nor do they believe things the first time they hear them; if they did, life would be all crisis. Perception is a process which develops slowly. Ideas burrow into the "psychological field." As they burrow, they must in a sense pass tests of harmony with other information. They gain significance and the power to throw their weight around and influence actions. So conceived, increased assurance is a form of a more advanced degree of perception.

A third way of thinking about the capacity of price expectations to influence behavior is to let oneself slip off the polished back of the *ceteris paribus* notion. Actually, as I continue to complain, it is exceedingly difficult to cling rigorously to this basic method of

Probability and Profit, Homewood, Ill., 1965. Donald Ellsberg discusses "ambiguity" and takes it into account as a discount for uncertainty in the form of an index. He points out that actions may frequently favor "those definable" as "status quo" or "present behavior" since for these the degree of confidence may be high and the range of probabilities narrow.

Price theory has long introduced the notion of a discount for uncertainty. Oscar Lange described it as *"effective* expected prices." "This is the most probable price minus the risk premium. For sellers the risk premium is positive, for buyers it is negative" (p. 31). Oscar Lange, *Price Flexibility and Employment,* Bloomington, Ind., 1944. These notions could be interpreted as simply resulting from the introduction of a probability distribution rather than a single-valued expectation. However, the fact that the direction of discount is different for buyers than for sellers tends to bring the ideas into closer relation to the slanting or ambiguity notion discussed in the previous paragraph.

scientific thought in a context where the causal process under examination necessarily *links* changes in independent variables in the system with changes in some of the elements confined within this *ceteris paribus* compound. In the context of price-timed buying, it is most unusual for prices to change without corresponding changes in quality, delivery periods, and the like. Indeed, such changes can readily be converted to a price dimension. Changes in these other market phenomena are sure to influence the subjective assignment of weight to possible price changes. They will, in other words, affect the assurance with which the price guess is made.

Finally, "expected values" or "best guesses" are often poor summaries for a probability distribution of expected values in the context of price-timed buying. They fail to take account of the differential utility of each possible price. The weighting system equates the utilities to the amount of price change, whereas actually they are often asymmetrical. Failure to anticipate a price rise means that goods have been bought at too high a price. But price-timed buying when prices fall means not only that the goods are bought at too high a price but also, in many cases, that less than optimal articles were purchased. In effect, then, the denominator of the right-hand side of the equation is, for price-timed ownership, inversely correlated with the numerator; risk of obsolescence (in the denominator) ought not to be set down at its average value but at values specifically related to specific values of the numerator, the expected rate of change in price. A further asymmetry in the utility of positive and negative error may occur at a personal level. If prices fall, a purchasing agent may be subject to criticism for advance buying to which he will not be subject for "missing the boat" if prices rise. Virtue's veil clothes the indiscretion of the resistant gambler but the mistaken gambler is fully exposed.

I conclude that whether one thinks of the "expected value" or "best guess" about prices as influenced by "slanting," the process of perception, inevitably associated market phenomena, or asymmetry of rewards and penalties, conclusions about behavior are the same; a best guess about price change will be associated with varying amounts of price-timed ownership as assurance or confidence in it, variously defined, grows or wanes.

The Ownership Surface

These behavioral characteristics prescribe that the levels of ownership implied by the structural assumptions must be viewed in the light of uncertainty about price expectations. The levels appropriate to sure price expectations, as illustrated in Exhibit 4, become the *limits* which would be appropriate as assurance builds up. They are shown along the back wall of an ownership surface in Figure 5.

Actually, price expectations are typically more or less unsure. Moreover, the structural as well as behavioral characteristics imply that many other aspects of the judgment of net advantage are also more or less unsure—those concerning future sales and various elements of holding costs. These judgments and those about prices are interrelated. On any or all of these counts, then, low assurance reduces the amount of price-timed ownership undertaken at each expected rate of price change. Assurance is lowest at the front wall of the surface.

The diagram should be thought of as representing potential ownership for a major material, a commodity, in an industry. Thus the CC'BB' rectangle represents zero price-timed ownership. Only such stocks as are needed for servicing sales and similar matters are held. Positive price-timed ownership is

FIGURE 5

Demand Surface for Price-Timed Ownership Sensitivity

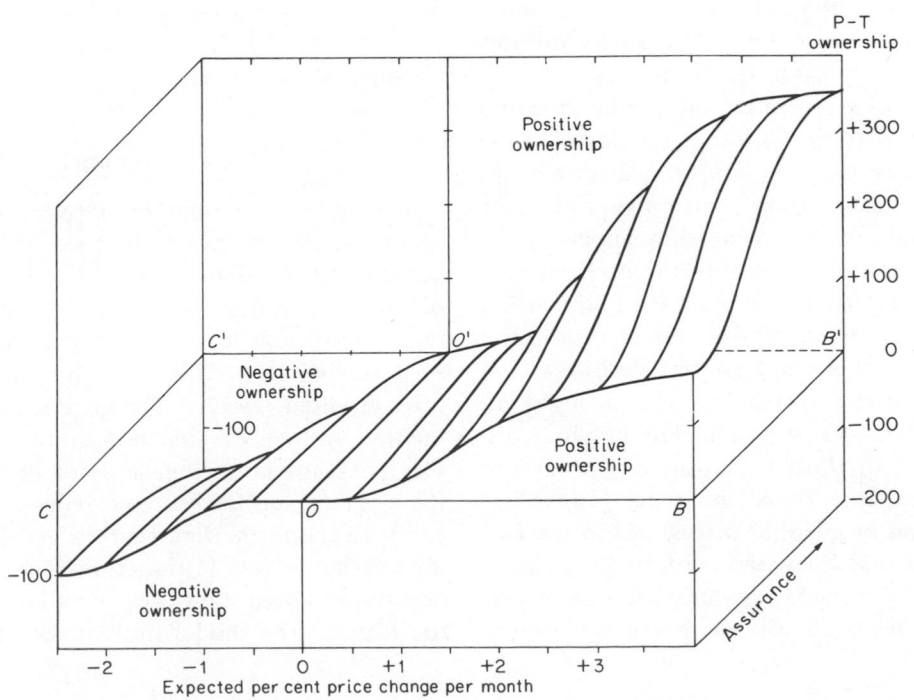

above the plane and negative ownership below it. If no price change is expected (center of the plane along the lines OO′), there is, of course, no P-T ownership. The rate at which prices are expected to rise are shown to the right, and to fall, to the left of the OO′ line. The higher the expected rate of increase, the more enterprise-commodity units may be involved in positive ownership, and the larger the extent of their involvement. That is, the surface rises as it moves to the right because of *both* additional units starting primary buying and continued secondary buying.

When the expected rate of rise is very low and also uncertain (front wall just to the right of O), no P-T ownership is indicated even for firms having a very high proclivity to benefit from price-timed buying. As we move to the right, the diagram suggests increasing rates of rise. But actually, it is doubtful that an expected rate has much meaning when opinion is very unsure. There are perhaps a series of overlapping probability distributions that are all so flat that their meaning is little more than "prices will probably rise"; how much they are expected to rise is hard to say except that at the right it is more than toward the center. That is why the surface is relatively flat at the front wall.

The backward dimension of the diagram depicts increasing assurance. It portrays the gradual accretion of price-timed ownership associated with more enterprise units for which additions to ownership appear justified, and more ownership for each participant. As depicted, the backward dimension accounts for much of the rise in price-trend ownership. This implies that decisions concerning desired ownership are strongly affected by degrees of belief. The previous discussion has attributed the impact of assurance to the changes in the shape of the probability distribution of possible prices, and to the further forms that increased confidence can take. The form of a more "advanced degree of perception" seems to assume particular impor-

tance as one thinks of the competition for executive attention among the wide variety of things that, minute by minute, take place in a business.

Negative price-timed ownership is a response to an expected fall in price. It is illustrated in the left lower section of the diagram. The structure is highly conjectural, but is based on the supposition that the minimum true hand-to-mouth position which would presumably be appropriate if serious price decline is expected is much nearer the normal efficiency levels for ownership than is the maximum extended position. For this reason the surface never falls much below −150 (back left corner), though it rises by over +300 (back right corner). Also, the difference between behavior under uncertainty and under certainty is less extreme.

Positive price-timed buying occurs when an enterprise-commodity unit wishes to move from a lower to a higher level of price-timed ownership, or from a larger to a smaller negative level of ownership. It occurs, in other words, when there is a wish to move upward on the ownership surface. A downward movement involves negative price-timed buying. Does this buying itself influence the markets in which it takes place?

Market Response

The analysis of market response needs to be formulated largely in terms of price-timed buying rather than ownership. Price-timed buying constitutes an addition to, and negative price-timed buying a subtraction from, such buying as would occur for other than price-oriented reasons. The greater or smaller buying influences demand-supply relationships; it generates other sorts of behavior in the contacts of buyers and sellers; it influences the information that is generated in the market place. It therefore influences expectations about how prices will change in the future. The model must make some presumptions about the character of the several market responses, and these need to be specified.

Market responses are of three sorts. None of the responses are immediate. They all take time, and how much time is a function of the things that need to occur. The several responses, each involving characteristic lags, concern market behavior, information and expectations, and income generation.

MARKET BEHAVIOR AND THE MARKET-BEHAVIOR LAG

Market behavior affects price, market conditions and levels of utilization.

Price Effect. Materials prices tend to respond to price-timed buying and the strength of the response is a function of the amount of buying, other things the same. Diagrammatically, positive price-timed buying represents a short-term *shift* of a demand schedule upward and to the right. Supply schedules may also shift upward and to the left as suppliers respond to the eagerness of buyers and perhaps also to some short-term rigidities in their own production scheduling. Negative buying causes shifts in the opposite direction. Thus, in terms of the usual demand-supply-price diagrams, a flock of small new short-term schedules for demand and supply are born and intersect at higher levels of the vertical price plane.

Effect on Other Market Conditions. Other conditions in materials markets also respond to the extra demand caused by price-timed buying. The amount of the response depends in part on the amount of the buying and on its rate of change. Thus the speed and reliability of deliveries may deteriorate simply because of short-term resistance to *changing* the level of output. This means that when once output has achieved a new level, the resistance will subside.

The character of market responses has two interesting implications. First, it seems clear that at this level it is not possible to isolate the impact of price-timed buying from that of all other market influences. Second, the lag associated with these aspects of market behavior could be very short indeed. Its length would depend largely on the institutions of purchase and sale. The action-reaction pattern of an open market are almost immediate. For individually negotiated deals, substantial time may be required before additional selling or buying is reflected in market conditions, including prices. Seasonal factors can be important. Sometimes it is conventional for prices to be changed only at certain times during the year, and a growing tendency for prices to rise or fall must wait for the appropriate months. If prices are going to be raised when the line is announced, some customers may be given an opportunity to stock up earlier at the old prices; this underscores the periodic influence. The annual trade association meetings may be the battleground for a campaign to change prices.

The Level of Utilization. All these market responses will tend to be more severe when the level of utilization is high than when it is low. This observation implies a further interdependency of factors affecting ownership. Market responses to price-timed buying or to buying associated with other market expectations cannot be disentangled from responses to the broader picture of supply-and-demand conditions. If so, lags may be introduced which can be far longer than any thus far considered. They involve cyclical rhythms of intensification of the shorter market-oriented responses.

EXPECTATIONS MULTIPLIER AND THE EVIDENCE LAG

Market responses carry information which is used by prospective buyers and sellers as a basis of judging the future course of prices. Consequently, the responses have potential multiplier effects via their role as evidence and the power of information to influence expectations.

Here again, the process takes time and therefore operates with a lag. Open-market prices are widely displayed daily if not faster. On the other hand, individual contracts between producers and buyers are often secretly negotiated, and the information may be slow to leak out, if indeed it ever does. The amount of buying being done by market leaders, the condition of inventories and order books of customers and of competitors, all constitute information which may take days if not weeks to become generally known.

However the point that I want to emphasize is simply that the actions listed as market behavior all convey information. This information, after it has had time to disseminate, influences expectations the next time around. The "feedback" thus consists not only of market actions and consequent changes in demand-supply relations but also of information which, along with behavior, influences further expectations with multiplier effects.

INCOME MULTIPLIER AND THE INCOME LAG

When price-timed buying causes output to be different from what it otherwise would be, the resultant income flows are subject to the usual multiplier effects. Because the situation can change rapidly, payroll and other adjustable income flows are doubtless primarily involved. Also, the short-term level of the propensity to consume, which, of course, varies widely, will affect the extent that positive or negative price-oriented demand is amplified. Expectations may also come into play to augment or mute the income multiplier effect. The lags associated with income multipliers have been widely discussed in the literature.

The Process of Change

The gadgetry of the model of price-timed buying has now been described in terms of a group of structural, behavioral, and market characteristics which interact after several short delays.

Aggregate change results from the shifting weights to be assigned to situations described in Figure 5. The weights indicate the number of enterprise-commodity units whose price-timed ownership is at some particular place in the ownership surface and about to shift to some other place. *The shifts take the form of positive or negative price-timed buying —movements upward or downward respectively in the vertical dimension.* Systematic shifts in the pattern of weights will occur as a result of forces set in motion by an initial dose of price-timed buying and the business environment in which it takes place. What is the pattern through time of the resultant buying?

It would be satisfying to be able to answer this question by a process table that spelled out the action, feedback, decision, action pattern; but the possibility of this tidy demonstration is barred by the basic construction. The result of the aggregate level is contingent on the character of the distribution within the aggregate of proclivity, impulse, feedback sets. Moreover, it is proper to stipulate these occurrences only in terms of probabilities, not as things that will happen. The magnitude of response will therefore depend on how sequences unfold. If so, the aggregate of occurrences this month has no prescribed single relationship to selected present conditions and the aggregate of occurrences last month or the month before.

Nevertheless, though statements must remain qualitative, reasonable and realistic assumptions about objectives, information, procedures, choices, and reactions seem to lead to the conclusion that, inherently, a spaced wave of price-timed buying will be generated unless intercepted by elements external to the model. Specifically: (1) cumulation is gradual and progressive—more buying is touched off per month as the situation matures than when it is young; (2) cumulation takes time; (3) reversal is inherent.

I want to discuss the processes of cumulation and reversal without admitting factors external to the model. Needless to say, they are present and important, especially in connection with the process of expansion.

CUMULATING EXPANSION

The course of a wave in price-timed buying of materials can be interpreted in terms of how and why enterprise-commodity units move from one position on the diagram to another. Start at a point where there is no longer a general belief that prices will fall and accordingly the desire for negative price-timed ownership has abated. This implies that positive price-timed buying has moved many firms from the lower left quadrant of the ownership surface to somewhere in the neighborhood of the origin, zero in Figure 5. I see no reason why price-timed buying in isolation could not cease at this point at which ownership tends to be at efficient levels, assuming that prices would remain stable. But I would like to suppose that there have been signs of renewed demand and other healthy underpinnings that lead to optimistic expectations.

Some firms in the industry, then, expect rises in prices, others declines. Most are unsure. There now occurs a moderate desire for price-timed ownership on the part of some firms with a high proclivity to gain. Price-timed buying would be governed by the difference between the previous and present ownership objective of the participating units.

Assume, now, that nothing from the outside occurs to counteract the effects of this initial dose of price-timed buying. Then market responses theoretically bring about a feedback: in minute quantities they would consist of behavior responses, expectation and evidence responses, and even an income multiplier.

However it seems clear that in reality there must be some threshold level below which feedback effects do not develop. How the threshold should be defined and how it operates need to be studied. It seems likely that the rate of change in final demand will be one part of the story; the sensitivity of in-formation systems and vulnerability to competitive behavior will be another.

The initial dose, and the feedback effects, can influence expectations in four ways, and actions in one further way: (1) fewer enterprise-commodity units will be subject to the expectation of falling prices; (2) more firms may expect a rise in prices of more materials; (3) the expected rate of increase may rise, though this may well tend to be a later manifestation; (4) expectations will gain in sureness. In terms of Figure 5, concentration of situations moves to the right and especially back. Price-timed buying is positive and there is more of it than at the time of the original dose.

As time goes on, there is a fifth way in which the situation matures. It involves the objective facts with which firms are faced; the need for defensive action increases. For example, competitors may be amassing low-priced inventories or suppliers working overtime. Consequently, the *action* based on a given set of expectations, held with a given degree of assurance, increases. Diagrammatically, the surface as a whole rises. The further buying will have its own round of feedback and multiplier effects, which in turn have further influences on new expectations.

All this takes time. It takes time for businessmen to perceive developments and learn their implications. The growth of assurance is particularly deliberate, since it waits on successive confirmations of expectations and events that deepen perceptions. After decisions are formed, administrative response, though swift, is not instantaneous. It takes time for market conditions, including prices, to reflect the impact of new buying. It takes time for the evidence to be displayed, perceived, and learned to the extent necessary to influence new expectations and the assurance with which they are held.

Will a snowballing process get under way, or will countervailing forces prevail? Countervailing forces internally generated consist of (1) reduction in initial buying because the

hump of the frequency distribution of proclivities has been passed; (2) reduction in
secondary buying because many units approach the long end of their long-short market
range; (3) negative (or zero) price-timed
buying to correct ownership based on disappointed expectations about price change.
Numbers 1 and 2 will not generally occur at
the early stage of movement having the basic
time-consuming characteristics that I have described. Number 3, disappointed expectations, is quite another matter, for its preva-
lence depends on whether the stimulation to
prices associated with price-timed buying is
*large enough to cause prices to increase as
much as or more than expected*. Is this likely
to occur?

The answer hinges, I think, on whether additional buying is contingent primarily on
the expectation that the price rise will accelerate (movement to the right of the diagram), or on the increasing assurance that
prices will continue to rise (movement in
the backward dimension). If the former governs, the situation is self-reinforcing only so
long as expectation-activated buying (along
with its ramifying effects) has a large enough
impact on prices to validate the expectation. This implies that the price rise is at
least seen to *accelerate*—a stringent requirement unlikely to be met. Moreover, the time
series showed that market-oriented ownership
did not parallel the rate of change in prices
(nor did change in ownership, hypothetically
buying, parallel the change in the rate of
change).

But this hypersensitivity is not likely to
be present if the growth of assurance were
the chief determinant. Assurance would increase as expectations are repeatedly confirmed. If expectations attended primarily to
the direction of change in prices, confirmation consists of continued change in the *same
direction*. The time series showed the implied
association between market-oriented ownership and prices proper (or change in ownership and change in prices).

The process, then, compounds in the five
ways previously mentioned and desired ownership moves backward and somewhat to the
right over the surface of the diagram. Feedback mechanisms provide a sixth mechanism
which, along with the fifth, causes the surface
itself to lift as the objective situation changes.
This implies cumulation of a progressive sort.
What brings it to a halt?

DOWNTURN AND REVERSAL

A *downturn* in price-timed buying occurs
after the amount of positive buying reaches
its peak. This definition parallels the usual
idea of a peak in any economic activity. Note
that even after a downturn, so defined, many
terms might still be moving upward on the
upper right segment of the ownership surface, but aggregate movement in the vertical
direction would have started to decrease. If
price-timed buying is visualized as superimposed on an upward phase of final buying, the
downturn in price-timed buying marks the
point at which its impact on total buying
starts to lessen.

But for some purposes the more significant
change in price-timed buying is the point at
which it turns from positive to negative. At
this point the influence of the timing of buying starts to depress rather than to stimulate
total buying. Call this point *reversal*, admittedly in this special sense. It will be useful to
note how both downturn and reversal in
price-timed buying occur as a result of elements internal to the model.

Structural characteristics require that price-
timed buying must turn down soon after participation in it has reached its maximum. That
it does reach a maximum is guaranteed by the
hill-shaped form of the proclivity to benefit
and by the ceilings to price-timed ownership.
Structural characteristics do not imply that
reversal must set in; they imply that price-
timed buying cease but not that it turn negative.

Behavioral characteristics, on the other
hand, can account for both downturn and re-

versal. Insofar as expectations about rates of rise in prices determine buying, a downturn would occur when the rate of rise in the rate of rise ceased accelerating; reversal would occur when it started to decline. Although, as previously explained, formulations of this sort seem totally unrealistic, it is possible that attention to rates of change becomes more common when a buying wave has lasted long enough for assurance about the direction of change to grow strong. If so, vulnerability to reversal, as well as to downturn, increases sharply at that time.

Insofar as the increasing assurance with which expectations are held constitutes a major aspect of the developing situation, a downturn occurs, other things the same, when the rate at which assurance (more specifically the action that it motivates) is building up starts to slacken; reversal occurs when assurance begins to lessen. And it seems likely that this lessening can take place as a result of the level of activity alone. At times, for example, factors directly associated with price increases of the past will raise doubt about their continuation in the future. For one thing, if prices reach levels that are high with respect to previous levels, this fact can raise doubt whether they will continue to rise. For another thing, operating margins may narrow after prices have risen for a while; a tendency of this sort is promoted by the fact that crude products respond more sensitively to changes in demand than do finished products. Narrowing margins often raise doubts whether prices will continue to rise. Structural and behavioral characteristics, then, guarantee a downturn and virtually guarantee a reversal in price-timed buying.

But in any event market response must, it would seem, convert downturn into reversal. The presumption rests on the supposition that the strength of the reaction of prices, delivery periods, or other market phenomena are a function of the amount of price-timed buying and perhaps also of its rate of change. Sensitivity to the latter would reflect, among other things, the difficulties that suppliers experience in changing production schedules. But within a wide range of functional relationships it would necessarily be true that the amount of market response declines when the amount of price-timed buying does. If so, the information feedback signals reductions in rates of price increase and less sureness that some prices will continue to rise. If expected rates of rise occur, or the assurance with which the expectation of some threshold rate is held declines, the ownership position that is justified is reduced. In effect, enterprise commodity units shift toward the front and left of the ownership surface and negative price-timed buying effectuates the shift. Market responses to these reductions further reinforce the messages that convey doubt about further rise. Aggregate price-timed buying turns negative, that is, reversal occurs, when the amount of negative buying exceeds that of positive price-timed buying, that is, when the sum of the vertical distance by which some enterprise commodity-units drop on the ownership surface exceeds that by which others rise.

DECLINE

The negative phase of a buying wave starts while most price-timed ownership is positive, but firms are trying to reduce their position by refraining from buying. Aggregate materials procurement is therefore less than the amount required to provide for final demand. However negative price-timed buying for any firm cannot be greater than the volume of orders that would otherwise be placed to meet final demand.

It seems likely that firms that had previously engaged in positive buying would try to unload in unison. Since there is a cost attached to positive price-timed ownership, uncertainty alone may be sufficient reason to forgo the possible benefit and engage in negative buying. Uncertainty may be more contagious in a business community than is the expectation of either a rise or fall. In terms of Figure 5, when uncertainty takes hold of industry opinion, there is a scramble of units to hop from wherever they are on the right-hand segment of the surface to somewhere on the left-hand side. Thus, though the slope of negative *ownership* is mild, negative *buying,* to effectuate downward shifts in desired ownership, can be relatively extreme.

The upturn in price-timed buying occurs as the number of firms, and the amount of the reductions desired, start to decline. Here, as for the upward peak, structural assumptions imply that the force of negative buying must decline. Indeed, the minimum hand to mouth position is doubtless far closer to the efficient service level of ownership than is the ceiling level; consequently declines must bottom off sooner.

Reversal, the start of positive buying, is brought on by the behavioral and market reaction aspects of the model in a manner generally parallel to the upper turn. However, as mentioned at the outset of this section, it seems likely that support from elements outside of the model—elements associated with final demand and other marked forces—are essential to launch price-timed buying on a climb over the positive sector of the ownership surface. However, if the support is present, the ground has been prepared for rapid and cumulating response. The decline of negative price-timed buying has already reduced the depressant influence on total buying of market oriented elements, and firms whose business has improved unexpectedly will be caught short and behave accordingly. Their behavior echoes in a manner previously described.

PRICE-TIMED BUYING AND THE INVENTORY CYCLE

A wave in price-timed buying has been described in terms of factors capable of producing self-reversing fluctuations of endogenously determined duration. It is shaped by the ecological process whereby opinion is formed, acted upon, diffused through the economy, and affected by it.

All Market-Oriented Buying

The model has focused on one aspect of market conditions—prices. Even so, changes in other aspects which are inevitably associated with changes in price—delivery period, assortments, quality—were recognized in discussions of market response to price-timed buying.

To admit these influences explicitly as part of the process embodied in a model would require, I believe, virtually no change in its basic structure. Indeed, the surface labeled price-timed ownership as shown in Figure 5 may well be a more realistic picture of market-oriented ownership than of expectation focused on price alone. The rise in expected rates of change in prices, measured along the horizontal axis, might well not actually occur unless the increase in expected costs represented by market prices were joined by costs associated with poorer selections or longer delivery terms. Likewise, the rising assurance diagrammed in the backward dimension could be caused by combinations of things that are likely to occur. For example, if, with a given degree of assurance, prices are expected to rise *and* delivery periods are expected to lengthen, there is far less to be risked by increasing ownership than if either were expected to occur without the other.

This implies that the model as described could doubtless be applied to the totality of market prospects without fundamental change.

Interindustry Diffusion

The ecology of a wave of market-oriented buying in a single industry may well also apply across industry lines. How this can and does occur needs study, but a few guesses may be in order. For one thing, the industries in a single vertical sequence are linked in many ways. Changes in the prices of raw materials such as cotton, hides, fats and oils, and scrap metals are known and watched by firms at later stages of an industry as indicators of prices and other market conditions in the more finished lines such as cloth, shoes, short-ening, autos, cooking ware, and electrical ap-paratus. From the finished end, the influ-ence of final demand has a significant bear-ing on raw materials as well as on finished goods markets. Between the two ends of a sequence the similar expectations are pro-moted by the hourly and daily contacts of buyer and seller over the telephone, in the office, and in the market; each firm is both buyer of materials and seller of a product, and thus a link in a vertical chain.[14] The link is specific in connection with unfilled orders. For a particular company, undelivered sales orders on the books can, of course, take a substantial part of the gamble out of price-timed buying of materials.

The closer are business ties, the more surely will diffusion occur, and the more promptly. Consequently, it is not difficult to visualize how a buying wave can develop within a single industry sequence. But were expecta-tions contained within these narrow channels, waves in various industries could counteract one another. If so, the quantitative impact on the economy as a whole would be small and the multiplier effects would be virtually nonexistent. Of great interest, therefore, are the factors capable of diffusing a disturbance across industry lines.

One can only guess what these are, since the subject has not been studied. The hints

of parallelism that we have observed in mar-kets so diverse as department store merchan-dising and durable goods manufacturing whet the curiosity to know more. One obvious car-rier of diffusion is the level of final demand and its rate of change, since most commodities share in some degree the fortunes of the econ-omy as a whole. Another candidate is the price of sensitive commodities not subject to strong independent variations in supply; for such commodities parallel price movements often occur. Here again, prices are one aspect of a more complicated set of market condi-tions, the influence of which spreads. It may also be that prices and market conditions in some commodities (steel is a good example) have a pervasive influence on a wide variety of other raw metals and finished goods. Other common influences—credit conditions, labor conditions, special situations of broad im-portance (national and international)—are likewise capable of some across the board in-fluence on market expectations.

The Pieces of an Inventory Model

Fluctuation in ownership associated with changing market prospects, in which ecolog-ical interplay is of special importance, is of course only one part of the total process of fluctuation in stocks on hand and on order. Consequently the model of price-timed buy-ing is only one piece of a complete model of fluctuation in materials inventories. Its par-ticular function is to explain why even this most volatile set of influences does not imply a sawtooth pattern of fluctuation but instead tends to cause inventories to build up more slowly and necessarily to retard and reverse. Other aspects of an inventory model were discussed in Chapter 11, where differences were indicated in the picture appropriate to de-partment stores and to durable goods man-ufacturers. The multiplier aspects associated with income and with expectations and their interrelationship were mentioned in Chapter 12. By way of summary I shall put the pieces

[14] Examples of linkages of these sorts appear in Thomas M. Stanbeck, Jr., "Short-Run Instability in the Cotton Broad Woven Goods Industry, 1946–1951," Un-published Doctoral Dissertation, Duke University, 1954; and Ruth P. Mack, *Consumption and Business Fluc-tuations; A Case Study of the Shoe, Leather, Hide Se-quence,* Princeton for NBER, 1956.

together largely as a sequence of empty boxes for which the previous discussions, especially the models of Chapter 11, serve to illustrate how they may be filled for various industries or other sufficiently homogeneous segments of the economy. A model for aggregate fluctuation in materials inventories would probably have to be built up by appropriate weighting of the segments.

The major pieces that need to be described and articulated are:

1. A forecasting procedure forming the basis of initial buying, which recognizes the information typically available to management and the time periods for which forecasts are actually required. This implies a basic distinction between firms having little advance knowledge of short-term changes in sales other than of a seasonal sort, such as retail stores, and firms for which sales orders or other trustworthy barometers provide a basis for reasonably good forecasts, such as many durable goods manufacturers. It also implies recognizing patterns of buying in terms of the overlapping time periods that the shingled structure of procurement frequently implies.[15]

2. A link of desired stocks to expected sales which for cyclical analysis is best formulated in incremental rather than average terms. My emphasis is negative—a constant average relationship ought not to be assumed. Even a constant incremental relation is of course a rough approximation, but perhaps close enough to realistic requirements to serve; presumably coefficients for increments would typically be smaller than the average ratio.

3. Changing opportunity costs of inventories which recognize changes in costs of carrying stocks, on the one hand (e.g., those associated with the presence of back orders or changes in the availability or cost of funds),

and, on the other hand, of alternative ways of performing the functions that stocks serve (e.g., flexible employment or selling policies).

4. The influence of changes in market prospects and expectations concerning them on the timing of buying. This covers influences originating primarily from the supply as well as the demand side and their ecological interplay.

5. Methods of defining, recognizing, and correcting error; this is a complex element. It involves in the first place the relative importance of inventory goals in the framework of all management problems—the opportunity costs of management attention to defining and enforcing precise inventory goals. It involves correction in the second instance for faulty initial guesses about future requirements; the shingled pattern of buying mentioned in paragraph 1 has relevance here. It involves correction of procurement based on expectations concerning market conditions or other matters which are found to have been in error or which no longer apply.

6. An income and expectation multiplier. At any particular time net capital investment in inventories is subject to some sort of income multiplier at an aggregate level. But its effect can be muted or amplified depending on the interpretation placed on the change in inventories on hand and on order and the expectations thereby aroused.[16]

If the model is constructed in terms of ownership, all of the prescriptions can be viewed as applying roughly to the present in the sense for which the objectives and realistic judgments call. This makes it possible to net out some of the anticipations-correction procedures, such as those implied in the shingled orders (paragraph 1) and corrections (paragraph 5). The income multiplier in paragraph 6 operates with the lag

---

[15] See the discussion of department store orders and manufacturers' orders and shipments in Chapter 11. Note in connection with the latter that orders can provide a forecasting instrument even when goods are not made to order.

[16] Multipliers are a central point in the analysis that closes Chapter 12. Other specifics on this point appear at many places in the book, but note particularly the discussion of Exhibit 2, Cases I and II in Chapter 3.

implied by successive income receipt and spending sequences. The expectation multiplier in paragraph 6 operates with such lags as the ecological process implies. The latter statement applies in some degree to the expectational elements in any of the paragraphs, but particularly to paragraph 4.

If the model is constructed in terms of materials stock on hand, it is necessary always to allow for the time required for orders to enter stock and the corrections that have been put into effect during that time. Even the allowance for deliveries is difficult to make in view of the long and changing leads of outstandings relative to stocks.[17] The implications seem to be that the model loses most of its potential *analytic* value if applied to stock on hand. But it would be useful in gauging the gross influences on stocks of previous levels of outstandings. For example, in 1961 and 1962, when these levels were low, stocks would presumably tend not to be as high relative to activity as at other comparable cyclical stages—1950, 1954–55, 1958–59.

The importance that I assign to expectations and to the information conveyed by orders rules out period analysis of the Lundberg-Metzler variety. Response in terms of ownership is visualized as potentially immediate, whereas the situation to which buying responds evolves over time periods inherent to each particular sort of situation or process.

DIRECTIONS FOR FURTHER STUDY

I mentioned at the close of Chapter 3 that the strategy of scientific advance often means that a good question answered badly may be a necessary prelude to a good answer some years later. The purpose of this book has been primarily to test the value of a question —How do flows of information, commands, expectations, contribute to the understanding of flows of goods and income? The broad question has sired a family of specific questions discussed at the close of Chapters 11 and 12. They are implicitly collected in a series of related boxes by the model that has just been outlined. Fill in the answers and the theory achieves a concrete form. At any rate, understanding grows. Work toward this end can, happily, utilize the great deal that has already been done. But it may be useful to discuss, without pretense of system, some of the work that needs doing.

Time Series. The most obvious need is for time series that reveal patterns of communication in the form of orders along with information about actions such as shipments or production. Required are data for the same firms on sales orders and purchase orders, shipments and receipts, and, if possible, flows at other critical points such as production starts or finished production. Information for the stock pools that these flows bound completes the statistical picture. By arranging the firms (or divisions of them) in vertically related sequences, it would be possible to trace the vertical transmission of demand through the economy. Such sequences could also be related to appropriate price information. Information for stages of an industry sequence would provide the wherewithal for examining how buying waves spread vertically. Information for groups of industries would provide insight concerning the lateral dissemination of fluctuation.

The report of the Consultant Committee on Inventory Statistics, made to the Subcommittee on Economic Statistics of the Joint Committee on the Economic Report in 1955, stressed the importance of information of this sort. It recommended improvement in the data for manufacturing stocks, shipments, and orders (Recommendation 10); it recom-

[17] See the discussion and illustrative example in Chapter 10.

mended that information on sales, new orders, stocks, and outstanding orders for major departments of department stores be collected (Recommendation 21). There has been a careful overhauling of the manufacturing data, but unfortunately the information is still less than what is needed to picture the flow of orders and output on a vertical or horizontal basis. For department stores the situation is sad indeed. Far from providing statistics on orders by departments, even the data for the total stores has been discontinued as of December 1963.

The capacity of time series to inform about vertical and horizontal communication of fluctuation would be greatly enhanced if data for individual firms were summarized in terms of distributions as well as in terms of the usual totals or averages. Certainly, for example, it would be useful to know something of the patterns of change in the distribution of firms in an industry with respect to the number of weeks' supply of materials held on hand and on order, and of rates of change in this supply.

Interviews. Statistical data of these sorts, data capable of indicating what is done with respect to purchasing and inventory problems, require the counterpoint of information bearing on why it is done. One way of acquiring this sort of insight is to ask the businessmen who make the decisions. I realize that the results of discussions are considered unscientific and subjective. Resorting to this method involves a trade-off: relevance is emphasized at the sacrifice of precision. But at the present state of the art, it seems clear that relevance is often a bargain purchase. In short, "It is better to be vaguely right than precisely wrong." [18] Specifically, systematic discussions with businessmen are required concerning the range of subjects covered in Chapter 2. We need to get richer and firmer knowl-

edge about the structure of costs and opportunity costs bearing on stocks and purchasing. We need to understand the information systems that help to formulate and validate objectives. Questionnaires are, of course, entirely useless for this purpose, at least until far more is learned about what to ask and how to formulate questions. Indeed, even in an open-ended interview, specific questions about stocks are likely at best to be only a point of departure.

For example, if a department store executive is asked whether, when sales increase 5 per cent, stocks also need to increase in the same proportion, the answer may be something like this: When sales first increase 5 or even 10 per cent, stocks *need not* increase at all. But pretty soon, often in connection with the next periodic planning procedures, management will start to think that the high level is going to last. Then stocks will move up to their customary ratio to sales. But the question, "Why do stocks need to rise that much?" provokes answers which do not, to the businessman, seem to hold their ground when probed. The investigations that need to be made consist of the discussions that follow, in which the man of affairs who knows the stuff of which good decisions are made is provoked to explore the grammar of the prose he speaks so well.

Discussions are exceedingly flexible techniques of study and accordingly are sensitive to the preoccupations of the investigator. If interviews are to be fully useful, they must probe the subjective as well as objective factors that determine how information is selected, appreciated, and acted upon. Of special importance in the context of the ecological aspects is the role of learning and assurance. Is there evidence of the gradual buildup that the ecological model assumes? If so, what information is watched, how does action depend on the perception of what competitors, suppliers, or customers are doing or have done? How is such knowledge conveyed among competitors, suppliers, indus-

---

[18] The remark was attributed to Wildon Carr by G. S. Shove, in "The Place of Marshall's Principles in the Development of Economic Theory," *Economic Journal*, December 1942, p. 323.

tries? Also of particular importance to the model are insights that can provide a basis for estimating how proclivity distributions are shaped. Interviews and other sorts of information, then, can in effect help to redraw Figure 5 and to suggest how units move from one spot on the surface to another. The answers would doubtless be found to differ for various sorts of industries.

Econometrics. As indicated toward the beginning of Chapter 9, econometrics was tabled for the course of this investigation. One would hope that its talents could be enlisted to test some of the notions that have been put forward and to add quantitative dimensions. As mentioned earlier, both the investigations described in this book and further information of the sorts just mentioned are prerequisites. But even so, formidable difficulties persist in incorporating the insights of this study into equations.

The study has shown that an understanding of the behavior of aggregate stocks must be built up out of an understanding of a number of parts for which causality is reasonably homogeneous. The analysis throws some light on how the parts should be defined. But even so there are major hurdles to be leaped or circumvented.

A convincing statistical "explanation" of the behavior of stocks or ownership must reconcile the observed magnitude and timing of aggregate fluctuations with a realistic view of business operations. My findings have presented the hypothesis that efficient servicing of sales, other things the same, does not require fluctuations as large as those which the statistics show and consequently "other things" do in fact appear to change with business conditions. Econometric analysis is thus asked to identify these other things and measure their impact.[19]

At a statistical level, this underscores the usual difficulties of isolating factors which tend to parallel one another at least most of the time—factors such as shipments, sales orders, labor costs, capacity utilization, market stringency, opportunity costs of financing or expectations about each.

At an analytic level, the potentially immediate response of ownership implies that distributed lags are a receptacle for ignorance; even for stocks, lags must have a duration that makes sense in terms of specific management problems and procedures in the context of cyclical variation.[20] Finally, the interpretation of the meaning of coefficients is confused by the possibility of multidirectional causal relationships, including those of an ecological sort.[21]

With the help of information from interview studies, the ingenuity of econometric work may contrive to circumvent the worst of these difficulties. If so, it seems likely that

---

[19] Needless to say, the effort to identify influences on stocks other than that of sales is familiar to econometric analysis. But, as I pointed out in Chapter 1, the results seem to be less than satisfactory. A major difficulty is the too powerful influence of orders. If ownership rather than stock is to be explained, the

difficulty can be described by saying that new sales orders (or backlogs) may be viewed as a cause and new purchase orders (or outstandings) are a result. The format of the analysis must somehow accommodate this distinction.

[20] In the context of seasonal variation, the lags would often be different, and this raises questions concerning the usefulness of analyses based on data that are not deseasonalized when seasonal patterns are strong. For example, unlike cyclical variations, seasonals in sales can often be quite reliably forecast; the relative importance of the several explanatory variables usually differs for cyclical and seasonal changes in stocks and ownership; the timing of the relations among the variables will differ. If seasonals are strong, the parameters of the equation system may tend to recite the seasonal rather than cyclical version of the story.

[21] These qualifications of the meaningfulness of gross correlation measures are superimposed on the worries expressed in Chapter 9, note 2, above. Indeed, perhaps the only honest test for association of these sorts abjures the comfort of the "one period change model" and endeavors to reproduce history by means of an equation system for a "process model"—one in which the influences presumed to be at work are fully specified and asked to churn out the resultant course of the dependent variable. (For an instructive comparison of the results of the two sorts of models, see Kalman J. Cohen, *Computer Models of the Shoe, Leather, Hide Sequence,* Englewood Cliffs, N.J., 1960.) Simulation may be a simpler and more flexible way to achieve a similar result.

individually fragile findings may gain collective strength by a comparison of the findings for a number of individual industries or departments of department stores. The coefficients developed for the several business situations ought•to differ in fashions that seem sensible in the light of other knowledge about each situation.

Simulation. Finally, there are serious gaps of knowledge concerning how the individual's view of the problem, the information that he uses, the responses that he makes, are influenced by the market and how it responds to and generates new information. Processes involving information have been studied under the titles of cybernetics and information theory. The particular sorts of processes involved in the model of price-timed buying could be explored with the aid of the massive capacity of the computer to manipulate and memorize numbers. The technique of simulation is suitable and flexible. It has been repeatedly put to work on the problem of tracing, in accordance with stochastic principle, how individual behavior builds into a time course of aggregate behavior.[22]

But my study seems to call for something more than the now familiar notion of analysis with a "feedback" from the environment. The character of the feedback is critical: it is one for which the coefficients of reaction (at the individual as well as at the aggregate level) themselves change. As far as I know, the

aggregate implications of this sort of process have not been explored. Interestingly enough, the closest thing to it that has come to my attention is in the field of epidemiology—the Reed-Frost model.[23]

One of the most attractive aspects of the technique of simulation is its capacity to test a theory constructed in terms of selected characteristics and behavior of individuals. The assumptions that are made must result in a spaced and self-reversing wave; of critical interest is the ten- to fifteen-month thrust. Simulation itself can indicate what values for chief components of the model will, and what will not, produce movements of the sort posited. It can indicate the support that is required from exogenous influences. It can indicate how sensitive the picture is to reasonable ranges of variation in critical pieces of the explanation.[24]

I have suggested a number of directions in which the effort to deepen understanding of the vertical diffusion of fluctuation associated with inventory waves may be pursued. They feature the effort to understand the behavior of individuals and how it generates

---

[22] See especially Guy Orcutt, "A New Type of Socioeconomic System," *Review of Economics and Statistics*, May 1957, pp. 116–123, and subsequent work of Orcutt and other contributors to the work of the Social Systems Research Institute, University of Wisconsin.

Needless to say, feedbacks can be represented in mathematical models also. James Duesenberry and Franco Modigliani took this approach in their models of consumer buying which introduced maximum past levels of income as an indication of changing standards of living. The advantage of simulation, as I see it, is simply, first, that a theory that proposes reactions of people to one another is put to a sharper test if the process is specified at the individual level. Second, the process is likely to imply response at an aggregate level which is nonlinear, and therefore likely to be lost if functional forms must be predetermined.

[23] Work in the field of mathematical analysis of epidemics started in the first decade of the century, when it was found that periodic recurrences of epidemics could be deduced from and described by information on the number of susceptibles, contact-rates, attack-rates, and recovery ratios. Theory developed over many years. However, deterministic models did not seem to square with the facts, and a stochastic model was introduced in the middle of the 1920's. Somewhat later, the notion of a threshold was introduced; the proportion of susceptibles in a community must be above some critical value.

The approach seems to be associated with the name of Lowell J. Reed and Wade Hampton Frost, who taught at Johns Hopkins University. But most of the written expositions and much if not most of the theoretical and empirical work appears to have been done by others. See Norman T. Bailey, *Mathematical Epidemiology*, London, 1957. There are also numerous articles in the journal, *Human Biology, A Record of Research*, September 1952, and in Jerzy Neyman, ed., *The Third Berkeley Symposium on Mathematical Statistics and Probability.*

[24] James Bettman intends to explore some of these questions through interviews and perhaps simulation in his doctoral dissertation at Yale University, Graduate School of Business Administration.

and feeds upon relevant information and changing objective situations. Knowledge of this sort seems to me to be necessary to scientific exploration of the process of economic change.

But it is perhaps not too visionary to hope that it may have some value in modifying the process. Most businessmen probably prefer to buy and sell in a relatively stable and predictable market. If so, fluctuations of the sort that have been discussed are undesirable. Understanding of how fluctuation is built up by the system whereby problems are perceived and solved by businessmen could be a first step in designing better ways of solving them—ways that subdue their innate tendency to generate and amplify fluctuation. Insights would bear particularly, I suspect, on the problem of sustaining business expansion.

If it is useful to trace the move-by-move pattern whereby expectations, actions, information, and situations feed upon one another in connection with the buying of materials by business enterprises, it should be useful also to trace analogous processes in other fields. Certainly, for example, the "fickleness" of consumers, or the lumped equipment purchasing of producers, or local "construction cycles" are not without strong elements of interplay among the actions of many individuals as well as between individuals and the business environment. Some elements of the price-timed buying model might be expected to apply—the hill-shaped frequency distributions of proclivities, the ceilings, the importance of assurance and learning, the time-consuming buildup of evidence, the changing patterns of market response. But many other elements would differ, particularly the length of most of the lags. Even trend growth, especially in developing countries, shares most of these elements.

Questions of these sorts, once raised, are hard to forget. Their hold is strengthened by the importance that we are learning to accord to rates of change in the economy— rates of rise during prosperity fast enough to maintain expansion but not too fast to be themselves maintained. Rates of change in ecological processes tend to be willful at the aggregate level. Hope of adjusting them to the requirements of stable growth seems to lie in understanding the underlying microprocess and how it cumulates. For this purpose the august tools of equilibrium analysis may be of limited use.

Index

(Page numbers in **bold face** refer to information in tables.)